READING DANTE

READING DANTE

A Theological Paraphrase of the Inferno

Kevin Dodge

ISBN: 0692560017
ISBN 13: 9780692560013

Credits:

Cover Art: *Allegorical Portrait of Dante,* Samuel H. Kress Collection, ©1995, Board of Trustees, National Gallery of Art, Washington DC
Cover Design: Courtney Barrow
Interior Art: Gustave Doré, *The Vision of Hell,* London: Cassell, Petter and Galipn, 1866.
Revised Standard Version of the Bible, copyright 1952 [2nd edition, 1971] by the Division of Christian Education of the National Council of the Church of Christ in the United States of America. Used by Permission. All rights reserved
The Holy Bible, English Standard Version, copyright ©2001 by Crossway Bibles, a division of Good News Publishers. Used by permission. All Rights Reserved.
The HOLY BIBLE, NEW INTERNATIONAL VERSION. NIV. Copyright©1973, 1978, 1984 by International Bible Society. Used by permission of Zondervan. All rights reserved.

For Father Billy Huete, S.J.

"People will not look forward to posterity who will not look backward to their ancestors"
(Edwin Burke, Reflections on the Revolution in France, 1790)

"It is in Christianity that our arts have developed; it is in Christianity that the laws of Europe have — until recently — been rooted. It is against a background of Christianity that all our thought has significance. An individual...may not believe that the Christian Faith is true, and yet what he says, and makes, and does, will all spring out of his heritage of Christian culture and depend on that culture for its meaning...If Christianity goes, the whole of our culture goes."
(T. S. Eliot, *Christianity and Culture*)

Table of Contents

Preface

About a decade ago, I picked up Dante's *Divine Comedy* for the first time. My wife and I decided to read *The Inferno* together at night. Like most first-time readers experiencing their initial trip through Dante's remarkable descriptions of the underworld, we were captivated by the vivid imagery and creative story-telling. Each new short Chapter (called a "Canto") brought vivid descriptions of sinners writhing under divine punishment. Although we had the best of intentions to keep going through the subsequent *Purgatorio* and *Paradiso* we stopped once we reached the center of hell. We also slept better once we did.

As it turns out, we missed the best part. Most readers of the *Divine Comedy* (hereafter called the *"Comedy")* become captivated by the lurid imagery of the *Inferno*, but fail to keep going. This is a pity because Dante's allegory of a soul seeking salvation is best read in light of its goal, which is the beatific vision. The story gets better and better as you go along.

I think it's hard to interact with Dante's vision well without recognizing that it finds its fulfillment in Christ at the top of a heavenly hierarchy. The idea that union with Christ is the goal of our spiritual lives comes directly from the Apostle Peter who said, God "*has granted to us his precious and very great promises that through these you may escape from the corruption that is in the world because of passion, and become partakers of the divine nature*" (2 Pet 1.4).

Dorothy Sayers, in her introduction to the *Comedy*, suggests the best way to read Dante initially is to read it through without trying to figure it all out. This is more or less what I did in that first reading. Sayers says it this way: *"The ideal way of reading the Divine Comedy would be to start at the first line and go straight through to the end, surrendering to the vigor of the story-telling and the swift movement of the verse, and not bothering about any historical allusions or theological explanations which do not occur in the text itself."*[1]

I basically agree. Ideally, the reader would do a quick read-through of a standard translation of the *Comedy* and get a sense for the big picture before returning to understand the details. Yet I fully recognize the reality that most don't have the time or interest to take Sayers up on her suggestion. The book you're holding is my response to the reality our busy lives and shortened attention spans demand.

When I returned to the *Comedy* after a long hiatus, I found myself dissatisfied with the quick read-through method. I decided I wanted to understand what was actually happening. Most commercially-available translations do a fine job of providing copious end-notes which explain aspects of what Dante is doing or saying. I discovered that without a very complex apparatus of notes (I used Robert and Jean Hollander's), it's very hard to understand what Dante is doing. Even reading at a superficial level, there are so many layers of allusion and symbolism to unfold, that it would take a lifetime to unpack.

I learned subsequently that readers of the *Comedy* have interacted with the poem from the beginning with an explanatory apparatus at their side. Even in Dante's day, where the history, politics and ecclesiastical polity would have been more readily clear to the average reader, few could keep up with Dante's massive learning. In other words, Dante was just too brilliant for anyone to appreciate in an unaided fashion. Just about everyone who has ever read this great poem has needed external helps to explain it and to enjoy it.

Methodology

Yet I found reading the *Comedy* while constantly paging back to consult end-notes a lousy way to read a story. It was annoying and time consuming. I tried several different methods to ease the annoyance. None of these worked very well.

So I decided to tackle the poem as a bigger project and the book you're holding is the result of my efforts. I spent time brushing up on my Italian (I lived in Florence briefly when I was younger). I started reading scholarly introductions to Dante. These were almost always helpful, but still confused me since the background history was so complex and hard to master.

Moreover, I bought several of the standard commentaries on Dante to try to read better. Most were very helpful. I then took several courses available on Dante offered by well-known scholars such as Dr. Giuseppe Mazzotta at Yale, Dr. Francis Ambrosio at Georgetown and Dr. William Cook at SUNY Geneseo. All of these fine scholars taught me a great deal.

Like so many before me, as I struggled through the text, I started falling in love with Dante and his work. It really is amazing. The more I learned, the better reader I became. And the better reader I became, the more awe-inspiring Dante's achievement seemed to me.

When Dante first released the text of the poem it was simply called *The Comedy of Dante Alighieri*. But, in a 1555 edition, the publishers added the word "divine" to the title and it stuck. The divine element of the *Comedy* is in its subject matter (remember, the goal of Dante's journey is the beatific vision in heaven). But, perhaps more pertinently, Dante's achievement is so remarkable it simply seems like he had heaven's help constructing it. For example, in the Introduction below, I explore very briefly the numerological elements embedded into the poem. Only a genius could have pulled this off. By the time we reach the center of hell, I hope you too will realize why most early readers thought Dante would have had divine help to write this. It seems beyond human capacity at times.

As I kept reading, however, many of my initial impressions proved inadequate. I initially thought the *Comedy* was Dante's chance to settle a bunch of old scores. After all, Dante places a whole bunch of Popes in hell. But I soon learned this was a popular, but ultimately inadequate way to consider the work. Dante needed to come to grips with his sin. He was hardly in a position to be condemning others (although he does do this in places as he grows in his moral and spiritual understanding).

In other words, I became far less interested in the lurid details of suffering and far more interested in asking why Dante was depicting these sins in this particular way. Very good interpreters such as Helen Luke, Dorothy Sayers, Mark Musa, Charles Singleton, Robert Durling, Robert and Gene Hollander, Justin Steinberg, Teodolinda Barolini, William Franke, John Ciardi, Allen Mandelbaum, Prue Shaw, Peter Hawkins, Richard Lansing and William Anderson all helped me to become a much better reader of Dante.

I also found myself drawing on my life experience. My years as a businessperson and Wall Street investor had given me an insight to how the world works. But my subsequent training in theology taught me how the world was *supposed* to work, but often didn't. This disconnect between the ideal and the real is a key aspect of the *Inferno*. The presence of sin explains the human condition very well, in my opinion.

Approach

This book tries to do something not available in most published treatments of the *Comedy*. I have written this treatment as a paraphrase. What do I mean by a paraphrase? Basically, what I've done is to imbed the interpretation of what's happening in the poem into the text of the story itself. My goal is to simply retell the story in an approachable way, but imbed into the story things most would miss without a scholarly interpretive apparatus at their side.

This, of course, has required me to make a series of interpretive decisions. Wherever possible, I've tried to be aware of issues the poem presents and to write with that in mind. I have a tendency to gravitate towards the scholarly consensus if I can find it, but I also take positions outside the consensus as well. Those who know the *Comedy* well will not like all my choices. But I believe those approaching the *Comedy* with less experience will find this method a much easier way to interact with this great work.

I don't at all claim my reading of the poem is necessarily the best reading. It certainly is not the only reading. It's simply my reading. By explaining what is happening within the text of the story, I hope to make the *Comedy* accessible to more people, especially those who might never otherwise have picked up the poem. By no means do I think my work should replace the many fine commercially-available prose or verse translations of the poem. My work is here primarily to assist the reader in interacting with Dante's poem in as approachable a way as possible. I simply hope to whet your appetite for what is one of the greatest literary works ever conceived.

Drawbacks/Criticisms

Let me be the first to admit that there are several drawbacks to what I've done. By writing a paraphrase of the *Comedy*, I have trampled on the poetry. I make no attempt to be sensitive to meter, to Dante's rhyme scheme or to assonance. My version reads much more like a prose story than an epic poem. In fact, I employ colloquial language throughout this work since this is how we normally communicate. Admittedly this differs from the style a reader of Dante's poem in Italian would encounter. However, at several points there are aspects to the poetry that drive the interpretation of what is happening (such as in Cantos Twenty and Twenty-One when Dante deals with the fraud of language amidst the Soothsayers and Barraters). Where Dante provides a poetic tour-de-force, I will point that out.

A second problem my work creates is its lack of subtlety. One of the truly marvelous features of the *Comedy* is Dante's masterful ability to allude to events, characters and ideas without overtly explaining what he's doing. While this subtlety is lost on most without a background in the literature of this era, I am changing the character of the work by deliberately destroying the subtlety Dante embeds. The point of this method of reading is to explain. Some will find that my focus on explanation tramples on Dante's art.

A third issue is the emphasis I place on pointing out allusions Dante makes to the Scriptures and explaining Dante's rather frequent employment of ideas from Christian theology. I am self-consciously emphasizing aspects that might interest Christians. I am doing this because I believe Dante has a lot to teach us not only about the spiritual life, but about the Christian faith as well.

This does not mean I want to sweep under the rug Dante's departures from the orthodoxy of his day. I rather enjoy pointing out these departures. But it does mean that I am much more interested in Dante's theological ideas than I am the subtleties of his art. Once again, many good readers of the poem handle these poetic features with greater skill in commercially available volumes.

In most cases, I quote the Bible from the Revised Standard Version (RSV). I do this because it is a modern, familiar text. However, we should keep in mind that Dante would have probably been more familiar with Jerome's Latin translation called the Vulgate. I recognize that there are significant differences between Jerome's translation and a modern one, but I opt for the RSV for the sake of clarity to the modern reader.

Unfortunately, there is a tendency among many readers of the poem to find this emphasis on theology and the Bible illegitimate. After all, Dante had a terrible time with the Church of his era. Some even go so far as to question how genuine his Christian beliefs were. He consigns most of the Popes who were alive during his lifetime to various levels of the *Inferno*. Why emphasize something he was clearly critiquing?

My contention is that Dante, despite being in exile because of a Church that failed him, never abandoned his faith. Dante believed that for a society to function well, it needs the Christian Church to perform its role properly, even though he has a strong critique to bring to the Church's shortcomings and its leaders' corruption.

Moreover, I believe very strongly Dante's first readers would have brought basic Christian assumptions to bear, not only in their reading, but in their lives. Biblical and theological language was in the air Dante breathed. To ignore this or to de-emphasize it because our culture is embarrassed by medieval Christian assumptions is to misread his work, in my opinion. Thus I believe emphasizing the Biblical and theological aspects of the poem is essential, especially since medieval conceptions of the Christian faith are less well understood today.

I have written this book primarily for those who already know something about the basics of Christian belief, but who would benefit from taking those beliefs and asking harder questions of them. My goal is to employ Dante's *Comedy* to enable a richer interaction with the Christian Scriptures and Christian theology. Those who do not hold Christian beliefs can certainly still benefit from this volume. Those who don't even know the basics of Christian belief will probably benefit a lot from it. In other words, the book assumes little in-depth knowledge, but is written primarily to explain Dante in Christian terms. If this leaves me open to the charge of bias, so be it. Every interpreter has bias. I am simply trying to be explicit about where I think my bias resides.

Translation Methodology

In writing this paraphrase, I first translated the poem into English from the Italian. I used Giorgio Petrocchi's critical text for this. Then, after surveying a whole range of secondary literature, I proceeded to retell the story in plain English, explaining along the way what I thought Dante was saying. If there were Biblical allusions in Dante's text, I made it a point to identify them.

This means I have not taken pains to stay particularly close to the original text. A paraphrase is not a translation. It's simply based on a translation, my own, in this case. This is why my work should not replace the reading of a more standard translation which adheres to the original text more closely. At times I have departed from the original text rather widely, but always with the goal of explaining what is there in the text of the poem.

For example, in the first Canto we will meet a kind of female trinity (the Virgin Mary, St. Lucy and Beatrice) who take pity on Dante and send Virgil, his guide, to aid him. We might be forgiven for not knowing who St. Lucy is. I explain this directly in the story as if Dante were telling us. In the original text of the poem, Dante simply assumes the reader knows who St. Lucy is. I assume otherwise.

One thing I have tried to preserve in the text is Dante's habit of not mentioning the divine names in the Inferno (God, Christ, Jesus, etc.). These names are almost never uttered by the mouths of sinners because they have no saving relationship with the three Persons of the Trinity. In their place, I use terms such as "Divine Son," "Maker," "Creator" and "Architect" as substitutes. Some readers may find this awkward (admittedly, Dante is much more subtle than I am), but I think it is important to preserve this feature. I do employ the Virgin Mary's name, even though she is only referred to as a "gracious lady."

On occasion, I deliberately introduce anachronisms into the story. An anachronism is the act of withdrawing something from its original context and placing it in another context. For example, at one point, I discuss "Faustian bargains." The legend of Faust long post-dates Dante. I do this simply for the sake of clarity.

Each Canto follows roughly the same format. I start with a very short explanation of what is about to take place. I then offer a paraphrase of the Canto, usually broken up into several sections to make the reading easier. After the paraphrase is complete, I then offer a Comment section that explains certain interpretative, literary, theological, philosophical or historical details that might not be immediately obvious from a simple reading.

My goal is to make reading the *Inferno* relatively easy and enjoyable. To be sure, the issues Dante grapples with are sometimes very difficult, but my goal is to explain them in as easy-to-understand terms as possible. Out of necessity, this means there is much more that could be said. However, I am trying to make the poem approachable. The vast secondary literature on Dante and his *Comedy* will handle many of the issues I raise if any reader would like to explore them at greater depth.

I also take pains to provide a long list of endnotes to help those who might want to track down my sources in the scholarly literature or to explore something deeper. One can legitimately spend a lifetime studying Dante. I encourage any reader who is interested to consult those scholars who have dedicated their lives to this great work. It will reward your efforts.

Acknowledgements

Although I have spent many hours writing alone, this has by no means been a solitary effort. I'm grateful for all the help I've received.

First, to the Dante scholarly community, particularly those I mentioned above, I extend my profound thanks. I would know little about Dante or the *Comedy* itself without the thoughtful efforts of many people. As teachers, you have enriched me greatly.

I'm also grateful to those who read the manuscript and provided helpful comments. In particular, David Baldwin, Guyanne Booth, Ellora Hermerding, Susan Skelton and Steve Wilensky were particularly helpful. Each provided feedback and pointed out embarrassing errors that has made this a better work. Thank you for the remarkable expenditure of time each of you gave this project.

Thanks also go to the clergy and staff at Church of the Incarnation in Dallas, TX for their encouragement, feedback and support. Special thanks go to Courtney Barrow for her design work on the cover.

As someone who lives with a chronic disease (MS), I am also grateful to those in the medical community who have kept me healthy enough to work on this project, especially Dr. Shin Beh, Dr. Jason Fish, Dr. Cinzia Levalds, and Diana Logan. Thank you for the great care you've given to me. I couldn't have done this without you.

I thank my wife, Lorelee, for her patience and good cheer, as she endured endless conversations (and, occasionally complaints) about

Dante. Lorelee reviewed most of the manuscript and provided helpful feedback.

I dedicate this work to Billy Huete, S.J., my spiritual director during the early days of writing this book. Father Huete led me through the Spiritual Exercises of St. Ignatius with great skill, sensitivity and insight. I learned much about the spiritual life from Father Billy and St. Ignatius. I also believe this work is much better because of that marvelous experience.

As always, however, any errors, omissions or other gaffes are my responsibility alone. *Sola Dei Gloria.*

November 2, 2015, All Souls Day

Introduction

Dante's Exile

One day, probably around 1304, Dante Alighieri was disillusioned, depressed and desperate for some good news. Two years prior, in 1302, through a series of circumstances largely beyond his control, Dante was thrown out of his beloved city of Florence on essentially trumped-up charges. Convicted of barratry (misuse of government funds), forgery and opposition to the Pope, Dante was forced to leave the city. Dante was a poet and statesman who had gotten his hands dirty with politics. This had cost him dearly.

For a Florentine, exile was the worst possible fate, in some senses, even worse than death. Ever since Aristotle identified people as "political animals" in his *Politics*, those in the west had come to define their identities as members of a *polis*, an earthly city. Even St. Augustine, picking up this theme in the *City of God* via Cicero, made identification with a *polis* — either the earthly city of man or the heavenly city of God — a key factor in one's eternal destiny.[2] Thus being tossed out of Florence wasn't a chance to start over. It meant the loss of Dante's identity.

It also meant Dante would be separated from his children, Jacopo, Pietro and Antonia and from his wife, Gemma. It meant he would lack funds. Dante became a kind of beggar, moving from city to city, looking for benefactors. We find him doing odd diplomatic, scribal and translation work along the way. He may have even taught and tutored a little.

But, in the early years of exile at least, his existence was like that of a poor mendicant friar.

In his philosophical work, the *Banquet*, Dante describes his exile with these poignant words:

> *Alas! Would that it might have pleased the Dispenser of the Universe that the cause of my excuse might never have been; that others might neither have sinned against me, nor I have suffered punishment unjustly; the punishment I saw, of exile and poverty! Since it was the pleasure of the citizens of the most beautiful and the most famous daughter of Rome, Florence, to cast me out from her most sweet bosom (wherein I was born and nourished even to the height of my life, and in which, with her goodwill, I desire with all my heart to repose my weary soul, and to end the time which is given to me). I have gone through all the land in which this language lives — a pilgrim, almost a mendicant — showing forth against my will the wound of Fortune, with which the ruined man is often unjustly reproached.*[3]

Thus two years into his exile, Dante is starting to figure out that it's going to last a while. We know Dante spent time in Forli in 1302, Verona in 1303-4, Arezzo in 1305 and Padua in 1306. [4] He may have even made it all the way to Paris between 1308-1309, though the evidence for this is thin.[5] His life in exile lacked any rootedness. He was a perpetual sojourner for about a decade.

Dante would stay in exile for the next twenty years until the end of his life. He would never see his beloved Florence again, nor would he have any physical contact with his wife Gemma. Because of Florence's antipathy for Dante, even his children would be threatened with exile once they reached the age of majority (Fourteen) because of Dante's conviction.

Toward the end of his life, Dante enjoyed a bit more stability, especially when he found his way to Congrande della Scala in Verona, the place where he perhaps completed the *Inferno* in 1314 and began much of the rest of the *Comedy*. Dante was always grateful to Scala for taking him in, so much so that he dedicated the *Paradiso*, the last of the three parts of the *Comedy*, to him.

One guest of Scala described Dante's living situation like this:

> *Different apartments, according to their condition, were assigned to the exiles in the Scala palace; each had his own servants and a well-appointed table served in private...On occasion Cane invited certain of his guests to his own table, notably...the poet Dante Alighieri.*[6]

After spending significant time in Verona, Dante spent his last years in Ravenna where he likely completed the poem and died in 1321. Dante became ill after conducting a diplomatic mission to Venice, made it back to Ravenna and passed away, likely from the effects of malaria. Thus exile is not just an interesting piece of background in Dante's story. It forms the significant context to why the poem even got written. In short, Dante's exile prompts his writing.

Originally, the governmental authorities of Florence had slapped Dante and several others with huge fines and a warning not to return. He heard of his sentence while he was staying in Siena on his way back from Rome.[7] Dante hoped that, given enough time, the fury in Florence would die down.

In 1302, Dante made an alliance with the Ubaldini family to try to secure his return.[8] This apparently went nowhere. New hope came in 1304 when Pope Boniface VIII, whose underhanded dealings Dante blamed for his exile, passed away. Dante thought these developments might be setting the stage for a comeback.

In fact, Boniface's successor, Benedict XI, was a good Pope (and the only Pope alive during Dante's lifetime he didn't condemn to the Inferno). The new Pope tried to negotiate a peace between the warring political parties in Florence, but failed. In this period, Dante's political allies tried to take back Florence by force. But they failed too.

At this point, Dante ended up severing his ties with his former political allies which meant access to funds was completely cut off. He even declared himself "a party of himself." He was disgusted with the corruption and division which factionalism had brought to his city and to the world around him. It was ruining his life. We will hear significant traces of this idea throughout the *Inferno* and the rest of the *Comedy*. In fact, Dante put the following lament into the mouth of Cacciaguida, his great grandfather, in the *Paradiso*:

> *You will leave everything that delights you most dearly; and this is the arrow which first sailed from the bow of the exile; you will experience how salt is the taste of the bread of others and how hard it is to descend that path and to ascend by other's stairs. But what will burden your shoulders the most will be your friends, wicked and foolish, with whom you will fall into this valley. They're all ungrateful, flippant and impious; they'll all turn against you, but in just a bit, they, not you, will have reddened faces. Their trial will prove their bestial behavior so that it will have done you well to have made a single party of yourself (Par, 15.55-69).*[9]

Dante had one last hope for restoration when Henry of Luxembourg, who became Holy Roman Emperor in 1309 and king of Lombardy in 1311, tried to reconcile the political factions living in exile.[10] Henry was well-known for his sterling character and excellent political leadership skills. He was also a bulwark against Papal power.

However, when Henry tried to assert his imperial authority, the King of France didn't follow him and the Pope delayed in crowning him Emperor.[11] The political faction in Florence which had exiled Dante basically ignored him.[12] Henry declared the Florentines rebels in 1312 and was getting ready to attack in 1313, but died of malaria before he could.[13] Once again, Dante's hopes for restoration came to nothing.

In 1315, while Dante was in Verona with Scala, Florence gave Dante the opportunity to return as long as he admitted his guilt.[14] There was one additional stipulation, however. Dante would have to beg for forgiveness from the city and do penance. Having already "published" the *Inferno*, Dante was becoming well known throughout Italy. He thought the terms ridiculous and said he would never admit his guilt. Dante thus spent his last years in exile.

To this day, there is an argument over returning Dante's remains to Florence. Florence has requested several times over the centuries to bring Dante back home. The city of Ravenna has understandably refused these requests, even when they have come from powerful people.

For example, in 1519, Pope Leo X ordered Dante's remains to be brought back to Florence. When officials came to collect the remains, however, they went missing. The remains were then rediscovered in 1865 when a workman was doing work on the walls of a church in honor of Dante's six-hundredth birthday and found them hidden behind a wall with a note on top confirming their authenticity. In the 1970s, the city of Florence issued an ultimatum to Ravenna to return the remains. This was met with a curt "no." Thus Dante's remains continue to rest in exile.

The Development of Florence

How did all this misery and exile come about? To explain it, we have to first answer how Florence became one of the wealthiest cities in Europe by the end of the thirteenth century. In 1200, Florence was fairly insignificant. It had no great university like in Paris or Bologna. It had few major cultural achievements to speak of.[15] It lagged far behind Pisa, Lucca and Siena in commercial development.[16] Its population was only between ten- and fifteen-thousand people.[17] Being inland without a port or a place on any major trading route, Florence was the last place anyone would have predicted to hit it big.[18]

By the end of the thirteenth century, however, Florence had rebuilt its walls several times to accommodate its staggering growth. Its population had swelled to over one-hundred thousand people.[19] One scholar has estimated this led to an almost fifteen-fold increase in the city's square footage.[20] Florence became a kind of boom town.

What made Florence great was its commercial success. Florence was not alone in the importing of wool, silks and spices from the Middle East. But through a proprietary manufacturing and dyeing process, Florentine merchants learned how to turn out the most luxurious textiles in all of Europe.[21] The almost insatiable demand for Florentine fabrics led to steady cash flows which, in turn, led to the huge increases in population described above. To be sure, textiles were not the only Florentine industry, but they were a significant driver of the boom.[22]

The expansion of business activity also led to the creation of a lucrative banking system which soaked up excess cash of the citizenry and used it to finance trade. The Florentine banks then began to finance not only the city government but also the Papacy. This allowed Florence to bargain for taxing authority within the city. The Papacy's support of the banking system is ironic given the Biblical injunction against usury, an incongruity Dante will happily point out in one of the lower sections of the *Inferno*.

By 1252, Florence had made its first gold florin, which would become the reserve currency for most of Europe. The city fathers also made plans for its magnificent Duomo (with Brunelleschi's spectacular cupola) which would become the largest church structure in Europe upon its completion in the fifteenth century. In short, the city prospered immensely because of the success of its businesses.

Politics

With prosperity, however, came political conflict. There were two major political factions in Italy during the twelfth and thirteenth centuries, the Guelfs and the Ghibellines. These factions were not just in Florence, but in other City-States throughout Europe as well. The Guelfs derived their name from an Italianized form of the word Welf, a family name for a series of twelfth-century Bavarian Dukes. The name Ghibelline probably derives from the name of a Hohenstaufen castle in Germany which was called Waiblingen.[23]

In its most basic terms, the Guelfs were generally pro-Papacy while the Ghibellines were supporters of the Holy Roman Emperor (although, as we'll see, it's quite a bit more complicated than that). It should come as no surprise that there was a power struggle going on between the Papacy, which wanted to expand its territory and power, and the Holy Roman Emperor, who wanted to resist further Papal encroachment. The Emperor in the first half of the thirteenth century, Frederick II, held most of Germany, but also controlled lands around Naples and Sicily. He was also pushing northward to check the Papacy's encroachment into Tuscany.[24]

As a generalization, the merchant class was associated with the Guelfs because they thought this was the best way to keep their independence. If the Pope needed the credit of the Guelf-run banks, it might help keep their taxing authority clear and their trade routes open. Thus the Guelfs allied with the Pope to maintain their commercial independence.

The Ghibellines, on the other hand, were generally aristocrats and didn't trust the Papacy. They much preferred employing the Holy Roman Emperor as a check against Papal power. What we should notice is that the various factions were often supporting different parties as a reflection of their monetary, business and power interests rather than out of a sense of loyalty to any particular institution.

In Florence, the conflict between the Guelfs and the Ghibellines came to a head early in the thirteenth century because of a family feud. On Easter morning in 1215, Buondelmonte de' Buondelmonti, from a well-known Guelf family, broke off his engagement suddenly to a daughter of the Amidei family, a prominent Ghibelline clan.[25] He announced his intentions to marry a young woman from the Guelf Donati family instead. This caused great offense.

In response, members of the Amidei family murdered Buondelmonte for the slight. The whole city then divided into two factions, the Guelfs, led by the Donatis, and the Ghibellines, led by the Amideis. Similar to what Shakespeare would later describe with the Montagues and the

Capulets in *Romeo and Juliet*, this division would last for over a hundred years not only in Florence, but throughout Italy.

This tension between the two groups spilled out into outright violence and warfare. For example, the Ghibellines forced the leaders of the Guelfs out of the city in 1248. But, when Frederick II, the Holy Roman Emperor died in 1250, the Ghibellines themselves were ousted from power.

Then, in 1258, the Ghibellines rose up to take back power, but lost, leading to their exile as well. The Ghibellines then returned to power in 1260 after defeating the city's forces at the Battle of Montaperti. This led to the widespread destruction of the property of the Guelfs who were still in Florence.

The Ghibellines ruled Florence until 1266 when the Guelfs pushed back and won a significant victory at the Battle of Benevento under Charles of Anjou. The Guelfs then returned to power and exiled the Ghibelline leadership.

This factional fighting never really ended, but did calm down a bit in 1282 when the Guelfs put a new system of government in place wherein representatives from the guilds of the city were put in charge of administration. This was a good idea and should have resulted in greater stability. The guilds sent representatives on a revolving basis, a reform which led to greater enfranchisement for the merchant and middle classes. The representatives, known as Priors, were sent to sit on the six-member town council for two-month terms.[26] This is eventually how Dante got embroiled in the political power struggles in Florence.

While this development in government should have mitigated the long conflict, the Guelfs split into two factions, the Whites and the Blacks. This happened because of another family feud. This time, the Cancellieri family split apart because of a series of gruesome murders. Vanni de' Cancellieri, better known as Focaccia, was a violent White Guelf in Pistoia who murdered Detto Cancellieri, a member of the Black Guelfs.[27] When violence erupted and the city of Pistoia appealed to

Florence for help, the conflict between White and Black factions of the Guelfs spilled over into Florence as well.

In Florence, the feud found expression in the hatred between the Cerchi and Donati families. The Cerchi family represented the Whites who were self-made merchants while the Donati family supported the Blacks who represented the older money in the city.[28] This White/Black split in the Guelfs would directly lead to Dante's exile.

If your head is spinning at this point, don't fret. We will meet representatives from many of these families as we journey through the *Inferno* and they will retell their stories. In fact, in many cases, Dante is our main source for much of this history.

The point to remember is that there was great fracturing of the body politic in Florence. Dante thinks the reason for this fracture is the presence of sin. It has ruined Dante's life and has brought needless division to his beloved city.

Dante's Rise

Dante's rise to prominence in the political sphere started with his participation in battle. The Ghibellines from the town of Arezzo met a coalition of Guelfs from Florence, Lucca, Siena and Pistoia in 1289. The Guelfs won this battle which helped solidify Guelf control in Florence (which they had won back from the Ghibellines in 1266).[29] Dante apparently did well enough in the battle that he caught the notice of some higher-ups in the city.

In 1295, Dante joined the apothecary's guild in Florence. If you're wondering what an apothecary's guild has to do with being a writer, books were sold in apothecary shops during this time in Florence. In fact, there is an inscription from the guild dating from 1296, describing Dante as a "poet of Florence."[30] That same year, Dante delivered a speech to one of the important political bodies in Florence.[31]

At this point, there were twelve major guilds in Florence, drawing members from about four-hundred families in the city.[32] This meant that when he said his intentions were to be an impartial mediator, he was let into the city.

As soon as Charles gained access to Florence, however, he threw his weight completely behind the Black faction, a move which apparently had been pre-arranged. The Whites, unable to withstand the power of the Papal forces, had to capitulate. The Blacks then rounded up all the White leaders, killed several, and exiled the rest from the city. They plundered White property wherever they went. This is why Dante is so mad at Boniface VIII.

In 1302, Dante was tried *in absentia* and exiled. After several months of non-response from Dante, the city fathers imposed a huge fine, confiscated his property and warned him on the pain of death never to return. This being the late Middle Ages, they were serious about their death threat. Dante went into exile for the rest of his life.

Dante the Poet

As intriguing as the political situation is, we know Dante as a great poet, not a great statesman. How did his artistic talent develop?

The details on Dante's formal schooling are sparse. We know he studied theology at the Cathedral schools of Santa Croce and Santa Maria Novella in Florence, which respectively were centers of Franciscan and Dominican learning. We also know he studied with one of the great intellectuals of his day, Brunetto Latini, since Latini appears in the *Inferno*. There is little evidence, however, that Dante was ever Latini's student in a formal classroom. Yet they seem to have been close.

We know that in the 1290s, Dante started to hit his stride as a poet. This is when he was composing one of his earliest works, *La Vita Nuova* (*The New Life*). Had Dante never written the *Comedy*, he would have still have made an important contribution to literary criticism and poetry through this work which is a complication of some of his early poetry.

Dante probably composed the *Vita Nuova* sometime between 1292 and 1294 when he was between twenty-eight and thirty-years old.[37] It appears that Dante had been writing poetry for quite some time prior to this composition, but the *Vita Nuova* is the first work which took shape in a form worthy of notice.[38]

The *Vita Nuova* is a series of love poems which are semi-autobiographical. A mixture of prose and poetry, the work can best be seen as a treatise on love, but also makes an important contribution to literary criticism through its prose sections which provide a running commentary on the poetry.[39] The work's primary importance in the history of literature derives from Dante's decision to compose the work in Italian, not Latin. This was a very radical decision since Latin at this time was the universal language of learning.

Through this collection, Dante tells the story of how he came to fall in love with Beatrice and, most importantly, how he failed in his efforts to win her hand. This is important because Beatrice is the true heroine of the *Comedy* and the *Vita Nuova*.

At the beginning of the *Comedy,* Beatrice takes pity on Dante when he's lost and is instrumental in sending Virgil, Dante's guide throughout the *Inferno* and *Purgatorio*, to his aid. Beatrice then plays an essential role throughout most of the *Paradiso* as Dante's guide through heaven. In many senses, Beatrice is the embodiment of love. Allegorically, Dante is trying to heal his soul, something which only love can do.

In the *Vita Nuova*, Dante met Beatrice when she was about nine years old. He fell in love with her at first sight. However, through a series of mishaps, some by coincidence and some deriving from character flaws, Dante's love for Beatrice was never returned.

The way Dante told the story in the *Vita Nuova*, however, Beatrice became ill and died as was prefigured in a dream Dante had. Dante was sure she had ascended to heaven.[40] Beatrice, thus, imitates Christ by coming to earth, taking on flesh, dying and ascending to heaven.[41] Once in heaven, she is able to assist Dante on his way.

Keep in mind that both Beatrice and Dante were married to others. We know Beatrice married Simone dei Bardi in 1287.[42] To understand Dante's love for Beatrice, we have to encounter it within the so-called "courtly-love" tradition. There was no actual love affair here. Dante's love for Beatrice is a metaphor and not to be taken too literally. Dante assures us that his love for Beatrice was "most chaste." Beatrice is a kind of mediator of love, the only thing which can heal Dante of his troubles.

This metaphor, however, plays an essential role in the unfolding story of the *Comedy.* Dante is incomplete without the love which he finds in his platonic devotion to Beatrice. Therefore Dante needs to seek forgiveness. He needs to learn to love in a way that will be returned. At the end of the *Vita Nuova*, Dante resolves to do the following:

> *After this sonnet there appeared to me a miraculous vision in which I saw things that made me resolve to say no more about this blessed one [Beatrice] until I would be capable of writing about her in a more worthy fashion…I hope to write of her that which has never been written of any other woman. And then may it please that One who is the Lord of Graciousness that my soul ascend to behold the glory of its lady, that is, of that blessed Beatrice, whose glory gazes upon the countenance of the One who is through all ages blessed.*[43]

Thus the *Comedy* is, in part, Dante's response to his failure at love in the *Vita Nuova*. If his entire life has fallen apart because of political intrigue and acrimony, Dante needs to find a way to make things right. Dante's task is to find forgiveness. He must seek love. He can do this only by coming to grips with his own inner wretchedness which keeps him from relating to others with authenticity.

The Comedy

The Comedy is arguably the greatest work of epic poetry ever written. Inarguably, Dante is the greatest Italian poet ever. His achievement is so important to the identity of Italy that the colors of the Italian flag come from the *Comedy.* In the *Paradiso*, Beatrice appears to Dante dressed in green, white and red, which represent the colors of the Christian theological virtues: faith, hope and love. It is not a stretch to say that Dante is the father of the Italian nation.[44]

Through his poetry and other works, Dante influenced scores of subsequent western writers and thinkers, including Boccaccio, Chaucer, Milton and Blake as well as Victor Hugo, Joseph Conrad, James Joyce, Ezra Pound, Charles Williams and Dorothy Sayers. T.S. Elliot describes his debt to Dante as follows:

> *Forty years ago I began to puzzle out the Divine Comedy...and when I thought I had grasped the meaning of the passage which especially delighted me, I committed it to memory so that, for some years, I was able to recite a large part of one canto or another to myself, lying in bed or on a railway journey....I still, after forty years, regard his poetry as the most persistent and deepest influence on my own verse.*[45]

Dante's decision to write the *Comedy* in Italian rather than Latin is monumentally important. This is one reason the *Comedy* was instantly so popular that no one could stop its publication despite its habit of offering critiques of the powerful. Dante may have placed Popes in hell, but the Popes did not even bother trying to suppress the *Comedy*. Even though it was being copied by hand, it spread too widely and too quickly.

Dante's decision to write in the vernacular also carries seminal importance for the Italian language itself. Modern Italian largely comes from Dante's decision to imbed his Tuscan dialect into the poem. We'll hear over and over again in the *Inferno* that people recognize Dante because of his dialect or his accent. Similar to the effect the King James Bible or the *Book of Common Prayer* had on the English language, the *Comedy* created such a level of uniformity in the Italian language that native speakers can understand close to eighty percent of the *Comedy* unaided today.[46]

The *Comedy* is also great because of its status as a kind of summa, or a summation of knowledge and experience. What Thomas Aquinas had done for theology twenty-five to thirty years prior, Dante did for literature with this epic poem. Dante was able to weave together pagan myth, literature, philosophy, Christian theology and doctrine, Biblical allusions, physics, astrology, cartography, mathematics, literary theory, history, and politics into a complex work that a wide audience, not just the highly educated, could read.

In terms of the poetry itself, each line of the poem is a hendecasyllable. This is just a fancy word which means each line contains eleven syllables.[47] This also contributes to the stability of the poem since anyone who wanted to alter it would have had to have kept the same pattern going. If they didn't, it would be immediately obvious that the manuscript wasn't genuine (more on this below).

The poetry of the *Comedy* is also unique because of the rhyme scheme Dante invented called the "*terza rima.*" The *Comedy* is subdivided into lines of three, a tercet. The last word of the first and third lines of a tercet rhyme together. Then, the first line of the next tercet rhymes together with the last word of the second line of the previous tercet. So the pattern is A-B-A, B-C-B, C-D-C, etc. This pattern then repeats itself over and over again.

Take this example from the first six lines of the *Inferno*:

Nel mezzo del cammin di nostra **vita [A]**
mi ritrovai per una selva **oscura [B]**
ché la diritta via era **smarrita [A]**

Ahi quanto a dir qual era é cosa **dura [B]**
esta selva selvaggia e aspra e **forte [C]**
che nel pensier rinova la **paura! [B]**

Translation:

In the middle of the journey of our life
I found myself in a dark wood
Since the straight path was lost

Oh, how hard it is to tell
what this wood was, how savage and severe and harsh;
The very thought of it renews the fear.

There are many theories about Dante's influences in developing this rhyme-scheme. But it appears to be original to him. What is most interesting is the stability and security it brings to the poem.

In the late Middle Ages, well before the invention of the printing press, all books were still being copied by hand. Hand copying presented a real problem for the transmission of ideas because one could never be completely sure one had an authentic copy of the original. Scribes were generally proficient at their task, but even the best scribes made mistakes.

The far greater problem for a popular work like the *Comedy* was that people would change the story to suit their tastes or interests. It was not unheard of to have a work edited beyond all recognition by someone trying to "improve" upon the work. As this "revised" copy gets recopied and circulated, the integrity of the work declines fairly rapidly.

With this rhyme scheme, Dante made such creative editing essentially impossible. If someone wanted to change the poem, he would have to keep it within the same rhyme pattern. Thus textual criticism — the comparing of one manuscript to another to see where errors have occurred — is by and large not a big issue with the *Comedy*. There are literally hundreds of early manuscripts of the poem, all of them reproduced by hand, which bear a remarkable similarity. Although there is no "original" copy of the *Comedy* which has survived, the great stability of the text is a testament to Dante's rhyme scheme.

There are a remarkable number of structures this rhyme pattern creates. Quite a number of readers have noted the link between the tercet, or the basic three-line unit of the poem, and the Christian Trinity. In Christian theology, there is one God who eternally exists in three persons, Father, Son and Holy Spirit. Thus God is both unity and diversity, unity in substance, but distinct in person.

Yet the worst punishments are reserved for traitors, those who violated some position or relationship of trust (Cantos Thirty-One through Thirty-Four). This might surprise the reader that the worst sin possible is betrayal, but it's important to keep Dante's own story in mind. He's been betrayed by those who were supposed to show him mercy. From Dante's perspective, betrayal is significant because it undermines the good order of the society. Put simply, a society cannot function without some degree of trust. Thus treachery strikes at the very foundations of society as a whole.

The corporate nature of sin is very much on display in the *Inferno*. Our society tends to think wrongdoing mostly affects individuals. From Dante's perspective, the whole society is imperiled when sin takes over the decision making of its leaders.

Contrapasso

One of the more unique features of the poem is how Dante deals with sin. We'll explore this in more detail as we get to the individual Cantos, but Dante's genius is fully on display as he metes out punishments in the *Inferno*.

Dante has a very Augustinian view of sin. To Dante, sin is misplaced love, an idea which derives from Augustine's *City of God*. When we love sex or food or money or power more than God, this leads to disorder in our individual souls and in the universe as a whole. From the Christian perspective, this is not how things are supposed to be. Sin has corrupted our lives and the creation itself.

One of the things that makes the poem so interesting is how sin is punished. The punishment always fits the crime in Dante's conception of hell. The term for this in Italian is called *contrapasso*. It's an essential feature of the poem.

We should think of *contrapasso* as a kind of retributive justice. The etymology of the word itself suggests this understanding. The Italian word *contrapasso* derives from two Latin words — "*contra*" (in return) and "*patire*" (to suffer).[50]

Contrapasso is Dante's way of dealing with the justice of hell itself. If God is so good and just, how could he allow anyone to suffer in hell? Isn't the very presence of the Inferno an affront to the claim of the mercy and kindness of God?

To Dante, the short answer is no. God has offered grace to everyone. Not everyone accepts His gift of grace. In fact, almost no one we'll encounter in the *Inferno* thinks they've done anything wrong. To be sure, they're not happy to be suffering. But sinners refuse to turn away from their desires, instead of toward the God who alone can save them from sin. The reason punishments in hell are just is because they're freely chosen. God simply gives sinners what they've really loved all along. God is not unjust for doing so.

But we should never forget that sin is a great mystery. Sin is a mystery because it makes no rational sense. It would seem that no one would consciously choose to be in hell. Yet this is exactly what's happened. In fact, Dante's point is that we don't have to wait to be in the Inferno to live in hell. By loving the wrong things, the wrong way, we can create hell on earth.

The vast majority of sinners we'll encounter in the *Inferno* try to justify their behavior when Dante meets them. Over and over again we'll find sinners who offer up a whole host of excuses for what they've done. Part of our job as readers is to figure out why the sinners' excuses fall short. What Dante needs to learn — what we all need to learn — is that sin clouds our judgment. Sin may make no sense, but we choose it anyway.

Because sinners in the *Inferno* have freely chosen to satisfy their desires at the expense of a relationship with God, they suffer because their love is directed toward the wrong things. To Dante (and to Augustine before him), changeable, material things can never really satisfy. No matter how much we enjoy food, we'll just get hungry again. No matter how much we enjoy sex, we'll just experience desire again. No matter how much money we have, it will never satisfy the hunger that's within all of us for transcendence. Created things cannot make one whole.

To be clear, it's not that any of these things is bad — food is necessary for life and is pleasurable. So are sex and money. The problem is not money, sex or food in themselves, which are all good things, but the disordered desire we have for them. The problem occurs when we fixate on created things without detachment. To prefer a created thing to the Creator is an apt definition of hell.

Each sinner in this poem was given the free offer of grace and a relationship with God and refused it because the sinner loved something temporal more. If a sinner rejects God in favor of something else, God's way of punishing that sinner is to give him the logical extension of what he really loves.

Thus we'll encounter the lustful in Canto Five who allowed their passions to overwhelm their intellects. They spend eternity in darkness, blown about by gale-force winds. The flatterers in Canto Eighteen spend eternity with human feces on their faces, a fitting punishment for the crap which came out of their mouths. The sowers of discord in Canto Twenty-Eight have various body parts severed on an on-going basis, thus experiencing the implications of what they did to rip apart the unity of the body politic. The results of all this are tragic.

Dante will often refer to the sinners in the Inferno as "shades," a concept C.S. Lewis borrows in the *Great Divorce.* They're still conscious, but have lost all the human vitality that an ordered life brings. These shades are literally shadows of their former selves. All the shades in the *Inferno* have a clear sense of the future — they know full well what is to come in the general resurrection and how they will miss out on the perfectly-ordered pleasures of heaven. They, however, have no concept of the present. Their hell is to experience the disordered desires they so craved (and continue to crave) forever. Their disordered desires will never satisfy them.

Symbolism

The last thing to mention is the symbolism of the poem. It will become clear quickly that the poem can be read on multiple levels. Although the literal story is very interesting and even entertaining, there's an underlying allegory that we're meant to uncover as well.

For example, the beasts in the first Canto are not just beasts. They're symbols of sins. Part of my job as your guide through the Inferno is to point out what the best explanation of the symbol is. I will try to do this as we go along in each Canto.

There are some fine readers who take issue with allegorizing the poem. To such readers, it's simply fanciful to think of Virgil as the embodiment of reason and Beatrice as the embodiment of grace and love.

I find most of these criticisms misguided and biased in favor of modern interpretive methods. To be sure, it's possible to read too much into any piece of literature. But the *Comedy*, of all works of literature, has taken on a life of its own. If we find significance or references that others deem fanciful, this shouldn't overly concern us. Dante has left plenty of room for us to read this text for ourselves. This is one reason why reading the poem over and over again is so worthwhile. We will see things we haven't seen before.

In fact, Dante is explicit in a letter to his patron Scala that there is an underlying allegory that he means for us to uncover and interpret. Scholars hotly debate the authenticity of the letter, but I have assumed its genuineness for the purposes of this presentation.

Our task is to read this poem like a medieval Christian would. Medieval readers were masters at reading a text contemplatively, a practice allowing the Spirit to bring to our minds that which it wants us to recognize and absorb.

My encouragement is to read it in whatever way brings you pleasure and allows you to process this great story. The point of this book is to translate into plain English Dante's symbolism, theology and philosophy so that anyone can approach the poem with ease and get a sense of what Dante is doing. I genuinely hope you enjoy the start of Dante's spiritual journey. I invite you to experience the *Inferno*, one of the greatest works of literature ever crafted.

The Inferno

1

Lost in a Dark Wood

THE PREAMBLE

Dante finds himself middle-aged, mired in a dark wood, having lost his way. He is lost not only physically, but spiritually as well. He tries to ascend to the light on top of a nearby mountain, but is forcefully repelled by three beasts, a leopard, a lion and a she-wolf. These beasts represent sins that have prevented the ascent not only of Dante, but of all souls. Virgil, Dante's poetic mentor, emerges to suggest a different path, prophesying not only the eventual return of one who will set things right, but also foreshadowing the journey Dante will undertake over the next ninety-nine Cantos of the poem. Dante accepts Virgil's gracious help and sets out on his journey. Canto One occurs during the early morning of Good Friday in the year 1300.

So there I was, stuck, lost in a dark wood. It was Holy Week in the year 1300.[1] I was thirty-five-years old, middle-aged, and in exile. I was estranged and alone. I was poor, cold and unhappy. I was exiled from my wife, my children and my beloved Florence. I had completely lost my way.

I have no idea how it all happened. It just started slowly. A little hatred here, a little power-grabbing there, a little discontent with what I had.[2] And, the next thing you know, my former allies, the Black Guelfs, had turned on me.[3] I thought they would have come to their senses by now and would have restored me back to the city I loved. How long could this madness go on? We're not built for exile, you know. Injustice, that's what I had experienced in life.[4] Yet the harshest thing of all — all that pride, envy and anger — all that sin, was eating me alive inside. Oh yes, I craved justice, but I was starting to think I would never find it.

They say that exile is a fate worse than death. I'm not so sure. It's close, but not the same. And, truth be told, I had recently seen what happens after we die. By some mystery, I had walked through the Inferno, Purgatory and Paradise, living to tell about it. I had observed things which were almost indescribable, even for me, a poet. But I'm guessing you don't want to hear about all my problems. So let me instead tell you about some of the good things I discovered when grace found me.

You see, I had been asleep for a long time. Not literally asleep, but nevertheless asleep to who I really was and what I had become. I was careless and had refused to accept responsibility for my life. I had misused my freedom.[5] I had many misplaced loves. So that dark wood, the one I described before, that's where I came to find myself. This is my painful story of how I found my way back to wholeness and found rest for my soul. Don't worry, my story is a comedy — it has a happy ending.

As I looked around, I noticed a large, towering hill at the end of the valley where I was. The hill held a strange attraction for me so I started to make my way towards it. When I got to the base of the hill, I looked up and saw rays of light breaking through at the top like hints of the sun peeking through the clouds. Looking closer, I caught a glimpse of something striking. I could barely make it out, but there seemed to be a kind of garden paradise up there at the summit, like the light shining in the darkness (John 1.5).[6] It was verdant and bright, a stark contrast to the foreboding, heavy gloom of the valley floor. I felt a sense of peace in my heart, a rare event for me, as if this is where I was supposed to go. If I could just get up that mountain, I would at last be at rest.

So I started bounding up the hill, huffing and puffing as I went. Before I got too far, I turned back to gaze at the long pass I had just come across. I was amazed that I made it. From what I understand, few mortals have ever come through that pass alive. There were just too many obstacles to traverse unaided. Here I was, physically alive, but still lost as I searched for the right path. It was like I had just emerged from the cleansing waters of baptism, and was starting my slow ascent to find sanctity, a kind of second stage of being born from above (John 3.3).[7] I knew I needed to repent and move toward virtue. I knew where I wanted to go; my heart just didn't know how to get there.[8]

Once I rested a bit, I started up the slope again, limping along as I went. My soul ached to be cleansed of the filth that was holding it back. I was attached to so many temporal things. I had freedom, but to this point, I had almost always used it in counter-productive ways. It was time to make a change, to turn, by ascending to the summit of that hill. There, I would find wholeness and peace. There, I would find rest for my soul. The problem was that my whole self — body, mind and spirit — was just limping along because I carried around so much sin. I was broken and hurting.

The Three Beasts

Just as I started to make some progress up the hill, a spotted leopard confronted me out of the blue. Startled, I jumped back and tried to maneuver around the beast, but it was too quick and nimble. The leopard's skin was patterned and bright, a ferocious beauty. The very fact that the beast scared me so much suggested that something was really wrong within me. I tried again and again to elude it, but the leopard kept forcing me back down the hill. As hard as I tried to maneuver around it, the lustful leopard made me go back down the hill. What was I supposed to do?

It was the morning of Good Friday and the sun was just coming up.[9] The stars, in the constellation of Aries, were supposed to be bringing me hope of spring's rebirth, a reminder of the hope that first ignited when the Divine Son came to earth, clothed in human flesh.[10] But, after my encounter with the leopard, hope was hard to maintain. So much had changed since the creation of the world, especially since many angels and all of mankind had fallen headlong into sin.

I started back up the mountain again when suddenly a violent lion appeared in front of me, blocking my way. Proud and majestic, the lion frightened me because of his ravenous hunger. He wanted to rip apart everything in his path, much like I wanted to do to those who had exiled me. Even the air trembled at his dreadful roar which forced everything he encountered to turn back. I found myself becoming angry at the impossibility of ascent.

In short order, I encountered a she-wolf, all emaciated and withered. She had consumed much, but was little nourished, kind of like a greedy person, embroiled in fraud, who lives out a wretched existence. She was so nasty that it frightened me. Despite her gaunt appearance, she laid a heavier burden on me than the other beasts, causing so much fear that I lost all hope of ascent. This was simply a barrier I could not cross. I was certainly not going to find peace by the direct route. So I retreated back down to the darkness below in the silence of the spiritual death which enveloped me.

At this point, I touched the bottom of the dark valley floor. For some reason, the words of Proverbs 4.19 came to mind: "*The way of the wicked is darkness, they know not where they fall.*" That described me pretty well, I thought. Except, was I really that bad? Wasn't the Divine Master supposed to be showing me mercy? Remember, I was the one who was suffering the injustice of exile. Why would the Master block my way to find him? Why did the Master let these beasts overpower my desire to ascend to him?

Virgil Appears

As I was wallowing in the quiet self-pity and depression of my spiritual desert, an odd figure appeared before me. I say odd because I couldn't really figure out what it was. He appeared fainter than a normal man, but had shape and form, which made me think it wasn't really a ghost either. It was a bit of an enigma. All I could think to do was to cry out a word from the mass: "*Miserere,*" have mercy on me (Ps 51.1), the very words King David used to cry out for forgiveness after his sins of adultery and murder.[11]

The figure answered, "Yes, I was once a man, but less so now. I'm a shadow of the man I once was. I hail from Mantua that town in

Lombardy." Mantua, I thought? Could it be? That's where my majestic mentor hailed from.

The figure continued, "I spent nearly all my early life under the reign of Julius Caesar, born too late for honor from him, but too early for salvation. I lived in Rome under the greatest ruler, Augustus Caesar, my patron for a time, even if the Roman habit of worshipping false and deceitful gods has caused me grief in my present state. I became a poet and composed timeless verses about Aeneas, the son of Anchises, and his journeys to found the city of Rome after the Trojan War. You've probably heard about me."

He continued, "But, tell me, why are you flailing around down here in the dark? Why not ascend the mountain — I hear it's delightful once you get to the top. Don't you want the joy the ascent up the hill will bring?"

My jaw dropped when I heard these words. I responded with excitement, "So you really are Virgil, the greatest of the poets, the one I draw on every time I sit down to write!" I lowered my head, not so much to honor him, as in shame that I could not ascend the mountain as he implored me to do.

I raised my head and continued, "I'll tell you what. There is no one like you. All the poets who came after you — some of whom I really admire — don't hold a candle to your work. I've spent years studying your verses with reverence and awe. You really are my master and teacher, the one I owe everything to for the sweet new style that has brought me not a little notice of late. I couldn't have done my work without you."

I continued, "But look, see that emaciated beast over there that keeps causing me to turn back? For some reason, I can't ascend the mountain to find the joy of which you speak. So I'm stuck back down here in the dark wood. Save me from her! I'll be eternally in your debt." I started weeping when I realized my own impotence in the presence of my hero.

Virgil answered, "I'll tell you what. You're going to have to go a different route, a far more dangerous, arduous and circuitous route, to find what you want. That beast isn't just a physical barrier; she's a spiritual one, too. You're going to have to confront her by leaving behind this savage and gloomy place. If you keep trying to ascend by force, she'll not only block you, but will eventually kill you, both physically and spiritually. You've got to go a different way."

Virgil continued, "That wolf has such a wicked nature that she's never satisfied. Even when she feeds, she just ends up hungrier than before. She mates with lots of different creatures, but produces little. So let me predict something for you, something I'm sure is going to happen: the Divine Son is going to come one day and deal with her and it will represent a painful demise. The judge will return with awesome power and might, with perfect wisdom, love and virtue. Yet, in this display, he'll demonstrate his great humility as well, just like his birth in a lowly manger. This is the one who will make everything right, who will restore Italy to its former glory, not like the glory of Camilla, Euryalus, Turnus and Nisus who died in the Trojan War without hope. No, the Redeemer will restore true order, hope and prosperity to Italy. Only he can pull it off."

Virgil persisted, "I think it's best for you if you follow me a different way. I'll be your guide. I don't promise ease and safety, but I will get you to the right place, first an eternal place, where you'll encounter the desperate squeals and aching pains of those who have abandoned hope, those awaiting the second death of John's apocalypse (Rev 21.8).[12] This is where we'll start."

But, then, you'll have the chance to move on from there to see those content to burn for a time as part of their purification, their preparation to be in the Divine presence. You'll see a glimmer of hope restored. But, finally, if you choose to, you'll ascend once more, under the supervision of a far more beautiful guide than I am. I'll leave you with her to ascend to timeless realms that I've never seen. The ruler of that realm doesn't allow me to enter because of the sin that is, and was, and always will be resident within me. You'll see his throne and all the blessed that he has chosen to be with him forever. This is where true beatitude resides."

I replied, "Poet, please help me! You may not have known the Master I'm trying to find, but I want more than anything to flee from this terrible evil that's hindering me. Let your words take on flesh that they may help me ascend. Please, I beg you, don't leave me here alone! Lead me to the gates of St. Peter and to those who are embroiled in grief. I accept your offer of assistance!"

With that, Virgil set out to depart and I followed along behind him. Our epic journey had begun.

Comment

As we begin our journey, we should be careful not to read Dante's story in an overly-literal fashion. There is an underlying allegory which holds a richer set of meanings. Dante would have been very well acquainted with St. Paul's words that "*The letter kills, but the spirit gives life*" (2 Cor 3.6). He's asking us to read the poem in a similar way to how a medieval interpreter would have read the Bible.[13] In the poem, we should assume that the literal story is true, much like we would as we suspend disbelief during a movie. This, of course, doesn't mean Dante's tale is literally true, even if it contains much truth. The poem contains many non-literal, but nonetheless true signs that lead to a deeper set of meanings. I believe Dante is asking us to employ this medieval reading strategy in the *Comedy*. To borrow the words of J. R. R. Tolkein, Dante's *Comedy* is a "true myth."[14]

Dante is explicit about this strategy in an important letter he wrote to Congrande della Scala, not long after writing the *Inferno*.[15] In his philosophical work, *The Banquet*, written a few years before Dante started writing the *Comedy*, he draws a distinction between the "allegory of the poets" in which we assume the underlying story is not true and the "allegory of the theologians" in which we assume the underlying story is true.[16] This is a crucial distinction.

As we'll see later on, Dante insists that this story really happened. He's willing to bet his life on it. Thus he's adopting the "allegory of the theologians." Dante wants us to lose ourselves in the story, assuming its truth, even though we might suspect that Dante didn't really experience everything he wrote here. Yet we must also take care not to push the allegory so hard that it muffles what Dante is trying to show us. Of course, this is not the only possible reading strategy, but it is the one we'll adopt in this retelling.

This means that as we read the *Comedy*, it's important to hold the literal and the allegorical senses in tension. The story really matters (and it's gripping), but it is supposed to lead to something larger than Dante's own life. It's not by chance that Dante employs a plural pronoun in the first line of the poem: "In the middle of *our* life," suggesting that the scope of the poem is about much more than one man. The poem is supposed to cause the reader to engage with her life as well. This is what makes the *Comedy* worth enjoying in every age. As human beings, we all have to live with the confusion that life brings. We all have to make the affirmative decision to respond to the grace that is offered to us. We all have to undertake a difficult journey in life if we're going to be whole.

So the *Comedy* is not so much one man's finding himself in the literal sense of the story. It's about a soul's journey to find what it has really always desired. And what our souls really want is to experience union with our Creator. No matter who we are or what our background is, rich or poor, Christian, Muslim or atheist, we all have an insatiable desire for transcendence (if we're honest). We all long for redemption and for a world that is at peace instead of at war, one redeemed instead of torn apart by sin, where harmony and order rule. We're at the start of our journey, and we're not there yet.

But why do we have to work so hard to experience this elusive wholeness? The short answer is sin. We need to be very clear from the beginning about what Dante means by sin. Dante is employing a very Augustinian understanding of sin, which he probably acquired through Thomas Aquinas. To Augustine, sin is about misplaced love. This means we either love bad things we shouldn't love, or we love good things that we should love in a disordered way. Thus sin leads to disorder in the creation through our attachments to temporal, created things.

Hence sin is misplaced love that manifests itself in a misuse of our wills. To Augustine, there's a distinction between the sin we're born with (original sin) and the sins we freely commit in our lives (individual sin). As we'll see, almost everyone is in the Inferno because they've freely chosen to be there by rejecting the forgiveness God offers to everyone. Each soul we'll encounter has refused to turn away from his misplaced loves. This is why the Divine Names "God," "Christ" or "Jesus" almost never show up in the *Inferno*. God cannot be openly acknowledged by those who have turned away from Him.

This is also why we can't undertake this journey by ourselves. The implication of the corruption in our souls is that we tend to delude ourselves. As a result, we all need a guide to help us navigate this journey. Perhaps our guide will be a loved one, perhaps a pastor or priest, perhaps a therapist, even a friend. For some, our guide may simply be the Scriptures, the tradition, the lives of the Saints or even this poem. Of course, we may know intellectually that we're imperfect, but most of us secretly think that we're really not all that bad, certainly not as bad as others we know or have heard about. We refuse to see the wretchedness within us that tears apart the fabric of the created order.

So this journey we're about to embark upon is for everyone, but unfortunately not everyone undertakes it. Why? Well, people don't undertake this journey because it's hard and risky. It's much easier to keep telling ourselves half-truths. It's much easier to demonize those we hate since it makes us feel better (for a time). It's far harder to risk being in relationship with other people and treating them with the dignity and the forbearance they deserve as those who bear the Image of God. In short, to find wholeness, we're going to need a guide to help us descend into the hell of the soul, the hell we've chosen to live in today. We're going to have to see that we've freely chosen to embrace our misplaced loves. And we're going to have to admit that in light of such an existential threat, there's little we can do about it without divine help.

This is where grace enters, God's unmerited favor, his love "*that he pours out in our hearts by the Holy Spirit which has been given to us*"

(Rom 5.5). The offer of grace is free, but so is our freedom to accept it or resist it. This journey that we're about to undertake isn't easy, but it might just reorient our lives both in the physical and spiritual realms. Whether your life turns out to be a comedy or a tragedy could just hinge on whether you receive the forgiveness and grace that are offered to you. Dante has accepted the free offer of grace mediated by Virgil. He's begun his journey. Let's follow him as it unfolds.

2

Embracing Grace

INTRODUCTION TO THE INFERNO

Dante's unsuccessful attempts to climb the mountain have taken most of the day. It is now early evening on Good Friday. Dante loses heart and his fear takes over. Realizing that he's no hero in the mode of Aeneas and St. Paul, Dante starts to doubt this journey is a good idea. In response, Virgil recounts the backstory to what has been happening. Dante's beloved Beatrice, the object of his love from his childhood, was concerned enough about his troubles that she left heaven and entreated Virgil to go help. Beatrice was prompted into action by the concern of the Virgin Mary and St. Lucy. This feminine trinity re-enacts the story of the annunciation whereby Dante must decide whether to cooperate with the Divine Grace offered to him. Dante accepts Virgil's help and they continue on their journey.

It was the end of a long Friday. The sun was setting, leaving behind only silhouettes in its wake. Virgil and I were together, he in the lead, and I following behind. Yet I was the only human in the mix. Virgil was just a shadow of a man, a shade. Having been blocked from taking the shortcut up the mountain, I had no idea what to expect. I couldn't imagine this journey was going to be easy, but I was pretty sure I was going to feel sorry for those poor souls I was about to encounter.

Now I want to emphasize something. This isn't some made-up story. I may be telling you a tale, but I want you to know my account really happened. You need to suspend disbelief and have some faith in what I'm saying. What I'm telling you came vividly from my memory. I'm bearing witness to the true things that I saw there.

Just like the great poets of old, let me call upon the Muses to inspire me with their genius. Let me entreat them to stir up my memory that I might write down what I really saw on that journey. The Muses will ensure that my writing is inspired.

Dante's Doubt

As we were walking along, I started to lose faith. What was I thinking, embarking on this journey? Was I really going to descend into the Inferno? Why not just stay up in the dark wood where it was safe? As far as I knew, no one had ever emerged from the Inferno alive. So why would I bother going there?

I asked my guide: "Virgil, you know I'm not that strong. I was just weeping a couple minutes ago. I'm nothing like the heroes you wrote about in your great epic, the *Aeneid*. Shouldn't we rethink this trip? Take, for example, Aeneas, the hero of your *Aeneid*. I've never been able to figure out just how he managed to descend into the netherworld. Of course, Aeneas made it out alive and went on to found Rome, but the Divine Master was on his side. He was the agent of divine providence, chosen to found the Roman Empire. The Divine Master was for him because this was the place the Almighty had chosen to establish St. Peter's seat.[17] As a result of divine favor, Aeneas couldn't help but secure a victory where so many others had failed."

"But it's not just Aeneas. I'm thinking also about St. Paul, too. The Master chose to disclose his mysteries to Paul when he elevated him by grace to heaven. As Paul describes it: *'I know a man...about fourteen years ago (whether in the body, I know not, or out of the body, I know not)...such a one was caught up to the third heaven...he was caught up into paradise and heard secret words which it is not granted to man to utter'* (2 Corinthians 12.2,4).[18] The Master had a purpose in mind in doing this, since he had chosen Paul to explain the way of salvation to those still on earth. Paul wrote a big chunk of the New Testament informed by what he had seen."

My voice became more agitated as I continued, "So let's be clear. I'm no Aeneas. He was a great leader and a war hero. I'm no Paul. He was a great missionary and a saint. Let's not kid ourselves. I'm not at all worthy to go down to the Inferno or to ascend into Paradise. This must be some mistake. It's insane to think that I'm in the same league as these guys. I'm not going to bet my whole life on this one crazy decision to follow some shade into the netherworld! Please, Virgil, help me figure this thing out because it's making no sense to me. How can you have faith in something when reason fails?"

Virgil listened patiently and then calmly answered me: "So, if I'm hearing you right, you're scared and your fear is assaulting your spirit such that you don't want to continue. How many times have I seen fear take over a man to such an extent that he turns back from an honorable undertaking? How many tales of terrible ghosts lurking in the shadows actually turn out to be true?"

The Female Trinity

Virgil continued, "The only solution for your fear is for me to tell you a bit of the back story for how I came to rescue you. You see, there are some pretty lofty people in the heavenly realms that have taken a keen interest in you. This is no chance journey. You're right to think it's risky, but people in heaven genuinely care about you. My coming to you happened like this:

I was biding my time in Limbo when I became aware that this unbelievably beautiful and chaste lady was calling me. Beatrice was her name. I get the sense that you used to know her when she was alive. This was not some apparition. I have to admit seeing a vision of this sort was very much out of the ordinary in my parts, so I begged her to tell me what she wanted."

"When I saw her glistening eyes that sparkled like the stars, I almost melted. Speaking with the voice of an angel, Beatrice told me about you, your history with her, and the predicament you were in. She told me how you were trapped by the beasts on the mountain. She also recounted to me the fear that had gripped you, causing you to turn back from the mountain. She was so concerned what the heavenly beings were saying about you that she fretted you might already be lost. She begged me to leave Limbo and come to you, to use all my powers of poetry and persuasion to provide comfort and help to you. You see, Beatrice, your long-lost love, the girl you fell for when you were nine years old, the one you dedicated all your earlier love poetry to, she travelled all the way from heaven to get me to help you.[19] Even if she spurned your advances when she was alive, she cares about you enough to have sent me to be your guide."

"Beatrice promised me that if I came and helped you, she would put in a good word for me with the Lord in heaven. Maybe there's a way of getting out of Limbo that I don't know about. I don't see how that's possible, but even a glimmer of hope would be better than what I have now. As you'll see, there's not much hope where I've come from."

Virgil continued, "Beatrice's virtue so overwhelmed me that I felt like reaching up to the moon. I was grateful that she asked me to undertake this task. Frankly all she had to do was ask. But there was one thing which puzzled me."

Virgil continued, "I asked her, 'Why aren't you scared to leave heaven behind and descend down here to the upper reaches of the Inferno? Aren't you worried you won't be able to get back to the eternal realms above?'

Beatrice then answered me, 'Your question is a good one. But, no, I'm not afraid. You see, there's nothing here that can harm me. I'm in a state of grace and nothing bad can befall me. I've experienced the perfection of faith, hope and love and because of that, the Inferno has no power over me. It's the Master, by his grace, who has enabled this. What I have can't be taken away from me."

"In fact, I'm not the only one interested in Dante. This all started with the Gracious Lady, who sits atop the heavenly hierarchy in the presence of our Lord. She felt so sorry for poor old Dante and the obstacles to faith before him that she had heaven suspend judgment on him that he might undertake this journey. Out of the wellspring of her love and mercy, she called first upon St. Lucy, that great martyr from the third century and the patron Saint of those with impaired vision, to do something about the situation."[20]

Beatrice continued, 'Lucy, who was seated next to Rachael, the wife of Jacob, in heaven, left her place and came down to call upon me. Lucy asked me to come to your aid since you loved her so much that you left the rabble behind. Moved by your tears and the torrent of spiritual death descending upon you, Lucy exhorted me to help. In response, I arose quickly. That's why I came to see you.'"

"Now this is all pretty remarkable," I thought. A female trinity, caring for me? As the Virgin was given a free choice to say yes or no at the annunciation, so I was being given the choice to respond to grace or not. What should I do?

Receiving Grace

Virgil took the story back up. "So, Dante, you see I've come here at the behest of the Virgin, St. Lucy and your beloved Beatrice. I'm mediating their offer of grace to you. That's why I rescued you from the beasts that assailed you while you were trying to take a short-cut up the mountain. It's no accident that you couldn't take the easy route. You'll never get to salvation that way. No, you have to decide here and now, in the absence of evidence, whether you're going to face your fears and follow me."

Virgil continued, "Dante, here's my question, what are you waiting for? Why all this fear? Why not have some courage in light of the three heavenly ladies who are calling you to examine your life? To find yourself, you're going to have to descend into the Inferno. There's simply no shortcut for this."

So I answered, "My strength may be wavering and my heart trembling, but what amazing compassion heaven has bestowed on

me. And what consideration you've shown me through your willingness to obey. Just as the Blessed Virgin, at the annunciation said, '*My soul magnifies the Lord and my spirit rejoices in God my Savior'* (Luk 1.46-47), so too I answer 'yes.'"[21]

"Virgil, I want to go with you into realms unknown. Our wills are knitted together. You'll be my leader and the Lord my Master."

Virgil then started again on his way and I followed behind, embarking on the difficult path before me.

Comment

Dante begins the Canto by calling on the Muses, asking for divine help in making sure his writing matches his memory. He is actually asking for divine inspiration as he writes. This is one reason why we should assume the literal story is a true myth. He asks the Muses to help him accurately reflect his memory as he writes. Hence, the idea of memory is very important here. To remember in an epic poem is actually to re-live, or re-present the experience.[22]

As Dante recounts his story to us, we should be aware that he has already lived through this journey. He is recounting what he has already seen. The very fact that he's alive to tell it makes us realize that everything is going to turn out well in the end, which is one reason we call it a comedy. At the completion of the one-hundredth Canto of the poem, at the top of heaven, after almost fifteen-thousand lines of poetry, all of a sudden everything goes black and we return to the beginning of the story again. In other words, there are both circular and linear movements happening in the story.

This combination of the circular and the linear is pretty remarkable because Christians, following St. Augustine, were well-known for having rejected the Greek view of circularity in favor of a linear view of history. Christians believed that the Incarnation and the hope of Christ's second coming created a trajectory for history. Yet, in the *Comedy*, Dante combines the two.[23] The poem is linear, in the sense that it's telling a story with a goal in mind, but is also circular in that we're supposed to encounter this journey over and over again. The poem's goal is the beatific vision in heaven, but the experience of the spiritual journey is something we're going to have to undergo if we choose to keep growing.

Why does this matter? Well, it helps to explain why Dante loses his courage in this Canto and why this is so important for us as readers. Dante has access to divine revelation and knowledge, but none of this helps him as he starts to go through the Inferno. He loses his courage and wonders why he's doing this. As he tells us, he's no Aeneas and he's no Paul. They're the heroes, not him.

The critical lesson we all need to learn is that doubt in the midst of a spiritual journey is normal. Yet everything depends on our decision of whether or not to keep going. Consistency is one of the keys to the spiritual life. Once again, we see Dante presented with a genuine choice — he could reject the grace of God that's being offered to him. He could reject Virgil's help and play it safe. But, as we'll see in the next Canto, it doesn't work out very well for those who decide to take the safe route. In other words, what seems like the height of folly and risk often turns out to be the very place that safety resides. The spiritual life is difficult because the decisions it demands are often bewildering.

Thus Dante is trying to encourage each of us to embark on our own journeys. As we do, we're going to encounter all kinds of troubles and doubts about whether we're on the right track. But, frankly, this is a normal part of a spiritual journey. In the end, we'll observe that taking the risk to examine our souls is the key thing we need to do to grow. There is little growth without risk and effort. Dante demonstrates that even though it feels very strange, the key to the spiritual life is to keep going, which is what he ultimately decides to do.

3

The Ante-Chamber

NEUTRAL ANGELS AND MISERABLE MODERATES

Dante and Virgil enter the ante-room of the Inferno through a large Romanesque gate, which warns all comers to abandon hope. Once through the gate, Dante encounters the souls of neutral angels and men who refused to take sides and thus are consigned to a place outside heaven or hell. Dante recognizes Pope Celestine V, who abdicated his Pontificate. Later on, Dante banters with Charon, the skiff captain who transports souls to the Inferno. He has a troubling encounter with the dead souls waiting to be transported across the river. Overwhelmed by the scene, Dante passes out, foreshadowing his need to fortify himself against the effects of sin.

As Virgil and I continued on our way, we came to a large gate. With my awestruck eyes, I surveyed the massive structure that reminded me of the architecture that the proud Romans employed to project their power.[24] My own hometown of Florence copied the Romans when it constructed its gates in order to keep the city safe.

The gate itself was foreboding. Tall and broad, it welcomed all comers. The Divine Son was right when he said "*The gate is wide and the way is easy that leads to destruction*" (Matt 7.13). This place was no joking matter.

As my eyes slowly made their way up the sides of the structure, I noticed some words written in capital letters scrawled on the gate:

THROUGH ME, GO ON TO THE CITY OF SORROW;
THROUGH ME GO ON TO EVERLASTING GRIEF;
THROUGH ME GO ON AMONG THE LOST.

I felt a kind of heavy pressure weighing down on me as I read these tragic lines. Sorrow? Grief? Loss? What kind of place was this?

But I kept going. As I moved my eyes down the gate, I noticed another triplet:

JUSTICE MOVED MY CREATOR ON HIGH;
SACRED POWER CREATED ME,
ABSOLUTE WISDOM AND PRIMAL LOVE.

My eyes then moved a little lower to where I saw the last part of the dark inscription:

BEFORE ME, CREATED THINGS DID NOT
EXIST, ONLY ETERNAL THINGS,
BUT I ENDURE ETERNALLY;
ABANDON HOPE ALL YE WHO ENTER HERE

These inscriptions seemed to be some kind of reference to the Trinity. Besides the obvious fact that there were three statements of three, all of these descriptions were of divine attributes.[25] I knew that the Father was pure justice and sacred power; the Son was absolute wisdom; while the Spirit was primal love. I also believed the Persons of the Trinity created the heavens and the earth. But, if the Master created everything, why did he create this place? Where's the justice in that?

Moreover, what's with this "abandon hope" language? This was more than a little ironic.[26] After all, I was trying to find hope! What good would it do me to walk through this terrible gate if there's no hope down here? I started to wonder whether Virgil really knew what he was doing, taking me down to such a foul place. Why would anyone want to go here?

Incredulously, I looked over to my guide and said, "Virgil, this is a really hard saying. It's not only hard to read because it's so dark, but it's hard to understand. And, frankly I find it intimidating.[27] In my mind, this was like when the Divine Son told the disciples '*to eat [his] flesh and drink [his] blood*' (John 6.53). Even with all the offense the Son caused in that statement, it's easier than understanding what this inscription means."

Virgil's response took me off guard. He didn't hesitate for a second, saying, "You're going to have to stop doubting. Your childish fright isn't helping you. In this place, the damned have lost the reasoning power of their minds because they've lost the Master who illumines the intellect. As you'll see, the damned don't think they've done anything wrong down here. They remain wholly unconcerned about the grief they've caused because they all think they've done the right things in their lives. Yet everyone here has misused their free will in one way or another. Don't look at the appearances of things, but consider their deeper meanings. Looks can be deceiving."

I marveled at Virgil's understanding of this place. He gave me a consoling look, placing his hand on mine to try to comfort me.

But as we moved on a bit, I started hearing frightful noises — the sound of sighs, cries and laments issuing forth from the darkness. At this point, the place was eerily dim because the stars that provided light to the woods above were absent down here. Startled by the wretched wailing, I started to sob.

There was so much noise. There were multitudes of foreign tongues and accents, all proffering accounts of suffering and anger. The cacophony of grief was almost overwhelming. The whole place seemed to be filled to the brim with misery. There was even the sound of people slapping each other around; it was like love had left completely. "What a colorless whirlwind of terror," I thought.

The Neutral Angels and Miserable Moderates

We then moved on a little further to a kind of ante-chamber. I could barely make out the faint resemblance of a large river off in the distance. I was so disoriented at this point that I asked my leader, "What am I hearing? Why is there all this pain down here?"

Virgil answered, "This ante-room holds the contemptible souls who tried to play it safe by refusing to choose a side. In life, they were the miserable moderates, never taking a firm position on anything. They're here together with the neutral angels who refused to take a stand when Satan led his rebellion in Heaven. These angels separated themselves, so they're not welcome anywhere — either in Heaven or in the Inferno." [28]

Still bewildered, I asked, "So what's the big deal? They're here on the outskirts of the Inferno. Why are they so upset?"

Virgil once again responded resolutely, "Let me be clear: these folks have no hope of death. They have no hope of moral improvement. Thus they have no hope of love.[29] They're stuck in their lamentable condition forever; and unlike most here, they're acutely aware of what they're missing. As a result, they spend eternity envious of everyone else.[30] Envy is something that never made anyone happy and these shades definitely aren't happy. What a waste, what a terrible way to end up, utterly bereft of hope. Frankly, no one cares about them since they didn't care about anyone else. So let's just ignore them and move on."

As we were passing by, I observed this miserable lot chasing around in circles an amorphous banner. Leaderless, they ran around without rest, demonstrating the absolute futility and purposelessness of their existence.[31] What really shocked me was the almost countless number of figures doing this. How could so many souls be in this miserable state? These were probably some of the ones the Apostle John had in mind when he said in his Apocalypse, "*And in those days men will seek death and not find it; they will long to die and death will fly from them*" (Rev 9.6).

The Great Refusal: Pope Celestine V

As I looked closer, I realized I recognized one of them, a shade who had affected my life considerably, Pope Celestine V. Let me admit that there was a lot to like about this pious man; he was a genuinely humble and peaceful monk who, despite the violence and corruption of the age, managed to become Pope because of his piety (it also didn't hurt that the Cardinals thought they could manipulate him into doing their bidding).[32] Yet he quickly realized he was totally out of his depth to deal with the corruption in Rome. When the going got tough — after five months — he abdicated his office when he figured out he wasn't up to the task.[33]

This cleared the way for my arch nemesis, Boniface VIII, to become Pope, the one I ultimately blame for my exile. I'm convinced the ambitious Boniface beguiled Celestine into abdicating. Well, no matter, this was a disaster and Celestine deserves his place down here for the misery he's caused so many by not following through on his divine calling. His great refusal allowed evil to triumph.[34]

When I looked back on them, I started to wonder if the Divine Master regretted even making these souls. They really had never lived.[35] They were naked and forever annoyed by horseflies and wasps circling around them, stinging them. The blood that flowed from their wounds mixed together with their tears was nourishing the lowly maggots at their feet. These lukewarm souls were the ones that the Divine Son called "*dead*" (Rev 3.1), even when they were alive. This was a pitiful sight.[36]

The River

I then looked farther on, past the dimly lit ante-chamber, and could barely make out the outlines of souls on the bank of the mighty river. It was almost as if I had seen all this before in my mind's eye, probably in something I had read. All these lost souls by the river? It reminded me of what Virgil had written in the *Aeneid* when Aeneas had to cross over the river to get into hell to see his dead father and to learn his fate.[37]

But just then another thing popped into my head. I realized I was in a kind of Exodus story.[38] If you think about it, the Israelites, when they were slaves, were in their own Inferno before the great parting of the Red Sea let them cross over. Still reasoning like slaves, they thought they had lost their freedom. My journey was starting to feel a bit like that. Just as the Israelites had to cross the Red Sea and wander through a desert, I was for some reason being led to wander through the desert of hell to find the Promised Land. I still didn't understand it all, but here I was, headed down to the Inferno.

I asked Virgil about the people I saw congregated around the shore. What was especially puzzling to me was how eager they seemed to be to get to the other side. In the case of the Israelites, I could understand — the Egyptians were chasing them. But why did these people want to get down to the Inferno so badly? What could possibly motivate them to do that?

Virgil curtly replied, "Be patient. This will get clearer for you a little farther on, once we get past the gloomy shores of the river Acheron." Worried about my impetuous tone and my impatience to see around the corner, I hung my head with shame, fearing my overly-confident speech had offended Virgil. I decided to keep quiet until we got to the river and kept walking forward in silence.

As we got to the shore, I noticed an old skiff coming towards us. Directing it was an old devil with a face crumpled up like discarded parchment. He had hair that was white as ancient wool and his eyes beamed with a seriousness that underscored his gruesome vocation. As he got closer, he cried out, "Woe to you, corrupt souls! You're never going to see heaven; I've come here to make sure of that! I'm here to take you to the Inferno, to the other shore, where eternal darkness, heat and intense cold all rule."

The figure in the boat was named Charon, the grim captain who ferried condemned souls to the netherworld.[39] Ignoring the others on the shore, he focused intently on me, raising his voice and saying, "Hey, you over there. Yeah, you: the one with the live body." I shrugged my shoulders and raised my eyebrows as if to say, "Who me?" He stomped his foot and exhaled loudly through his demonic nose, "You, the not-so-bright one. Get away from the other folks. You're not supposed to be down here. I haven't come for the living, but for the dead." I froze in place, Virgil by my side, not knowing what to do.

Charon, when he saw that I didn't move, grimaced and said something cryptic: "Look, you're destined for other ports of call, not this one. No doubt, I've seen it — you're going to pass by a different way. A lighter ship needs to bring you home."

What kind of strange prediction was this? Could I trust what a demon was telling me? I liked the idea that there might be a happy ending to this story. But who knows who you can trust down here. I just let his comment pass. "Better to be realistic than optimistic," I thought.

Then Virgil spoke up. "Look, Charon, heaven has already worked this whole thing out." He then continued slowly and clearly: 'There it's so willed, where what's willed, is done'. Just let us cross with the rest and we'll be on our way."

I was pretty impressed with Virgil, who showed some backbone there. He seemed to know the shibboleth, the secret password to get us by the gatekeeper.

Upon hearing the password, good ol' wooly cheeks finally relented. I was glad he did. I didn't much care for him.

I started to feel uncomfortable when I became aware of all the dead shades surrounding me on the shore. These souls had shape, but no flesh. It was like they were worn out and naked. For some reason, they were all in a hurry to get to the other side of the river.

As Virgil was speaking, they ceased their incessant chattering for a short while. But, as soon as he finished, they let loose what was really in their hearts: spewing invectives against the Divine Master, their parents, even humanity. Some cursed their place and time of birth. All their hearts were filled with darkness, anger and vitriol. They were just like Jeremiah, the weeping prophet, who said, "*Cursed be the day I was born*" (Jer 20.14).

They all started weeping in unison and drew back to the shore. What a sight! It seemed their confusion and torment was the tragic result for those who did not fear the Master.

Unimpressed with their weeping, Charon fixed his eyes on them and scooped the dead souls up into his boat, striking anyone who lagged behind with his oar. It was just like in autumn when the leaves fall to the ground. These souls, who died in their fallen condition, were tumbling down to their doom. As they disappeared on the skiff through the dark water, a whole new crowd of dead shades lined up to take their place, a limitless sea of depressing ruin.

Seeing the distress in my eyes, Virgil spoke like a comforting father, "Oh my son, this is the meeting point for everyone who dies apart from grace. Did you see how eager these souls were to cross that river? Well, that's the power of divine justice at work. The Divine Master turns their fear into desire. They can't wait to get to the Inferno, thinking it's their preferred place. The Master gives them exactly what they ardently desired in life."

He continued, "No good soul right with the Master ever passes over here. This is why Charon gave you such a hard time. All these souls misused their free will to be here. Thus they freely chose their own Inferno. For our choices to be free, the Inferno has to be a genuine possibility."

When he finished speaking, the earth shook with such staggering force that I was scared to death. My body's trembling only increased as I felt the subterranean wind that came up from the earth, the probable cause of the earthquake.

Overwhelmed by the scene and its attendant reality, I fainted like one caught in a deep sleep. My head hit the ground and I passed out.

Comment

Canto Three introduces the reader to one of the most difficult issues in the poem — how to grapple with the justice of hell. After all, if God truly loves his children, how can it ever be just to consign a large portion of his sons and daughters to eternal torment? The division of humanity into the sheep and the goats is one of the more troubling aspects of the Christian faith. How can this particularity square with a God who reveals himself as loving, long-suffering and compassionate? Dante expects large masses of people consigned to eternal torment to bother us.

Dante introduces the reader to a creative way of dealing with this dilemma. He helps us grapple with the justice issue through his belief that God has endowed his creatures with genuine freedom. In Dante's world, each person is given the grace to choose for himself whether to attach to transcendent eternal things or to the temporal things of the world. Without exception, since all bear the Image of God, all have some desire for something transcendent. And, thus, radical human choice is one of the central themes of the poem.

Put simply, those who are in the Inferno have freely chosen to be there. God has not sent them there as some kind of punishment for their bad acts. In fact, as we'll see, souls usually are not in the Inferno for something they've done that violates some arbitrary set of rules. Rather, souls are usually there for something they did not do; namely, their refusal to accept God's free offer of forgiveness.[40] Dante was probably very aware of St. Peter's statement that God does not wish "*that any should perish, but that all should reach repentance*" (2 Pet 3.9). The Inferno exists because people prefer their own misplaced loves to God's forgiveness.

Hell is a necessary counterpart to God's creation of humans with free will. Some — maybe even many — will use their free will consciously to reject God and to refuse anything transcendent in their lives. The Inferno, then, is not just a future reality, according to Dante, but is an ever-present reality for those who try to live without forgiveness while they're on earth. There are lots of people walking around in their own private hells today. All God does in consigning people to the Inferno is to give them what they really wanted in this life. To Dante, this is why hell exists.

Dante also introduces us in this Canto to a central feature of the poem called in Italian "*contrapasso.*" I discussed this in the Introduction, but want to make sure we understand it because it is so central to the poem. This key concept derives from two Latin words: "*contra*," meaning "in return" and "*patire*" meaning "to endure, suffer or bear."[41] *Contrapasso* is Dante's way of describing God's retributive justice in the *Inferno* (and later in the *Purgatorio*).

Dante's unique contribution is to insist that every soul suffers according to his sin on earth. As we go through the *Comedy*, we'll observe that this retribution comes in the form of either a parallel equivalence or a contrast.[42] Thus, in a sense, the Inferno is merely a continuation of what the person chose while he was alive. John Ciardi describes this well: "*The law of Dante's Hell is the law of symbolic retribution. As they sinned so they are punished.*"[43]

One of the key activities we need to do as readers is to try to understand these punishments because they provide much of the rich symbolic texture for the poem. In Dante's world, God's retributive justice is never arbitrary. So, for example, the *contrapasso* for the "miserable moderates" is to be stung by horseflies and wasps for all eternity. The blood which flows from their wounds feeds the worms and maggots at their feet. For souls (either angel or human) who felt no passion for others in this life, but played it safe by not choosing sides, they're consigned for all eternity to be pricked in their skin so they feel something. Their blood, which they refused to shed during their lives, then feeds the maggots on the ground, a symbol of their moral uncleanness. [44] Dante makes it clear that these souls, by having no passion or concern for others, never really lived. Or, as Helen Luke memorably writes, "*to [Dante], they are more contemptible than the damned.*"[45]

A word of caution is in order, however. We ought to be careful as we read the *Inferno* to recognize the punishments as metaphors. John Freccero describes this well when we he writes, "*The punishments fit the crimes, provided we understand 'fittingness' as an aesthetic category.*"[46] This doesn't make the punishments less vivid or real, but more so.

We have to ask: Is it really so bad that people tried to stay on the sidelines? Don't we get tired of loud-mouthed extremists? To understand this, we should recall that Dante is dealing with some serious injustice in his own life. He's in exile because of a power struggle. Dante wasn't a dogmatist, but he cared enough about his city of Florence to stand up for what he thought was right. He was suffering — really suffering — for it and this is probably driving his contempt for those who played it safe. He was probably also aware of James' statement: "*Whoever knows what is right to do and fails to do it, for him it is sin*" (Jas 4.17).

One last item of note in Canto Three is that Dante probably just invents the concept of neutral angels. Although a vigorous scholarly debate has popped up around this question, there's nothing in the Bible that teaches this.[47] It's a good example of Dante's keen imagination. He's pushing the boundaries of Christian teaching in the poem. You might wonder why the Church allowed this. No doubt, the Church wasn't very happy about Dante's doctrinal innovations, but the *Comedy* was so popular from the moment it came out there was simply no way to stop it.

Although most of the time Dante faithfully reflects the Christian teaching of the late Middle Ages, he was perfectly willing to question the tradition at times (within limits) — an example of his remarkable achievement. One might even say that coming to grips with a God beyond human comprehension requires the sensibility of a poet to imagine what is beyond reason. This is what Dante does with such remarkable success in the *Comedy*.

4

The Virtuous Pagans

CIRCLE I: LIMBO

After passing out, Dante awakes to find himself across the river Acheron. With Virgil, Dante starts his descent into the first Circle of the Inferno, called Limbo. Great sighs greet the pilgrim as he descends. Limbo is where the virtuous pagans come who lack faith given by grace. There is no active punishment here, only unfulfilled desire. Dante meets many souls, including great epic poets, political and military leaders, philosophers, doctors, scientists and mathematicians, representing the glories of pagan learning. In the end, Dante discovers that while learning can enhance human virtue, it cannot save the soul. All the virtuous pagans are deficient in the theological virtues of faith, hope and love.

Crash! I awoke suddenly to a heavy peal of thunder that shook the ground beneath me. I was groggy and disoriented as I came back to consciousness. I had been so sound asleep that it took me a while to become aware of where I was or even what was happening. It was kind of like the disorientation I felt when I awoke to find myself lost in the dark wood at the start of this journey.[48]

When I arose slowly to my feet and looked around, my surroundings seemed unfamiliar. I could see the broad river that I recognized from my previous conversation with Charon, the one who ferried souls across the Acheron River. Yet somehow I had managed to get to the other side of the river. I had no idea how. Charon or Virgil could have carried me over here after I passed out, but how it all worked is still a mystery to me.

As I surveyed the landscape, I noticed I was standing on the edge of a deep pit, kind of like the abyss in John's apocalypse. There, John "*saw an angel coming down from heaven, holding in his hand the key of the bottomless pit and a great chain*" (Rev 20.1). A thundering wave of lament was rising up from the abyss into my ears, which made me recoil.[49] The murky fog within the ditch made it impossible to see down into it, but the foreboding sounds rising up from below made me tremble.

Virgil was also there, standing close to me. When I looked at him, I noticed his face was drained of all color like an empathetic father waiting to tell a worried child about impending danger. Virgil said, "Let's go on down there into the blind world below. I'll be in the lead and you follow on behind."

I couldn't let his creepy face go by without comment, so I said, "Just wait just a minute. If *you're* afraid to go down there, where does that leave me? You're the one who's supposed to be leading me and bringing me comfort. Are you sure this is such a good idea? Let me just say: I have my doubts."

Virgil responded, "You're mistaking my pity for fear. I'm not afraid, just feeling sorry for the people we're about to meet. You see, they're my friends and colleagues."

He continued, "Let's go now since we've got a long journey ahead of us." So Virgil struck out in the lead and we entered into the first Circle of the Inferno.

Limbo

Now I had heard a thing or two about this place, this so-called Limbo, from my studies. But, as I started down, it was quite a bit different than what Thomas Aquinas and the others had taught me. They all emphasized the Divine Son and his leading the Old Testament elect out of the Inferno at his resurrection.[50]

Maybe they were right, but there were a whole bunch of other things I encountered that surprised me. For example, Limbo was within the Inferno itself, not outside it.[51] As a result, there was no hope of salvation down here.

And, surprisingly to me, there were a lot more than children down here — I could hear adults as well.[52] This was all very puzzling and different than what I expected. Only unbaptized infants were supposed to be down here. Why were there adults, too?

As we made our descent, I was surprised to hear no weeping, just collective sighs. It reminded me of what Moses had written in the Psalms: *"For all our days pass away under your wrath, our years come to an end like a sigh"* (Ps 90.9). The very sound from the sinners' exhalations made the air shake with lament.

These sighs came from a huge crowd of people that ranged from infants to grown men and women. Their sheer number startled me. My unaided reason wasn't going to be able to figure all this out. Seeing my confusion, my good leader said to me, "Why don't you ask one of them about the spirits you're observing. It's important that you know about these souls before we go any further."[53]

I didn't want to say anything to these strange souls. I was too scared. When I didn't respond, Virgil said to me, "The souls down here were virtuous, at least in a philosophical sense. Most had justice, temperance, courage and wisdom. For this, they had merit. But merit is simply not enough; they needed faith too. And, for that, they needed grace, which comes by the Spirit. They needed forgiveness for original sin, not their actual sins, of which they had few."[54]

"Moreover, they just didn't know about the theological virtues of faith, hope and love, which come only from the worship of the Creator.[55] Now some of those in Limbo also had the misfortune of living before the Divine Son came and thus didn't have the chance to worship aright. Having died about twenty years before the Son was born, I know something about this; I am one of those myself."

Virgil went on, "We missed out on the Divine Son and thus we're lost, devoid of hope and living with unquenchable desire. As Virgil was speaking, I thought this sounded just like what St. Paul described: "[*You were*] *separated from Christ, alienated from the commonwealth of Israel and strangers to the covenants of promise, having no hope and without God in the world*" (Eph 2.12).

Virgil continued, "You see, the desire for the Creator is only a foretaste of grace.[56] To die unbaptized and without the Son, is to die with eternally unmet desire."

When Virgil stopped, I felt sick to my stomach. I was overwhelmed with sorrow at the seeming injustice of all this. There were really good people down here — people I respected — who were forever held in Limbo.

I immediately started to worry about my own lack of fidelity. I myself was baptized, of course, but what about sanctifying grace?[57] I was, after all, very fond of the budding humanism of my day. Did I prefer Virgil's writings to the prophets? Would I end up down here, too?

So I asked, "Tell me, sir, has anyone ever left Limbo either by his own merits or by the merits of others who made it to Paradise? Thomas Aquinas seemed to think that a bunch of Old Testament souls did."

Recognizing what I was getting at, Virgil responded, "I had been down here a few years when the Divine Son descended to Limbo after his crucifixion. Let me tell you, it was quite a sight. When the Son came down, he was full of power and already crowned with the laurel wreath of victory."[58]

As Virgil spoke, it seemed to me this was a lot like St. Peter described: "[*Having been] put to death in the flesh but made alive in the spirit, he went and preached to the spirits in prison*" (1 Pet 3.19).

Virgil went on, "The Divine Son first drew to himself a number of famous souls from the Old Testament. First, he lifted up Adam, the parent of the human race, along with his son Abel, murdered by his brother Cain. Then, he rescued Noah, who built the ark, along with Moses, who gave the law and led Israel through the desert. He did the same for the patriarch Abraham as well as for David, the great king of Israel.

He then lifted up Isaac, son of Abraham, and Jacob, Isaac's son. He did this together with Jacob's wife Rachel for whom Jacob worked an extra seven years for her father Laban to win her hand. There were a bunch more — a giant throng of them, enough to fill half of heaven. But, before this happened, not a single human soul was saved — they were all waiting for the Divine Son to come."

The Virtuous Poets

As we went along, we were passing through an area thick with spirits. We weren't that far down when I saw a flaming light, which lit up the darkness — a symbol of the heroic work of these virtuous pagans in preserving ancient wisdom.[59] The light was off in the distance, coming from a group of honorable souls who had gathered together.

As their forms became a bit clearer, I asked my guide: "Oh lover of the liberal arts, who are these souls, thought worthy to be set apart from the world and from the others down here?"

Virgil answered, "Their great works have won renown for them even in Paradise, allowing them to progress beyond others." I was starting to get the sense that Virgil was the very embodiment of human reason himself.[60]

As we got closer, a voice bellowed out that I later realized was Homer's: "All hail the greatest of the poets, that shade who has joined our Circle again."[61] He was talking about Virgil, my guide! I had never read Homer directly since I couldn't decipher Greek, but I certainly knew of Homer's reputation. This was undoubtedly high praise.

After Homer quieted down, I saw four great shades coming towards us. They appeared a little bit plain. They were neither sad nor joyful, but were lacking in passion, which was somehow fitting for this Limbo.

Virgil said, "See that one over there with the sword in his hand walking before the three other shades as if he were their noble master? That's Homer himself, the great epic poet of the Trojan War, who wrote the *Iliad* and the *Odyssey.* You would do well to learn Greek so you can read it."

Virgil continued, "His sword reminds me of what an important source he was for my own epic poem, the *Aeneid.* The other one there is Horace, a contemporary of mine, best known for his moral satires.[62] Ovid is third, from whose *Metamorphoses* I learned Greek mythology.[63] Lastly, there's Lucan, the historian of the Roman civil war between Pompey and Caesar.[64] He was the one who fell out of favor with the Emperor Nero and committed suicide.[65] Each of these writers shares with me a commitment to the greatness of poetry and learning. In honoring me, they honor our common vocation.[66]

These four writers gathered together around Virgil, who in my opinion, soars above the others as the greatest of the poets. After briefly catching up with each other, they turned to me and greeted me. I noticed out of the corner of my eye that Virgil smiled broadly, something I wouldn't see him do again in the *Inferno.*[67]

This was a significant gesture. They were honoring me, a fellow poet, by welcoming me in their midst. I was standing on the shoulders of giants.[68] I fell in among their rank and was pleased to count myself the sixth member of this august and wise gathering. To tell the truth, I was pretty sure I belonged among this throng, but only time would tell if I was right.

We moved further on towards the light, chatting about various things, which I'll decline to recount. All I can say is that our talk was fitting for the place where we were.

The Citadel of the Liberal Arts

We came next to the base of a lovely castle that had seven layers of walls surrounding it. The walls were towering and strong, symbolizing the fortress of the seven liberal arts — grammar, logic, rhetoric, math, geometry, astronomy and music.[69] Behind the walls, the castle was majestic, lofty and fair, symbolic of philosophy, the height of all rational knowledge.

A small creek flowed around the castle, which protected it. We managed to skip over the water, just like we were walking on solid ground, much as Peter did when *"he got out of the boat and walked on water"* before he started doubting (Matt 14.29). The water was there to remind us of the work of the Spirit (Gen 1.2), who illumines the intellect and consequently is responsible for all true learning. John had written about this when he said that the true light *"enlightens every man coming into the world"* (John 1.9).

After passing through the seven gates, we came into a lush, verdant meadow. The souls I encountered there had weighty eyes and were moving slowly about the place. Their upright stature bespoke great authority. They demonstrated wisdom by only speaking infrequently and with voices sweet as honey.

Virgil and I went off to one side to an elevated perch where we could observe the venerable bunch. The place where we stood was expansive, open and bright. As I witnessed the procession of the virtuous pagans, I was greatly transfixed and exulted.

First, I saw a whole company of Trojans. I saw Electra, who was the mother of Dardanus, the founder of the City of Troy.[70] With her, I saw Hector, the Trojan hero killed by Achilles in the Trojan War as well as Aeneas, the star of the *Aeneid* and the founder of the city of Rome. With them also was Julius Caesar, the great Emperor of Rome and a distant son of Aeneas.[71]

Next, I saw a group of those early Latians who fought Aeneas when he came to Italy to found Rome.[72] Camilla, daughter of king Metabus, assisted in Turnus' fight against Aeneas.[73] Then there was Penthesilea, the lovely queen of the Amazons who helped the Trojans against the Greeks and was killed by Achilles.[74] On the other side was King Latinus who gave his daughter Lavinia to marry Aeneas.[75] In her marriage to Aeneas, Lavinia became the mother of all Romans.[76]

Further on, I saw a group of Romans led by Brutus who, driven by his rage at the rape of his daughter Lucretia, helped found the Roman republic after driving out the Tarquins.[77] Standing with him were four Roman women: the above-mentioned Lucretia; Julia, who was Julius Caesar's daughter; Marcia, the second wife of Cato; as well as Cornelia, the daughter of Scipio, known for her strength and fortitude.[78] Standing by himself off to the side was the great Muslim caliph, Saladin, foe of the crusaders but gentleman to all.[79]

As I raised my eyes a bit more, I saw several famous Greek philosophers. First, I noticed the great master of those who know, Aristotle, whose re-discovered works excited my times. Everyone was looking up to Aristotle, appropriately showing him honor. In front of him were both Socrates and Plato, Aristotle's venerable teachers.

I saw several Pre-Socratic Philosophers as well: Democritus, known for his theory that everything came from atoms and thus was subject to chance.[80] With him were Diogenes, a founder of cynic philosophy; Anaxagoras, who discovered a spiritual basis to material things and Thales, who thought water was the primal substance.[81] Alongside them were Empedocles, who thought the universe was governed by love; Heraclitus, who posited fire as the primal substance; and Zeno, the founder of the Stoics.[82]

Next, I saw a grouping of poets: Dioscorides, the Greek natural philosopher; Orpheus, inventor of poetic song; Cicero, the great Roman statesman and philosopher; Linus, inventor of the dirge as well as Seneca, the great Roman stoic and tutor to the Emperor Nero.[83]

Finally, I saw several doctors, scientists and mathematicians: Euclid, the geometer; Ptolemy, the great astronomer and cosmologist; Hippocrates, founder of the field of medicine; Avicenna, the famous Muslim physician and philosopher; Galen, the greatest Greek anatomist and medical researcher; as well as Averroes, the Muslim whose commentary on Aristotle prompted Thomas Aquinas' writings.[84]

There were many more Great Ones I have not included; we'd be here all day if I did. No, the subject of my quest calls me onward. Keep in mind that often what is told here pales in comparison to the real thing. Written words can't do it all justice.

Our group was reduced to just Virgil and me as we turned a different way, moving out of the quiet and into the trembling air. I then came to a place where nothing shines.

Comment

We see Dante's departure from Christian teaching once again coming through in this Canto. Dante completely re-imagines Limbo in Canto Four. Christian theology had taught that Limbo was the place where unbaptized infants went when they died. Although there had been some significant development in this theology over the years, the real purpose of Limbo was to hold unbaptized babies.

In western theology, the reason unbaptized infants were kept in Limbo was because of original sin. St. Paul had written that "*death spread to all men, because all sinned*" (Rom 5.12). Thus, to St. Paul, the reality of death is the result of sin. Picking up on this, St. Augustine taught that all are born in a sinful condition. The proof for this was the death of infants, who had committed no actual sins.

The fact that infants die, having not committed any actual sins, demonstrated to Augustine that they were born in a sinful state. The remedy was infant baptism, which the church believed washed away original sin (Acts 2.38, 22.16; Titus 3.5; Rom 6.4; Gal 3.27). For those infants who died without baptism, they were not punished in hell, but they went instead to a place outside hell called Limbo, which was not unpleasant, but not heaven either. By placing Limbo within the Inferno, Dante has innovated significantly.

Those from the Old Testament who did not know Christ, but nevertheless worshipped the true God, were traditionally thought to be in a different place. The Church fathers knew this place as "Abraham's Bosom," from the Biblical story of Lazarus and the rich man (Luk 16.22).

Dante's innovation causes him to introduce a subtle problem into the narrative.[85] It is problematic that Moses is in Limbo and is not led out until after the resurrection. After all, Moses appears at the transfiguration, which occurred before Jesus' death and resurrection.

Yet notice the contrast Dante offers. Dante spends almost no time on unbaptized babies. Rather, he populates Limbo with his heroes from classical antiquity. Keep in mind that Dante had likely read few of the long list of names he places here, either because he didn't have facility with Greek or because their works weren't available to him.

Thus what is important to Dante is less the details of who these people were and more the importance of classical culture. Dante was a budding renaissance humanist and was very supportive of scholarly efforts to recover the wisdom of the ancient world. He thought these scholarly efforts brought light and truth into the world.

But there's just one problem. Dante shows us in no uncertain terms that humanist learning is not enough. Learning without faith can blind us to reality. Dorothy Sayers says it well: "*It is the weakness of humanism to fall short in the imagination of ecstasy; at its best it is noble, reasonable and cold, and, however optimistic about a balanced happiness in this world, pessimistic about a rapturous eternity.*"[86] Unaided reason can only get you so far.

What should we say about the justice of all this? Is it really just that Virgil, who could not have known Christ because he died in BC 19, is in Limbo? The simple answer why Virgil is in Limbo is that, like everyone else we will encounter in the Inferno, he lacked faith.[87]

Virgil is a very effective guide, especially in the upper reaches of the Inferno, but there's something that prevented his ascension with other souls after Christ's crucifixion. That something is his lack of faith. What Dante seems to be implying is that once Christ descended into hell after his crucifixion, he sent to heaven those in Limbo who received his message. Like the rest, Virgil heard Christ preach, but refused to go with him. He preferred to stay where he was and to enjoy the honor of the other poets in Limbo rather than experience the glories of heaven.[88]

In a sense, there's a delicious irony here. The great poets of classical antiquity, whose job it is to help us imagine, are in Limbo because they couldn't imagine well enough. They could not imagine their need for redemption, and when it was offered to them, they refused. The virtuous pagans do not miss out on heaven because of ignorance (Christ preached to them, too); they miss out on heaven because, like everyone else in the *Inferno*, they misused the talents and freedom God had given to them.

Ring I:
The Sins of Incontinence

5

Blown by the Wind

CIRCLE II: LUST AND ADULTERY

Dante and Virgil continue down to the second Circle of the Inferno where the sin of lust is punished. The lustful are those who allowed passions to overwhelm their intellect. To Dante, true love never allows the intellect and love to be at odds. The consequence is death. The lustful spend eternity in darkness, symbolic of the intellect they've abandoned. They are blown about by gale-force winds, symbolic of the unsettled state of their souls. After meeting several famous shades, we encounter the lovers Francesca and Paolo whose illicit affair is perhaps the most famous vignette in the entire Comedy.

Minos

Virgil and I kept descending, this time into the second Circle of the Inferno, the region where we met those who gave into their passions. We were heading down along the edge of a kind of funnel-shaped path that went ever-lower. Although we had passed the great Romanesque gate warning us to abandon hope some time ago, I got the sense that we were coming to the place where the Inferno really started.[1] In contrast to the sighs we heard above, we could hear the faint sounds of wailing and grief as we descended.

We came to a clearing where the bestial Minos stood as a kind of infernal magistrate. In mythology, Minos had been a son of the gods. As ruler of the island nation of Crete, he had gained renown for his fine sense of wisdom and justice.[2] Down here, however, Minos had been transformed into a snarling, grotesque monster.

Minos would receive messages from the Maker about how far down into the Inferno to send each condemned sinner. When a soul would come before him, he would hear its confession and then wrap his tail around himself. The number of times he wrapped his tail corresponded to how many Circles down that soul was to be placed, thus carrying out the unerring judgment of the Maker.

It impressed me that the confessions I witnessed rang frank and true — there was no equivocation or deception down here, no ability to hide what was true.[3] The sheer brutishness of Minos seemed like an outward manifestation of the inner ugliness of the confessions he was hearing.[4] At any rate, he was the worst-looking confessor I had ever seen.[5]

The sheer number of souls that I encountered continued to shock me, a sea of shades heading to perdition. The souls would line up, make their confessions, hear their judgments and would disappear from sight, sent down to their eternal abode. It was a gruesome sight.

When Minos saw me wincing, he paused from his infernal vocation and addressed me directly: "Hey you! You, who thought it would be nice to come to this hospice of grief, don't be fooled by your guide! I know you're impressed with the spaciousness of the entrance to this place. Anyone can come in; but no one gets out. You'd better be careful who you trust down here, especially the one leading you lower."

A hospice of grief? I figured he was describing a corrupted monastic guesthouse, but I didn't find it particularly amusing.[6] Frankly, there wasn't much to laugh about down here. I found myself wondering about the justice of all this again. Sure, the Divine Son had said that the "*gate is wide…that leads to destruction and those who enter by it are many*" (Matt 7.14), but didn't the Creator also desire "*all men to be saved*" (1 Tim 2.14)? Were these souls really so bad that they were going to suffer eternally?

When Virgil saw the confusion on my face, he spoke sharply to Minos, "Why are you such a big mouth? Did anyone ask for your opinion? Since

I have the password, it's going to do you no good to impede our progress. Here it is: 'It's so willed where what is willed can be done'. Why don't you just go back to your infernal judgment now and stop bothering us?"

"Well," I thought, "Virgil is handling this pretty well. I'm sure glad he's on my side and knows his way around this place. I don't think I could manage this journey very well on my own."

Let me also admit that I didn't find Minos overly harsh.[7] He was just doing his job. Maybe he was right. How did I really know I could trust Virgil anyway? Despite my lingering doubts, we just kept going.

The Regal Licentious

However, as soon as we descended a little way from Minos, I started to hear great moans and weeping. We came to a place without any light. Even as my eyes adjusted, the only thing I could really make out was the souls themselves.[8] The place was annoying because of the severe gale-force winds that opposed and harassed everything not fastened down. The whirlwind rarely let up, leading the spirits on with its persistent plundering and refusing them any rest. This whirlwind appeared to be a direct punishment for those who gave into their fleshly passions and ignored the light of reason.[9]

We came down a little farther to discover an ugly landslide, which (I learned later) was caused by the great earthquake that shook the whole earth after the resurrection when *"the angel of the Lord descended from heaven and came and rolled back the stone"* (Matt 28.2).

When those who lacked self-restraint — better known as the incontinent — would arrive, they would squeal, moan and lament. They would then blaspheme the divine power that had put them here. In this, they showed the ugliness that was really in their hearts. The sight was detestable.

I came to understand that these sinners were here at the upper reaches of the Inferno because they had given up on reason and surrendered to their passions. They had all perverted the love that was in their hearts, since their desires literally overwhelmed their judgment, reducing them to the level of animals. They were blown about by the wind, just like a flock of starlings in migration season. The wind blows here and there, up and down, but surrendering to lust did little to provide peace, comfort or diminished suffering.

I saw a long trail of judged sinners coming down, bewailing their state as they went. They reminded me of the long trails of crabby cranes who wander about with the wind in anticipation of the fallowness of the winter season.[10] The cranes' long necks, squawking calls and territorial disposition as they breed were all emblematic of the sight in front of me.

When I saw all this, I asked my leader, "Who are all these people blown about by the black wind?" Virgil replied, "The first of them that you'll want to know about was a great Empress. Semiramis was her name, and her claim to fame was that she was the promiscuous founder of Babylon. Her untrammeled lust led her to have incestuous relations with her son.[11] Despite this, she provided strong leadership for her kingdom for forty-two years following the death of her husband Ninus."[12]

Virgil continued, "The next one is Dido, who in my epic poem, the *Aeneid*, killed herself for love because of her grief over the sudden departure of Aeneas. In her lustful relations with Aeneas, she was unfaithful to the vow of chastity that she had made to her late husband Sichaeus. Next to her is the lustful Cleopatra, the Empress of Egypt, who had intimate relations with both Julius Caesar and Mark Antony, corrupting both of them. Cleopatra then tried to seduce Octavian, Antony's successor, but his refusal prompted her disgraceful suicide."[13]

Virgil went on, "Notice as well Helen of Troy, whose beauty and uncontrolled passions brought so much misery to both sides in the Trojan War. With her is the great Achilles who, weakened by the beauty of Polyxena, ended up losing his life to Paris at the end of the war."[14]

Virgil continued, "As Helen of Troy's abductor and lover, Paris himself is there, too.[15] So is Tristan, the archetypal hero of French and Celtic Romance literature. Tristan carried on a love affair with Isolt, even after her marriage to the king, Mark of Cornwall.[16] Both Isolt and Tristan lost their lives when they drank a poisonous concoction intended for the king."[17]

Virgil went on and on, naming shade after shade, over a thousand of them. All of them had perverted loves and had given into lust. In their passionate attempts to satisfy their animal desires, true love — and even life — had departed from them.

My reaction to this terrible scene was to pity the souls I encountered. Hadn't we all felt the pangs of lust at one point? Hadn't we all surrendered our reason and given into passion? I felt lost, just as lost as I was above in the dark wood. Again, I wondered, where was the justice in all this?

Francesca and Paolo

When Virgil had finished with the regal bunch of reprobates, I turned and zeroed in on two sinners in particular. I noticed them because they were joined together while being blown about by the wind. Somehow the two figures managed to be both gallant and hollow at the same time.

Virgil said to me, "Let them come a bit closer and you'll see who they are, if you ask. They're being driven by the same love that drove them to this place. Ask them about it. I'm sure they'll tell you."

I hung back briefly until the wind blew and moved them over toward us. I drew in a deep breath to power my voice above the tempest and said loudly, "Oh exhausted souls. Would you please come over here and speak to me, that is, unless it's otherwise forbidden?"

As they made their way over to us, it seemed like they were doves, called to their resting place by desire. But, unlike every other dove I had observed, these doves were not innocent but were rather being blown about by their passions. It was almost as if these two were a perversion of the Christian symbol of the Spirit who, at the Son's baptism, "*descended upon Him in bodily form, as a dove*" (Luk 3.22).[18] Their uplifted wings let them fly through the darkened air, but their unrestrained desire had caused their souls to reside in the Inferno. Something wasn't right here.

They had been standing next to Dido before they made their way over toward us. But, beckoned by my warm-hearted call, they came closer.

I recognized the woman as Francesca da Polenta of Ravenna. In my day, everyone knew her story. She had been engaged to Gianciotto Malatesta, the heir-apparent to be governor of Rimini. Unfortunately, Gianciotto wasn't very attractive, and had a crippled body.[19] Yet, through a strange set of circumstances, Francesca fell in love with Gianciotto's brother, Paolo.

The marriage of Gianciotto and Francesca had been arranged by their parents, meaning they had never met each other. Because of Gianciotto's disability, Paolo was sent to be his proxy at the betrothal. Mistakenly thinking she was to marry the handsome Paolo, Francesca immediately fell in love with him. When the wedding-day came, she was heartbroken to learn that she was to marry Gianciotto, not Paolo. Her love for Paolo was thus thwarted by marriage. But they clandestinely found ways to be together, which led to her downfall. Francesca and Paolo were stabbed to death by Gianciotto when he surprised them and found them in a compromised intimate position.[20]

When Francesca saw me, she began, "Well, you're a sight for sore eyes. A living creature…down here? Your grace and kindly disposition do you well. It's not every day that a creature travels through the wine-dark air to visit us, especially since our blood was left to stain the world."

Francesca courteously continued, "If the King of Kings were a friend, Paolo and I would pray for your peace since you've rightly had compassion on our perverse state. But, while you're here, we'll tell you anything you want to know as long as the wind dies down a bit."[21]

Francesca continued, "I was born in Ravenna, on the coastal plain where the River Po slopes down and meets its tributaries. ***Love***, which swiftly ignited my gentle heart, seized Paolo when he encountered the fair form of my body. He made the first move.[22] How is it right that this fair form has been taken from me? It offends me just to think about it."

Francesca went on, "***Love***, which releases no one from returning it, seized me so mightily with pleasure in Paolo that it still hasn't gone away from me. This is why we're still together, forced to ponder our actions for eternity."

Francesca continued, "***Love*** led us to a joint death when my husband killed us in cold blood. Where's the justice in that? Caina, a section in the lowest realm of the Inferno, awaits Gianciotto; of this, I'm sure."[23]

These were the words that came to me from Francesca. She's convinced that she's done nothing wrong, I thought. It can't be healthy for us to deny love, can it? Where's the benefit in that? And, no doubt, she's a victim of injustice. Her husband murdered her and her lover, after all.

As I struggled with what I had just heard, I lowered my head in deep sympathy for Francesca's plight. It seemed to me that Gianciotto should be at the lower reaches of the Inferno along with Cain who "***was of the evil one and murdered his brother***" (1 John 3.12).[24]

After pausing to think, I raised my head and said, "Francesca, your martyrdom brings tears to my eyes. I'm sorry for what's happened to you and to Paolo. Maybe you're right. You're both victims here, the targets of brutal murders."

I continued, "But tell me something. If you're not responsible for what happened, is love to blame? How did your passions bring out these dangerous desires in both of you?"[25]

Francesca responded, "As I'm sure Virgil can attest, the remembrance of this is grievous unto us. To recall happier times makes my suffering worse since the wretchedness we're experiencing is so unfair.[26]

Francesca continued, "Despite this, let me recount to you our tale of woe. Paolo and I were together one day minding our own business, simply basking in each other's company. We were reading for pleasure the great French romance novel about Lancelot and Guinevere, *Lancelot du Lac*.[27] While we were alone together without any realization of the feelings we had for each other, we read about how love grasped Lancelot."[28]

Francesca continued, "As we were reading, luxuriating over every sweet word, our eyes locked several times as we glanced knowingly at each other. Flooded with feelings of love, the reading drained all the color from our visage. Helpless in our passion, one spot in the novel simply overpowered us. As we read in the story how the desired lips were kissed by such a lover, Paolo reached over and passionately kissed me on the mouth. Oh, sweet luxury!"

Francesca went on, "Trembling all over, we lost control. That book made us do it! Galehot, Lancelot's sidekick and trusted go-between, was the instigator of this whole mess.[29] That day, consumed with passion, we had no need to read any further."

As Francesca was speaking, Paolo kept silent and wept. Their punishment was to be joined together forever, consumed with unfulfilled desire. Overwhelmed with compassion and pity at this sorry sight, I lost control and fainted, falling down as if dead.

Comment

Francesca and Paolo's romance is one of the best known scenes in the entire *Comedy*. It demonstrates Dante's mastery of subtlety, and shows off his poetic powers.

There are a number of things lurking in the background that will make the story even more vivid. Perhaps the most important are the subtle fabrications to the story that Francesca offers. Earlier readers of the poem would have readily recognized these alterations since they would likely have been very familiar with the story of Lancelot and Guinevere.

When Francesca tells us about Lancelot, she describes the story by saying, "love grasped him." Yet, in the story of *Lancelot du Lac*, Lancelot is very shy. This is why he needs his trusted sidekick, Galehot, to be the intermediary between Guinevere and him. He's too shy to talk to her or to approach her.

In the original story, it's Guinevere who boldly seizes the moment and kisses the taciturn knight. Yet Francesca quietly reverses the roles and portrays Lancelot as kissing Guinevere so as to claim Paolo kissed her.

The point is that she's not telling Dante the truth. It's likely that she, not Paolo, initiated the kiss and thus couldn't control herself. This could be why Paolo never speaks, a subtle way of underscoring his passivity in the affair. Hence, in the end, Francesca is really responsible for her own sin. She couldn't say no.[30] Her passions overwhelmed her intellect.

Yet, in Francesca's world, no one is really to blame. She claims she was helpless in following love. Francesca wants to blame the book they were reading for igniting the passions that were too overwhelming to control.

This, of course, is absurd. Should Francesca have been alone in a bedroom with her former lover reading a romance novel? She is not nearly as innocent as she presents herself.

This is important because the big problem in the Inferno is that no one is willing to take responsibility for what they've done. Francesca doesn't think she's done anything wrong, even though, if we read between the lines, we can readily surmise she carried on an affair with Paolo. To make matters worse, we'll learn right at the beginning of the next Canto that Paolo is also Francesca's brother-in-law.

What Francesca is trying to do is to claim not only helplessness, but also that what she was doing was right. She's actually trying to make us believe that she was engaged in self-sacrifice by cheating on her husband.[31] She does this by claiming she was acting out of obedience to love.

This story stands at the beginning of the Inferno-proper, and thus provides the classic case for what is wrong with the sinners who we encounter there. They've misused their freedom and refused to seek forgiveness for what they've done. There is nothing disordered with desire, per se.[32]The problem is that Francesca allowed her passions to overwhelm reason. Hence, what she experiences can't be true love.

Thus Dante, the pilgrim, is conflicted. He doesn't handle himself particularly well. When he faints at the end of the Canto out of compassion for Francesca, we, as readers, should realize that Dante has failed his first test. He's supposed to see through the half-truths and smoke-screens Francesca is offering and instead see things from God's perspective. Francesca sinned because of her adultery with Paolo. She's trying to justify herself. But her excuse that "the book made me do it," should ring hollow both to us and to Dante. Dante still has a lot to learn.

In that light, there's a very important literary allusion that many miss at the end of the Canto, when Francesca tells us "That day, we had no need to read any further." This is an allusion to the climactic scene in Augustine's *Confessions*. After hearing a child chant "take up and read," Augustine takes up the Bible, decides to embrace "Lady Continence," and to commit to celibacy. As Augustine puts it in the *Confessions, "I neither wished nor needed to read further."*[33]

Hence Dante is making an important point about the essential character of human freedom. Augustine stopped reading the Bible, humbled himself by converting to celibacy, and went on to become one of the great Saints of the Church. His intellect kept his passions under control. Francesca and Paolo, on the other hand, kept reading their medieval romance, had an affair and ended up in hell. Differences in outcome result inescapably from the free choices of the will.

With freedom comes the responsibility to choose the good. Francesca has taken something very good — the pleasure of sex — and perverted it. Her lack of repentance and inability to see her own guilt is why she winds up in hell.

The last thing to notice in this Canto is that sexual sin is at the beginning of the Inferno, not at the bottom. To listen to some today, one would think that sexual sin is the single worst thing a person could do. But this is a perspective at odds with the history of Christian teaching. Traditionally, sexual sin is the least punished sin, not the most. The punishment meted out to Paolo and Francesca is to dwell in darkness and to be blown about by a strong wind. It's not pleasant, but, comparatively, it's relatively mild. As we'll see, punishments become ever-more severe as their effects involve more and more souls.

6

The Gluttons

CIRCLE III: CERBERUS AND CIACCO

Dante wakes up to encounter the third Circle of the Inferno. Here, gluttons are punished by submersion in putrid slush that forms from persistent rain and hail. All the gluttons' bodies have gone limp, the result of their unfulfilled desire for food and drink. Dante encounters Cerberus, a monstrous dog and the guard of the Inferno, as well as Ciacco, a fellow Florentine, who prophesies about the political future of Florence and its citizens. Dante learns some troubling facts about what the future has in store.

When I came to my senses after passing out, I was in a new place.[34] Just like before at the River Acheron with Charon, I had no idea how I managed to get down here. The pitiful sight of Francesca and Paolo, the ill-fated and lustful in-laws, was still in my head. Overwhelmed with sadness, I couldn't get over my feelings of pity for them. Why couldn't their search for love be forgiven? It was all very puzzling to me.

To make matters worse, I started seeing things around me that were even more troubling. I was trying to get used to these new, dismal surroundings. I moved about and looked around as much as I could. Yet everywhere I turned, I saw dim indications of fresh torment and woe. There were new victims that I needed to investigate.

As I looked around, I realized that somehow I had come down to the third Circle of the Inferno. It was not pleasant at all, even worse than the gale-force winds above. There was a persistent rain, cold and heavy, which drenched everything. Nothing ever changed — it was like a dreary Monday morning that lasted forever. I frankly couldn't imagine living like this.

As I walked around, something kept pelting me in the head and on my shoulders. I realized after a while that large hailstones, along with wet snow, were intermittently, but steadily, showering me. As the unclean water made its way through the besmirched air, it created a kind of putrid and stinking soup on the ground that reeked horribly. It was almost like a reversal of the Maker's care for Israel when he sent manna from heaven and ***"each gathered according to what he could eat"*** (Ex 16.18). Without the Maker, we would only encounter squalid mush.[35]

I came to realize that the cold rain, hail and snow were the reality of overindulgence in food and drink. What seemed so convivial and pleasing in life formed a cold, stinking slop on the inside. My, how different things looked from this perspective!

Cerberus

As I continued looking around, a loud set of barks startled me. They came from a cruel canine monster who was yelping at the shades submerged in the stinking filth. He had three heads and ruby red eyes, exercising his authority with a bloated belly. He had three human faces and a greasy black beard. With talons on his large hands, he would scrape the shades, then flay and quarter them. Just like a glutton, his throats never seemed to be satisfied. Observing his three heads, I quickly recognized him as Cerberus, the guardian of the Inferno.

I had read quite a bit about Cerberus in my studies, especially from Virgil. In classical literature, Cerberus was the one who would devour corpses.[36] Here, with his clawed hands, fat belly and slimy beard, I found him to be every bit as terrifying as I had read, but also a lot more human.[37] It was just like St. Augustine had suggested in the *City of God*: the false gods of antiquity were really just evil spirits wreaking havoc on the earth.[38] This was certainly an apt description of Cerberus.

The souls he had trapped had been reduced to animals. Following Cerberus' lead, they were howling like dogs as they suffered under the unrelenting showers. They were immersed in disgusting slush, yet trying desperately to find some rest. The sinners did this by periodically flipping their bodies over to try and screen themselves from the oppressive pelts of hail, and from the assaults of the infernal canine. One thing was clear — there was no rest to be found down here.

Cerberus was like a gigantic worm, burrowing his way through the mush. As he passed by Virgil and me, he made a threatening gesture toward us, opening wide his mouth and showing off his sharp fangs, dripping with saliva. His three heads looked like an unholy trinity of unfulfilled ravenousness.

Undeterred, my leader countered this threat by stretching out his hand, picking up a fist-full of smelly dirt lying on the ground and throwing it inside Cerberus' rapacious pipes. Just like the Creator had cursed the serpent after he tempted Adam and Eve by saying "*dust you shall eat all the days of your life,*" (Gen 3.14), so Virgil shut up Cerberus with this act. Once again, Virgil's quick thinking was an impressive sight.

I was surprised when Cerberus quieted down as he irrationally chomped on the rotten, filthy dirt. Cerberus struggled to devour it piece by piece, looking pathetic as he chewed. His lust for sustenance seemed to know no bounds. Yet his unrestrained craving for food, even grotesque food, never satisfied him.

I turned to Virgil and asked, "In the *Aeneid,* didn't you have Aeneas pacify Cerberus by giving him tasty cakes to eat? Here, it seems to be different. Cerberus has settled for putrid dirt. I guess that's what gluttony does to people." Virgil offered no reply to my observation.

Ciacco

As we left Cerberus behind, chomping greedily on filth, we were traipsing over shades submerged in the soupy muck. This was a strange sensation since shades have no physical bodies. All we could feel was their profound emptiness, the natural result of the emptiness of their lives.[39] They didn't move an inch as we walked over them.

As we moved along, however, one shade sat straight up when he saw us passing by him. He spoke up, saying, "Hey, you over there, the one being led through this terrible place, do you remember me? You were born before I passed away."

I looked over and said, "The anguish I'm witnessing down here is perhaps blocking my mind. I don't think I've ever seen you before. But, please, tell me who you are. Why have you been sent to such a deplorable place? I can't imagine a fate worse than this smelly mire!"

He said to me, "Your city of Florence is so full of envy that the cup of uncleanness overflows (Matt 23.25). I lived there, at least during better days. Your fellow-citizens called me Ciacco. It won't surprise you to learn that I'm all limp in this rain for the destructive fault of gluttony."

He continued, "Let me tell you, I'm not alone either. Everyone you're walking over is being penalized for the same error." With that curt speech, he became silent.

"How strange," I thought. "I don't think I've ever encountered this Ciacco before. But I also had to chuckle at this absurd sight because Ciacco's name means "pig" in my native tongue. The pig is being punished for gluttony. Apparently the Maker has a sense of humor."

Standing over him, I decided to ask something important, "Ciacco, your difficulty is weighing on me. It almost brings me to tears. But, if you can, would you please answer three questions for me? First, tell me what the future holds for my beloved Florence. It's a divided city right now, as you probably know, and I somehow suspect that you can see the future. Second, is there anyone just in the city? Finally, please, if you would, tell me the root cause of why there's so much discord within Florence."

I wasn't sure he was going to answer me. He didn't seem too eager to talk.[40] But, after sitting quietly for a while, Ciacco said, "The city of Florence will come to blood and the White Guelfs outside the city will drive out the Black Guelfs with great force. Then, it will come to pass, that the Whites will fall within three years and the Blacks will overcome it with the help of the one feigning neutrality."[41]

As he paused, I thought, "I knew it: Pope Boniface VIII is just pretending to be neutral in the struggle between the White and Blacks Guelfs in Florence. He sent Charles of Valois as a mediator, but intended all the while to usurp power. I think I'm right to blame Boniface for my exile."

Ciacco continued, "For a long time, the Black faction will hold their heads up high, subduing the Whites under heavy burdens. The terrible suffering they'll cause or the shame they'll bring on themselves simply won't trouble them. Honor has little currency when leaders lust for power. In fact, to answer your question, there are two just men in the city, but no one will favor them, as pride, envy and avarice will have exploded their hearts."

Only two just men, I thought, I wonder who they are? Ciacco's speech reminded me of how the Maker agreed with Abraham that he would spare Sodom "*for the sake of ten*" just men in the city (Gen 18.32). It seemed no one righteous was left in my hometown. I'm guessing Florence was doomed because of its terrible corruption."

After Ciacco finished his sad speech, I said to him, I'd still like you to tell me more. If you would continue your discourse, I'd gladly listen. You still haven't answered all my questions.

Ciacco curtly continued, "You'll see a whole host of Florentines down below. For example, you'll run into Farinata degli Uberti, Tegghiaio Aldobrandi and the venerable Jacopo Rusticucci. They were all accounted as worthy by worldly standards when they led the Guelfs in different generations.[42] But you might also run into Arrigo di Cascia and Mosca dei Lamberti, both of whom had a hand in the murder of Buondelmonti,[43] the one who started this whole political mess when he backed out of his engagement to Lambertuccio's daughter.[44] Rest assured, they're all down there below."

Ciacco's answer confused me a bit, so I asked, Weren't all these inclined to do good? I have great respect for Farinata, and Jacopo's memory is revered by all. Arrigo and Mosca were trying to right a grave injustice. Why should they be punished so harshly for this?

Ciacco said, "Dante, don't be fooled by appearances. All these I've just mentioned are among the darker souls down below. Their various sins encumber them in lower Circles of the Inferno. If you keep going on your descent, you'll see some of them down there, I promise. Let them recount their own stories to you."

Ciacco then looked up, changed his expression, and asked me tenderly, "But when you return again to the sweet world above, would you please bring my name to men's minds? Write about me. I'd really like my memory to live on in Florence. Yet I will tell you no more. Please be off on your journey."

While still looking at me, Ciacco turned his head away. A blank, empty stare came over his motionless face. With envy written across his visage and with pride having filled his heart, he would converse with me no more out of sheer exhaustion.[45]

I have to admit that I was really confused at this point. Ciacco told me I would return to the sweet world again. Was his prophecy directed at me? How did I know that Ciacco could tell the future accurately? Should I listen to a glutton? I was eager to discern all this, but realized that I would only discover the truth by continuing on my journey.

Seeing my concern, Virgil said to me, "Ciacco is not going to wake up again until the angelic trumpet sounds and the hostile ruler, the Divine Son, returns for the final judgment. It's then that "***the dead shall rise again***" (1 Cor 15.52). At the resurrection, these shades will reassume their flesh and hear the final judgment pronounced against them for refusing grace."

Once again, Virgil surprised me. Who knew that a pagan could have such a grasp on Christian theology! I guess he has a pretty good idea about what the future holds for everyone down here.

The Prophecy of the Resurrection

As we slowly made our way through the filthy mixture of shades and slush, Virgil and I kept talking. Since he knew so much about the resurrection, I decided to inquire about what was in store for the shades suffering down here. I asked, "After the second coming and the great judgment, will the torments of the souls down here be increased or decreased"?

Virgil looked right at me and said, "You should recall the scholastic philosophy you've studied, based as it is in Aristotle's great work *On the Soul*.[46] You must be aware that when a thing is more perfect, it feels both more of the good and, consequently, more of the pain. At the resurrection of the dead, the souls down here will be perfected in their lack of being, which is their wickedness. I'm afraid this necessitates more suffering for them, not less."

I grimaced at these sad words. The resurrection of the dead, which unites body and soul, was supposed to bring all souls to perfection, I thought. Yet all of these accursed shades will only ever attain perfection in a negative sense. Only their wickedness will be perfected, not their goodness. So they'll be more perfect than they are right now when their flesh is reunited with their soul, but this only portends more suffering for them. A horrendous future was in store for each shade I encountered.

As we were walking, the path started to curve. Speaking far more than I've recounted here, we came to the point where it began to descend again. There, we encountered Plutus, the great nemesis, the god of riches and wealth.[47]

Comment

We have already had hints about the political dimensions of the *Inferno*, but they form a significant part of Canto Six. As such, it might be helpful to recount once again what was happening in Florence before the time the *Comedy* was written. For a more detailed treatment, please see the Introduction.

Most of the events of Ciacco's prophecy, while occurring right around the time the poem supposedly takes place (in 1300), would have been well-known to Dante. Dante is not making wild-eyed predictions about what would happen in Florence in the future. By writing several years after 1300, he describes "prophecies" of events he knows have already transpired.

Florentine politics is a big reason why Dante is in exile, forced to live outside his beloved city without his family. As he writes this early Canto, he might have had some hope of return, but this was not to be. Dante would stay in exile for the rest of his life.

The big rivalry between the two political factions of Florence, the Guelfs and the Ghibellines, began in 1215 when Buondelmonte dei Buondelmonti was engaged to a daughter from the prominent Amidei family. In a fit of youthful flightiness, he rejected his fiancé at the last minute and decided to marry another woman from the rival Donati family. When Mosca and others had Buondelmonte murdered, this led to an armed uprising. Over the years, this also resulted in a ferocious blood feud between the two Florentine families, which, in turn, caused the city of Florence to break into two factions. Control of the city of Florence passed periodically between the Guelfs and Ghibellines for the next century.

Dante was a White Guelf, but not a particularly partisan one. He had won some respect for his participation in 1289 in a great battle in which the Guelfs defeated the Ghibellines, thus solidifying their power. But it doesn't appear that Dante was particularly caught up in the feud underlying the factions. He was more a Guelf by birth than by conviction. Nevertheless, as a member of the town council, he was branded as a partisan. The result was exile.

When we get a hint that Dante is going to put both his allies and his political rivals in some of the lowest Circles of the Inferno, we get some indication of how he felt about the politics of the time. Put simply, politics had ruined his life. He believed that he was unjustly treated. As prophesied, we'll observe the political dimensions of the poem unfolding as we continue on through the Inferno.

We should also note the prominent place the Christian doctrine of the resurrection of the dead receives at the end of the Canto. At the end of the Nicene Creed, Christians confess: "*We look forward to the resurrection of the dead and the life of the world to come.*" Hence, Christians believe that all souls will receive their bodies again at Christ's return. The Apostle Paul says it this way, "*In a moment, in the twinkling of an eye, at the last trumpet. For the trumpet will sound, the dead will be raised imperishable, and we shall be changed*" (1 Cor 15.52).

Dante employs this teaching on the resurrection to demonstrate what will happen for those who are in the Inferno. It's not good. Those who are damned will experience a more intense bout of suffering after the resurrection because they will be perfected in their lack of being.

To St. Augustine, evil was not a substance that was warring against the good. Rather, because God had created all things good, evil must be a privation. Thus, because their wickedness will be perfected at the resurrection of the dead, the logical implication is that eternal punishment will become even more intense.

This can be a very difficult reality to swallow. Yet notice how different Dante's reaction is from what has come before. We began the Canto with Dante's waking up after passing out subsequent to his encounter with Francesca and Paolo in the previous Canto. Yet, in Canto Six, Dante comes to grips with an even more difficult truth — there's worse suffering to come for those who are in the Inferno, and he accepts this almost without complaint.

What we're supposed to see in this "new" reaction is that Dante is learning. He's still puzzled by what he's observing. But, instead of swooning and whining about the injustice of it all, he seems to accept the truth of the matter without complaint. This is a very small step that Dante takes, but it's an important one.

He's starting to see that God's justice isn't capricious or arbitrary. He's starting to see that the punishments he's encountering are fair since they merely tell the truth about the sin that had so engulfed the souls we met. Punishment in the *Inferno* always fits the crime.

In our day, gluttony is often seen as a "good" or "harmless" sin. Gluttons often are prosperous and have a high living standard.[48] Many look up to them.

The jolly Santa Claus figure is hardly seen in our culture as one who merits punishment. Yet the reality is that uncontrolled eating and drinking has nothing to do with pleasure. It's a destructive addiction that destroys the body, ruins relationships and causes its perpetrators to lust after food and drink. Gluttony is a perversion of the good things that God has provided. And, to Dante, it's no laughing matter (the pun on Ciacco's name excepted).

In this Canto, no soul we meet ever interacts with anyone else. This is a distinct contrast to the previous Canto where the sin of lust required a partner.[49]

Here, the gluttons experience solitary indulgence. The result is that all they do is focus on themselves. We observe this most vividly when Ciacco, the pig, begs Dante to keep his memory alive in the city of Florence. He's not sorry at all for his gluttony. He has little awareness of the pain it has caused himself and those around him. He just wants the focus to be on him as he pursues the satisfaction of his unquenched desires for eternity.

Hence, addiction is never good. It ruins lives. It destroys families. It causes communities to crumble. It brings no lasting pleasure. The happy drunk or the jolly glutton might seem harmless, but Dante is showing in no uncertain terms that they are not. Sin is like that — it eats at the very fabric of our being and is never satisfied. Unordered desire is a perversion of the good.

7

The Wheel of Fortune

CIRCLES IV-V: GREED AND WRATH

Dante and Virgil enter the fourth Circle where the sins of greed are punished. They encounter Pluto, the god of wealth. Pluto collapses at a simple spoken word from Virgil. Dante then encounters souls, some of whom are misers and some of whom are big-spenders, clashing while pushing around large weights. Their love of material goods causes Dante to ask Virgil about the concept of Fortune, initiating a detailed explanation. After descending into the fifth Circle at the banks of the river Styx, the pilgrim encounters the wrathful and the slothful before reaching a large tower.

"Papa Satan, Papa Satan, Aleppe!" What annoying gibberish, I thought, when I heard his brooding cry. I couldn't quite make out what Pluto was saying. Maybe he was complaining about the Pope and his greed?[50] I had no idea what he was talking about.

In fact, exactly who was screeching, trying to frighten us off the path, I didn't really know. It seemed like it was Pluto, the ancient god of wealth, who was in our way, but he could have just as well have been the Pluto who guards the netherworld.[51] I thought these were the same. But, whoever he was, he gave me the creeps.

Virgil, my gentlemanly and scholarly guide, saw my bewilderment and said, "Don't let your fear get the best of you. No matter what power he thinks he has, he can't prevent our descent down this cliff. Virgil then turned to the fat-faced Pluto and said, "Shut up, you accursed wolf! Why don't you just let your rage keep consuming you from within?"

Virgil continued, giving a modified version of the secret passcode that he had used to great effect before: "The journey into the gloom isn't without reason; it's willed on high where Michael, the archangel, exercised revenge on the proud revolt."

Once again, this seemed to work. However, I had to wonder how Virgil knew anything about Michael, the archangel. I didn't want to ask, but I guessed Virgil must have learned something about Michael during his time down here in the Inferno. Virgil must have somehow learned that Michael waged war against the fallen angels. At that point, "*The great dragon was thrown down, the ancient serpent, who is called the Devil and Satan, the deceiver of the whole world — he was thrown down to the earth and his angels were thrown down with him*" (Rev 12.9). The devils down here probably didn't like Michael very much since they lost a war to him.

As soon as Virgil had finished speaking, Pluto collapsed. He was like a mainsail entangled behind a ship's mast that snaps in the wind, bringing the whole vessel down. When Pluto crumpled after just a few short words, I realized that it said something about his character. Pluto looked formidable on the outside, but was rotten and weak within. I guess this is what the incessant pursuit of wealth does to a soul.

The Greedy and the Profligate

We then descended into the fourth Circle, coming upon the miserable shore that sucks in all the evil of the universe. What was intriguing as we walked along was that our descent was becoming familiar. I had passed out the first couple of times we transitioned to various Circles. But now the path was becoming a little less murky to me. I was worried that I was getting used to all this sin.[52] It never seemed natural, just familiar.

"Oh, the justice of the Creator," I thought, "who crams in so many new travails and pains. Why does our iniquity spoil us so?"

We came to a ledge, and I observed a strange sight. I saw souls recklessly crashing into each other down below. They reminded me of the terrible sea current Charybdis, which sucked in sailors and sea vessels who overconfidently tried to navigate its treacherous flux. Their violent crashes had a certain synchronicity to them, so they looked as if they were engaging in a round dance where they would weave in and out.[53] Seeing them was a good reminder about the ultimate futility of human accumulation.[54] They just went round and round, trying to find order.

This group contained a much larger number of souls than in the other Circles I had encountered above. When I looked closer, I noticed there were two groups positioned in half circles, rolling weights around with their chests. The two groups were constantly crashing into each other. When they would collide, one group would look back and cry out, "Why do you hoard?" The other would shout, "Why do you squander?"

I remembered from my time reading Aristotle's *Ethics* that the virtue of moderation was in charting a middle course between the prodigality of over-consuming and the poverty of hoarding. Being greedy and being miserly were two sides of the same coin.[55] Their selfish lives of immoderation inevitably caused these souls to collide with the needs of others, creating a terrible morass of confusion.

From my vantage point above, their colliding paths somehow looked like a full circle.[56] But their screams toward each other showed their hatred, blinding them to the symmetry of their movements. Their world was a zero-sum game. Money and exchange had made it impossible for them to be in genuine relationships with each other. By obsessing over material things, they lost sight of the reality only a loftier vantage point could provide.

My heart was almost wrung out when I asked Virgil, "Please explain to me who these shades are. I see a bunch of tonsured foreheads down there to our left where the greedy are. Were these all clerics?" Now I asked this because both Thomas Aquinas and Aristotle had taught that being a miser was worse than being a big-spender.[57] But were all these Clerics spendthrifts, sworn as they were to poverty?

Virgil said, "Yes, everyone you see down there who is greedy was a member of the clergy.[58] They squandered the Church's resources, which belong to the poor, on themselves.[59] Their judgment was so confused in the first life that they didn't keep their outlays in any kind of moderation. As you can hear from their yelping voices, this simply caused division and got them nowhere. But it's not just clerics — Popes and Cardinals are down there, too — avarice has infected the whole lot and is destroying the Church."

I responded, "Master, given how many are down there, I thought I'd be able to recognize a few who soiled themselves in such filth."

Virgil tenderly answered, "This thought of yours is futile. Their undiscerning lives, which polluted their souls make them almost unrecognizable down here. By maximizing individual desire, they've lost their individuality. For all eternity, these two groups will collide. Even at the general resurrection when the Divine Son returns, the avaricious will rise up with closed fists and the spendthrifts with cropped hair. Their perverse spending and hoarding has stripped the world of its beauty, and has put them in conflict forever. Words can't express the damage money does to people."

Treatise on Fortune

Virgil continued, "My son, now you can see the farce of goods committed to Fortune. People squabble constantly over these things, but they have no eternal value. All the gold that ever existed will never give a moment's rest to these tired souls. It all comes down to Fortune, nothing else. Fortune is a terrible burden to bear."

I answered, "Please tell me more about this Fortune. Why does it hold the world in its clutches?"

With a hint of pity in his speech,[60] Virgil said, "Oh foolish creature. Why are you still so slow at getting this? Do I have to spoon-feed you so you can learn to judge rightly?"

He continued, "The Master, whose wisdom transcends all, made the heavens and gave them the angels so that each part of the heavens shines perfectly on the other, distributing light equally. This means that there is a perfect harmony between the heavenly realm and the earthly realm. Since these heavenly bodies are responsible for the changeability of the material world, there must be harmony between the two."

Virgil went on, "At the same time, the Creator appointed a general minister and guide to be over the splendors of the world. This is Fortune. In time, Fortune transferred vain goods from one people to another and from one tribe to another without the mediation of human good sense. As a result, one realm rules and another languishes on the earth. It looks random, but it's all happening according to Fortune."

Virgil continued, "With the verdict of Fortune, hidden like a slithering serpent in the grass, human wisdom can't stand up to her. Fortune foresees, judges and pursues. There's just no getting around it. Divine providence among the heavenly hierarchies is in perfect harmony with what actually transpires on earth, even if it appears to make no sense from our vantage point. Nothing happens by chance, but only according to the Creator's plan."

Then, Virgil said, "Fortune's permutations don't stop; necessity makes her swift. This is why changes in Fortune happen with such rapidity. So those who whine against Fortune are wasting their breath. Even when things go against them, they ought to be praising Fortune instead of blaming and speaking ill of her since everything is divinely providential. Fortune is the one who is blessed and thus whining doesn't reach her. The Wheel of Fortune turns continuously, rotating between blessing and suffering. She won't stop her wheel for you. Fortune is inscrutable."[61]

Virgil paused to get his breath and said, "Let's continue on down to see even greater woe. It's now past midnight — notice that every star that was rising when we first set out is sinking.[62] Loitering is unwise down here."

The Fifth Circle: The Wrathful and Sullen

Moving on, we traversed the boundary of the fifth Circle to reach another shore. We were walking alongside a spring that was gurgling up and then flowing down through a ditch. A quick review of the Inferno's geography that I had seen so far made me realize the waters were coming from Acheron, the River I had crossed earlier at the start of my journey. [63] Acheron's water had apparently run beneath the four prior Circles I had crossed and was flowing down the cliff into the River Styx below.[64]

Now the name Styx derives from the Latin word meaning "hatred."[65] This seemed like a pretty good signal of what I was about to encounter. As the sad brook descends, it goes all the way to the foot of the menacing gray shores that I could see off in the distance.

Gazing intently, I saw all kinds of people muddied in that muck. They were completely naked with irate looks about them. They were smacking each other around, not only with their hands, but with their heads as well. Some used their chests and feet to attack other people. Periodically, they would gnash their teeth and then use them to tear at each other's flesh piece by piece. What can I say, it was an ugly sight.

Virgil said, "My son, what you're observing is the souls of those overcome with anger. There are two kinds of anger in view down here, the wrathful and the sullen. The wrathful are the ones you just saw — naked and doing violence to the others they're around. They are all stuck in the mud of their hearts' wrath."

Virgil continued, "But I want you to realize that there are more souls submerged under the water. You can tell by the bubbles that gurgle up to the surface periodically. The bubbles come from their sighs wherever they wander. Stuck under the water, they are sullen, having been slothful in the sweet air above. Their repressed anger causes them to be stuck in the black mire.[66] They can't even talk anymore, as their gurgles form a perverted hymn to their unending grief."

As we turned away from the disgusting puddle, I shook my head in disbelief. I always suspected sloth was the most prevalent sin in monastic communities. So it seemed that the greed of the clerics and the sloth of monastics uniquely went together.

Yet, out of the corner of my eye, I saw something I don't think I'll ever forget: the ugly sight of angry souls guzzling down the mud that was consuming them. This was a community that was completely out of control.

We came at last to the end of the Ring of Incontinence, having reached the foot of a large tower.

Comment

As noted in the last sentence, this concludes our journey through the first of the three major divisions of the *Inferno*, the Ring of Incontinence. In the last few Cantos, we have observed the lust of Francesca and Paolo, the gluttonous Ciacco as well as the avaricious clerics and the slothful monastics. It's been quite a journey so far.

What we've seen, particularly in Canto Seven, is the breakdown of community that happens when souls sin. The wrathful are using all their body parts to tear at the flesh of others. The avaricious are so intent on gratifying themselves that they don't care about the community anymore. The sullen are so withdrawn in their repressed anger that they can't even speak with one another. This is what sin does to communities — it rips them apart.

But Dante singles out one particular community that is dear to his heart — the Church. When clerics squander the Church's resources or live in luxury (in violation of their vows), when monks squander their vocations to laziness, when Cardinals and Popes incite discord, wars and strife, this doesn't just hurt the Church — it harms the entire society.

This is why the discourse on Fortune that occurs right in the middle of the Canto is so interesting. Given the depths to which the Church had fallen during Dante's day, it would seem common sense that this was all happening without the knowledge of God.

But Dante is compelled to remind us that divine providence has never ceased working. We should remember this today in light of modern-day scandals in the Church — the greed of ministers who use media outlets to enrich themselves, the sex scandals that have occurred throughout the universal Church, the alignment with power elites over the poor, the seeking of political power over humility. These are all modern examples of the same thing. Looked at rationally, it seems the Church will fall apart under its own weight, having lost its first love and its mission.

Yet it was Christians of the Late Middle Ages who transformed the idea of what Fortune was all about. In antiquity, "*Fortuna*" was the goddess of luck. She was always depicted as fickle (thus Virgil's analogy of Fortune being like a snake hiding out in the grass). Fortune was the very thing that would give disease, kill children or bring poverty without warning. Fortune struck randomly (and usually perversely) and everyone was subject to her whims.

Yet medieval stained glass windows would typically depict Fortune differently. They would show a wheel with four stages. At the top would be "The Reign," suggesting that you're on top of the world and have conquered. The second stage would say "I have reigned," suggesting deterioration. The third level would say "I have no kingdom," which depicts utter desolation and total loss. But, at the bottom, a fourth level would say "I will reign again," thus depicting the hope of resurrection. In the middle of the wheel, one would often find a cross, reminding onlookers that all things in life, good or bad, happen according to God's providence. Thus, with a focus on Christ at the center, peace can come even in the midst of turmoil. In short, Fortune works according to a higher authority.[67]

This is Dante's point. The avaricious, the spendthrifts, the wrathful and the slothful all have the focus on the gratification of their own temporal needs. The result is a surface-level disaster for the communities that they serve. They spend eternity either doing violence to themselves or to others. They live pushing around meaningless weights or submerged in the filthy runoff of the streams of hell. As usual, their punishment is their own doing.

Surprisingly, Dante doesn't seem to be interested only in a caricature of the Church's shortcomings. He cares deeply about the Church, yet thinks its current leadership, which has caused him so much grief, isn't contributing to human flourishing. He ardently seems to believe that a well-functioning Church, along with a good secular ruler, is part of the basis for a flourishing society. Dante believes that both the Church and the State need to be performing their proper roles for the people to prosper. In Dante's day, the Church, in its Babylonian captivity in Avignon, was decidedly not performing its proper role. This forms the basis for his strong critique in this section.

Yet Dante's big point in this Canto is that none of this is a surprise to God. Importantly, Dante introduces the reader to the idea of heavenly harmony here. In the *Paradiso*, this will be on display almost in every Canto. The world seems to us like it's all messed up. This, of course, isn't wrong. It is decidedly not the way it's supposed to be because of the presence of sin.

However, just as medieval stained glass transformed the wheel of Fortune through the cross, so, too, our views of Fortune can be transformed through belief in God. Hope is not the ill-fated belief that everything will just work out in our lives — life decidedly might not work out according to our plans. Hope, rather, is the belief that true happiness is never fully found in this life when it is attached to temporal things.

True happiness comes when communities are integrated, not at war. True happiness comes when we detach from created things and attach to the only thing that can satisfy us — that is, Christ. True happiness is ultimately found in a spiritual life lived in concert with that which is eternal.

8

Stymied at the Gates of Dis

CIRCLE V: RIGHTEOUS ANGER

Dante continues his discussion of the fifth Circle, which deals with the sin of anger. He encounters Phlegyas, whose anger at the rape of his daughter led him to torch the temple of Apollo. He ferries Dante and Virgil to the entrance of the city of Dis, which is depicted as a series of red Mosques. It is like a city overrun by the Turks. On the way, Dante meets one of his Florentine arch-rivals, Filippo Argenti, whose pent-up rage causes a significant confrontation. Finally, Virgil and Dante, failing to gain entrance to the city of Dis, find themselves unable to make further progress on their journey.

Let me take us back to what happened while we were on our way to the foot of the large tower, the one I described reaching at the end of the last Canto.[68] I need to fill in some of the important details about what I saw there.

Before we got to the tower, while we were still a long way out, Virgil and I had our eyes drawn up to the top of the structure that was in the distance. We noticed two flaming lights on top of the tower's spire, which were sending signals to someone below. I learned later the lights were signaling demons, who weren't too happy about our approach.[69]

I noticed that signals from the tower were quickly returned by another source, suggesting continuous communication was occurring. It was just like I might have seen from the watch posts that served as early warning signals for Italian cities.[70] It was troubling that their back-and-forth communications were abuzz with news of our impending arrival. But my eyes couldn't make out what they were saying.

In my nervousness, I turned to Virgil, who had proved himself stalwart and sensible up to this point, and asked, "What's with these lights? Can you make out what they're saying? Who is it that's sending the signals?"

Virgil responded, "If you look over the filthy waves we're on, you'll be able to spy out what's to come. The marsh fumes are concealing it a bit, but what's coming isn't pretty."

In the distance I saw a small ship coming toward us sleekly and swiftly. The skiff was moving like a skillfully-fired arrow from the bowstring of a master archer piercing the air. It was upon us in what seemed like an instant, captained by a single oarsman who was yelling at the top of his lungs, "Now you're under arrest, fallen soul!" He was looking right at me as he said this, his anger symbolizing the speed with which wrath can take over a person.[71]

Virgil retorted with derisive verve, "Phlegyas, Phlegyas, your shouting is pointless. This time, you're not going to get us any longer than it takes to pass over this swamp!"

Now I had heard about this Phlegyas from Virgil's own writings. He was the son of Mars,[72] the god of war, and was eternally angry because of the rape of his daughter Coronis by Apollo.[73] When he burned Apollo's famous temple at Delphi in livid revenge, he was condemned to be the one to ferry the damned into hell. Apparently, he was coming toward me, thinking I was one of the damned. The very etymology of his name ("*Phleg*") suggested one who would transport unlucky souls into the fire.[74] It was a brutish business.

Phlegyas also seemed to be representing the bitter resentment exhibited by those who are deceived.[75] It was readily apparent that Phlegyas was the very embodiment of the wretchedness that comes from pent-up anger. He was decidedly not happy when he saw that I was still embodied, thinking he had been tricked.[76]

Virgil went down and got into his boat, motioning for me to follow after him. Strangely, it was only when I got inside the boat that it seemed to have any weight. If St. Augustine had famously said that "*My weight is my love,*" there was evidently no genuine love to be found down here.[77]The irate Phlegyas demonstrated that quite clearly.

Filippo Argenti: Quick to Anger

As soon as we were in the skiff, the old prow, which is the forward-most portion of the boat, set out for deeper waters. My weight made the boat cut through the waters more lethargically.

While we were running over the dead millpond, one who was encased in sludge rose up and said incredulously, "Who are you that comes before your hour?"

With a moment's hesitation, I burst out angrily, "Look, you filthy wretch! Unlike you, I'm just coming for a visit. I'm not staying. But you, who are you who is made so rotten?" I reacted swiftly because there was no way I was going to let a shade in the Inferno draw equivalence between us. Let me tell you, I was better than this slime-ball.

So I continued, tears welling up as I spoke, "Accursed spirit, you stay right where you are! I know you despite all the filth encasing your putrid frame."

I said this because I recognized this foul creature as Filippo Argenti, a man who had slapped me on the face when we were in Florence together, reflecting our differing places in the political spectrum of the day. Argenti's family had been instrumental in my not being able to return to my beloved Florence.[78] As a result, I couldn't stand him.

With that, Argenti stretched out both of his hands toward the boat in a fruitless effort to attack me, but Virgil just pushed him away, saying firmly, "Get away from us. Why don't you stay over there with the other dogs!"

Virgil, in a torrent of esteem, then threw his arms around my neck, kissed me on the cheek and said excitedly, "Disdainful soul, '*Blessed is she whose womb conceived you*'" (Luk 11.27). I guess he was really happy I had told off Argenti. Virgil's praise warmed my heart. But I also chuckled a little bit when Virgil tried to quote scripture. Apparently, he had forgotten about the next verse when the Divine Son corrects the woman who said it by asserting, "*Blessed rather are those who hear the word of God and keep it*" (Luk 11.28), something which, unfortunately, Virgil had not done.

Virgil looked intently at me and continued, "In the world above, Argenti was full of pride. He's named "Argenti" because he actually had his horse's shoes bedecked with silver.[79] That's how arrogant he was. No good deeds adorn his memory. That's why his shade is so furious down here. His anger has eaten him alive."

Virgil went on, "How many in the world above thought of themselves as great men who are now nothing better than swine in the mire down here? The angry leave behind a wake of horrible contempt."

Then, continuing my disdain, I said, "Master, I'd like to see Argenti thrust down like a pig in the mire before we exit this swamp!"

Virgil responded, "Before the landing comes, you'll be satisfied. Your wish has to be fulfilled."

Just after Virgil said that, I saw Argenti being torn to shreds by a muddy mob. I still praise God and give thanks for it. He got what was coming to him.

The whole mob was crying out, "Get Filippo Argenti! Get Filippo Argenti! Before they could get to him, the bizarrely quick-tempered Florentine spirit turned and started mauling himself with his own teeth, thus showing what unquenchable anger was doing to his putrid soul.

Now did I do the right thing here? I think

so. Thomas Aquinas had taught me that not all anger is sin.[80] Thus I think my anger was different than Argenti's. After all, the Divine Son got angry when he threw out the moneychangers from the temple (Matt 21.12). David even commanded us, saying "***Be angry and do not sin***" (Ps 4.4). I was starting to figure out that to pity those in the Inferno would be to question the perfect judgment of God.[81] I think this was a sign of my progress, not regress. Maybe I'm right, but, who knows? Maybe I'm wrong.

The Entrance to Dis: Sullenness

We left Argenti there. I'll refrain from telling any more of the gory details. I'll just say the sight was pretty ugly. But, as soon as we were clear of him, I heard terrible sounds of mourning. I opened my eyes wide to focus on what lay ahead.

My good leader said, "Now, my son, our journey is getting serious. We're approaching the city named Dis with its severe citizens and great host. As you know, the city gets its name from Pluto, the god of the underworld.[82] The great host is none other than Satan."

I said to Virgil, "Well, master, I can already make out its infernal mosques. They're as red as if they had just exited a blazing fire." The mosques and the burning within the city suggested that something was wrong not just morally, but politically as well.[83] It was almost as if the infernal Turks had taken over the world.[84]

Virgil said, "The eternal fire that burns within Dis is glowing red, just like you're going to see in the lower Circles of the Inferno. From here, we're going to start seeing some much more serious punishments than we've encountered so far."

More serious? I have to admit that the incontinence and anger we had encountered so far weren't trifling. I guess the deliberate sins of a corrupted will are more severe than those of the passions that we had seen so far.

We came at last to the deep moats that provide a defensive barricade for that disconsolate city. Dis' walls seemed to be made of cold iron, emblematic of the calcified wills of the residents down below.[85] We circumnavigated the entrance widely to avoid the barricades. Then, our boatman cried out with a booming voice, "Get out! Here's the entrance."

Above the gate, I saw more than a thousand angels who had fallen from heaven. Speaking with one voice, they said, "Why is this one, who is without death, going through the kingdom of the dead?" When he heard this, my savvy guide immediately indicated that he wanted to speak with the devils privately.

So they put their disdain away, at least for the moment, and said, "You come alone; send the embodied one away. He's got some nerve thinking he can enter into this kingdom. In fact, let him return on his crazy way. Better said, let him *try* to return, if he can."

Looking at Virgil, they said, "You, who escorted this one through such a dark land, you're are going to stay right here."

Oh Reader, let me tell you how discomforting this was. These were threatening words and I was worried that my journey was going to end right here, in hell, and that I might never make it back to the world above. I had no idea how I would navigate the Inferno without Virgil's help.[86]

As Virgil was turning to speak with the fallen angels, I cried out as if undone, "Oh beloved leader. You've rescued me from deep dangers and restored my confidence more times than I can count. Please don't leave me here! If our entrance into Dis is refused, let's just turn around and go back. I don't want to get stuck down here in this terrifying place."

Virgil, ever the gentleman, said to me, "Don't be afraid. There's no one who can prevent our passage."

He then came over and whispered to me, "It's been granted to us by you know who. Just wait for me here and let your spirit take comfort. Don't lose hope. I'm not about to leave you here in the underworld."

Then, my sweet father proceeded to go away and totally abandon me there. To tell the truth, I was starting to lose a little faith in Virgil. There were all kinds of competing things swirling around in my head, but most of them filled me with doubt.

I wasn't able to hear the negotiation going on a little way off from me, but it didn't go on long before it ended and they parted. Our adversaries slammed the gate in the face of Virgil. We were left outside feeling rather helpless. Virgil slowly and sullenly returned back to me.

Virgil lowered his eyes to the ground as he came back. His face was devoid of all assurance. He sighed and said, "Well, they've denied me entrance into the sorrowful city." I had never seen Virgil so utterly lacking in confidence. For once, his great rhetorical skills and secret passcodes had no effect on these gatekeepers. We were stuck outside the gate.

Virgil said to me, "Don't be alarmed at my agitation since I'm going to overcome this test, just wait and see. Their inward defenses have outflanked me for now. But this hubris of theirs is nothing new. They used it before when the Son came down and "*led captivity captive*" (Ps 68.17).[87] Their resistance didn't work then and it won't work now. The gate above, that once was locked, now stands unlocked."

Virgil continued, "In fact, you saw the fatal warning written above the gate — 'Abandon hope all ye who enter here'. A Great One is going to have to descend, passing through several Circles to let us in."

Virgil continued, "All I know is that I'm out of tricks. We're going to need some Divine assistance for Dis to be opened to us. I guess we'll just have to sit here and wait." With that Virgil sat down on the ground, shrugged his shoulders, put his head in his hands, and motioned for me to sit beside him.

Completely uncertain about what was going to happen, I sat down beside him and waited. Without the power of grace, my guide seemed to be ineffective and faltering.

Comment

Both Aristotle and Thomas Aquinas tackled the question of anger, and Dante is following their thinking in this Canto.[88] They saw anger as coming in three different categories: the enraged, whose anger is expressed with quick emotional outbursts; the sullen, who repress their anger; and the vindictive, who act out their anger with calculated clashes.[89] We observe examples of all these in this Canto.

When Phlegyas lashes out at Dante in the beginning of the Canto, this is a good example of an emotional outburst. Later, Filippo Argenti provides an example of what pent-up anger brings. He ends up trapped in the filthy mud. Lastly, one might argue that Dante's vindictive reaction to Argenti is an example of the third category of calculated anger.

Argenti and Dante were enemies when they were neighbors in Florence, as Argenti was a Black Guelf while Dante was part of the White faction. We have evidence from the great medieval writer Boccaccio that the Argenti family played a key role in keeping Dante in exile.

Yet Dante hits right back at Argenti and Virgil praises him for it, giving him a big hug. This might seem to be a strange reaction. Why would Argenti be rotting away in the mud because of his anger while Dante is praised for his?

Here, Dante is depicting the concept of righteous anger. Anger, in and of itself, is not necessarily sinful. Thomas Aquinas explains it this way: "*If one is angry in accord with right reason, anger is not a bad thing.*"[90]

Thus anger only becomes a problem when it is not acted out in accord with reason. Aquinas puts it this way: "*If one desires revenge to be taken in accordance with the order of reason, the desire of anger is praiseworthy and is called zealous anger. On the other hand, if one desires the taking of vengeance in any way contrary to the order of reason, for instance if he desires the punishment of one who has not deserved it, or beyond his deserts, or again contrary to the order prescribed by law...then the desire of anger will be sinful.*"[91]

Dante is trying to show us that his anger toward Argenti is justified. Dante has been wronged for nothing he did. He was in the wrong place at the wrong time, caught up in the politics of the day. The action of keeping him in exile has ruined his life. Thus his lashing out at Argenti is justified, at least in his mind.

But should *we* see it this way? Dante says some pretty cruel things, gloating in the end that Argenti is writhing in hell. I think Dante keeps this issue deliberately ambiguous to trouble us. He is not lashing out in love and thus the merit of his actions is certainly open to question. At the very least, he has not learned to love his enemy and is still quite immature in this thinking. Yet there is no clear answer on whether he was right here. Dante leaves it up to us to figure out.

But what Dante has done, perhaps for the first time, is to start seeing things from God's perspective. To reiterate: no one we encounter in the *Inferno* is innocent. Up until now, Dante keeps feeling pity for the souls he encounters. But this has not been the correct response. In this Canto, he lashes out with righteous anger at the sin he encounters, sin that has injured him grievously. Perhaps he takes it too far, but his perspective about the sinners he encounters is changing. In other words, he's learning.

This becomes significant when Dante ends this Canto in a helpless state. He's very worried that Virgil can't come through and so he's stuck outside the gates of Dis waiting for assistance. This is a marvelous description of the reality of the spiritual life. We have our guides, our practices, our belief systems, our creature comforts. But, then, something happens and we get stuck. There is no more forward progress to make unless God shows up to help us. Thus Canto Eight is a very important transition point for Dante in his journey, which holds critical lessons for how we should live the spiritual life.

Anyone who is living the spiritual life knows there are points of dryness on the journey. There are seasons of absolute futility and bewilderment when we think about turning back. We get frustrated with the seeming ridiculousness of praying to a God who doesn't answer or with eating the flesh of a God in the Eucharist that tastes and smells an awful lot like plain bread or with watching the suffering that exists in the world without being able to do much about it. Dante is trying to show us that waiting is a normal part of the spiritual life when lived out in a genuine way.

Lastly, there is an important interpretive issue in Canto Eight. In this paraphrase, I have been frequently interjecting explanations in order to make things clear. But the interjection to the reader at the end of this Canto is the first time Dante addresses us directly. Why is this significant?

It's significant because Dante is breaking up the action to point us to something deeper — namely, the underlying allegory that's here. Dante's journey almost comes to an end in this Canto because his forward progress has been blocked. The devils won't let him into the city, and Virgil, his heretofore stalwart guide, is proving to be helpless when his smooth talk and mysterious amulets don't open doors. Without divine assistance, Dante and Virgil can't continue.

Just as Dante breaks up the story by his interjection, the journey is also broken up. Dante and Virgil are at risk of failure here. The interpretive issue posed by Dante's direct address of the reader will be the focus of the next Canto. But we should realize that direct addresses are alerting us to something important underlying the story.[92] More on that as the journey continues.

9

Dante and the Gospel

CIRCLE V (PART II): THE CITY OF DIS

Dante and Virgil, stuck at the gates of Dis, are unsure what to do next. After learning that Virgil has made this trip to the depths of the Inferno before, Dante comes under threat from a perverted trinity of Furies. The Furies threaten to send Medusa, the sight of whom would turn Dante to stone. Dante, the author, then breaks into the narrative to encourage searching for the "doctrine behind the veil." A heavenly messenger, typologically representing Christ and his grace, comes down, forces the demons back, and opens the gates of Dis for the pilgrim. Inside Dis, Dante and Virgil encounter heretics who are lying in sepulchers, having misused their intellects. This takes place in the wee hours of the morning on Holy Saturday.

Virgil and I were sitting there at the iron gates of Dis, trying to figure out what to do next. Truth be told, I was really scared. The color had drained from my face after I saw Virgil turn back following his unsuccessful attempt to negotiate with the demons. One look at his vexed visage told me that, for once, he had no idea what to do next.[93]

Virgil was just sitting there, staring silently into the thick fog that obscured all sight. The fog was a kind of metaphor for our confused state. It was as if Virgil was expecting the demons, who had walked away, to come back to the negotiating table. But all we could hear was deafening silence.

Breaking the quiet, Virgil proclaimed, "Look, we have to win this battle. You definitely don't want to get stuck down here. If we don't... well...let's not even think about it. I mean, there's no way we can lose this; Beatrice told me we'd be fine.[94] I just don't understand why heaven is taking its good old time before showing up to help us. But until it does, I think we're stuck here."

I didn't want to say anything, but it seemed to me that Virgil was holding back on me. He wasn't letting on how serious the situation was. I'm not sure he had any hope that we'd be rescued. After all, hope is one of the theological virtues that Virgil couldn't claim. All I knew was that his initial confidence was gone and his words now seemed different than before. This hardly filled me with confidence.

In fact, my fear ratcheted up a notch when I started to realize that this situation was a whole lot worse than he was telling me. Was I going to be stuck here for all eternity in an embodied state before the gates of Dis? Oh no, this is not what I had signed up for!

Somewhat tentatively, I asked, "Has anyone *ever* come down to this awful place from the first Circle where your friends, the virtuous pagans, reside? Up there, it seemed to me their only suffering was being devoid of hope."

Virgil answered, "Well, it rarely happens that anyone from Limbo makes his way down here, but it's not unheard of, either. In fact, I myself made this journey once before. It happened when Erictho, that harsh witch, used her powers to recall my body for a time. I had only been down in Limbo for a short while, when she exhorted me to go down to the lowest Circle, where Judas is, and retrieve a shade for her. I'll tell you what, the very bottom of the Inferno, in the middle of the earth, is the farthest place from heaven you can get. So I know the way down to that dark and doleful place quite well. Feel secure and don't worry."

Wow, I thought, I had no idea that Virgil had actually done this before. Maybe we will get through this mess after all. But I still didn't trust him completely.

Virgil continued, "This stinking swamp, which surrounds the whole lower area of the Inferno, can't be entered without wrath."

I wasn't exactly sure what Virgil meant by that. I couldn't help but remember what Jeremiah had said while in prison: *"The Chaldeans are coming in to fight and to fill them with the dead bodies of men whom I shall smite in my anger and my wrath, for I have hidden my face from this city because of all their wickedness"* (Jer 33.5). Just like Jeremiah, we weren't going to make any progress unless the Master forced open the gates of the city for us.

It seemed to me the futility I was feeling had something to do with all the violence and cruelty that was surrounding me. I really didn't want to hurt anyone, but the fact was that I was being forced into a position to accept the necessity of violence in order to make progress.[95] I was hoping someone would come down here and turn things around.

Medusa and the Furies

Virgil said a whole bunch of other things that I honestly don't remember. He went on and on, but I really wasn't listening to him. Instead, my eyes turned to fixate on the top of the spire that was glowing red-hot as the city of Dis girded up for battle. From the top of the spire, three blood-soaked Furies, female in both feature and form, showed themselves. They were strange-looking creatures with poisonous water snakes for hair.[96]

Now everyone knew about the Furies in my day, since we had read Virgil and other authors, but no one could quite agree on what they represented.[97] Usually, the Furies were the ones who punished blood-crimes.[98] Their presence was signifying the transition we were making from the Ring of Incontinence to the Ring of Violence within the Inferno. I think the Furies' female form derived from the timeless proverb that *"hell hath no fury as a woman scorned."*[99] All I know is that you didn't want to mess with these snake-coifed Furies.

In literature, the Furies were attendants of Persephone, the queen of eternal lament, who ruled this part of the underworld.[100] The daughter of Jupiter and Ceres, Persephone had been carried off by Pluto to be his queen down below.[101]

Virgil said, "Look up there and notice the ferocious Furies, the handmaidens of the queen. That's Megaera on the left. On the right is Alecto; she's the one who is constantly weeping. Tisiphone is in the middle." Each was using her nails to tear at her breast and using her palms to beat her figure. They were screeching so loudly that, out of total fear, I scurried closer to Virgil.

Despite my fear, I was pleased that Virgil knew these Furies pretty well. I couldn't help but notice these embittered women were a kind of perverted female trinity. Just as the Gracious Lady originally called Virgil to my aid, thus raising up Lucy and Beatrice, now a trinity of women were resisting us here.[102]

The Furies cried out as they looked down at us from atop the tower, "Let Medusa come forth and we'll turn him to stone. It was bad enough that we didn't avenge the assault of Theseus!"

In Virgil's *Aeneid*, Theseus was the king of Athens who went down to the Inferno to abduct Persephone, Pluto's queen.[103] During the attempted abduction, Theseus got stuck in the Inferno and couldn't get out.[104]Hercules had to intervene on his behalf, leading him to safety to the chagrin of the devils.[105] Apparently, the Furies were still mad about this rescue of Theseus.

This seemed like a real threat to me. Medusa had the power to turn people to stone if they looked at her. Although she was powerless against women, her sensual beauty was a mortal threat to men.[106] Being the only living male here, that threat was directed against me. So Medusa represented yet another threat to my progress on this journey.[107] The Inferno was pulling out all the stops to keep me from advancing and I wasn't at all sure what to do about it.

Virgil said sternly, "Turn around and keep your eyes closed. If Gorgon shows herself and you see her, there will be no upward return at all."

Now Gorgon was another name for Medusa. She had originally been mortal, but when she got pregnant by Poseidon, Athena turned her hair into serpents, causing all who looked upon Medusa to turn to stone.[108]This is, at least, the story that I had been told.

At this point, Virgil did something surprising. Worried that I might peek through my closed eyes, he turned me around and used his own hands to cover up my eyes, thus adding a layer of protection. I take it that Virgil's actions carried a deeper meaning, namely the important interpretive intrusion that was to come next.[109]

The Interpretive Crux: The Harrowing of Hell

Now, Dear Reader, let me pause from the story for a moment to address you directly. I know this might seem a little jarring — my just talking straight to you — but I want you to get this point. I want you to read beneath the surface level of the text here. There's an important teaching hidden beneath the veil of this strange story that I want you to understand. There's a danger in reading superficially here — so much so that the poem will turn to stone if you only stick to the literal sense of the text and don't go beneath the veil to uncover a deeper meaning.[110] Remember what St. Paul said when he talked about his unregenerate Jewish countrymen:

> *Since we have such a hope, we are very bold...But their minds were hardened...Yes, to this day whenever Moses is read a veil lies over their minds; but when a man turns to the Lord the veil is moved* (2 Cor 3.12, 14-15).

While my eyes were still closed, there came a loud, disturbing sound, full of fright. It was like a mighty wind violently stirring up chaotic waves of heat brought on by opposing air masses. The wind was blowing against a nearby forest on the opposite bank without restraint.[111]

The wind shattered branches, demolishing and carrying them off. Dust went forth without regard for life, the kind of wind that makes both beast and shepherd flee in terror. While my eyes were closed, the mighty wind reminded me of the early church at Pentecost, when the wind was the sign of God's presence on the fledgling church (Acts 2.2). What I was experiencing in the Inferno was its opposite. The wind was destructive, but not edifying.

After the wind died down, Virgil released my eyes and said, "Now direct your attention toward that old scum where the smoke is most acrid."

Just like frogs vanishing through the waters away from their arch-nemesis, the snake, I saw more than one-thousand ruined souls scurry away from the one who was walking on the water of the Styx as if on dry land. He was swatting the greasy air with his left hand and was tiring of doing so.

I quickly figured out this messenger had been sent from heaven. I turned to Virgil. Looking intently, he motioned for me to be quiet and bow down to the messenger out of respect. This was none other than a Divine Messenger sent to re-enact typologically the Divine Son's harrowing of the Inferno.[112] A messenger of the Divine Son had come to intervene on my behalf.[113]

He seemed full of contempt, as he strode confidently to the gate. With a scepter in his hand, he effortlessly opened the locked gate. Not a single demon dared to get in his way. Just then, I wanted to cry out with the words of the Psalmist: "*Your throne...is forever and ever; a scepter of uprightness is the scepter of your kingdom.* (Ps 45.6). But I remained silent, in awe of what I was witnessing.

The heavenly messenger spoke in a booming voice from the dreadful doorstep of Dis, "Oh vexed shades driven from heaven, how did this bitter end come to you? Why do you kick against the will that can never be cut off from its goal and so often has amplified your grief?"

He was paraphrasing the words of the Divine Son to St. Paul at his conversion on the Damascus road, when the Son asked in a blinding light from heaven: "*Saul, Saul, why do you persecute me? It hurts you to kick against the goads*" (Acts 26.14).

The heavenly messenger continued, "What good does it do to clash with destiny? Remember Cerberus, the hound of hell, who had his chin and neck peeled off when Hercules came down here to rescue Theseus! You know, I'm coming down here to help this lost one on his on-going journey."[114]

With that, he turned back toward the disgusting road without uttering a single word to me or to Virgil. It seemed like his attention was fixed on other cares than the ones right before him. He truly was a figure of the Divine Son.

Inside the City of Dis

Virgil and I entered the gates without any resistance. I was eager to check out this place that had been denied us for a time. It was like I was entering a metropolis vanquished after a long and bloody battle. We were the victors, but the heavens had done the fighting.

This infernal city had several parallels. St. Augustine's *City of God* came immediately to mind, where there was both an earthly and a heavenly city — which were mixed for a time — but would be separated in the end. But perhaps more importantly, Dis seemed to me like the opposite of the heavenly Jerusalem promised in John's apocalypse: "*And I saw the holy city, the new Jerusalem, coming down out of heaven from God, prepared as a bride adorned for her husband*" (Rev 21.2). Ultimately, Dis resulted from the pride and arrogance of people who try to live for their own desires.

Once I was inside, my eyes darted around. On every side, I saw a broad plane filled with distress and terrible torments. It was like I was observing several famous ancient cemeteries — in particular, Arles in Provence, Pola in Yugoslavia, and Quarnero Bay on the Adriatic Sea, which is on the other side of Italy.[114] In each of these locations, graves dotted the landscape. In a similar way, I observed sepulchers all over the place as we entered the city. The difference was that the ones here in Dis were far more bitter.

On the outside, the sepulchers were flames that made them so aglow with heat that they were like iron being smelted. All their covers were in an open position and from them issued forth bitter laments, as they were coming from those miserable and injured souls within.

After observing this disturbing sight, I said: "Master, who are these buried inside those arks who are letting out such woeful sighs?" As I was saying this, I noted that their ark-like shapes made them into a kind of perversion of the ark that saved Noah and his family from the deluge of the flood.[116]

Virgil responded, "These are the heretics with all their followers. Every cult is here and many more than you're thinking of right now."

I gave Virgil a puzzled look after he said this because it was becoming clear to me that somehow Virgil could read my thoughts. I cringed at this, realizing that Virgil all along knew about my doubts regarding his leadership.[117]

Virgil continued, "Here, like is buried with like, and the sepulchers are more or less hot."

I had an idea of what heresy was from Thomas Aquinas. Heresy only concerned those who were in the Church, who willfully distorted its teachings. To Thomas, the degree of heresy depended on one's attitude. If someone rejected the teachings of the Church ignorantly that is one thing, but to willfully and obstinately reject the Church's teachings was to impose the heretic's own will over the Maker's.[118] Thus heresy is grave, willful rebellion against the truth and against the Creator.

We then did something we had never done before in the Inferno. We turned to the right as we moved along between the fortifications and those being tormented. Up until this point, we had always been descending in a leftward direction. I'm not exactly sure why Virgil decided to switch directions all of a sudden. All I know is he did.

This is the mixed-up condition that sin creates: we get turned in the wrong direction in our intellects which, in turn, perverts our wills.[119] We think we're going right, when in fact we're going left. And it all starts with pride, the very thing that instigates heresy in the first place. Thus heresy is a grave offense against God and truth, a willful rebellion among those who know better. It leads to the messed up world in which we live.

Comment

We end Canto Nine with Dante's entrance into the city of Dis and into the second Ring of the Inferno. Having left the sins of incontinence behind in Canto Seven, which deals primarily with the passions, we start to observe from here the sins of violence. As we get behind the walls of Dis, the sins of violence carry with them a far greater degree of premeditation.[120] Thus we start to encounter more willful sins that are treated more harshly because they affect more people and involve more calculation.

As usual, Dante inserts a transition into the journey before we get too far. This transition has as its subject the sin of heresy. Simply stated, heresy is an error of the intellect. In Dante's world, there were no heretics who were outside the Church since it was always a willful and obstinate rejection of the Church's teachings that led to heresy. Those unfamiliar with Church teachings could not be heretics. Hence heresy is punished outside the standard structures of incontinence, violence and fraud that form the broad geography of the Inferno proper.

Although it is transitional in function, Canto Nine is one of the most important Cantos of the *Inferno* from an interpretive perspective. When Dante pauses to address the reader directly, we need to pay particular attention to what Dante is doing. He is halting the narrative to tell us, as readers, to look out for something important.

We already have seen the need to dig underneath the surface of the story to discover its deeper moral meanings. All along I have been trying to point these out within the text of the story itself.

But, with the jarring break in the narrative that the direct address to the reader introduces, Dante is now insisting that we stop and take a closer look. It's almost like Dante is making himself out to be the omniscient author of his own text.[121] He's telling us, "Don't miss this part. It's important."

When Dante tells us to look behind the "veil" to find the "doctrine," he's making an important point about how we're supposed to be reading his poem. This scene has obvious references to Moses. When Moses was in the presence of God, this would cause his face to shine as he reflected God's Shekinah glory. Moses would then come out and speak to the people, telling them what God had commanded (Ex 34.34). But, after he was done, Moses would put a veil back over his face because the people were unable to look upon Moses' face and were afraid to come before him (Ex 34.30).

The Apostle Paul, in the New Testament, makes the point that Christ has removed the veil from those who turn to him (2 Cor 3.16). Those who have the grace of God are being transformed into the likeness of God, which was marred in the Fall.

When the heavenly messenger appears in this Canto, we should not read this as just another scene in which gets Dante out of trouble, enabling entrance into the city that had been closed. The surface story is important, but there's something more significant at work underneath the literal sense of the text.

The messenger who comes from heaven is clearly a figure of Christ. In a way similar to how Jesus came down earlier in the story to lead out the Old Testament elect from Limbo, thus harrowing hell, this mysterious messenger is trying to do something similar for Dante. Dante is stuck on his journey. He can go no farther and needs divine assistance to make any more progress.

So one comes down who is worthy of great honor (Virgil has Dante bow down out of reverence), can walk on water and holds a scepter in his hand that opens the door to Dis. By the way, the scepter is the same instrument the author of Hebrews uses to demonstrate the supremacy of Jesus when the author says "*Your throne, O God, is for ever and ever; the righteous scepter is the scepter of your kingdom*" (Heb 1.8).

In fact, this messenger is so powerful that demons are silent in his presence, much as the demons were in Jesus' presence when the Son commanded, "*Be silent and come out from him! And when the demon had thrown him down in the midst, he came out of him, having done him no harm*" (Luk 4.35). This messenger is typologically playing the role that Jesus played when he harrowed hell.

But, at a more allegorical level, this heavenly messenger is representing grace. It was St. Augustine who, more than anyone, taught the Church about the essential nature of grace in salvation. Without the grace of God, no one can be saved. Said differently, you can't get to heaven or make progress on a spiritual journey by your own efforts alone. In one of Augustine's most famous statements on grace, he writes the following in the last chapter of the *Confessions*:

> *In your gift we find our rest. There you are our joy. Our rest is our peace. Love lifts us there and your good spirit exalts our humble estate from the gates of death…My weight is my love. Wherever I am carried, my love is carrying me. By your gift we are set on fire and carried upwards: we grow red hot and ascend. We climb the ascents in our heart and sing the song of steps. Lit by your fire, your good fire, we grow red-hot and ascend, as we move upwards to the peace of Jerusalem.*[122]

Now, in the Inferno, we're not yet ascending. We're still descending through the lower Circles. But, in no uncertain terms, Dante is trying to convince us that our salvation comes about as God's gift to us.

Yet Dante is also describing this in terms he would have learned from Thomas Aquinas: that grace "perfects our nature." In other words, grace is a cooperation, a dance, as it were. To Dante, God does not force us to come to him; he doesn't override our wills. But, if, like Dante, we start on our journey, realize the gravity of our sin and turn to God, he meets us and enables our progress.

Thus "the doctrine beneath the veil" is the Gospel itself, the good news that a restored relationship with God is possible if we humble ourselves and turn to Him.

Dante still has much to learn. He has most of the Inferno yet to see. But, through no real effort of his own, he's experienced the grace of God in a significant way in this Canto. As a result, his journey can continue, where before, it had been blocked.

The last thing we should notice is the contrast that Dante, gifted with grace, sets up with Virgil, who does not have the same gift of grace. If the messenger who comes from heaven with his scepter typifies Christ and the grace he brought to the world, Virgil represents the coldness of humanism. To be clear, I mean humanism in the best sense of the term here — the great striving that ancient authors encouraged in order to achieve a life of virtue. Humanists of all ages have taught that man can strive toward the goal of a happy life by maximizing the cardinal virtues — justice, wisdom, moderation and courage.

But Virgil, representing the greatest achievements in humanist learning, is of no help when it comes to entering Dis and thus to continuing on his spiritual journey. Why? He's no help because he himself has not experienced grace and thus has no ability to grow in the theological virtues of faith, hope and love.

Virgil is great — the best the world has to offer — but when it comes down to it, Virgil's great learning is stymied in the face of a spiritual battle that must be fought with spiritual tools. Virgil may be the greatest of the Latin poets and may have been a very effective guide for Dante up to this point, but he hits a wall. Only the grace of God, which enables us to do things which, by nature, we cannot do on our own, is able to break down the wall and enable Dante's journey. Only grace makes a spiritual journey possible.

10

Divided Sepulchers

CIRCLE VI: THE HERETICS

Dante and Virgil head down to the right into the Circle of the heretics. Here, the Epicureans, who deny the immortality of the soul, are punished. Fulfilling Ciacco's prophecy from Canto Six, Dante meets two prominent Florentines. The first is Farinata, the former head of the Ghibellines, who won a resounding victory against the Guelfs at the battle of Montaperti. Farinata "prophesies" Dante's exile from Florence. The second is Cavalcante, father of Dante's best literary friend, Guido, and an important Guelf official. Farinata and Cavalcante spend eternity lying together in a sepulcher, forcing them to face the divisions they created. Dante misleads Cavalcante who asks about his son Guido, which Dante later regrets.

Virgil and I went on along a narrow path that wound between the city wall to our right and a series of sepulchers on our left.[123] The path was narrow enough that we had to walk single file.[124] I didn't much like walking so close to the sepulchers, so I stayed as close as I could to the back of Virgil.

As we were going along, I reached out to Virgil, the embodiment of reason, "Oh highest virtue, leading me along through this strange turn to the right, please speak to me and satisfy my desires."[125]

I asked, "These shades in the sepulchers, can they be seen? I note that all their covers have been raised and no one is keeping watch over them."

It was almost as if these tomb covers, laid as they were to the side, were there to remind us of the Divine Son's escape from the grave at his resurrection when the great stone was rolled away (Luk 24.2).[126] Yet this scene was different because these condemned souls weren't going anywhere.

Virgil answered, "After the last judgment in the valley of Jehoshaphat, all these covers will be put back on and securely fastened.[127] These shades will be reunited with their bodies, but they'll spend eternity down here."

I knew Virgil's reference to Jehoshaphat came from the prophet Joel: *"Let them arise and let the nations come up into the valley of Jehoshaphat: for there I will sit to judge all nations round about"* (Joel 3.12). It was a reference to the Divine Son's second coming when he would win a great victory over the forces of darkness and finally conquer death, reuniting the souls and bodies of the dead.

Virgil continued, "It's here that Epicurus, with all his followers who teach that the soul dies with the body, will spend eternity."

Now I was aware the Epicureans were often misunderstood as perpetual pleasure-seekers. They were actually more interested in the pursuit of virtue in the world above. But, in the Inferno, it's their heretical view of the soul that has gotten them into trouble.[128] The Epicurean denial of an afterlife leads to the pursuit of pleasure as one of the highest goods. Even though the Epicureans claimed to be pursuing virtue, their mistaken notions of the soul surely prove that they fell short.[129]

Virgil continued, "Look, the questions you have posed to me as well as the desire you're holding back, will soon be satisfied."

Once again, I realized that Virgil could read my thoughts.[130] I should be careful what I wished for. How did he know that I wanted to see some souls from my hometown of Florence? Earlier, Ciacco had told me that I'd see some Florentines.[131] I was hoping that he was right.

Farinata

So I said, "Good leader, I'm not trying to keep much of anything in my heart hidden from you. Besides, what's the point if you can see into it anyway? This isn't the first time you reminded me of..."

Just then, a loud voice interrupted my speech: "Oh Tuscan, who goes about Dis, the city of fire, with such courteous speech, please pause here for a bit and talk with me. It's not every day that we get someone alive down here. Your accent makes it clear that you're native to that noble homeland where I caused some trouble."

My accent? It was almost like I was the Apostle Peter coming under suspicion because of his Galilean speech before he denied his Master for the third time (Matt 26.73). I couldn't see who was talking, but the voice seemed to be coming from behind me to the left.[132]

All of a sudden, a figure sat up in one of the sepulchers. I shrank back in fright, standing just a little bit closer to Virgil.

Virgil, annoyed at my clinging, said "Why are you looking at me? Turn around. Over there is Farinata, who sits upright. You can see all of him from the waist up."

Now Farinata was someone I was eager to see. I wondered how Virgil had recognized him, since they had apparently never met. Farinata had been the leader of the Ghibellines, the rival faction in Florence, and had crushed the Guelfs at the battle of Montaperti in 1260.[133] He then died in 1264,[134] one year before I was born.[135] After losing a major battle at Benevento in 1266, many Ghibellines (including Farinata's own descendants) had been banished from Florence. Spitefully, the city posthumously condemned Farinata and his wife as Cathar heretics.[136]

Turning around, I locked my gaze on Farinata as he was lifting himself up by forehead and chest. Farinata's stature was powerful and impressive.[137] Just like the Divine Son, he looked as if he held the Inferno in utter scorn.[138]

I kept staring at his chest because I was looking for signs of a heart. Heresy is ultimately a sin against the theological virtues that come from the heart, the place where the emotions and the intellect come together.[139]

Virgil, courageous as always, put his hands on me and nudged me toward Farinata's sepulcher. He said, "Make your words count." Virgil was acting like the preacher Qohelet in the book of Ecclesiastes who said: *"Do not be rash with your mouth, nor let your heart be hasty to utter a word...therefore let your words be few"* (Ecclesiastes 5.2).

When I was at the edge of his tomb, Farinata looked at me for a while and then, almost contemptuously asked me: "Who might your ancestors be?"[140] There was monstrous pride just oozing from his lips.

Eager to oblige, I held nothing back. I opened up completely to him and told him about my Guelf lineage. He raised his brow ever so slightly as I was speaking, clearly not very impressed with my stature.[141]

Farinata said, "Your allies, the Guelfs, were ferociously opposed to me, my ancestors and my party. Let me tell you, not once, but twice I expelled them from the city. They ran away like scared dogs."

Not wanting him to get away with that last quip, I responded: "You're right, the Guelfs were exiled twice at your hands. But I'll have you know that they came back from exile both times. This is one art your colleagues have not mastered very well. We came back and yours didn't." I paused just a bit to let those last stinging words sink in.

Cavalcante

But, during my brief pause, there arose a second shade who was in the same sepulcher alongside Farinata. I could only see this one from the chin up, as he must have been holding himself up on his knees. He looked around to both sides of me, apparently hoping to find out if there was someone else with me. Not seeing anyone, this sadly muffled his hopes. It was almost like he was blind.

I didn't recognize this one, but he looked kind of like a friend of mine. He said, "If great poetic genius has allowed you to come through this blind prison, I have to ask, 'Where's my son? You know, my son, Guido, who was the greatest of all the lyric poets. I was hoping he might be with you since you were friends.'"

Guido? My friend? This shade must be Guido's father, Cavalcante de' Cavalcanti! Both his words and his placement among the heretics identified him to me. You see, Guido's father was a fellow Guelf who was also an Epicurean.[142] This must have ultimately been his undoing.

But I also needed to correct Cavalcante, who didn't seem to realize I was down here because of the grace of the Master. I said, "Look, I didn't come down here on my own accord. That one, who is waiting over there, he's leading me through here. I don't know, maybe he'll lead me to someone your Guido held in disdain."

All of a sudden Cavalcante straightened up to his feet and cried out, "What's that? Did you say, 'held'? Is Guido not still alive? Does not the sweet light still strike his eyes?"

I simply stayed quiet. When he noticed a delay in my response, Cavalcante fell back into the tomb face up and no longer appeared outside.

Now I knew that Guido was still alive, but I was starting to worry about his fate, since I thought he might have shared the Epicurean leanings of his father.[143] Frankly, it confused me why his father didn't know that.[144] I guess shades down here could foresee the future, but were ignorant of the present. I started to feel a twinge of guilt that perhaps I should have told him the whole truth.

Farinata, Round II

But Farinata, the great-souled one, having considered what I said before, simply picked back up where he left off.[145] He didn't move at all, neither his neck nor his side. If there was a shred of emotion in him, I couldn't see it. He just continued his original speech and said, "If my Ghibellines didn't come back from exile, it torments me more than this tomb."

"Really," I thought, "Farinata is damned for all eternity and he's worried about some thirteenth-century political conflict? Maybe, I was seeing a flicker of empathy left in him for his family."

Then he turned to me and issued a prophecy: "Not fifty moons from now, you'll know quite well how hard it is to come in from exile."[146]

I wondered what this meant. I was afraid he might be right. I might never get back to my beloved Florence!

Farinata continued, "If you ever hope to return to the sweet world above, tell me, why are people there so utterly cruel with their laws against my family?"

Farinata was referring to the legislation I helped pass that allowed Ghibelline sympathizers to return to Florence, but specifically excluded his own descendants because of their role in the slaughter at the Battle of Montaperti.[147]

I responded, somewhat defensively: "The torment and terrible slaughter that colored the river Arbia red, caused such vindictive political speech to be raised."

Sighing, he shook his head and said, "In doing this, I was not alone, nor without reason. I would have taken part with the others simply because I wanted to come in from exile."[148]

Then, turning his face upward, he emphatically said, "But let's be clear. I did stand alone when my compatriots wanted to level Florence to the ground in retribution. I'm the only one who held back the floodgates and prevented the slaughter of my beloved city. I defended her openly before everyone."

I was almost feeling sorry for Farinata by this point. What he was saying was true. He was well-known for standing alone against the other Ghibellines after the battle of Montaperti, saving Florence from sure ruin.

So I said, "May your kin find some rest at some point." I went on, "I need to ask a small favor: could you please help me untie the knot that has snarled my judgment down here?"

I continued, "If I've heard it right, it seems that you can observe beforehand what time will bring. Yet the present seems to depict a different story. So you can see the future, but have no knowledge of the present down here. Is that right?"

Farinata said, "We observe things dimly as one who has deficient light. Yet in knowledge of future events the Sovereign Ruler still shines on us. When things draw near or are happening, our whole intellect goes dark. We need another to bring it out for us. Thus we know nothing of what's happening back on earth. This is why poor Cavalcante didn't know anything about his son."

So regretful of my silence toward Cavalcante, I said, "Could you please tell him that his Guido is still alive? Before, I was tongue-tied in my answer. Please tell him that I thought he could see what was happening with his son at present and thus didn't understand his predicament. If you'd help resolve this error for me, I'd appreciate it."

But, already, Virgil was calling me back. Quickly, I asked Farinata to tell me which spirits were with him down there.

He said, "Well, there's more than a thousand spirits down here. Here with me are both the second Frederick, the Holy Roman Emperor (the one friendly to the Muslims), and Cardinal Ubaldini, the powerful Ghibelline who was Bishop of Bologna.[149]

Then Farinata hid himself and I turned back to Virgil, thinking over his words that once seemed so hostile to me.

Virgil set out and while he was walking, he asked, "Why are you so lost?" I answered him fully, which seemed to satisfy him.

Then Virgil said, "Let your mind preserve what you've heard uttered against you. Now pay attention here."

With that, Virgil raised his finger, a sign of instruction.[150] Continuing, Virgil said, "When you come before the sweet rays of Beatrice, that one whose beautiful eyes see everything, you'll learn much more about your life's journey."

Then he started moving his feet again to the left. Leaving the wall, he turned toward the center through a path that drops into a valley. Even here, the stench of the valley below was putrid.

Comment

Odd directional notations both begin and end this Canto. We start with Dante and Vigil turning to the right. This is strange because so far they've only been travelling to the left, winding down a spiral as they've descended ever deeper into the Inferno. But, at the end of the Canto, Virgil starts turning to the left again and begins heading down toward the center of the earth by resuming the usual direction. This may seem insignificant, but, as we'll discover, there's little that is irrelevant in this poem.

Since heresy is in view in this Canto, this is probably why the directions shift. As we've seen, heresy is both an error of the mind and of the heart. It turns the world upside down. When heretics within the Church distort the truth and teach incorrectly, this causes a spiritual journey to get mixed up and headed in the wrong direction.

But, as John Freccero has pointed out, left and right aren't relative in the Inferno, they're absolutes.[151] We ought to understand the seemingly irrelevant stage directions as issuing forth from a fixed vantage point — God's. This ends up being an important detail because Dante, imitating Christ by descending in humility, is trying to discover what is eating at his soul.

But in the Inferno everything is mixed up. In fact, by descending, everything is upside down (this fact will become important at the very end of the *Inferno*). Dante is journeying into the middle of the earth, the farthest possible point away from the heavenly realms and the beatific vision.

As we'll see later, it's only when Dante emerges from the Inferno and starts his ascent upward that the directions are put "right" again. He'll start to ascend in a leftward direction when he reaches Purgatory, having passed through the Inferno. He'll then start to experience a world turned right-side up. Thus Dante has to descend into the Inferno in order to get turned around so he can ascend again. He needs to find his "true up," where his will be made "right."[152]

But what about the Epicureans? If heresy involves those within the Church who distort its teaching, why do the followers of Epicurus get so much scrutiny in this Canto? Well, first we should note that it was those who still claimed to be Christians (Farinata and Cavalcante) who are in view here.

The Epicureans denied the immortality of the soul. Suffering in sepulchers, they discover very quickly in the Inferno they were wrong. Their souls have survived the death of the body and thus the punishment they've brought on themselves is to sit in a grave for all eternity and contemplate that they're not dead and that there is an afterlife. They misused both their wills and their intellects so much in life they cannot now intuit anything going on in the present. Even worse, they can see, dimly, what will happen in the future. None of it turns out very well for them.

Dante wants to present heresy as something inherently divisive. It divides the will from the intellect in individuals. Heresy divides whole societies as well, as it destroys the natural order that God has made.

Thus Dante depicts two heretics here as leaders of rival political factions — the Guelfs and the Ghibellines. They're forced to lie together for all eternity in recognition of their actions, which did so much to divide their city. Their personalities might be very different — Farinata is stern and stalwart, while Cavalcante is emotive and flighty — but their actions have divided what God intended to be united. To Dante, suffering as he is in exile, heresy is a grave sin because of the harm it does to whole communities.

One other thing to note about Farinata is his prophecy about Dante's impending exile. Of course, Dante, as he's writing, is already in exile, and has been for some time. But Dante sets the *Inferno* in the year 1300 right before his exile so he can "prophecy" things that will take place. When Farinata says that "fifty moons from now" Dante would know how hard it is to come back from exile, this is a reference to the White Guelfs' last-ditch effort to come back to Florence in 1304. Farinata's prophecy is simply saying something Dante already ruefully knows — the negotiations wouldn't be successful.

At the start of this Canto, Dante gives us a quick lesson in Christian eschatology with the idea that Christ will return at "the end of days" to restore order to his creation. According to the prophet Joel, the valley of Jehoshaphat, located between the city of Jerusalem and the Mount of Olives, will be the place where the final judgment takes place. This is where souls will be united with their bodies for all eternity.

Don't confuse Jehoshaphat and Mt. Megiddo, the sight of "Armageddon." Mt. Megiddo is where the final battle will take place between Christ and his army of angels and the powers allied against him from the four corners of the earth (Rev 16.16). The valley of Jehoshaphat is where the final judgment takes place.

Notice, once again, this carries the image of unity. It envisages the unification of soul and body, the unification of the body of Christ and the unification of the nation of Israel. The resurrection of the body at the last judgment is what will bring things back together that were separated because of sin.

Dante is learning something about Christian hope, the hope that God will make all things right in the end. That which is turned upside down will be made right-side up. The death of sin, which will result in the death of death itself (1 Cor 15.54), is what will re-unite the intellect, the will and the heart and will put an end to the divisions that so typify both Dante's world and ours.

11

Intermezzo

THE GEOGRAPHY OF THE INFERNO

Virgil provides Dante with a lesson on the geography of the lower regions of the Inferno as they pause at the edge of the seventh Circle. Although they are only about one-third of the way through the Inferno, there are just three more Circles to go, encompassing violence, simple fraud and complex fraud. The sins of fraud and violence will come with ever-more subdivisions as we move forward through the poem. This means the punishments will become ever-more severe as love grows ever-more dim. This Canto takes place on Saturday morning between 3:00-4:00 AM.

Virgil and I then came to a steep embankment formed by rocks broken in the shape of a circle. Looking down, we saw scores of souls packed very tightly into the ever-narrowing spirals below.[153] As soon as I peered over the edge, a horribly putrid odor assaulted me from the abyss. It was simply awful.

Virgil and I then withdrew a bit behind the cover of a sepulcher to get our bearings amidst the terrible smell. Over the tomb, I noted a sign that read, "*I contain Pope Anastasius.*"

This was apparently the place assigned to Pope Anastasius II, the arch heretic, who became convinced by the deacon Photinus to deny the deity of Christ.[154] Although heresy is no laughing matter, I had to chuckle at the obvious irony of Anastasius' name since it means "resurrection." Not to be outdone, Photinus' name means "the little light."[155]

If the Divine Son isn't God, there was no resurrection. Moreover, if Photinus convinced the Pope that the Son was the natural-born child of Joseph and Mary, he had little illumination to his intellect.[156] I guess the Creator has a sense of humor even down here.

A Geography Lesson

Virgil and I decided to stay put for a while simply to get used to the awful stench. To make forward progress, we were going to have to get accustomed to the terrible fumes welling up from the abyss below. While we were waiting, I asked Virgil to fill the time by explaining the remaining geography of the Inferno. I wanted to know what we might encounter on our journey to the center of the earth.

Virgil said, "You're reading my mind." Continuing, he said, "My son, within these boundary stones are three Circles, each smaller than the one before and ever narrower than those we've left behind. The remaining three Circles go down to the center in the shape of a funnel. All are full of wicked spirits. Just the sight of them will confirm why they're all impounded together."

Virgil continued, "Every malicious act despised in heaven has injustice as its end. And this injustice injures others with either violence or fraud. But listen closely: because fraud is an evil act unique to humans, it's more grievous to the Maker than violence.[157] Hence you'll find the fraudulent placed farther down in the Inferno than the violent, and also assailed with greater degrees of grief.

Violence

The first Circle down from where we are now belongs to the violent. But, because violence can be subdivided into three different manifestations, it's dealt with in three different rings.[158] This is because violence can be perpetrated against God, against the self or against one's neighbor, as you'll discover quite clearly below.

Moreover, violence against others can be further sub-divided into injuries done against a person, himself or against his possessions. Further, violence against property can then take the forms of pillage, arson or violent extortions, while violence against other people includes those who ransack and plunder. These are all punished below, but in different groups.

This all seemed a little complicated to me. I knew what Virgil was saying was similar to what Thomas Aquinas and Cicero had written, but I was going to have to see it for myself to understand what he was really talking about.

Virgil continued, "Now one can perpetrate violence either against oneself or against one's goods. This is punished two levels down. These souls ought to repent, but, as you'll see, they won't. As you know, in Roman law, to damage property by gambling it away or by melting it down, is treated as an extension of the person.[159] So these sinners end up weeping."

Virgil went on, "Yet violence can also be perpetrated against the Creator himself by denying or blaspheming Him with the heart. One can also be violent toward the Maker by disdaining his nature and its goodness. You'll soon see those that do this very thing."

Virgil continued, "So the bottommost rings of the violent deals with those who commit violence against nature, dealing with sodomy and usury. These violent despise the Maker with their hearts."[160]

Fraud

Virgil said, "Ok, so much for violence. Let's talk about fraud, which is even worse. The fraudulent not only deny their consciences, but eat away at them to the point where their consciences no longer function well. So fraud is ultimately a crime against reason, betraying the trust of another.[161] The explanation of why this is so terrible is that it dissolves the bonds of love made by nature. We'll see all kinds of examples of the loss of love. We'll see hypocrisy, flattery, sorcery, falsehood, theft, simony, panderers, embezzlers and other filth.

Virgil continued, "But it gets worse. The other kind of fraud utterly destroys the bonds of trust that hold the world together. This is the worst kind of fraud, the kind that is premeditated. Betrayal is what I mean. At the very bottom of the Inferno you'll see Satan, the ultimate betrayer, sitting as the perfect exemplar of treason against right reason.

At this point, I stopped Virgil and asked, "But, tell me, why are those in the Circles we've already passed — those in the thick lagoon punished for anger; those the wind drives along, punished for lust; those the rain batters, punished for gluttony; and those colliding with such terrible tongues — not punished inside the flaming city of Dis? If God is so angry with them, why is there a division between those who are inside the city and those who are outside?"

Virgil shook his head and asked, "Why does your mind wander so far off course? Where is your sense? Don't you remember Aristotle's *Ethics,* which discusses this point so thoroughly? Don't you remember the three dispositions that heaven doesn't want: incontinence, malice and mad bestiality? Don't you remember how incontinence offends God less because it's a crime of passion and thus accrues a lesser censure than those crimes perpetrated with intent that affect whole societies?"[162]

Virgil's rebuke stung a bit. I guess I hadn't understood completely what we were about to see. From his answer, I surmised that Virgil was saying that there were two types of fraud — fraud that occurs in normal human terms and "mad bestiality," a kind of fraud that was so heinous it was beyond belief.[163] I have to admit this was pretty much as Aristotle had put it.[164]

Virgil continued, "If you consider well this finding and bring to mind who it is who undertakes penance above and outside the walls (in Purgatory), you'll see why these souls are separated from the still sin-stained spirits punished above and why divine judgment hammers them with slightly less wrath."

I still didn't understand it completely, so I cried out: "Oh Sun, who cures every troubled sight, you make me content when you resolve my doubts; please help me to know." Here, I was asking for some divine illumination for my intellect. I still didn't quite understand how the usurers fit into this whole scheme. How exactly did usury offend the divine goodness?[165]

Virgil invoked philosophy, saying, "Consider Aristotle's *Physics.* You'll find, after reading not too long, that God's children, as much as they can, follow nature, as does a disciple his master.[166] So it's almost like your nature is God's grandchild. From these two things — nature and human industry — a person earns his living and advances along his path.

Virgil continued, "Because the usurer takes a different path, she disparages nature itself and her offspring, which is human industry.[167] This causes the usurer to invest hope in other things."

Having finished his speech, Virgil said, "Come on, follow me now, since I want to go. Pisces, the fish, is just appearing on the horizon and the Great Bear is lying just to the northwest.[168] The way down the cliff is still quite far off."

Comment

In many senses, this is a transitional Canto without a lot of action. Dante is giving us the lay of the land for what we're going to encounter from here to the end of the Inferno. However, Dante's geography lesson is usually confusing for new readers. Put simply, we learn that there are three Circles left, which punish the sins of violence and fraud. All these subdivisions become clearer as we descend farther down.

As Dante explains, however, fraud is the worst sin, even worse than violence, because it is uniquely human and breaks the bonds of love. It represents the ultimate betrayal of trust and the ultimate misuse of the intellect that God has given to us. This is why we'll discover Satan at the very bottom of the Inferno — he's the worst betrayer of all, to Dante.

One thing to mention briefly is that Dante makes a mistake with history in this Canto. It appears that Dante is confusing Pope Anastasius II with the Emperor Anastasius I.[169] Dante also seems to be a bit confused about who misled whom.

Even if Dante is a bit confused here, the issue he is raising is real. Anastasius denied that Jesus was God. This is known as the Ebionite heresy, which is the earliest Christological heresy that we have on record.

Named after Ebion (derived from the word for "poor" in Hebrew), the Ebionites were Jews who were drawn to Christianity at an early stage.

Yet they had trouble recognizing that Jesus was something more than a great prophet. They wanted to see Jesus as one of the greatest of the prophets, but also wanted to deny that he was God. Irenaeus, the great Christian theologian of the second century, describes them as follows:

> *The so-called Ebionites admit that the world was made by the true God, but in regard to the LORD they hold the same opinion as Cerinthus and Carpocrates. They use only the Gospel according to Matthew and reject the Apostle Paul, saying that he is an apostate from the law...they circumcise themselves and continue in the practices that are prescribed by the law and by the Judaic standard of living.*[170]

So heresy is a big deal to Dante because of its ability to divide that which should be united (namely, the Church). Heresy also causes division in the broader Christian community as well. Dante, suffering as he is in exile, cannot get over the idea of the inherent injustice of those who ruin others' lives by dividing, instead of uniting. We'll observe this as a fairly constant theme in the Cantos that follow.

Lastly, Dante places small details into the poem, which are designed to give us hints as to the time. Remember, the poem began on Good Friday in the year 1300. Dante began his descent into the Inferno on the evening of Good Friday (just as Christ did after he was crucified).

When Dante tells us at the end of the Canto that the constellation Pisces was coming up over the horizon and that the Great Bear (the Big Dipper) is in the northwest part of the sky, this must mean that it's just before sunrise (probably close to 4:00 AM). Thus, measured in chronological time, Dante and Virgil have been on their journey through the Inferno for only a few hours. They entered into the Inferno during the evening of Good Friday and we're just about to come upon the first light of Holy Saturday.

Ring II:
The Sins of Violence

12

The River of Boiling Blood

CIRCLE VII (RING I): VIOLENCE AGAINST OTHERS

In this first section of the seventh Circle of the violent, Dante encounters the sin of violence against neighbor. After descending a landslide of broken rocks (caused by the harrowing of hell described in prior Cantos), Dante and Virgil encounter the violent. They meet several bestial creatures, a Minotaur, who is half-man and half-bull, and several Centaurs, who are half-man and half-horse. Along the way, they encounter several figures being punished in a river of boiling blood for their acts of violence against their neighbors.

As Virgil and I got up to go, I noticed some things about the landscape. Before us was a sheer cliff, descending down into a gulch. There were mountains of broken rocks all around, which had been a constant feature as we had been making our way around the rim of the gulch.[1]Although I couldn't quite make it out, there was something else there, lurking in the shadows. Whatever it was, it was a sight that would cause every eye to turn away.

The landscape was like that landslide in the Tyrolian region of Northern Italy near Trento along the river Adige.[2] The landslide in that place was so severe that it actually changed the direction of the river.[3] Most thought an earthquake or water erosion caused this landslide.[4] Down here, however, it was pretty clear that the Divine Son's harrowing of hell was the precipitating cause.

The result of the massive landslide in front of us made it possible to make our way down, using the broken rocks as steps. It was a long way down, so our path was about to become even more perilous.

The Minotaur

Right there, at the point where the broken rocks cleared the way for our descent, we encountered a grotesque sight stretched out along the path.[5] We saw the Minotaur, a hideous figure that was half-man and half-beast.

The Minotaur was created when Pasiphae, wife of Minos of Crete, had sexual relations with a bull while disguising herself as a wooden cow.[6] Imprisoned in a labyrinth, the Minotaur was eventually killed by Theseus who ended the Athenian practice of sacrificing children to satisfy the ravenous hunger of the Minotaur.[7] I guess this is what Virgil meant before when he described this place as being beset by "mad bestiality."

When the Minotaur saw us, he was chomping on himself, as one whose unquenchable anger burned within. In a very real sense, he was doing violence to himself, suffering from the anger that was consuming him. Yet, all the while, his rage was impotent.[8]

Virgil reacted swiftly, crying out against the Minotaur: "Do you think Theseus, the Duke of Athens, who ended your life up above, has come down to get you? Get away from us, you beast, since this one beside me wasn't trained by your sister Ariadne. She may have conspired with Theseus to put you to death up above, but this one has come down just to observe your punishments. Look at him, he's stunned at the sight of you. The Minotaur is like a bull, mortally wounded by a sledgehammer, who can't move, but just thrashes about in shock."[9]

With that, I saw the Minotaur thrash about violently on all fours, utterly enraged and devoid of sense. While the man-beast was disoriented, Virgil sternly charged me to run to the opening of the path, saying, "It would be a good thing for you to go on down while he's still in a fit."

So Virgil and I moved on past the Minotaur and we took the path that went down through the landslide. The rocks were unstable under my feet because of the weight of my body. Apparently shades can't move rocks down here.

As I was trying to make sense of what I had just seen, Virgil said, "Maybe you're thinking about these rocks, which are guarded by that bestial wrath that I just stamped out. I want you to know that the other time I travelled down here to the lower Inferno, these rocks had not yet fallen because the Divine Son had not yet descended down to Limbo."

Virgil continued, "The Son's harrowing of the Inferno shook every part of this loathsome valley because of his intense love that enabled some to believe. So violently was this place shaken that all the fundamental elements of the universe, formerly separated by hatred and chaos, were fused together, unifying what was once separated."[10]

Virgil's words stunned me when I realized that this is exactly what happened in the direct aftermath of the Divine Son's death. Matthew said it this way: *"And behold, the curtain of the temple was torn in two, from top to bottom and the earth shook and the rocks were split"* (Matt 27.41). Matthew's rocks were apparently the ones I was seeing down here.

Then Virgil said, "Fix your eyes yonder to the abyss because we're approaching the river of boiling blood that consumes those who harmed others with violence."

The Centaurs

At the sight of boiling blood, I cried out, "Oh blind greed and insane wrath that so goad us on towards violence in this brief life, and then, in the afterlife, bathes us in such evil!" Here, I couldn't help but associate anger and greed as the central causes of all the violence I had seen around me and had experienced in my life.

Just as Virgil had instructed me, we were about to encounter those who had killed out of malice and those who robbed for gain. I saw right in front of me the first ring of the violent in a wide pit, enclosed in an arc. I could only see the part sticking up, which suggested to me this was just the top portion of a complete Circle that had more layers below.[11]

Between the rocky base of the cliff and the precipice of the gulch ran a bunch of Centaurs, who were half-horse and half-men.[12] Armed with bows and arrows, the Centaurs guarded the banks of the river, picking off any shade that attempted to escape.[13]

The product of an unholy union between Nephele, the cloud-born princess and King Ixion, the Centaurs were the guardians of the violent down here.[14] Yet the Centaurs were also different from the Minotaur since their intellects weren't thrashing about, dominated by violent anger. Instead, they channeled their anger to carry out cruel and violent acts against others. This seemed to be more serious than the violence that comes simply from the exercise of the passions.

As they saw us coming, each of the Centaurs stood still, while three broke formation to come out in front with bows and arrows drawn.

Then one of them cried out from afar, "What are you doing down here? To what martyrdom have you consigned yourself and where do you come from? Tell us, or I'll shoot you right now!"

Virgil responded, "We'll only answer to Chiron the Wise once we've come over there beside you. You are always so rushed that you lose your judgment."[15]

Now I figured Virgil wanted to speak with Chiron because he was the leader of the bunch. He stood in the middle between Nessus and Pholus. Chiron was probably smarter than the others because he hadn't been sired from King Ixion, like the other Centaurs, but rather from the god Saturn. This Chiron had been Achilles' tutor before the Trojan War, so he must have had something going for him.

Virgil then nudged me and said, "That one over there is Nessus, who died after trying to rape the fair Deianira, Hercules' wife."

This must have been what Virgil was referring to when he accused Nessus of constantly rushing. When Hercules saw what Nessus had tried to do, he killed Nessus with one of his poisoned arrows. But, when Deianira took the now-poisoned shirt off Nessus and gave it to her husband, this caused Hercules' death as well, thus demonstrating the tragedy of violence that perpetuates itself over and over again."[16]

Virgil continued, "Pholus, the one standing to the other side, was full of anger because of his bellicose nature. [17] He died when he dropped one of Hercules' poisoned arrows on his foot."[18]

What I observed was a pretty remarkable sight. Scores of Centaurs were roving around the gulch, shooting at any one of the violent who tried to emerge out of the bloody river. Since the souls trapped in the river sunk down under the weight of their transgressions, those submerged in the deeper part of the river were constantly trying to get to more shallow parts. The Centaurs made sure this didn't happen.

As we kept coming closer, Chiron took out an arrow and scratched his beard with the notched end, moving it away from his jaw. I thought this was a very strange sight since I was under the impression that none of the spirits down here had a physical body. But this Chiron seemed to have a beard and a moustache that appeared very real. [19] I never did quite understand how this could be.[20]

Chiron had a huge mouth and with it he said to his companions, "Have you noticed that the one behind moves the rocks he's walking on? That's something you don't see every day among the dead." Apparently, he realized I was still embodied.

As Virgil approached Chiron, his eyes only came up to his breast, where the horse part and the human part are joined.[21] It was almost like Virgil was trying to cozy up to Chiron as a friend.[22] Virgil looked up at him and said, "That one behind is quite alive and so is very unique down here. I'm showing him the dark valley. We're doing this because we have to; this isn't a joy ride."

Virgil continued, "Up above, the fair Beatrice charged me with this unusual office, and signed off her call by singing alleluia. Let me vouch for this one: he's neither a robber nor a thief."

Virgil then said, "I need to ask you a favor; by the power on high that moves me to take this journey here below, please lend us one of your Centaurs to lead us on our way. We need someone to show us where the ford of the river is and to bear this one behind me on his back since he's still embodied and can't fly through the air."

Chiron wheeled around to his right and said to Nessus: "You turn about and guide them. If anyone gets in your way, you know what to do."

The River Tour

Virgil looked at me and said, "Now let's go on with our faithful escort along the banks of the river of blood where those being boiled are uttering loud cries of lament."

In the river, I saw the gruesome sight of souls sunk down to the brow. The great Nessus explained what we were seeing: "These are tyrants who took to blood and plunder. Here, they lament the merciless damage they caused."

Nessus continued, "Over there is Alexander of Pherae, a tyrant from Thessaly, who was so vindictive that he used to clothe men with the skins of beasts and sic dogs on them.[23] Beside him is the cruel Dionysius the Elder, the tyrant of Syracuse, who brought so much distress to Sicily."[24]

Nessus went on, "The one over there with the jet black hair sticking out is Ezzelino, a prominent Ghibelline who loved to torture the Guelfs and who massacred the inhabitants of Padua.[25] The other head sticking up with the blond hair is Obizzo d'Este, a murderous Guelf who was taken out by his debauched son in the world above."[26]

Now this surprised me and so I turned to Virgil with a puzzled look. I had heard the story a bit differently, but decided to hold my tongue.[27]

Virgil said, "Let Nessus go on ahead of you. I'll follow along behind. You get up on his back."[28]

As we went on a little further, Nessus stopped to look over the souls who were submerged in the river only up their necks. This was apparently murderers' row. He pointed out a shade off to the side by himself and said, "That one is Guy de Montfort who killed his cousin, Henry of Cornwall, while he was in church. He did this right at the words of institution in the Eucharist when the host was transformed. [29] Henry's heart still drips blood on the River Thames."

I think Nessus was describing the legend that Henry's heart was preserved on the London Bridge where it was venerated.[30] Apparently, Henry's murder had still not been avenged.[31]

Finally, I saw the third grouping of souls who were violent, but not with murder. These lifted their heads and chests up out of the river. I have to say, I recognized a bunch of them. As the river became more and more shallow, I noticed it only scorched their feet, suggestive of the property they took away through pilferage and pickpocketing.[32] We used the shallowness of the river as our spot to cross over.

Nessus turned to his right, allowing us to see from where we had come.[33] All along, the boiling stream had been diminishing in depth. Then, as Nessus looked to his left to observe the ever-deepening portion of the stream, I realized that we had gone along in a kind of semicircle.[34] At the end, where the river reached its maximum depth, tyranny let loose its wailing.

Nessus said, "There, midway along the portion of the river where we didn't go are those who have destroyed property. The first one divine justice stings is Attila the Hun, who destroyed everything in his sight before Pope Leo the Great convinced him to turn around, thus sparing Rome.[35] With him are Pyrrhus, who defeated the Romans three times, the source of the phrase "pyrrhic victory." Beside him is Sextus, who became an outlaw after the murder of Caesar, thus causing severe famine in Rome when he cut off the North African grain supply."[36]

Beside them were also the two Riniers — Rinier da Corneto and Rinieri da Calboli who I knew from my day. They held up the roads through robbery and produced so much war.

Then, turning around, Nessus crossed over the ford of the river once more. All the while I continued to cling to his back.

Comment

In this Canto, Dante sees violence against others as having two causes: greed and anger. This is why the violent are punished in a river of boiling blood, the Phlegethon. This is the third major river we have encountered so far in the Inferno (the others were Styx and Acheron). Like the others, this river runs around the pit in a circular fashion. [37]

The river of boiling blood is an especially apt description of what leads to violence against one's neighbor. Ultimately, to Dante, this is a crime against reason, when the desires of the animal part of the soul overcome the reason of the rational part of the soul. Hence, when Dante encounters the Minotaur (half-man and half-bull) and the Centaurs (half-man and half-horse), he is demonstrating the victory of our animal natures over our rational natures.

It might be instructive to consider the various levels of punishment in this Canto. Notice that the worst perpetrators are those whose violence affected whole societies. Both Ezzelino and Obizzo caused great harm to others because of their violence. As a result, only their hair is protruding from the river.

To Dante, the constant strife brought on by the Guelfs and the Ghibellines is counter-productive. In no way could these conflicts be counted as just wars because they were not defensive. Even worse, they often had greed and the desire for power as their chief motivators.

Notice as well that Dante is not partisan in his condemnation of violence. He puts a Guelf right next to a Ghibelline at the deepest part of the river. The type of killing that ravages entire communities is an especially heinous sin to Dante.

In fact, notice that it's even worse than murder. The murderers are punished in a shallower part of the river than those who perpetrated organized violence. This makes some sense given that murder's effects are relatively isolated compared to the wide-spread violence perpetrated by the Guelfs and the Ghibellines.

This is something we will observe with ever-greater clarity. The worst sins are those that affect the most people. In Dante's world, crimes of passion are much more limited in effect than the pre-meditated crimes of violence that rip apart communities. The problem with violence is ultimately its scope and its ability to tear apart the fabric of God's creation.

13

Losing Hope

CIRCLE VII (RING II): SUICIDES AND PROFLIGATES

Virgil and Dante descend to the second ring of the seventh Circle where the violent, the suicides and the profligates are punished. The suicides have been turned into large bushes that bleed from their wounds. We encounter the Harpies, strange bird-women who eat the foliage of the bushes, thus severely injuring the suicides. One of them houses the soul of Pier delle Vigne, a famous rhetor, poet and advisor to the Emperor. Having committed suicide after a falling out with the Emperor, Pier is concerned with restoring his reputation in the world above, a sign of his continued pride. Dante also encounters spendthrifts who have destructively squandered their goods, a kind of suicide. Finally, Dante meets a nameless suicide from Florence who tells of the exchange of loyalties at the Christianization of the city.

Nessus, who had guided us around the river, hadn't yet reached the other side when we starting moving through a pathless forest. The forest's lack of order was a troubling sight to our minds.[38] It was colorless too, no green leaves, no smooth branches and no fruit. Everything seemed negative, flat and sullen.[39]

In fact, the forest was marked by gnarled and warped branches surrounded by poisonous thorns. It reminded me of the region of Maremma in south-western Italy, bordered as it was by the stream Cecina in the north and the small town of Cornetto in the south. Even that swampland wasn't as impenetrable as this place.[40]

I also noticed that some loathsome Harpies had made their nests in the trees. These strange creatures were half-bird and half-woman.[41] I knew all about these Harpies since they had chased the Romans from the Greek islands in Virgil's *Aeneid,* on their way to Italy. The Harpies had prophesied starvation and failure for Aeneas' travelling band, causing them to lose hope.[42]

The Harpies had broad wings connected to human faces and necks. They had feet with ferocious talons and prodigious, protruding bellies. These Harpies rested in the trees above and did nothing but utter laments over the souls of the suicides.

Virgil, my good master, began to speak: "Before you enter into the forest any further, I should tell you that we're in the second ring where the violent are punished. We're going to be here until we come to the horrid burning sand down below. So keep your eyes peeled. You're going to see things that you simply wouldn't believe if I just described them with words."[43]

On every side, I heard horrible wailing, yet didn't see anyone in particular before us. This confused me, so I just kept still. It was like I was all the way back at the start of my journey — bewildered and lost in a dark wood.[44]

I didn't know what to make of all this. Virgil's explanation didn't tell me much. He was probably trying to make me think the voices were coming from people hiding among the branches. Yet I was really thinking about Adam and Eve, who, after they sinned, *"hid themselves from the presence of the Lord among the trees of the Garden"* (Gen 3.8).[45] This part of the Inferno seemed eerily similar to that famous garden after the Fall. Virgil was going to have to do something to help my skepticism.

Pier delle Vigne

Virgil said, "Just lop off a little twig from one of those branches and see what happens. If you do, those doubts of yours will be cut short."

I slowly stretched out my hand just a bit and snapped off a tiny twig tip from a huge thorn bush. At this, the trunk shrieked and cried out, "What the hell are you doing? Why are you mangling me?" At this, I noticed the trunk became dark with blood, prompting it to cry out again, "Ouch! Why are you mangling me? Don't you have any pity?"

The branch continued, "We were men once, but now we've become mere twigs. Your hand might well have been more merciful if we had had the souls of serpents." Apparently, with the reference to the serpent, the voice in the trunk really wanted me to notice the allusion to the Fall.

It seemed that it actually hurt the creature to utter these words.[46] The trunk was like a green log burning from one end, which causes hissing at the other end, dripping and spitting as the air goes out from it. Its wounds affected everything, as words and blood fell out from the broken twig. I dropped the twig in horror and stood still, like one overpowered with dread. It was like this soul had been reduced to mere materiality.[47]

Seeing my fright, Virgil said to the voice in the trunk, "Look, I know tearing off the twig hurt you. But I'm trying to demonstrate something to this skeptical one with me.[48] If he had just believed what he saw from my verses in the *Aeneid*, I wouldn't have had to do it. What can I say, he lacks faith. Your sight is so unbelievable it made me do something that still weighs on me."

Virgil continued, "But tell us who you were. Maybe, in return, your fame will be restored in the world above and you'll get to clear your name."[49]

Then the trunk said, "With your sweet words, you entice me so I can't be silent. Don't be dismayed at what I'm about to say."

He continued, "I'm the one who held both keys to the heart of Frederick. I turned them as skillfully as I could, locking and unlocking so subtly that I kept almost every one of his confidences. I was so faithful to that glorious office that I lost my sleep and then my nerve."

As soon as the trunk mentioned Frederick, I recognized the voice as Pier delle Vigne, the chief advisor to the Emperor, Frederick II. Known for his poetry and the principles of law he crafted, Pier fell out of favor with Fredrick, was thrown into prison and was blinded.[50] No one really knows what he did to incur the ire of the Emperor, but he was probably the victim of some intrigue at court.[51] While awaiting trial, Pier committed suicide by bashing his head against a stone wall.[52]

Pier continued, "The harlot of envy, the typical downfall of courts, never took her whoring eyes away from the domain of Caesar and inflamed every soul against me. So inflamed, they incurred the ire of the Emperor, and my pleasing honors were turned to miserable bereavement. My soul, in disdainful zest, seeking to flee from contempt by death, made me unjust, contrary to what is right."

I thought to myself, he must be talking about his own suicide. Even he knows it was wrong to take his life. He makes himself guilty with his own speech.[53]

Pier went on, "I vow to you that never once did I break faith with my lord who is so worthy of honor. I was unjustly treated at court! If either of you returns to the world, please support my fame, which is still lying under the wound envy gave it."

Ok, I thought, but if he knows what he did was wrong, why is so insistent on his innocence? But I couldn't help it. Pier's words caused pity to well up in my heart. I suspected he might have been falsely accused, just like I was.[54]

After waiting a bit, Virgil said to me, "Don't miss your chance. While he's gone silent, question him further if you want to."

I turned to Virgil and said, "No, *you* should keep questioning him about what you think will satisfy me. I don't think I can. My pity for him grieves me too much."

Virgil then said to Pier, "If this man should freely do for you what you've requested, may it please you, O jailed spirit, to tell us how your soul is bound in these gnarled scrubs. If possible, please tell us if you ever expect to get out of here."

Pier then exhaled strongly. His breath turned into a voice, which uttered this brief answer: "At death, when the savage soul departs from the body that uprooted itself, Minos, the infernal judge, dispatches it here to the seventh Circle. It falls into the forest in a place not chosen."

Pier continued, "But wherever Fortune shoots it, it springs up like a clump of wheat plants. Then it grows into a sapling, then into a wild shrub. When it has fully grown, the Harpies graze on its foliage, thus bringing pain and a window into the soul. The bushes express their pain through wailings."[55]

This sounded to me a lot like the Divine Son's parable of the sower when *"A sower went out to sow his seed; and as he sowed, some fell along the path"* (Luk 8.5).[56] It seemed to me that Pier's faith hadn't taken root, as could be seen by his suicide when Fortune hadn't gone his way. His was the seed that was choked by the thorns in which *"the cares and riches and pleasures of life"* (Luk 8.14) bring destruction.

Pier continued, "The others down here will eventually be reunited with their bodies, but such an outcome wouldn't be right for us. We can't put our bodies back on in the general resurrection, which we took away from ourselves with suicide. No, our flesh will hang from our own branches forever." [57]

The Big Spenders

We were still paying attention to the trunk of Pier, thinking he wanted to say something more, when we were startled by a noise. The sound was similar to a hunting party chasing after a wild pig, snapping off twigs as the hunt hastened by.

From our left side, two shades, naked and scratched, were fleeing so hastily that they were breaking nearly every branch in their way as they ran along. The one in front cried out, "Hasten, hasten, O death!" And, the other, thinking him too slow, cried out, "Lano, your limbs were not so nimble at the jousts of Toppo!" And then perhaps because his stamina was failing him, he got himself tangled into a single clump.

I had heard of this Lano before. He was from Siena and was famous for being such a big spender that it was destructive. In fact, he spent so much he completely blew through his substantial wealth. Lano had let himself be killed at the ford of Pieve del Toppo in Italy. Apparently, he could have saved himself, but consigned to a life of poverty, he allowed himself to be killed, a kind of passive suicide.[58] The one running behind was Jacopo of St. Andrea, another prodigious spender, who had famously burned his own house to the ground, thus committing a kind of suicide with his goods.[59]

A whole pack of black dogs, ravenous and swift, was chasing the two souls through the forest like hounds let loose from the chain. They represented the fierce violence that drove these spendthrifts to their doom.[60] The dogs caught up with them, sunk their teeth into the one who had crouched down, tearing him apart piece by piece, and carting off his dismembered limbs.

The Nameless Suicide

After seeing this, Virgil then took me by the hand and brought me to a bush, which wept in vain over its bleeding abrasions. The bush said, "Oh Jacopo, what good was it to make a screen of me? Why is your sinful life my fault?"

When Virgil halted over the bush, he said, "Who were you that through so many bleeding wounds, you blow out your doleful speech?" The bush replied, "Oh souls who have come to see the unfair torment that has ripped me from my leaves, gather them up for me at the foot of this wretched shrub."

The bush continued, "I was from Florence, the city that exchanged Mars, its first patron, for John the Baptist when the Christians came to town. Because of this exchange, the gods are forever unsettled, as the temple of Mars was turned into a Church, and Mars' statue removed to the Ponte Vecchio.[61] If it weren't for the passing of the Arno River over the bridge that still affords some sight of him, those citizens who rebuilt the city on the ashes that Attila the Hun left, would have done their work in vain. As a result, I turned my home into a gallows."

Comment

Canto Thirteen is one of the more memorable in the *Inferno*. Here, violence against the self in the form of suicide and profligacy is punished. Dante intends the reader to see this scene as a metaphor for what destructive behavior does not only to the individual soul, but to the broader society as well.

Dante is writing the *Comedy* as he's in exile, falsely accused and struggling to survive. Dante views violence against the self as wrong, but it also invokes pity in him. The root of violence is ingratitude, which makes human relationships untenable.[62] Dante is suffering mightily because of the breakdown in society and because no one in Florence would give him a fair hearing. In a sense, ingratitude has had a hand in ruining his life.

But Dante is still learning. He is not yet convinced God's justice is always right, nor is he convinced yet that Virgil knows what he's doing. This leads Dante, at Virgil's behest, to perpetrate violence unknowingly against Pier delle Vigne. There is painful irony imbedded in the very action of learning.

In fact, Dante is unable to question Pier because of the pity Dante feels for him. But Dante still needs to learn that his pity is misplaced. Despite of his protestations to the contrary, Pier sinned grievously and refuses to recognize the sin that he freely admits led to his demise — envy. Instead of putting away his pride and envy, Pier is desperate for his reputation to be restored. He tries to employ Dante as his agent in carrying out this task.

When Jesus gives the so-called Golden Rule, *"Do unto others as you would have them do unto you,"* (Matt 7.12), we observe the tie between love of self and the love of neighbor at work. Suicide is the negation of the love of self.

Without a healthy love of self, we cannot really love others. And, if we are unable to love others, the entire fabric of society falls apart. Suicide harms not only the body of the one killed; it harms families and even societies as well.[63]

It's important to note that Dante is not rigid on this point.[64] One of the more surprising features of the *Divine Comedy* is that we'll find suicides among the redeemed. For example, Cato (who we will encounter briefly by analogy in the next Canto), governs the entrance to Purgatory. This is against typical Christian teaching, but it reflects the idea that God is the author of salvation, not people. Dante is trying to show that while suicide is a grave crime against nature, God will show mercy to whom he will.

Dante sees lots of complexity behind the motivations for suicide rather than simply issuing a blanket condemnation of the practice. For all those who have been affected by someone's suicide, we can be thankful that Dante handles the subject with some sensitivity, even if that sensitivity isn't immediately obvious.

Dante's departure from standard Christian teaching is also on display when Pier describes the fate that awaits suicides in the general resurrection. Pier says suicides will receive their bodies in the general resurrection, but they will not be able to inhabit them. Dante simply invents this.

To Pier, suicides will hang from their own branches forever, a parody of suicide.[65] This is also something Dante makes up. There's no evidence for this idea either in the Bible or the tradition of Christian teaching. This is another example of how those in the *Inferno* can see very clearly see the future that awaits them, even if their own self-knowledge continues to be warped by sin.

This is also why the bleeding trees are a poignant image for the effects of suicide. Because suicide is a crime against one's own body for which one has a stewardship responsibility, the trees are denied any human resemblance. As Dorothy Sayers puts it, "*As they refused life, they remain fixed in a dead and withered sterility. They are the image of the self-hatred, which dries up the very sap of energy and makes all life infertile.*"[66]

We shouldn't miss the word play that Dante is making with Pier delle Vigne's name. The English form of "Pier" is Peter, while "vigne" in Italian is the plural form of the word "Vineyard." Both of these terms are held in tension in this Canto.[67]

For example, Pier makes an allusion to St. Peter when he says he held "both keys" to the heart of the Emperor. This is an allusion to St. Peter's status as the keeper of the keys which enables a Pope to bind and loose sin. As Jesus says to Peter, *"I will give you the keys of the kingdom of heaven; whatever you bind on earth will be bound in heaven and whatever you loose on earth shall be loosed in heaven"* (Matt 16.19).

To Dante, the Bishop of Rome, as successor to Peter, held the power to bind and loose sins on earth. By analogy, Pier held the power to influence the Emperor through his counsel and law code. In Pier's legal reforms that drew heavily on natural law, Pier was also in a sense defining right and wrong.

We also get a reference to a vineyard with Pier. This whole Canto takes place in a kind of ruined garden, full of bleeding bushes. Jesus warned his followers in the Parable of the Vineyard that to mistreat the messengers of God is to incur God's wrath. As Jesus said in the Parable, *"What will the owner of the vineyard do? He will come and destroy the tenants and give the vineyard to others"* (Mark 12.9).

Pier has brought disorder to the society through his suicide. This is why at the beginning of the Canto, Dante sees only negativity as he enters the forest. There has been a total breakdown in order. Ironically, Pier delle Vigne, the great expositor of natural law, has broken the law by committing suicide himself, thus incurring the wrath of God.

Hence, the central problem of suicide is the loss of hope.[68] Since hope, along with faith and love, are theological virtues, its loss is devastating. By contrast, Dante is still clinging to the hope he will be restored someday from his exile. He's also clinging to the hope that he'll emerge from the Inferno unscathed.

But Pier also speaks ironically when he insists that he was faithful to his "lord" (Frederick II). We encountered a brief mention of Frederick in

Canto Ten when we learned that he was already in the Inferno. The irony here is that by claiming to be faithful to his earthly lord (who winds up in hell), Pier is tacitly admitting that he was unfaithful to the true Lord. He misused his many gifts, attached himself to political power and wound up in an even lower state than his master.

We also encounter some interesting statements at the end of the Canto from the nameless suicide, who discusses the change in authority from Mars to John the Baptist in Florence. Anyone who has visited Florence can see the baptistery that is named after John the Baptist, the patron Saint of Florence. Prior to Florence's adoption of Christianity, the god Mars (the god of war) was the city's patron. After Christ, the statue of Mars, which used to guard the city, was moved to the Ponte Vecchio (literally, the "old bridge"). The statue reportedly remained on the bridge until Attila the Hun attacked the city in AD 450 and it fell into the Arno River.[69]

The association of Mars with Attila the Hun is probably not coincidental. All throughout this Canto, Dante has been discussing the breakdown in society that he's witnessing. Dante is probably both wistfully remembering his beloved city, but also providing a negative critique of it by ending the Canto with an image of the gallows.

He's claiming the city has turned away from its Christian roots. There is no justice or normalcy in Florence anymore. The society had been ruptured because of sin.

14

The Burning Sand

CIRCLE VII (RING III, PART I): VIOLENCE AGAINST GOD

Virgil and Dante enter the third ring of the violent, a wasteland of burning sand, surrounded by the forest and the river of blood, which punishes violence against God through blasphemy and usury. Sinners are punished with flakes of fire coming down slowly like snow over the barren landscape. The travelers meet Capaneus, a figure from Roman mythology, who demonstrates the sin of blasphemy. The Old Man of Crete, drawn from Daniel's prophecy of the four kingdoms in the Bible, shows the degradation that comes to society when parts of it resist God. The Canto closes with a tutorial on the river system of the Inferno, fed by the tears of the Old Man of Crete. This provides a preview of Cocytus, the bottommost section of the Inferno.

Virgil and I came to the border where the second ring of the violent is separated from the third. Here, we encountered an incredible form of justice, where violence against God himself was punished. The sight brought both wonder and horror to our eyes.[70]

Now to make these strange things clear,[71] I certify that we arrived at a plain, a wasteland that rejects every plant from its bed. The desolate landscape brought to mind the description of Sodom and Gomorrah after God destroyed "*the land of the plain*" (Gen 19.28, NIV).[72] The barren landscape symbolized the resulting punishment which comes for violence against nature.

The grieving suicides, encased in the trunks of the forest, enclosed the wasteland like a wreath. A miserable river of blood encircled the wasteland like a trench. Here we halted our steps at the very edge.

The ground was made of arid and thick sand, no different from what Cato saw as he marched across the Libyan Desert before eventually killing himself.[73] Cato was known for his discipline and defense of his aristocratic heritage, but died when Caesar got the upper hand in battle in North Africa.[74] Cato gave his life so that others might be free.[75]

I cried out, "Oh vengeance of God, how much you ought to be feared by those reading about what I saw before my eyes!"

I observed many flocks of naked souls who were all wailing with equal misery. Their nakedness was similar to others we had encountered so far in the Inferno. But here it was even worse. There was nothing to protect the sinners from the punishments that were being unleashed.[76]

Some souls were lying face up, in a supine position. These were blasphemers who cursed God to his face.[77] Another group sat all hunched and motionless. These were usurers who sinned against the art of human industry.[78] A final group went about in perpetual motion. These were sodomites, who, overcome with incessant desire, could not sit still.[79] The group moving about had the most souls in it. Those lying supine were fewer, but their loose tongues were in much more pain.

Just like the fire and brimstone that rained down on Sodom and Gomorrah, swollen flakes of fire were floating down ever so slowly over the barren landscape. The eerie scene was like a flaming snowfall in the mountains devoid of wind.

This must have been similar to what Alexander the Great experienced when he marched across the hot parts of India, first encountering snowfall and then a shower of fire.[80] Alexander apparently commanded his troops to flatten the soil, which extinguished the vaporous flames before the fire spread. But, here, the unquenchable flames were coming down, igniting the sand like tinder underneath flint, thus doubling the misery. The flames never ceased.

All around there was frenzy, as the naked souls tried desperately to swat away the flames. It was kind of like a "*tresca*," a vigorous dance involving the waving of hands that afforded no rest. The sinners' wretched hands, now here, now there, attempted to shoo away the fresh flames.

Capaneus

I began to speak: "Master, you've helped us overcome all things. Well, almost all. There was that incident with demons who barred us outside the gates of Dis."

"But, anyway, who is that giant that seems to scorn the fire, the one who lies there on his back, spiteful and disdainful, so the fiery rain doesn't humble him?"[81]

That same giant, when he realized I was asking Virgil about him, cried out: "What I was alive, that I am dead! Jupiter, the god of the sky, exhausted Vulcan, his blacksmith. (Jupiter was the one who made that sharp bolt of thunder that knocked me out on my last day.)"

He continued, "Even if Jupiter were to wear out all the others at the black forge at Mt. Ida in Sicily, he couldn't get me down here. On the day of my death, he asked Vulcan to forge some more thunderbolts to use against me in battle. Vulcan did this. Even though Jupiter hit me with all his might, he couldn't have enjoyed the vengeance. All I know is Jupiter's bolts can't get me down here."

I realized this must be the great Capaneus. In Roman mythology, Capaneus arrogantly attacked Jupiter at Thebes and knocked him down with a thunderbolt.[82] Capaneus' blasphemous actions against the gods were impetuous and unwise. He paid the price for it when Jupiter and the gods won the battle of Phlegra.

What I was seeing was different than the myth, however. Capaneus was depicted in the myth as heroic and strong. But there's nothing attractive about him down here.[83] He's suffering under the weight of his own sin.

Then Virgil, with force I had not seen before, said, "Oh Capaneus, since your pride is not snuffed out, you are punished even more. No torment, except for your rage, would complete your painful fury. You're afflicted with something much worse."

This was the first time I had heard anyone actually use the word "pride" in the Inferno. Of course, pride was implicitly underneath everything we had seen so far, since all sin derives from pride. But Virgil was saying something important: the giant's own pride, the worst of the sins, was endlessly torturing him.[84]

Then Virgil, putting on a kinder face, turned to me and said, "This was one of the seven kings who laid siege to Thebes. He held — and still seems to hold — God in disdain and to regard him little. But, as I told him, his own disparaging outbursts are quite fitting."

Virgil continued, "Now follow along behind, and watch that you don't set your feet on the scalding sand. Always keep your steps close to the edge of the forest."

The Rivers of the Inferno

We advanced in silence, arriving at where a little streamlet spurts out from the wood. As it glowed against the backdrop of the forest, the redness of the blood-soaked river still makes me shudder.[85]

Out of the hot spring Bulicame (near Viterbo) flows a little stream that prostitutes divide among themselves to ply their trade.[86] This little streamlet in front of us looked similar as it moved down across the sand. The sides of the rivulet along its edges were made of stone, which enabled us to walk along it.

Virgil said, "I've pointed out many things to you since we've come to the Inferno through the gate whose threshold is denied to no one. But nothing can compare to this particular stream that quenches every flame over it."

I really wanted to know more about this stream. It was like Virgil's words had set the table for the meal that I now wanted to consume. I begged him to serve me the main course for which he had stoked the desire.

The Old Man of Crete

Virgil continued, "In the middle of the sea, there sits a wasteland, which is called Crete, under whose king the world was once chaste."

Now everyone in my day thought Crete was at the center of the earth. After all, this is why our forefathers named the sea that surrounds it the Mediterranean ("in the middle of the earth").[87] The first king in Crete was the god Saturn, who reigned over a kind of Golden Age on the island. Crete was also famous for being the birthplace of the Trojans. After Aeneas' journey to Italy, the Trojans became the Romans.[88]

Virgil said, "Mt. Ida is still there on Crete, and is known as the birthplace of the gods. The mountain was once perfectly happy with water and foliage. Now it's forsaken like a thing decayed. Mt. Ida was a kind of Eden before sin ruined everything."

Virgil continued, "Cybele, Jupiter's mother, once chose Mt. Ida as the trusted cradle for her son to better conceal him when he cried. She used to have her servants scream aloud to protect her son from his father, who used to eat his sons after they were born.[89] Saturn was cannibalizing his children to try to forestall the prophecy of his eventual dethroning by his own son."[90] The screams were supposed to cover up the sound of her crying babies.

Virgil went on, "Within the mountain stands a tall old man who keeps his back to Damietta, an important seaport in Egypt in the East, and instead faces toward Rome in the west. This posture symbolizes the divide of the pagan world from the Christian world."[91]

Virgil said, "The man's head is formed out of fine gold; his arms and chest are of pure silver. Then, the fork of his legs, below his groin, is made of brass. From there down, he's all choice iron except for his right foot, which is made of terra cotta. He stands erect on that right foot more than on the other."

Virgil words amazed me. This was just like Daniel's famous prophecy of the four kingdoms of the world and how they stood distinct from the kingdom of God.[92] The four kingdoms in Daniel's prophecy were the Babylonians, the Medes/Persians, the Greeks and the Romans.[93] In the movement from one dynasty to another, Daniel prophesied (with remarkable accuracy) that we would witness deterioration in the quality of the kingdoms. Further, in Virgil's writings, he had prophesied that Augustus Caesar would restore the Golden Age in the Roman Empire, something that the Divine Son's resurrection ultimately ensured.

Virgil said, "Each part (except for the gold) is broken by a fissure, dripping with tears. When gathered together, it hollows out that cave. From rock to rock, the streams take their course, forming the rivers Acheron, Styx and Phlegethon. They all head down further through this narrow conduit, finally stopping where no more descent is possible, to form Cocytus, the fourth river of the Inferno. You will see Cocytus for yourself farther on down. Yet here I dare not say anymore."

I realized all the rivers of the Inferno came from a common source.[94] This must be symbolic of sin. After all, sin emanates from a single source, pride. The Golden Age of Christianity is supposed to give the world no tears.[95] But this certainly hasn't been true in my case because sin is ever-present in the world.

Since the Old Man of Crete was standing on one foot, this shows the problems that occur when corruption affects the Church. The Church was supposed to guard the health of the society, but this was breaking down in my day.[96]

Infernal Geography, Continued

I asked Virgil, "If that stream before us flows down like this from our world, why does it emerge only here?"

Virgil said to me, "You've seen that the Inferno is round like a funnel. As we're going along, we've been mostly descending to the left. As we've been making our descent, we've been getting closer to the bottom. But, even though we've been going in a circular direction, we haven't made a full circle yet. This is why you think you haven't seen this stream of blood before. Let this be a lesson to you: if we encounter something new, don't let it astonish you."

Then I responded, "Master, where are the rivers Phlegethon and Lethe found? You omitted any discussion of Lethe. As for Phlegethon, you've only said that it's made into a river by these tears.

Virgil said, "You certainly do please me with all these good questions. But the boiling red water you saw up above when we encountered the wrathful (Canto Twelve) should have jogged your memory. You actually have seen its source before. As far as Lethe is concerned, you'll see it again when you get to the top of Purgatory.[97] That's where the redeemed spirits go to cleanse themselves. There, their guilt, having been repented, is washed away."

Then Virgil said, "Now it's time to leave this forest. Take care to stay close to me. The sides, which are not on fire, form a way for us. Over them, every flame is quenched."

Comment

There's a lot going on in this Canto. Many of Dante's allusions draw from classical mythology which may prove confusing to readers not familiar with the works Dante cites. Dante may be drawing on the classical tradition to demonstrate its sterility. As much as Dante admired classical culture, the gods of classical antiquity are, by nature, opposed to the one true God of Judeo-Christian teaching. Thus they become the paradigmatic examples of blasphemy against God. Although Dante is usually seen as the bridge between the late medieval and renaissance periods, here we observe Dante being more of a medievalist with his skepticism about the Roman gods.

This sterility becomes clear right up front when we observe the landscape of the Canto itself. No longer are we in a verdant (but corrupt) forest. Not only is the landscape sterile, but the sinners are naked as well. They have nothing to protect them from the flakes of fire that are falling on them. The analogy to Sodom and Gomorrah is fairly obvious here, an analogy that will continue in the next Canto as well.

Dante's depiction of violence is very interesting. We observe sinners punished with physical violence. But the root of the problem is a spiritual one. This is what sins against nature do. Such sins take what is productive and turn it into something sterile.

The root problem is the sin of pride. This is what really gets Capaneus in trouble. Capaneus is a mythical blasphemer whose pride manifests itself in fits of rage. He's condemned for his blasphemy against Jupiter, who stands as a symbol for the Christian God.[98]

We also observe the sin of usury in this Canto. Usury brings sterility to monetary exchange and thus to productive human activity.

But what does usury have to do with blasphemy? Today, we understand usury as the sin of charging excessive interest on loans. In Dante's day, usury was charging interest at all. Consider Lev 25:36: *"You shall not lend him your money at interest, nor give him your food for profit."* Ezekiel writes: *"[If] he does not lend at interest or take any increase...that man is righteous."* (Eze 18.8-9). It appears the Old Testament had a clear prohibition against lending at interest, which was known as usury.

The connection between blasphemy and usury for Dante is the disorder it brings to the society and the universe. As Dorothy Sayers puts it, *"'The usurer makes breed that which was mean to be sterile;' Money breeds money — but in so doing makes sterile everything else."*[99] Once again, sin takes God's good creation and twists it until it becomes almost unproductive.

As usual, there is a hierarchy of suffering in this Canto, but even this gets turned upside down. Normally, the punishments become evermore severe the farther down we go. But, here, blasphemy is punished first with sinners forced to lie on their backs and bear the full brunt of the falling flakes. Those face-up are forced to suffer the most. By contrast, the usurers are in a sitting position, thus reflecting the harm they've done against productive activity.[100]

Lastly, there is vocal discussion among commentators about the hydraulic river system of the Inferno. Since Dante teaches us about the rivers Phlegethon, Styx, Acheron and Lethe in this Canto, this has led to attempts by commentators to harmonize the whole system. The problem is that it is very difficult to do this successfully. I will make no attempt here. It's a testament to Dante's genius that we are still trying to figure out his world seven-hundred years later.

The most important thing Dante tells us is not the names of the rivers, many of which we have already encountered. The most important disclosure concerns Cocytus, which we will visit at the very bottom of the Inferno (starting in Canto Thirty-One). The point Dante is making is that all rivers lead there.

The prophecy of the Old Man of Crete is also pointing forward to Cocytus, which sits at the literal center of the earth. Dante cites the prophet Daniel's prediction of the four kingdoms of man (which correspond to four political dynasties) — the Golden age of the Babylonians under King Nebuchadnezzar, which leads to the Silver Age of the Medes and Persians, which leads to the Bronze Age of Greeks and which culminates with the Iron age of the Romans. The point of Daniel's prophecy is the degradation that society will endure before a Redeemer comes to make things right.

With the reference Dante makes to the founding of Rome (while the Old Man turns his back to the eastern port city of Damietta), Dante is saying that the society he's living in has been torn apart because Papal power is seizing the prerogatives of imperial power.[101] This is why the Old Man of Crete rests off balance on his right foot, thus symbolizing the lack of harmony in early fourteenth-century Europe.

Dante is hoping not only for an honest Pope who can bring justice to the spiritual realm. He's hoping for a just Emperor who can bring balance to the secular realm as well. As Dante writes, the Papacy is about to be kidnapped by the French King to Avignon. Further, the Holy Roman Emperor is no longer able to perform his role adequately. From Dante's perspective, the result is his exile and the remarkable level of turmoil and unrest evident in the society. This imbalance of power is dangerous for everyone.

In the world Dante has created, Cocytus is the literal center of the earth. To the medieval mind, which has the earth at the center of the universe, Cocytus is the most distant point away from God. It is where love has completely grown sterile. The Old Man of Crete is pointing us there. Cocytus, the very center of the Inferno, is where we're headed.

15

Fire and Brimstone

CIRCLE VII (RING III, PART II): VIOLENCE AGAINST NATURE

Dante and Virgil continue in the third ring of the violent where violence against nature is punished. The pilgrims meet Brunetto Latini, one of Dante's intellectual mentors, whose besetting sin was sodomy. He is relentlessly in motion with a band of sodomites, whose constant activity depicts the problem of unrestrained desire. Latini delivers an important prophecy about how Dante's journey will turn out.

Virgil and I were walking along the hardened embankment that kept the boiling rivulet of blood separated from the desolate plane of burning sand. We were headed on a downward slope toward the center of the abyss.[102] Vapor from the brook kept rising up like a mist, which sheltered the water of the stream and the embankments from the flames that continued to fall on the sand.[103]

These banks were like the dikes one finds in the Netherlands between Wissant and Bruges, both notorious centers of sodomy as commercial ports.[104] The citizens of these cities erected dikes to hold back the tides that sweep down on them and to put the sea to flight.

The dikes were also like those the Paduans constructed along the Brenta River to defend their towers and castles in Northern Italy from the heat that melts the snow and causes such terrible flooding in the summer.[105]

The banks down here were formed in a similar way to how the Creator willed to construct them. But who knows who really built things down here. They weren't as high or thick as the ones in Padua or in the Netherlands, but were about the height of an average man.[106]

We were already far enough away from the forest that I couldn't have told where I was, even had I turned back towards the woods. I didn't turn back. Just remember what happened to Lot's wife when she turned around to look at Sodom's destruction: *"She became a pillar of salt"* (Gen 19.26).[107]

Brunetto Latini

We encountered a platoon of souls coming along the bank below. All of the shades were peering at us like it was evening and hard to see under the light of a new moon. They gazed at us with knitted brows, like an old tailor does when attempting to thread the eye of a needle. I had no idea who these strange souls were.

As they squinted their eyes, one of them recognized me. One shade reached up, grabbed me by the hem of my garment and cried out, "How incredible!"

When he extended his arm to me, I fixed my eyes on his charred face. Behind his scorched visage I realized I knew this shade. As he lowered his hand to his face, I asked, "Are you down here, Mr. Brunetto?" I spoke to him with the formal address his stature deserved.[108]

This was simply amazing. Brunetto Latini was my favorite teacher, not someone I actually knew from a classroom, but know him I did indeed.[109] Mr. Brunetto was a lot like me. He was a famous Guelf political figure who, after an embassy to France, was forced into exile after the battle of Montaperti.[110] He eventually came back to Florence, which is what I was hoping to do.

Latini was best known for his vernacular works, especially his French encyclopedia and his verses.[111] He died beloved and honored by all.[112] A whole bunch of people would have been shocked to find him down here, given how respected he was at the time of his death.

Latini answered as he looked up at me on the bank, "Oh my child, let it not displease you if Brunetto Latini turns back with you for a bit and lets the company go on."

I replied, "As much as I can, I pray you, if you want me to sit with you, I'll do it! Well, I'll do it as long as it pleases the one with whom I'm going." I looked ahead toward Virgil, but he didn't turn around and did nothing to stop me.

Latini said, "Oh child, if one of this pack stops, even for a moment, then he gets held up down here for another thousand years without brushing off the attacking fire. I couldn't stand the increased punishment.[113] So let's go on. I'll follow below at your hem. Then I'll return to my band that goes on weeping over their eternal brokenness."

I didn't dare to go down from the embankment to walk with him below, but I kept my head bowed as a man who goes about reverently. This was out of respect for my teacher. Yet there was a kind of role reversal going on here. Latini was my intellectual mentor but he was forced to look up toward me. I, his student, had to look down to talk with him below. The role of teacher and student was somehow reversed.[114] The Inferno is always messing up the proper hierarchy, I thought.

Mr. Brunetto said, "What fortune or destiny leads you down here before the last day? And who is this that shows you the way?"

I answered, "There above, in the good life, I was lost in a dark wood before I reached the peak of my years. Only yesterday morning I turned my back on my life. When I was returning to that place, the one leading me appeared. He's directing me home by this path."

Latini said, "If you follow your star, you can't fail to reach the glorious port, at least if I have perceived it correctly in the good life. Had I not died so soon, seeing that heaven is so inclined toward you, I would have given you support in your political work."[115]

This was a remarkable statement, I thought. Mr. Brunetto, who could tell the future, was saying that I was actually going to get through the Inferno and find my way back home. I sure hoped he was right.

Latini continued, "But that malicious, thankless rabble that came down from Fiesole a long time ago (and still holds the mountain) will become an enemy for you because of your good works. Among the bitter berries, it's not right for the sweet fig to bear fruit."

Mr. Brunetto continued, "An old rumor in the world suggests these old usurpers are a blind, avaricious, envious and prideful people. Keep away from them and their morals. Your destiny holds so much honor for you that both sides, the White and the Black Guelfs, will hunger for you eventually."

Latini continued, "But let the grass be far from the goat. Let the usurpers make hay of themselves, but don't let them touch the plant (if anything still springs from their dung). The offspring of the Romans lives again, since the usurpers staying in Florence caused it to become the seedbed of so much wickedness and malice."

To be honest, I didn't like this part of Latini's prophecy since it was less optimistic. He was making reference to what the usurper Cataline did after he plotted against Caesar and then fled Rome to Fiesole, the hill town above Florence.[116]

It was the descendants of Cataline, after the Romans destroyed Fiesole, who founded Florence along with a remnant of Romans, at least according to legend.[117] This was a rather tragic mistake when they intermixed. This might have contributed to the injustice I was experiencing from the city leadership. Mixed company makes for bad politics.

But was Mr. Brunetto right? He seems to think my experience was going to be worse than his. I might never get back to my beloved Florence.

This was terrible news! Both the White and Black factions in the city were going to unite to keep me out. This was almost too much to bear!

I answered him, "If I had my way, you wouldn't still be banned from humanity. In fact, my mind is steadfast (and my heart grieved), since my remembrance of you — good and paternal that it is, is full of hopeful memories. I remember when, in the time-bound world, you showed me how a man can become eternal through literary fame.[118] I'm in your debt as your student. My tongue, while I'm alive, compels me to declare it."

I continued, "What you've just prophesied about my progress, though, I'll store up in my heart. I'll wait and let it be interpreted later by a subsequent text.[119] There's a woman in my future, Beatrice, who cares for me a great deal. She'll know what to make of all this if I'm able to reach her."

I couldn't help but think that Mr. Brunetto was the antithesis of the heavenly figure of Beatrice. Whereas literary fame used to be my goal under my teacher, now my goal was just to reach her. Both Beatrice and Mr. Brunetto deserve admiration, but his tortured soul is not something I wanted to emulate.[120] I really didn't want to stay in the Inferno forever. As much as I respected him, his teaching was evidently flawed.[121]

I went on, "This much I want to make clear to you, as long as my conscience doesn't reprove me. I'm ready for my fate, come what may. Such a pledge is not new to my ears. Let Fortune spin her wheel as she likes, just like the peasant whirls his scythe."

Then, Virgil, who was walking ahead of me, turned around over his right shoulder, looked at me and barked out a proverb: "He listens well who marks what he hears."

Virgil was trying to warn me that what Latini said was important. I realized that. So I went on speaking for bit. As I walked along with Mr. Brunetto, I asked which of his current companions were the most notable and eminent.

He said to me, "To know some of them would be good. But, as for the others, it might be more praiseworthy for me to keep quiet. Time is too brief for there are too many. If I can summarize, you should know all were clerics, great and famous men of letters. They were all soiled in the world by one single sin, a crime against nature."

I thought to myself, I guess that means they were all sodomites. This is probably why he didn't want to get into too many details. They were all clerics? Shudder the thought!

Mr. Brunetto went on, "Priscian goes with that wretched crowd as does Francesco d'Accorso as well."

Priscian wrote the best-known Latin grammar that we used in school. His crime could have just been idolizing the Latin text. This was most unnatural. [122] Latin teachers beware! Francesco, on the other hand, was a famous lawyer and judge who spent most of his life in England.[123] Who knew he was a sodomite, too?"

Latini continued, "If you had any itch for such filth, you yourself would have seen Andrea dei Mozzi, a Bishop deposed by Pope Boniface VIII, the so-called servant of servants. Andrea was removed from Florence on the Arno to a less important See at Vicenza along the Bacchiglione River because of his immoral lifestyle and ineptitude.[124] There, the disgraced bishop died, leaving behind his sinfully erect muscles."[125]

Mr. Brunetto continued, "I would say more, but to speak longer, that I'm not able to do, since I see new smoke coming up from the sand over there. Souls are coming with whom I must not mingle. Let my *Tesoro,* my literary treasure, on which I still live, be commended in the world above. I ask for nothing more."

Then, like Lot's wife, reduced to a shadow of his former self, he turned back.[126] He was sprinting so fast that he seemed like someone running the races at Verona through the fields for the green cloth. In fact, he seemed more like those who win than those who lose. I watched him take off and dash at full speed to catch up with his company of sinners.[127]

Comment

One hotly debated issue in this Canto (and the next) is whether the sin of sodomy is the correct reading for those shown here in perpetual motion over the burning sand. This has been the consensus among readers from the earliest days, but has been questioned of late. The problem is that there seems to be no obvious reason why being in perpetual motion is an indication of homosexuality.

The reason that readers of the *Comedy* have traditionally come to this conclusion is because of the references to Sodom and Gomorrah in the last Canto. The traditional understanding of the sin at Sodom is sodomy. When the three angelic visitors went down to see Sodom, the men of the city rose up at night and demanded that they be brought out to them. The Bible describes it as follows: *"Where are the men who came to you tonight? Bring them out to us, that we may know them"* (Gen 19.5). Although some debate the intended meaning of the word "know," the men of Sodom appear to be demanding sex from the male visitors. God then rains down fire and brimstone in punishment for the city's sin.

Yet later prophets saw it somewhat more ambiguously. Isaiah, for example, charges Sodom with lacking justice (1.10, 3.9) and Ezekiel criticizes the city for its lack of social justice (16.49). Ezekiel's statement in the next verse (16.50) that the citizens of the city acted "abominably" is a reference to their pride, arrogance and gluttony.[128] Thus there's no mention of sexual sin in these later prophets.[129]

The New Testament (and the subsequent Christian tradition) interprets the sin of Sodom in a more familiar way, however, claiming that *"Sodom and Gomorrah and the surrounding cities, which likewise acted immorally and indulged in unnatural lust, serve as an example by undergoing a punishment of eternal fire* (remember the burning sand!). *Yet, in like manner, these men in their dreamings defile the flesh, reject authority and revile the glorious ones"* (Jude1.7-8). Thus sodomy is likely to be the sin in view in this Canto.

The other concern raised is that there is absolutely no evidence that Brunetto Latini was a homosexual. While true, this perspective largely misses the point. We need to remember that Dante was in perpetual exile because the authorities in Florence had judged him by his reputation.

Dante had never be able to appear before a tribunal to answer the charges brought against him (mismanagement of funds), yet the city had found him guilty *in absentia*.

By making Mr. Brunetto guilty of a crime with no external evidence to back it up, Dante is providing a commentary on what had happened in his own case.[130] Thus, to the original readers of the *Inferno*, Brunetto Latini's placement among the sodomites would have been shocking.

This is not to say that Dante just makes this up. Of course, we don't know if Dante had first-hand knowledge of Brunetto's homosexuality or not. Yet, if we read between the lines, Dante might be trying to tell us that Latini had made sexual advances toward Dante while he was alive.

Admittedly, this is a speculative claim. As Ronald Martinez points out, the changes in direction, the reversal of roles and most importantly, the act of grabbing Dante by the hem of his garment, all seem to suggest subtly that Latini had made advances.[131] He turned around briefly when Dante rejected his sexual advances. It's doubtful that Latini is making a pass at Dante here, but his action could a reminder of something which happened in the past.

Yet Latini continued in his sin.[132] In other words, while there is no independent textual evidence to confirm it, it appears Dante knew Latini was a homosexual because his teacher had made sexual advances toward him while in Florence. Given that Latini died in 1295, it is possible, but by no means certain, that this happened.

One of the things to note is that to the medieval mind, homosexuality was an issue not just because a few Bible verses condemned it, but primarily because of the disorder that it brought to the society. As we will see more clearly later in the *Paradiso*, society was a perfectly ordered hierarchy that God had created. Everything had its right place. Sin destroyed the order in the universe, thus corrupting the hierarchy.

One of the main aims of modernity, especially in America, has been the destruction of this idea of hierarchy in favor of a more flat, egalitarian society. To those in the medieval period, one could not do anything to alter the reality of hierarchy in a universe given by God. Hierarchy was simply built into the creation. To undermine it was to act against God's will.

But we will also discover when we get to the *Purgatorio* that there are homosexuals among the redeemed. Dante will remind us that almost all sin can be redeemed by God's grace. Thus it is clear that Dante has great respect not only for Brunetto, his teacher, but also for the Florentine Guelfs we will meet in the next Canto. Dante's main concern is the lack of fecundity that comes with sodomy. Sodomy takes sex, which is supposed to bear the fruit of children, and instead makes it sterile. In choosing to pursue illicit pleasure, Brunetto has injured the society as well as himself, in Dante's opinion.

Yet this creates a delicious set of ironies. Dante is extremely courteous toward his own teacher. He does not condemn him at all. He clearly wishes he did not find his teacher in the Inferno. However, the topography of the Canto undermines this respect. After all, Brunetto is walking on burning sand while fire and brimstone fall from the sky. Dante may hear in the prophecy that he will make it out of the Inferno, but Brunetto is going to spend eternity down there. In essence, Dante's empathy for Mr. Brunetto has more to do with his own situation than with his teacher's. He's showing us that outward reputation does not matter much before a God who knows us completely.[133]

But could it be as well that Dante sees himself in his teacher? He realizes the sterility of his past life and how he needs to overcome his inherent narcissism and his desire for fame if he is to reach a better life. This is why Latini's prophecy that this story really will turn out to have a happy ending is so important. Dante is going to reach his goal, and his more detached position toward those he used to admire shows the progress he is making as he continues on his journey.

Sodom is not some far-away place in a far-away time. Sodom, in Dante's world, is Florence itself. His beloved city is a cesspool of partisan politics and continues to show injustice in choosing to exile him. Brunetto is trying to get Dante to condemn his old city and the "rabble" that are in it. But, in another sign of growth, Dante refuses to do this.

In the end, Dante sees that he's no better than his teacher. The only difference is the direction they are headed. Brunetto embraced a life of sin, refuses to repent for it, and is consigned to be in constant motion, symbolic of what the persistent pursuit of pleasure does to a person. By contrast, Dante heads lower and lower into the depths of the Inferno and comes to grips with the idea that it is only the grace of God that is keeping him from such a fate.

Dante's most ardent desires have changed. While on his journey, Dante's goal is to see his beloved Beatrice. But this means turning his back on the sparkling pleasures of the world. Thus Dante takes an important step in the right direction on his journey.

16

Dante's Knotted Cord

CIRCLE VII (RING III, PART III): THE SODOMITES

Dante and Virgil encounter three more sodomites, men of renown from Florence, who demonstrate the political damage done when God's order is disrupted. Dante strips off the cord he's been wearing since employing it in an attempt to capture the Leopard in the first Canto. He offers it to Virgil, who throws it into the abyss, thus arousing a strange creature who comes up from below.

We got close enough to the edge of the Circle that I could hear a rumbling waterfall down below. The sound was similar to the one a bustling beehive makes.

Three shades detached themselves from the group that was passing by us under the harsh, tormenting rain. Coming toward us, they were calling out together, "Stop! Oh you dressed like you've come from a depraved land." Somehow they recognized me as a Florentine.

I saw sores all over the bodies of these shades, some fresh and some dated, which were left by the continual shower of flaming rain striking their flesh. It pains me even now to recall it.

Their cries caused Virgil to pause attentively. He turned back toward my face and said, "Now let's just wait a second. To such as these, it's necessary to be polite. Were it not for the nature of this place with its flaming rain shooting out like arrows, I would tell you to hasten toward them since it would be more fitting. But in this case I wouldn't do it."

The band of three stopped and recommenced their eternal wailing. But, when they joined us, they combined themselves into a wheeling dance.[134] As Mr. Brunetto told us before, the shades had to keep moving lest they incur greater punishment.[135]

They were just like Greek athletic champions, all oiled and naked, who take care to get their grip and advantage right before they wield their blows and bobs.[136] Their feet kept going straight ahead while their heads turned to converse with us.[137]

The one began, "If the misery of this sandy place and our singed and hairless faces make us and our prayers contemptible, let our fame prevail upon you to tell us who you are and how your living feet move so securely through the Inferno. This one, in whose footsteps you see me following, was of a better station than you might think, despite the appearance of his naked and peeled skin."

Three Florentine Guelfs

He continued, "He was the grandson of the good Gualdrada. Guido Guerra was his name in his life; he acted wisely and wasn't afraid to wield the sword."

Guido Guerra was famous in my day as one of the most important leaders of the Guelfs in Tuscany.[138] Having survived the battle of Montaperti in 1260, Guido was a hero at the Battle of Benevento in 1266. Guido led four-hundred knights into the fight, thus restoring power to the Guelfs.[139] It was once again surprising to see such a distinguished citizen down here in the Inferno.

He continued, "The other one, who tramples the sand close to me is Tegghiaio Aldobrandi, whose voice should have been more welcome in the world."

Aldobrandi was a contemporary of Guerra on the Guelf side.[140] He famously warned the Florentines against going to war with Sienna at the

Battle of Montaperti where they lost miserably.[141] I guess they should have listened to him. His counsel was first-rate, I thought.[142]

He continued, "And I, who bear this cross with them, was Jacopo Rusticucci. It was certainly my bestial wife, more than any other, who harmed me and put me down here."

Was Jacopo really blaming his sin of sodomy on his wife? That's novel. She was so repulsive to him that he became a homosexual? Who knows, maybe their sexual practices were unnatural like sodomites.[143] I shudder to think about it.

Jacopo and Tegghiaio had houses next to each other in Florence.[144] They were both well-known political figures. And, yes, as everyone knows, Jacopo hated his wife.

I think if I could have been protected from the fire, I would have just thrown myself down there to be among them. I even think Virgil would have let me do it. But, since I would have been burned and baked, fear conquered my good intentions that made me eager to embrace them. I instead stayed on the embankment and talked with them from afar.

I began, "Grief, not vexation, makes me fixate on your condition. When Virgil made me realize people like you were coming near, I was ransacked with sadness for no short while. I am a fellow Florentine, like you! Your venerable names and your deeds have been told and retold over and over again. What are noblemen like you doing down here?"

I continued, "I am leaving behind the bitter gall of sin and going on toward the sweet fruit of paradise, promised to me by my good and true leader. Before I get to ascend to paradise, however, I have to go down first to the very core of the abyss. Just like Paul, '*I press on toward the goal for the prize of the upward call*'" (Phil 3.14).

Jacopo replied, "Then may your soul conduct your members on your journey. May your fame shine forth after you!"

Jacopo continued, "But, tell us, are gentility and valor still at home in Florence as they were before or have they been utterly discarded? I ask this because Guglielmo Borsiere, who has been tormented with us for just a short while, and is over there with our company, has mortified us with his recent report of mores in the city. The new people and their sudden wealth have generated such pride and excess that Florence is already up in arms about it."

I had never heard of this Borsiere before.[145] But if he reported a breakdown in courtesy, generosity and nobility in Florence, that wouldn't have surprised me at all.[146] My dear city just wasn't what it used to be.

I turned my face up toward Florence and wept.[147] The three shades took this as my answer. They all looked at each other with a knowing glance.

Jacopo said, "If you leave these dark places and return again to look at the beautiful stars above, it'll profit you to tell others you were down here. Make sure you speak of us to others when you do."

With this, they broke their dancing circle and fled. Their legs were so swift it seemed they had wings. Saying an "amen" couldn't have been uttered fast enough since they disappeared so quickly. Virgil then thought it was time to get going.

Dante's Cord

I was following along after Virgil. We had not gone too far before the sound of the waterfall was so loud we couldn't even hear each other speaking.

The river Phlegethon below us was just like the Acquacheta River in Italy that flows from Mt. Viso on the western shore of the Apennines before it descends to and then eventually dumps into the Adriatic Sea.[148] There, at the monastery of San Benedetto de l'Alpe, the water drops in a single cascade with enough force that it sounds like a thousand tributaries combined.[149]

Down from a steep bank, we encountered roaring water tinged with red. It was so loud and ferocious that, in a short time, it assaulted our senses.

I had a cord around my waist, like the Franciscans wear.[150] All the way back at the start of the journey, I tried to use it to capture the violent

Leopard with his spotted pelt.[151] This cord I had used as a kind of girdle, which had strengthened me thus far on my journey. But it also contributed significantly to my overwrought self-confidence. I had seen down here that many things were beyond my control. I needed to embrace humility like St. Francis did.[152]

Virgil motioned for me to loosen the cord and take it off completely. I was reminded of the Divine Son's statement to Peter, "*Truly, truly, I say to you, when you were young, you girded yourself and walked where you would; but when you are old, you will stretch out your hands, and another will gird you and carry you where you do not wish to go*" (John 21.18).

I wouldn't need the cord to confront the Ring of fraud below.[153] So I gave it to Virgil, still knotted and coiled. Then, turning to his right, he flung the cord just a short distance over the ledge. It plunged into the depth of the abyss. In so doing, I was trying to crucify the sins of the Leopard with the cord.

I said to myself, I bet something strange is going to respond to this symbol. I watched Virgil follow the cord with his eyes until it disappeared into the abyss below. Ah, how cautious men have to be with those who not only see our deeds but peer into our thoughts with their judgment as well.

Virgil responded cryptically, "Soon will come what I expect. Your dreamy thoughts are about to be exposed to your sight."

Now it's imperative that a man should close his lips as much as possible to that truth that has the appearance of a lie, since it causes shame without guilt. But, here, I'm not able to stay quiet. I really saw what I'm about to describe.[154]

By the lines of this Comedy, Dear Reader, I swear to you (so that they might be well received) that I saw a figure swimming up through the dark and thick air, the sight of which would have been incredible even to the most self-confident heart. It was like something returning, which had submerged itself for a time, to loosen an anchor clutched by the reef. It looked like something hidden in the sea, reaching up, extending its arms and pushing off with its feet. Whatever it was, the sight of it took my breath away.

Comment

The political overtones in this Canto are obvious. When we meet the three Florentine Guelfs, these were all leading citizens of Florence. Thus Dante's placement of them down here would have been shocking to his original readers. His accusation that they were sodomites continues the discussion we observed in the last Canto about the difference between public perception and hidden reality.[155] Given Dante's exile, this has great importance for him.

But Dante is also engaging in a political polemic in this Canto. He is saying that all is not right with the city of Florence, which has exiled him. As Susan Noakes has noted, politics for Dante isn't as much about struggles between political parties as it is an effort to organize people to seek the highest good.[156] The central problem is that no one is really seeking the highest good in Florence right now. This is why Dante thinks he is suffering in exile.

We have already heard about two of the three Guelfs in this Canto when we met Ciacco the pig in Canto Six. Ciacco predicted Dante would encounter them on his journey through the Inferno.

The question arises, however, why Dante would criticize some of the older heroes of his own political party, the White Guelfs? It appears that Dante was claiming that the Guelf political ideology — his own political ideology before his exile — was bankrupt.

Remember, the Guelfs were on the side of the Pope, but as a bulwark against the Holy Roman Emperor. What they most wanted was to maintain their political autonomy as an independent city-state.[157] But Dante realizes, having suffered through exile because the Papacy was asserting its own interests, that complete autonomy is a fallacious political goal. Just as sodomy is a sin against nature and represents the desire to be free from God's order, Dante was guilty of a similar sin in desiring autonomy in the political realm.[158] Sodomy and political autonomy are thus closely linked.

When Dante encounters the three Guelfs with sores all over their bodies from the fiery rain, this is making an allegorical statement about the damage done to the body politic by those in power. In Dante's day, there was an increasing tendency to investigate after considering hearsay evidence.[159] This practice was justified from the Bible. When God sent his messengers to Sodom to *"See whether they have done altogether according to the outcry that has come to me. And if not, I will know"* (Gen 18.20-21), this led to an investigation of what was happening at Sodom. Thus God heard and he investigated. In canon law, an investigation could be commenced on the basis of a reasonable suspicion even it came from common knowledge acquired by hearsay.[160]

In Dante's case, there was no evidence he had actually misused public funds, one of the charges that got him exiled, but the accusation was enough to ruin his reputation.[161] Just like he did with Brunetto Latini in the previous Canto, Dante places souls with stellar public reputations who were heroes for his own political cause into this ring to protest against hearsay evidence. [162] Dante was willing to call into question the reputations of some of Florence's leading lights to expose how he had been treated.[163] In so doing, he implies that salvation is not something that can be determined humanly by outward appearances. It is God alone who looks on the heart (1 Sam 16.7).

This Canto is also important because this is one of the only places in the *Inferno* where Dante refers to the poem as a Comedy. In other words, Dante essentially names his poem here. This is obviously significant. Dante is not really making a statement about the happy ending that will come in heaven at the end (the usual meaning of what a comedy entails). Rather, as Justin Steinberg has perceptively noticed, Dante is making a kind of contract with the reader.[164]

If we will suspend disbelief and take in the story as he tells it, Dante will show us something pretty amazing. But if we refuse to suspend disbelief, Dante will never succeed in the case he's trying to plead. He is asking us, as readers, to become involved in his own plight. But he's also showing empathy to the reader if we start to doubt his trustworthiness as an omniscient narrator when he describes flying monsters coming up from the deep.[165]

Yet Dante's strategy for convincing us to suspend disbelief is characteristically clever. Dante sympathizes with our plight as readers.[166] Are we really supposed to believe all this happened? Dante tells us he didn't believe when he first saw these events either, but he insists that they did, in fact, happen. Thus Dante connects the inherent uncertainty of language with truth.[167] He draws us in and persuades by admitting his story seems hard to believe.

The problem is that the contract he's trying to make with the reader comes with flimsy terms. Dante swears an oath on the "lines" of his Comedy that he really saw the infernal monster that came up from below. But, as surety for the contract he wants to make, he offers us his own words (the thing that was most valuable to him), suggesting that the "notes" of the poem are true because they're guaranteed by those same words. The argument is circular. We have to learn to trust Dante (our omniscient narrator), just as Dante needs to learn to trust in God's providence.

Ultimately, Dante is showing us that legal contracts are an important component to the poem.[168] All along, Dante and Virgil have been negotiating to get information or to make progress. These all involve implicit contracts. But, since we're in hell, there is no legitimate legal authority to back them up. This is why Dante's oath comes with such flimsy terms. The oath is simply reflecting how hard it is to negotiate when there is no rule of law and no one can be trusted. Dante will explore this issue in much greater detail in the next section, the longest portion of the Inferno, which explores the sin of fraud.

Lastly, Dante's cord is also a central event in this Canto, not least of which because it begins to mark the transition to the next Ring of the *Inferno*. There's a lot of scholarly debate about how to understand the cord. It is by no means certain that we should associate the cord with the

Franciscans, as I have done (following Francesco da Buti). The standard interpretation is to link the cord to sin of the fraud explored in the next Ring.[169] But what is interesting is that the five-fold knots on the cord (representing charity, obedience, chastity, penance and detachment) are precisely the things Dante needs to learn.[170]

This is the very cord that Dante used to try to corral the leopard on the mountain at the start of the poem. He failed to do so in his own strength. Thus his loosening of the cord is an important symbol of humility and obedience. It's another sign that Dante realizes he can't complete this journey on his own. He cannot be autonomous and reach heaven. He needs to submit to the God whose grace is leading him along.

Notice the cord returns as a kind of hybrid creature. It changes and thus initiates his coming descent through the Ring of fraud, which will eventually bring him to the center of the Inferno itself.[171] Dante is realizing the depths of his own sin here. Just as he was intimately involved in the violence that brought about a ruptured community in Florence, Dante will find his own connection to the fraudulent down below. He is learning that while his sins are different than others, he is still guilty. The only difference is his acceptance of grace, the help that God offers to all of us for the journey.

17

Wasting Time

CIRCLE VII (RING IV): USURY

Dante reaches the end of the Ring of the violent, where he encounters a small band of usurers who are punished by being forced to sit still and do nothing. Geryon, a three-natured beast who represents fraud, transports the travelers down the steep cliff to the lowest section of the Inferno.

Geryon

"Check out the beast with the scorpion's tail," began Virgil, as we watched Geryon pass by, who had come up from the deep. He was so fierce-looking that I couldn't imagine anyone standing against him.[172] Geryon's association with the filth below stunk up the whole place.

Virgil beckoned the beast to come toward us at the edge of the cliff by the stone walkway where we were perched. He was a pure personification of fraud. As he came closer, his filthy three-fold nature became clear. His head and chest came to rest first, but he kept his treacherous tail away from the shore.

Geryon had the face of a just man, benign in its outward appearance. The rest of his body was that of a serpent. He had two paws like a lion. Yet his defining trait was not his claws, but the almost human-like hair running all the way down to his armpits.[173] This meant that he was part-man and part-beast.

Geryon's back, chest and sides had skin covered with knots and little circlets. These had more color in embroidered patterns than any bright Turkish or Tartar garment.[174] In fact, even the work of the weaver Arachne, who was undone because of her pride in the multi-colored tapestry she made, couldn't compare to the hues of Geryon's skin.[175] Arachne was usually associated with the devil, which made me cringe at what lay ahead. [176]

Now this Geryon was a figure born out of mythology. Usually depicted with three bodies, Geryon was a beast who lured in strangers and then consumed them.[177] Hercules finally stopped him.[178] Down here, Geryon was a bit different, with his three natures and all. He had an innocent face attached to the body of a snake and the tail of a scorpion, just like one who fraudulently preys on the unsuspecting innocent. He was like an unholy trinity, much as Cerberus was with his three heads, at the entrance to the Inferno.

Geryon reminded me of the covered rowboats I had seen that sometimes rest on the beach, partly in water and partly on land. Geryon's head and body were on the ledge and his tail was hanging off. He kind of looked like the drunken Germans who were known for their gluttony.

But he was also like the ravenous beavers who employed their tails to prey on fish. Geryon was just like the worst of these beasts crouched down, looking for prey on the edge of the rock that encloses the sand. With his tail hanging off the ledge, Geryon was on the prowl.[179] Into the void, Geryon's whole tail was quivering, twisting upward its venomous fork that looked just like a scorpion's. His appearance reminded me of the terrible scorpions from John's apocalypse: *"[The locusts] have tails [with stingers] like scorpions and their power of hurting men for five months lies in their tails"* (Rev 9.10).[180]

Virgil said, "Now we have to adjust our route a bit until we reach that wicked beast lying over there." Then, for only the second time, we switched our direction and turned to the right, taking ten careful steps on the far ledge to keep well away from the sand and flames. I was afraid to even ask what this change of direction implied. It probably meant that fraud is rarely approached head-on, but crookedly.[181] It might also have suggested the intellectual correction I was going to need to make as we transitioned to the next Circle below.[182]

The Usurers

When we reached the beast, I caught a glimpse of figures a little farther down sitting on the burning sand near the barren place. When Virgil caught me looking he said, "Why don't you go over there and see what their punishment is like so you might get the full experience of this place?"

Virgil continued, "But let your investigation be brief. While you're there, I'm going to negotiate with Geryon to grant us passage down to the next Circle on his strong shoulders."

This worried me a bit. Virgil had left my side only one time before in the Inferno, right outside of the gates of Dis. His negotiations hadn't gone so well there. In fact, I had never talked to sinners down here by myself before.[183] So I went alone to the extreme edge of the seventh Circle where a group of doleful souls sat still.

Their mourning burst through their eyes, while their hands sought relief from the burning sand and the fiery rain. It was evident to me that these souls were being punished for usury. Just as the usurers had gone from city to city plying their infernal trade of money lending, their punishment was to sit immobile on the sand.[184] They were like a pack of dogs in the summer, chomping at the air with their jaws when fleas, flies and horseflies bite. None of them said anything.

I didn't know any of them, but I noticed that each had a moneybag hanging around his neck. Each bag had a unique background color and a family crest that occupied their unbroken gaze. Each was finding pleasure in contemplating his money.[185] All I know is that "*He who loves money will not be satisfied with money; nor he who loves wealth with gain*" (Ecc 5.10).

As I continued looking at them, I noticed a blue shape on a yellow purse that held a lion's face. The colors and the crest resembled that of the Gianfiglizzi family in Florence.[186] Some from this family were notorious for practicing usury.[187]

As I continued on, I saw another crest of red blood that depicted a goose more white than creamy butter. This was similar to the crest of the Obriachi family, which was prominent for their banking and lending activity in Florence.[188]

Another crest on his white money pouch depicted a blue, pregnant female pig. This crest looked like that of the wealthy Scrovegni family from Padua. Reginaldo degli Scrovegni was an epic usurer.[189]

Opening his mouth, Reginaldo said to me, "What are you doing in this pit? Now get out of here. Since you're still alive, know that my fellow townsman Vitaliano will soon sit here on my left side!"

I thought it was pretty bold that this Reginaldo wanted me to tell about the alleged misdeeds of another. Reginaldo seemed to be drawing attention away from himself, which was a pretty novel practice, since most others I had met in the Inferno so far wanted to plead their innocence.[190] Reginaldo, by contrast, just wanted to be forgotten.

Reginaldo said, "I am a Paduan. Many times they filled my ears by shouting, 'Let the sovereign knight come who will bring the bag with the three goats.'"

I knew the reference to the three goats was referring to Giovanni Buiamonte who fell out of favor in Florence when he was accused of running off with others' money and goods.[191] He, too, was a moneylender, but went bankrupt and died poor.[192]

After Reginaldo was finished speaking, he scrunched up his mouth and stuck out his tongue at me. He looked like the oxen that lick their noses. Similar to the pig on his pouch, Reginaldo was so corrupted he had degraded himself to the point of being a beast.[193] There was no gentility left.

Then, afraid my staying any longer might annoy my leader — who, after all, admonished me to be brief — I turned back and left these weary souls.

Descent to the Abyss

I found Virgil already mounted up on the back of the fierce beast, Geryon. As I drew near, he said, "Be strong and bold!" This was similar to the charge the Maker had given to Joshua when he took over from Moses as the leader of Israel, before he led them over the Jordan River and into the Promised Land, saying ***"Be strong and of good courage"*** (Josh 1.6). The obvious difference was the place we were headed was no Promised Land. We were headed to the lowest Ring of the Inferno.

Virgil continued, "From this point on, we're going to make our descent with Geryon and others like him. You'll sit upfront; I'll be in the middle so that his tail can't reach us and do any harm." Since Geryon's scorpion-like tail was still quivering, this seemed like a good idea to me.[194]

I was scared and started trembling all over. I was like someone who had a fever brought on by malaria, which induces uncontrollable chills and paleness.[195]

At Virgil's words, I was completely gripped by fear. Yet I felt shame come over me, realizing how great and courageous my master was and the striking contrast his cool resolve made to my abject terror. His courage continued to strengthen me on this journey.

I was worried Virgil might rebuke me, so I hoisted myself up onto Geryon's broad shoulders. I wanted to speak, but my voice failed me. All I could manage to utter was, "Make sure you hold me tight!"

So Virgil, who had helped me out of so many tough spots, clutched me in his arms, steadied me and then got situated behind me.

Virgil said, "Geryon, move along now! Make a large circle and descend slowly. Keep in mind the new load you're carrying."

As a small boat goes out bit by bit from its berth, so the beast took off backward at first. Then, having got himself wholly free, he turned his tail to where his chest once was. Stretching out his tail, he started moving like an eel. With his arms pumping like a swimmer, he flew through the infernal air.

I don't think I've ever been so scared. It must have been similar to how Phaeton felt when he abandoned his reins that cooked the sky, a sight visible even today. Phaeton, when he heard reports that Apollo, the sun god, wasn't his father, begged Apollo to drive the chariot of the sun for a day.[196] Apollo thought this was a bad idea, but didn't think he could go back on the oath he had made to grant Phaeton's wish.[197] When Phaeton proved too unskilled to maintain control of the chariot, its erratic flight almost set the earth on fire, which caused Jupiter to kill Phaeton with a thunderbolt before he did.[198]

The flight of the miserable Icarus also came to mind, since he had his wings stripped of feathers from melting wax. Icarus was trying to fly away from the labyrinth of King Minos with waxed wings fashioned by his father.[199] Ignoring the advice of his father to steer a middle course between the sun and the earth, Icarus flew too close to the sun, which melted his waxed wings, causing him to fall back to earth, plunge into the sea and drown.[200] This was a fate I was hoping to avoid.

I couldn't really see anything, but Geryon, as we flew through the air. All perception of space and time vanished around me.[201]

Geryon kept up his swimming motions as we moved very slowly through the air. I think we were wheeling around in a wide arc as we descended. I couldn't perceive anything but the wind in my face coming up from below.

As we moved lower, I was hearing on my right side the waterfall striking the whirlpool down below us, which made a horrible roar. Judging the distance by the sound, I leaned out a bit and let my head look down.[202]

This caused me to become even more sheepish about our descent, since I caught the sight of fires and heard wailings down below. I pulled my head back in and grabbed onto Geryon even tighter.

I couldn't have perceived it before, but I became aware that our descent was made by a series of spirals that spun around great torments, threatening us from every side.

Our trip at the end was like a falcon, long at flight, but catching nothing, causing its falconer to exclaim, "Oh, so you're coming down now?" This falconer was a symbol of Satan.[203]

Without seeing any signal like a lure or bird-call from the falconer, the falcon descends, fatigued from lots of movement. Through a hundred rotations he lands well away from his master's arm, sullen and disdainful.[204]

This was how Geryon placed us on the bottom at the very foot of the jagged cliff. He wasn't happy at all. Having dropped us off, he bolted out of there like an arrow being shot from a bowstring.

Comment

Canto Seventeen marks the half-way point on Dante's journey through hell. It also provides an important transition between the Ring of violence and the Ring of fraud. Given Dante's decision to devote half the poem to the sin of fraud, this provides some indication of how important this subject is for him.

Canto Seventeen is also remarkable because of the unsurpassed imagery and descriptions Dante employs to describe his flight on the back of the beast Geryon. Dante uses sight, sound and tactile sensation to illustrate his voyage. It's a marvel of poetic construction and well worth reading in the original. Once again, at a key transition point in the journey, Virgil and Dante are forced to rely on outside help to make forward progress. As in the case of the Divine Messenger who unlocked the gates of Dis in Canto Nine or Charon who ferried them across the river at the gates of the Inferno in Canto Three or Nessus who helped them navigate the river of boiling blood in Canto Twelve, the travelers have required outside assistance along the way.

In fact, structurally, Canto Seventeen appears to be directly linked to the transition Dante needed to make in Cantos Eight and Nine at the gates of Dis. In both instances, interruptions imperil forward progress.

This provides a kind of allegorical commentary on the journey of life, where often we are forced to go backward in order to go forward. This is the very nature of beginning and ending.[205]

Geryon is one of Dante's most memorable characters. Although Geryon is usually depicted in mythological texts as having three bodies or three heads, Dante has re-envisioned him as having three natures. Geryon has the innocent face of a just man, the body of snake and the tail of scorpion. He is the personification of fraud, which looks innocent on the outside, but is ready to pounce on those who are unsuspecting. Thus Geryon serves as a kind of fraudulent trinity, the embodiment of the corruption of God's order.

One key allegorical element that could be easy to miss is Virgil's continuing role as the personification of reason in this Canto. Throughout the poem, Dante has needed grace to make forward progress. But he has also needed Virgil's guidance, as well. Virgil, as we have seen, is stuck in Limbo as one of the virtuous pagans.

Reason can be very helpful, even necessary to this journey, but at certain key points, Virgil has proved unable to navigate the labyrinth of the Inferno. This will become ever more pronounced as we observe the journey unfold.

We see reason at work, for example, when Virgil has Dante sit up front while he himself takes the middle position on Geryon's broad shoulders. Virgil does this specifically to guard against Dante's being stung by Geryon's quivering tale. Hence, reason is protecting Dante against fraud (represented by Geryon). Another example occurs when Virgil goes to negotiate with Geryon, thus leaving Dante on his own to observe the usurers. Dante needs no assistance from reason to see the obvious harm done by the usurers.[206]

What is the harm of usury? In Canto Fourteen, we learned that usury was not really about charging excessive interest, it was about the disorder moneylending brought to the society. Usury was thought to be unseemly because moneylenders were using money to make money. Our society's embrace of finance would have been thought deeply corrupt by Dante.

To the medieval mind, there was nothing productive about usury. In fact, the contemplative gazes of the usurers directed toward their money pouches, which Dante observes, is the reversal of contemplation centered on God that will preoccupy those in heaven.

Unlike tangible goods, money, by its very nature, is meant to be used, not amassed and lent out.[207] Thus to charge money for money was a perversion of its proper use. Therefore usury is a serious crime against nature, just like sodomy. It sins against the very nature of money itself.[208] This is why the punishment for the usurers is simply to sit still. Their incessant activity is reduced to silence and motionlessness. Just like the sodomites, they bring sterility to what should have been productive activity.[209]

One other interesting aspect of this Canto is that Dante never speaks out loud, but for one brief phrase. This is one of the few times in the whole Inferno where this is the case.[210] Dante is paralyzed by fear most of the time and cannot speak. Moreover, most of the usurers have nothing to say to him. They're too busy thinking about money. The only one who speaks, Reginaldo, uses his tongue to impugn the character of someone still alive.

But the usurers also perform a structural role as well. Dante places them at the very edge of the Ring of violence. This suggests that while usury does violence to God's order, it exhibits elements of fraud, as well. Thus the usurers employ many of the same coarse gestures, bad language and ill-treatment of others that will be characteristic of the Ring of fraud below.[211] In a sense, the usurers provide a preview of coming attractions.

What Dante has learned is that he is really not in control. He demonstrates in no uncertain terms that spiritual growth is not a matter of just trying harder.[212] The usurers are great examples of those who attempt to achieve human flourishing with frenetic activity. Yet, in the end, they have nothing to say and can do nothing but gaze on their moneybags. They've made so little spiritual progress that they sit silently.

Dante has seen again and again that this journey is a cooperation with grace. We all have to descend into hell and face our own demons to make progress. In the end, Geryon, the infernal beast, becomes the servant of Dante's continuing journey.[213] Thus the personification of fraud becomes the key for Dante's attempt to discover the fraudulent elements of his own life, elements that he will explore in the next Circle below.

Ring III:
The Sins of Incontinence

18

Pimps, Seducers and Flatterers

MALEBOLGE I: DITCHES 1-2

Virgil and Dante enter the second half of the Inferno through the third Ring of fraud. They encounter the first of the ten ditches of Malebolge ("evil pouches"), which examines the sins of fraud. In this ditch, Dante first encounters sinners running in opposite directions, a reminder of the perversion of the Year of Jubilee by Pope Boniface VIII. The souls, having encouraged sin through pimping and seducing, run along being scourged by angry demons in punishment for their incitement of animal passions in the society. Dante then encounters flatterers, who have their faces caked with human feces, emblematic of the crap that spewed from their mouths during their lives.

There is a place in the Inferno called **Malebolge**, full of evil pouches surrounded by dark-grey rock that forms the encircling walls.[1] The torments would be even worse down here.

In the exact center of the malicious field, an enormous pit gapes open, massive in breadth and depth. I'll wait until later to describe it in more detail once we get to the lowest part of the Inferno, the region known as Cocytus. The pit is almost too ghastly to describe.

The eighth Circle went around like a belt about the shaft of the pit along its sheer, foreboding bank. Its bottom was divided into ten successively-narrowing ditches where ten varieties of fraud are punished.[2] These ditches are like moats that protect the castle walls, thus rendering strange patterns in the places they were set. With such patterned details were these ditches made down there. They looked like an infernal spider web.[3]

The ditches had bridges jutting out from their rocky foundations to the outside bank, just like fortresses are known to employ. Out of the rock at the foot of the cliff ran ridges that stretched across the embankments and ditches, up to the shaft that divides them and connects them together.

In this place, Virgil and I found ourselves jettisoned from the back of Geryon. Virgil turned to the left and I took my usual place behind him.

As we were walking along the pit, I saw new miseries, new torments and new agonies off to my right.[4] We were only in the first ditch of this new Circle and yet it was full of all these things.[5]

At its base, two lines of naked sinners passed by us. The pimps were moving toward us in the middle on our side in a counterclockwise direction, while, on the other side, the seducers went along with us in a clockwise direction.[6]

I was stunned by this sight. It looked just like the city of Rome during Pope Boniface's Jubilee year. The Jews had celebrated the Jubilee every fifty years at which they were to *"grant redemption of the land"* (Lev 25.24), meaning all debts were cancelled, slaves were freed and property was returned to the original owners. The Jubilee ensured there was never a permanent underclass in Israel.

But something different happened when Pope Boniface called his Jubilee. Out of necessity, the city authorities invented two-way traffic to control the crowds cramming into the city on their pilgrimages. This was a pretty clever invention if you ask me. One group faced front as they headed toward the Castel Sant' Angelo and St. Peter's on the right, while the others went on the left toward Mount Giordano.[7]

You want to talk about fraud? This was a great example of it since the Pope offered a plenary indulgence to all comers who visited the basilicas of St. Peter and St. Paul on pilgrimage that year.[8] Boniface just wanted to fill his coffers from the crowds, a pretty spectacular misuse of the Jubilee, if you ask me.[9]

The Pimps

On both sides, on that same dark rock, I saw (for the first time) horned demons with huge whips, beating the naked souls cruelly from behind.[10] Oh, how the demons made them scamper at the first scourging! To be sure, no one was waiting around for seconds or thirds.

While I was going along, my eyes locked on one of them. As soon as I saw him, there was no doubt in my mind that I had seen this one already. So I ceased walking for a bit to check out his traits. My sweet leader paused with me and let me go back a little. This was a little like the spiritual life — two steps forward and one step back.

The one being flogged thought he could escape my sight. He hid his face, to no avail. I said, "You, over there, with eyes cast down to the ground. If the features you wear about you aren't deceiving me, I recognize you as Venedico Caccianemico. What in the world could have led you to such an infamous place?"

Venedico had been the head of the Guelf party in Bologna.[11] He was exiled from his city twice for detestable behavior, including handing over his own sister to the Marquis of Ferrara for sexual favors in exchange for cash.[12] That's right, he sold his own sister.[13] I wonder how he'd respond to what I knew.

Venedico answered, "Well, reluctantly, I'll explain it. Your clear speech compels me, as it causes me to remember the old world up above."

He continued, "It's true, I was the one who pimped out my sister, Ghisolabella, to the Marquis. You've probably only heard the whitewashed version of the indecent tale, though."[14]

He went on, "But let me be clear, I'm not the only one from Bologna down here weeping. This place is full of them. I'm not by any means the only one who said "Oh, yeah, yeah" in my native dialect, the one spoken between the Savena and the Reno rivers bordering Bologna."[15]

He continued, "If you want evidence or attestation, just keep in mind our avaricious hearts. We earned money gambling, stealing, pimping, whatever it took to fill our coffers."[16]

While Venedico was still speaking, a demon beat him with his whip and said, "Get lost, pimp! There are no women down here to connive!"

I couldn't help but notice that the pimps who had served as illicit go-betweens for all kinds of bad behavior had incited the animal passions of scores of people. They stimulated and fulfilled the perverse desires of sinners.[17] Therefore it seemed right that they would now be driven on an endless march, scourged in their flesh.[18]

The Seducers

I then rejoined Virgil. After just a few steps we came upon a ridge jutting out from the bank. We easily climbed up it. Turning to the right on its chipped peak, we removed ourselves from their endless circling and turned around to see the group going the other way. As we came to the point where the ditch opens wide to make way for the scourged, we looked down on them as they passed below.[19]

At this Virgil said, "Hold on! Get a look at these other badly-born souls. You've not seen their faces before since we've been walking in the same direction as they were." At the old bridge, we saw a train of souls coming toward us along the other side, driven along with whips like the others.

Without my asking, Virgil said to me, "Notice the big one coming. He doesn't shed a tear in spite of his pain. What a noble aspect he retains. That one is Jason, who by courage and gumption made off with the ram from the Colchians. Then he passed through the Isle of Lemnos after its daring and ruthless women had consigned all their males to death."

Virgil continued, "There, with tokens of affection and with fancy words, he tricked the young Hypsipyle who earlier had beguiled all the other women. Jason left her there at Lemnos, pregnant and abandoned. Such guilt condemns him to his agony and Medea gets revenge as well."

Jason was one of the most famous characters from mythology because of his quest for the Golden Fleece. He had gotten Hypsipyle pregnant after seducing her with beguiling words at Lemnos, promising to return after his quest for the Fleece was complete. But Jason ended up betraying Hypsipyle for Medea, whom he married after she helped him defeat a set of fire-breathing oxen and a massive dragon.[20] Jason later deserted Medea for Creon's daughter, Crusa, confirming his detestable character.[21]

Virgil continued, "With Jason go all who deceive in such a way. I think this is sufficient knowledge of the first ditch and of those who are locked within its jaws."

The Flatterers

We had already come to where the narrow inner bank of the first ditch intersects with the outer bank of the second to form the shoulder of another arc. There, we heard people griping in a different ditch, wheezing with their muzzles and beating themselves with their own palms.

The banks were caked with muck from the vapor below that sticks to them, assaulting their eyes and nose. The bottom is so dark that no place had sufficient light to see unless we climbed up on the back of the arc where the ridge is highest.

As we arrived there, in the ditch below, I saw people smothered in dung, which perhaps came from human privies. While I was searching down below with my eyes, I saw someone with his head so besmirched with disgusting crap that you couldn't tell if he was laity or clergy.

Their punishment seemed just. They had forced others to swallow their crap in the life above. Now, in the Inferno, the flatterers walk around encrusted with excrement, swallowing it whole just like a beast ingests his dinner.[22]

One chided me, saying, "Why are you so eager to gawk at me more than other sullied souls?"

I replied, "Why? If I remember right, I saw you once when your hair was dry. You're Allessio Interminei from Luca! That's the reason I eyed you more than the others."

Allessio answered, slamming his noggin, "My flatteries that never ceased from my tongue have submerged me down here."

Then Virgil said to me, "Set your gaze a little farther forward so your eyes can get a better look at the face of that filthy and disheveled hooker down there. Do you see the one scratching herself with her shitty fingernails, the one opening her legs and then standing up on her feet?"

Virgil continued, "She is Thais, the wench who answered her paramour when he asked, 'Do I find abundant favor with you?' Then, she replied, 'Oh, Magnificently.'"

Thais was a character from one of Terence's plays who symbolized the degradation to the society caused by prostitution.[23] Her illicit flatteries were certainly fraudulent.[24] Like everyone else down here, she incited scores of people to sin.

Virgil said, "Our eyes have had enough of this place. Let's keep going."

Comment

This Canto begins the third (and most extensive) Ring of the Inferno where the sins of fraud are punished. The reader should immediately notice the change in tone that occurs. There is vulgar language, harsher punishments and obscene gesturing all over this place.

Also, for the first time, we encounter a demon in the flesh. Here, the demons are whipping pimps and seducers as they go along. When readers get ideas about the harsh medieval views of punishment in hell, they often think of this section of the *Inferno*. This, of course, distorts Dante's perspective since it ignores the first half of the poem. But the rather stark imagery is a reminder of just how serious Dante thought fraud was.

For the next twelve Cantos, we will be travelling through the eighth Circle, known as Malebolge. Almost forty percent of the *Inferno* is taken up by Cantos that are in the eighth Circle. Within the next twelve Cantos, these "evil ditches" are a series of trenches traversed by a series of rock spurs that serve as bridges. All the pockets are arrayed in a spiral configuration. In other words, the pouches get ever-narrower as the travelers go through the Circle and encounter different aspects of fraud.

Malebolge serves as a kind of microcosm of hell itself.[25] The punishments become ever more severe because the sins increasingly affect the entire society, not just the individuals involved. In general, the more impact a sin has, the harsher the punishment that ensues.

We will also notice that there is no movement between ditches in Malebolge.[26] This sends an important message about how divisive fraud is for a society. It breaks apart families, friends, governments and businesses. Because relationships are the basic associational building blocks of societies, fraud contributes to the breakdown of order. Fraud negatively affects every activity in a society, from sex to the Church, to public administration, to spiritual and material well-being.[27]

At the very center of Malebolge is a giant ditch called Cocytus, the epicenter of the Inferno at the very middle of the earth. Thus we're headed to the very center of hell, the place farthest removed from the light and love of God.

19

Simony and the Papacy

MALEBOLGE II: DITCHES 3-4

Virgil and Dante encounter those who have bought and sold Church Offices and Sacraments, the Simoniacs. These sinners are stuffed head-first into small, round fissures in the rock and have their feet sticking out, tormented with flames. This positioning demonstrates how corruption in the Church turns the entire society on its head. Dante encounters Pope Nicholas III, a notorious seller of Papal privileges, who mistakes the pilgrim for Dante's arch-nemesis, Pope Boniface VIII. Dante issues a strong polemic against the corruptions of the Papacy and the Church hierarchy, focusing especially on Popes Nicholas III, Boniface VIII and Clement V. Dante's strong rebuke meets with Virgil's immediate approval.

"Woe to you, Simon Magus, and your despicable followers. You should have devoted yourself to the good things of God. But, in your predatory profession, you instead prostituted yourself for gold and silver. Now we're sounding the trumpet of judgment against you, as we look upon you in the third ditch."

I don't exactly know what came over me to utter such a stark invective.[28] I simply couldn't stand the sin of simony that presented itself before me. Simon was a magician who had astounded people in Samaria with his magical arts in the first century. After being baptized by the Apostle Philip, Simon tried to buy the gift of the Spirit with money. Peter rightly rebuked Simon for his vulgar request, saying, *"Your silver perish with you because you thought you could obtain the gift of God with money... Repent therefore of this wickedness of yours, and pray to the Lord that, if possible, the intent of your heart may be forgiven you"* (Acts 8.20, 22).

Ever since then, sinners who have tried to purchase ecclesiastical office or sacramental favors have been called Simoniacs. Such wicked souls, by embracing political power and unmitigated avarice, were ruining the Church.[29]

I was just itching to hear the sound of the seventh angel's trumpet ring forth from John's *Apocalypse* when *"There were loud voices in heaven saying, 'The kingdom of the world has become the kingdom of our Lord and of his Christ, and he shall reign forever and ever'"* (Rev 11.5). I think simony destroys the purity of the marriage between the Church and the Divine Son.[30] Simon Peter, the mediator of that marriage as the first Pope, strongly disapproved of Simon Magus and his simony. Yet his successors were willfully disdainful of this fact.

We had already come to the next tomb and were standing over it, having climbed up to the rock bridge jutting out over the middle of the ditch. Once again, prompted by sheer amazement for what I was observing, I cried out, "Oh Loftiest Wisdom, how great is the art you show in heaven, on earth and in the wicked world. What justice your great might conveys!"

The Divine Architect's art was his creation, which pointed beyond itself, participating in the heavenly realities above it. Such a great Artist had every right to render harsh judgment against those who trashed what he had so carefully crafted.[31]

Baptism and the Baptistery of San Giovanni

Along the sides and on the floor of the ditch, I noticed the iron-colored rock was full of holes. This was different from what I seen in the first couple of ditches. Each of the holes was round and similar in size. The holes seemed very similar in appearance to those in Florence's baptistery named after St. John, the patron Saint of my beloved city.

That baptistery had special significance for me. In the first place, I myself was baptized there, as were all of Florence's children.[32] There were four round stations in the baptismal font,[33] which the priests used to manage the crowds of people seeking baptism for their infants during the Easter season.[34] These stations were the place of new birth for the inhabitants of our fair city, and thus were of central importance for all Florentines.

One day, I accidently broke one of the circular stations while rescuing a young child drowning in it. The child, a disobedient lad to be sure, was clowning around in the font, replaying the act of baptism for fun when he got caught in one of the holes and started to drown.[35] I rushed in to save him, but inadvertently ruptured the sacred font in the process.

I set my seal before you — I am not lying — I did profane the holy font, the instrument that seals the baptized with the promise of the Spirit. This I confess openly. But I did so for good reason. As I saved that child those many years ago, I was trying here to save the Church from its errant ways now.[36] And, as the indwelling presence of the Spirit saves sinners, so my motives are pure in what I'm about to tell you.

From the opening of the holes protruded a startling sight. I saw the feet of sinners with their legs up to their calves sticking out. The sinners were upside down in the holes with their heads and chests submerged. The soles of their feet were on fire. As a result, their legs were twitching so furiously they could have snapped the sturdy bands used to tie up firewood or bundles of leather.[37]

The irony here was striking. St. Peter had gone to his death as a martyr, demanding to be crucified upside down because he didn't consider himself worthy to die in the same way as his Lord. But these Popes, the successors of St. Peter, had so perverted the Office that they were suffering Peter's fate with none of the glory.[38] Their perversions caused such suffering that it seemed right to me that they should grieve down here.

The flames scorching the feet of the sinners were moving from heel to toe, just like fire in motion over an oily surface only passes over its outer husk. I was amazed at the ironic reversal going on here.[39] At Pentecost, with the sound of the rush of a mighty wind, flames of fire rested on those gathered, who received the Spirit and began the Church (Acts 2.3). Down here, everything was upside down, so the flames of fire were scorching the feet of those who had corrupted the Church. Moreover, the oil, that had anointed these souls at their baptisms, was now being used as fuel to burn their feet.[40] This represented the logical outcome of profaning one's baptismal vows so completely.[41]

Pope Nicholas III and the Fourth Ditch

I asked Virgil, "Master, who is that who mortifies himself in that hole over there, the one writhing more vigorously than his compatriots around him? If I'm not mistaken, I think I see a redder flame that drinks him in." The redder flame was an indication that this sinner, whoever he was, was receiving a more intense punishment.[42]

Virgil answered, "If you want, I can take you over to that lower bank. You'll learn some important things from him about who he was and what his wrongdoings entailed."

I replied, "If it would please you, it would certainly be gratifying to me. You're my leader. I know by now that I can't depart from your will since you can read my silent thoughts."

So we came to the fourth ditch. Turning, we went down toward our left into a narrow porous gulch. Virgil was still attached to my hip and didn't let me go until we had reached the place of the one wailing with only his lower legs visible. It was a pathetic sight to take in.

Once we came upon him, I addressed the sinner sternly: "Oh wretched soul, whatever you are, planted like a stake and holding your upper parts below, if you can, say something."

I stood like a friar hearing the confession of a treacherous assassin, one begging for mercy despite the overwhelming evidence against him. In Florence, convicted assassins were executed upside down with their heads planted in a hole.[43] But here I was, a layperson, about to hear the confession of a terrible sinner. Things sure seemed upside down here.

The sinner cried out, "Are you already standing there?" He then cried out even louder after I didn't respond right away: "Are *you* already standing there, Boniface? I guess I misread the prophetic writings. I thought you wouldn't be down here for three more years!"

The sinner continued, "Were you so quickly sated with the proceeds of your simony, which you didn't hesitate to take by trickery from our Fair Lady, the Church? Did you then use the proceeds to commit outrages against her? This is what I've heard about you."

I simply froze at his outburst. His feet sticking up from the hole, the sinner thought I was Pope Boniface VIII, the one who I've blamed for my exile! He had apparently heard about the rumor that Boniface had persuaded his predecessor, the humble monk Celestine V, to abdicate the Papacy so Boniface could pursue his underhanded dealings from the seat of Peter.[44] I guess the rumors were true.

But how could this sinner mistake me for my arch nemesis, Boniface? I simply couldn't comprehend it and didn't know how to respond.

Seeing my hesitation, Virgil leapt into action. He told me firmly, "Tell him *right now*: I'm not the one you think I am." I did just as he ordered me.

At that, the nasty soul wrenched both his feet even more violently than before. Then, sighing, he said to me with a weeping cry, "What exactly is it you require of me?"

The sinner continued, "If you want to learn my name so badly that you've come all the way down to this ditch, you should know that I once was clothed in the great mantle of the Papacy. Truly, truly I say to you, I was the son of the she-bear, of the Orsini clan. So intent was I on helping my dear cubs get ahead in the world, that I pocketed wealth. I admit it. I guess that's why I'm stuck down here in this infernal ditch."

From his speech, I realized that the sinner was none other than Pope Nicholas III. Although Nicholas had a respected career as a Cardinal, he was really known for his needless nepotism as Pope.[45] Three of the Cardinals he created while Pope were close relatives, not to mention the almost endless flow of high appointments to other family members.[46]

I was also amused by the pun on his name, as the moniker of the Orsini clan came from the Italian word for bear (*orsa*)[47] and rhymed with the Italian word for moneybag (*borsa*).[48] What wasn't funny was the utter lack of concern Nicholas was demonstrating for his actions.

He went on, "Below me in this hole are others that preceded me in simony. They're stuffed down there below all crushed and flattened into the fissures in these rocks. This previews my fate as well. Once Boniface, the one I assumed you were when I questioned you just now, comes down here, I'm going to be pushed farther down, too."

Nicholas continued, "I'm telling you that after Boniface, another will come from the west, a lawless pastor, with even fouler works to his name. He'll cover both Boniface and me. He'll be a new Jason, the one you can read in about in the book of Maccabees. As King Antiochus IV was permissive to Jason, so the king of France will be to him."

I surmised he was talking about the man who would become Pope Clement V, the successor to Boniface, and the one who did the unthinkable and transferred the seat of the Papacy from Rome to Avignon in France. Clement's whole reign was illegitimate as he functioned as a puppet for the French King, Philip IV.[49]

In fact, Clement only became Pope by promising to free the French King from the excommunication Boniface had placed on him.[50] This is probably why he ended up in Avignon. Clement thus began the so-called Babylonian captivity of the Papacy in France which lasted for almost seventy years. This was one of the worst periods in the history of the Church.[51]

The comparison to Jason in the book of 2 Maccabees was also apt. Jason was the High Priest under King Antiochus IV in the second century

BC.[52] Jason promised the king three-hundred-sixty talents of silver and another eighty talents from a different source of revenue if he would appoint him as High Priest (2 Mac 4.7-8). There was even more cash available if the king would grant him the authority to establish a school and a body of youth for it. These huge sums demonstrate the corrupting influence of money in ecclesiastical ministry.

This was all pretty startling news that confirmed my opinions about the state of the Papacy and the Church. Most of the Popes I knew during my lifetime were already here or were about to come here. Their insatiable desire for money and the things of the world had caused the Papacy to abandon its role as the spiritual leader of mankind.[53] No wonder the world was so messed up.

Polemic against the Papacy

I'm not really sure if what I did next went too far. But I was just too fed up with all the corruption I was seeing. I asked Nicholas with an almost mocking tone, "Please, do tell me now, just how much treasure did our Lord require from St. Peter before he entrusted the keys to his keeping? Did he ask for anything more than just 'follow me'"?

The keys I'm talking about are the keys of binding and loosing sins, passed down through the ages to the successors of St. Peter. The Divine Son had originally given them to Peter when he said, *"I will give you the keys of the kingdom of heaven and whatever you bind on earth shall be bound in heaven and whatever you loose on earth shall be loosed in heaven"* (Matt 16.19).

I went on, my disdain growing, as I spoke, "Neither Peter nor the other apostles asked for gold or silver from Matthias when he was appointed by lot to replace the guilty Judas among the apostles after he killed himself. So stay there since you're rightly castigated. Watch over all your ill-gotten gains that you made during your intrigues against Charles of Anjou."[54] I spoke in such a tone to a former Pope because he had surrendered his authority. I saw no need to treat him with any respect.[55]

Charles of Anjou fomented a rebellion in Sicily as a result of the heavy burdens placed on its inhabitants in paying for his acquisitions of Jerusalem and Achaia.[56] It was widely assumed that Nicholas, drawing on funds from the eastern Emperor, used them to stoke the fires of rebellion in Sicily.[57] Both rulers brought instability where they were supposed to be bringing order.

I continued, now venting my anger at the whole panoply of corrupt rulers in the Church's hierarchy: "I would employ even severer words because your unabated greed and desire for material things saddens the world. You've trampled the good by lifting up the depraved."

I went on, "Pastors like you are just like the whore of Babylon whom St. John the Evangelist wrote about in his *Apocalypse*. John saw a vision of the whore, sitting upon the waters, fornicating with the rebellious kings of the earth. She was endowed with seven heads and gained strength through ten horns."

St. John described what he saw this way:

> *Then one of the seven angels who had the seven bowls came and said to me, 'Come, I will show you the judgment of the great harlot who is seated upon many waters with whom the kings of the earth have committed fornication and with the wine of whose fornication the dwellers on earth have become drunk'. And he carried me away in the Spirit into a wilderness and I saw a woman sitting on a scarlet beast which was full of blasphemous names and it had seven heads and ten horns. The woman was arrayed in purple and scarlet and bedecked with gold and jewels and pearls, holding in her hand a golden cup full of abominations and the impurities of her fornication; and on her forehead was written a name of mystery: 'Babylon the great, mother of harlots and of earth's abominations'. And I saw the woman drunk with the blood of the saints and the blood of the martyrs* (Rev 17.1-6).

Although most in my day interpreted this passage morally in light of the judgments that would come upon the reprobates of the world, I knew that the woman John envisioned in this passage was actually a symbol of Rome.[58] But what I hadn't understood until I journeyed down here is that the Popes, who ruled Rome as the Emperors used to, were also in view. The corrupted Papacy was the whore drunk with her fornications. The Popes, who were supposed to be humble servants, had turned into monstrous, thieving whores, committing abominations across the whole sweep of humanity in their savage search for wealth and power. It was a sorry sight.

I continued, "You have made for yourselves a god of gold and silver. What difference is there between all of you down here and the idolaters? The only difference is that they worshipped one idol — a proverbial golden calf — while you worship hundreds! You Popes were prostituting the Church with these reprehensible actions."[59]

The Donation of Constantine

I went on, "Oh, Constantine, how much evil did you bequeath to the world not by your conversion, but by your Donation that the first rich father assumed from you?"

I was speaking here of the Donation of Constantine. Constantine was the Roman Emperor early in the fourth century who moved the Empire toward acceptance of Christianity.[60] Constantine enabled the Church to come out of hiding after centuries of periodic persecutions and vastly expanded its acceptance.

But Constantine's Donation is a different story. This document, which I was convinced was genuine, justified Papal claims to political authority. As the story goes, Constantine offered his Donation to Pope Sylvester out of gratitude for curing him of leprosy in AD 337.[61]

No matter what the document said, I thought giving direct political power to the Papacy was a terrible idea since it played a direct role in the corruption of the once-venerable institution. The Pope was supposed to be watching over spiritual matters, not political ones.[62] As such, I thought the Donation was illegitimate.[63]

While I was sending such notes his way, Nicholas started kicking fiercely with both feet. I wasn't sure if he was bitten by anger or conscience. But, clearly, my tough words had an effect on him.

I think what I said really pleased Virgil. His countenance sparkled as he listened to my diatribe. He knew what I was saying was true and seemed especially pleased with my confident tone.

Virgil couldn't hold back his glee so he grasped me with both his arms and gave me a bear-hug. Having taken me to his breast, he literally carried me up onto the path we had descended. He didn't even tire of holding me so close. In fact, he kept carrying me all the way up to the top of the arch that connects the fourth ditch to the fifth. With Virgil's embrace, I couldn't miss the symbolic clasp of reason here.

Once we got up there, he gently set me down. I say gently because the surface of the ridge was uneven and steep. It would have been tough going even for a goat used to the treacherous terrain of the mountains. I just hoped at the separation of the sheep and the goats, I would be counted among the righteous.[64] I sure didn't want to end up down here.

Once I got down, I looked around and saw another gulf open up before me.

Comment

Dante pulls out all the stops in this Canto in his polemic against the Papacy. We should realize that Dante was not against the *idea* of the Papacy; he was steadfastly opposed to its corruption at the hands of those greedy for gain and for power. The good shepherd is supposed to lay down his life for the sheep (John 10.11). By contrast, many of the Popes of this period had lost this perspective.

Dante, of course, is caught up personally in this power grab. Writing as he is from exile, Dante believes that his difficulties could be traced, at least in part, to the corruption of Pope Boniface VIII. If Boniface had been a fair dealer, he would never have sent troops to Florence to try to expand his power base. Further, had Boniface been more honorable, Dante would not be suffering in exile, or so he thinks.

There are ironies all over the place in this Canto. The *contrapasso* is especially apt that has the sinners in this part of Malebolge upside down in circular holes with only their feet sticking out. Church leaders who were supposed to have their gaze pointed to heaven instead are stuffed face-down into the earth.[65] When Church leaders are greedy for power and gain, this turns the whole society upside down.

The Papacy's failings are also an ironic perversion of the martyrdom of St. Peter, who demanded to be crucified upside down at the hands of the Roman government. This idea comes from Eusebius' *Church History*, the oldest extant extra-Biblical history of the Church, which claimed the following: *"Peter seems to have preached in Pontus, Galatia, Bithynia, Cappadocia and Asia to the Jews of the Dispersion. Finally, he came to Rome where he was crucified, head down-wards at his own request."*[66] Although later Protestants would question Eusebius' claim that Peter died in Rome, the evidence is strongly in its favor.

Dante blames this situation with the Papacy on the Donation of Constantine, which purported to grant political control of Rome to the Papacy. While Dante assumes the Donation of Constantine is genuine, it turned out to be a forgery. This discovery that the Donation was a forgery undermined Papal claims to temporal authority over certain territories in Italy. We can only imagine how Dante might have used this fact if he had known it.

In the fifteenth century, the Renaissance scholars Nicholas of Cusa and Lorenzo Valla, demonstrated definitively from the language of the document that the Donation must have been an eighth-century forgery. In particular, Valla analyzed the document from both a rhetorical and philological perspective, proving convincingly from an analysis of the Latin employed that it had to be crafted much later than originally believed.[67] Valla's work shows the careful linguistic skill of Renaissance humanism at its best.

Even though Dante did not know the Donation of Constantine was a fake, he had rejected the close marriage of Church and State in his political writings. Dante wrote the following in his treatise on government (*On Monarchy*):

> *But to divide the Empire is contrary to the office committed to the Emperor; for his office is to hold mankind in all things subject to one will...Therefore, it is not permitted for the Emperor to divide the Empire...The Church may not go contrary to its foundation, but must always rest on its foundation [which is Christ]...In the same way I say that the Empire may not do aught that transgresses human right.*[68]

One easy thing to miss is Dante's switch to plural pronouns in the midst of his polemic against the Papacy. In Italian, writers can draw a distinction between second person singular (*tu*) and second person plural pronouns (*voi*). In English, the pronoun "you" is the same in its singular and plural forms, so the distinction becomes lost.

When Dante is in the middle of his polemic, right before he equates the Roman Papacy to the whore of Babylon, he switches from addressing Nicholas III directly to addressing the entire Church hierarchy.[69] In other words, he switches from singular to plural pronouns. This distinction does not come through very well in English, but is striking in Italian. Dante is addressing the corruption of the whole society as he goes along, not just individual Popes. As servant-leaders, the Popes should have set a better example for the society and are a significant reason why the society has become corrupt. But the Popes were not the only ones who were at fault, and thus the punishments in this part of the *Inferno* are not reserved for Popes alone.

Finally, Dante's use of the Book of Revelation both begins the Canto and plays a prominent role throughout it. When Dante equates the Papacy to the whore of Babylon in Revelation 17, he was doing something radical. Whereas most had interpreted this passage in allegorical or moral terms, Dante reads the text in its literal sense, but then takes the further step of saying that the woman in Revelation 17 is the Pope in Rome.[70]

Although many different interpretations of this passage have come down through history, the text itself interprets the reference to the woman with seven heads as follows: *"The seven heads are seven mountains on which the woman is seated"* (Rev 17.9). Many would come to see this reference to the seven hills as a reference to Rome (which was built on seven hills), thus making the link between the whore of Babylon and the Papacy more concrete.

Even here, we observe the corruption of the Church at work because the seven heads can also been seen as a reference to the seven Sacraments or the seven gifts of the Holy Spirit, while the ten horns is usually read as a reference to the Ten Commandments.[71] All the gifts of God are corrupted when the leadership of the Church goes bad. Dante believed he was suffering in exile because of it. He does not hold back his disdain for those who had ruined his life by corrupting the Church.

20

Soothsayers and Astrologers

MALEBOLGE III: DITCH 4

Virgil and Dante encounter those who were soothsayers and astrologers. These sinners have their heads turned almost completely around backwards and are forced to walk in reverse. They looked too far into the future and now have no idea what is in front of them. Virgil does the vast majority of the talking in this Canto, recounting literary figures such as Amphiaraus from Statius' Thebaid*, Tiresias from Ovid's* Metamorphosis*, as well as Aruns and Manto from Virgil's* Aeneid*. As Virgil recounts these tales, he changes important details from the "official" version, thus implicating himself in fraud as well. This Canto ends at about 7:00 AM on Holy Saturday morning.*

We came to a whole new set of strange punishments, so I'm constructing fresh verses to describe them.[72] We'll give attention to the twentieth Canto, whose first refrain tells of those submerged in the abyss of the Inferno.

I thought I was now ready for all this, and wanted to check out the open ditch bathed in tears of woe. I saw people silently coming through the rounded valley, weeping as they went along. Their pace was slow, like those processing through a basilica while chanting the Great Litany during Lent. Their turgid pace and silent expressions seemed appropriate for those who had spoken too much in the world above.

As my gaze fixed on them, it was an amazing sight. They had contorted bodies between their chins and the top of their chests. Their faces were turned almost the whole way around backward which compelled them to go about in reverse. Any ability to look ahead was withheld from them.

Maybe as a result of some strange medical disorder, someone had been twisted back like that before. But I had never seen anything like it. Even if I had seen it previously, I also wouldn't have believed it.

Now, Dear Reader, if God lets you take away fruit from your reading, consider for yourself how it was that I could keep my tear ducts dry. After all, I was seeing the very human image that we all share so contorted, that tears from their eyes were bathing their butts down through the crack. Tell me if you could have kept yourself from crying at this terrible sight![73]

I wasn't so skilled. Of course I had bowed my head and was weeping at the sight, perched as I was against one of the rocks of the rough reef.[74] I was weeping over the lost state of the souls right before me in this miserable ditch of the Inferno.[75]

In an uncharacteristically strong outburst, Virgil rebuked me, saying, "Are you still as foolish as the others? Here pity lives even when it's dead. Who is fouler than the one who brings passivity to God's judgment?"[76]

I guess this sight didn't move Virgil at all.[77] The differences in our reactions to this place were striking. Virgil must have thought my compassion for these miserable sinners was foolish.[78]

Three Literary Soothsayers

Virgil commanded me, saying, "Raise up your head. I said, raise it up. See the one the earth opened up and swallowed before the eyes of the Thebans when they all cried out, 'Where are you rushing off to, Amphiaraus?' 'Why are you leaving the war?' 'Why don't you just tumble down to Minos who lays hold of each one?'"

Amphiaraus was one of the kings in the Theban war, who tried to avoid fighting since it would inevitably lead to his death. However, he ended up playing an important role in the war after his wife, Eriphyle, gave away his hiding place,[79] only succumbing when Zeus caused the earth to swallow him alive. [80]

Virgil said, "Look how he's made his chest out of his shoulders. He wanted to look too far ahead in life. Now he looks back and makes his way in reverse." Once again, everything seemed out of its natural order down here.

Virgil continued, "See also Tiresias who changed his looks when he turned from male to female, thus transforming his members. Later on, he had to strike two coiled serpents with his staff before he could regain his masculine plumage."

Tiresias was a well-known soothsayer in Thebes from Ovid's *Metamorphosis*. He separated with his staff two copulating serpents he encountered.[81] But, in turn, he was changed into a woman for seven years.[82] After the seven years, he found the same serpents again, struck them with his magic staff, and was turned back into a man. [83]

I have to admit that I didn't remember Ovid's depicting Tiresias in such a negative light. Ovid seemed to like Tiresias in his story, especially the part when the gods were fighting over who (men or women) experience more sexual pleasure. When Tiresias agreed with Jupiter that women experience more pleasure, Juno, in her rage, struck him with blindness.[84]

Virgil went on, "Aruns is the one who backs up to Tiresias' belly. In the hills of Luni where the Carraresi work, he lived down in the plains below in a white marble cave as his home. There, he observed with an unobstructed view, the stars and the sea."

Aruns was an Etruscan soothsayer, as Lucan described it.[85] From the innards of an ox, Aruns foresaw the coming civil war between Caesar and Pompey, but didn't warn anyone.[86] This became especially problematic when Caesar won such a resounding victory.

So I guess Virgil thought Aruns was living in the outskirts of Luna, not in his hometown of Luca like I thought. Virgil seemed to be subtly changing the details of all these stories from how they were originally told, turning Virgil himself into a kind of astrologer.[87] Whatever the case, I couldn't miss the irony that Aruns who could see so far ahead in life, now couldn't even see beyond himself since he backed up against Tiresias' belly.

Manto and Virgil's Fraud

Virgil continued, "Look at that one over there, whose breasts are hidden by her loose, flowing hair so that you can't see them. This one was Manto, who searched through many lands before she set herself down in Mantua, the place I was born."

Manto was a very strange sight. All her hairy parts — from armpits to pubic hair — were facing the wrong direction.[88] I knew from Virgil's writing that Manto was the daughter of Tiresias.[89]

Virgil said, "After Manto's father departed from this life, while the city of Bacchus was enslaved, she wandered for quite some time through the world. High up in the northern part of fair Italy lies a lake named Banaco. This lake lies at the foot of the Alps near Tyrol, which borders Germany."

Virgil continued, "At Garda, Val Cammonica and Pennino, the mountains are bathed by the waters of a thousand springs, and maybe more, which gathers in that lake.[90] There is an island in the middle of it where the Dioceses of Trent, Brescia and Verona come together. The Bishops of these three Dioceses could bless it if they ever bothered to journey there for Mass."[91]

Virgil said, "Peschiera, a beautiful and mighty arsenal, which opposed the Brescians and the Bergamese, rests on the banks at its lowest point. There, all the water that tumbles into Benaco that can't be contained, overflows and descends into a river, streaming through green fields. When the water is at its head, it's no longer called Benaco, but Mencio, until it reaches Governolo, where it spills into the Po River. It doesn't run far before encountering a lowland where it spreads out and forms a bog. Because of the prevalence of malaria in summer, the bog is sometimes treacherous."

Virgil continued, "Passing through, the untamed virgin, Manto, saw land in the middle of the bog without cultivation or inhabitant. There, to flee all human cavorting, she stood with her servants to ply her trade. There she lived and there she left her lifeless body."

Virgil continued, "Afterward, men from all around gathered at that place that was so well protected by the bog on all sides. They built the city over those dead bones. The city is named Mantua, named after her who originally chose the place, without resorting to sorcery to choose its name."[92]

I wondered what had gotten into Virgil. What was with this pointless geography lesson?[93] I had never seen him drone on and on like this before. I take it that he had a point, but I wasn't sure what it was. The character Manto was from his *Aeneid.* But, down here, Virgil yet again changed the story. It was like he was recanting what he had written.[94]

In the *Aeneid*, it was Ocnus, son of Manto, who had founded the city Mantua. But now, in this retelling, it was Manto herself who founded it. [95] This was all a bit confusing, especially since Virgil had been born in Mantua. Didn't he know the founding myth of his own city?

Virgil continued, "The people within Mantua were, at one time, more abundant before the foolishness of the Counts of Casalodi endured the trickery of the Pinamonte."

Here, Virgil was talking about the incident in 1272, when Count Alberto was deceived by Pinamonte dei Bonaccolsi into removing supporters from the city. This resulted in a huge slaughter of the nobility in the city.[96] The people had turned on their leader, just like the people of Florence had turned on me.[97]

Virgil said, "Therefore, I admonish you, if you ever hear otherwise about the origin of my land, let no lie defraud the truth."

Again, I was confused. Virgil seemed to be indicating the lack of truth in his own work, the *Aeneid.* Was Virgil accusing himself of fraud? It seemed strange to hear such a thing this far down in the Inferno. I think this demonstrates that Virgil's poem, as a tragedy, could err.[98] I decided to not to confront my guide over this.

But I no longer had any doubt. Virgil was showing that language could be both fraudulent and truthful.[99] In a sinful world, it was hard to tell which was which.

Eight Astrologers

I replied, "Master, your way of thinking is usually so certain and receives my full trust such that anything else would be spent coals. But, tell me, of the people slowly processing, do you see any worthy of note? My mind reverts back to this alone."

Virgil replied, "That one over there whose beard protrudes from his cheeks onto his dark shoulders used to be a fortuneteller. (This was true, at least when Greece was so lacking in males that the only ones left were babies in the cradle.) Eurypylus was his name. Along with Calchas, he foresaw the time for cutting the ship's anchor at Aulis. My High Tragedy sings of him in a certain place. But I know that you're well familiar with my work."

Eurypylus was another character from Virgil's *Aeneid* who learned from the god Apollo that the Greeks' voyage to Italy from Troy would require a human sacrifice.[100] This was similar to the sacrifice of Iphigenia for favorable winds in the journey from Aulis to Troy that was foreseen by Calchas.[101]

Virgil continued, "That other one, whose hips are so lean, was Michael Scot, who really learned how to play the game of defrauding with magic."

Scot was someone who learned Arabic and was able to translate Aristotle into Latin.[102] But he also worked extensively with astrology and alchemy, which were responsible for popular opinions of him as a great wizard.[103]

Virgil said, "Notice Guido Bonatti; notice also Asdente, who now wishes he had attended to leather and thread, but he repents too late."

I knew Guido was a famous astrologer.[104] Rumor had it that Guido da Montefeltro won his great victory over the French because of Bonatti's astrology.[105] Asdente, which means toothless, was famous for predicting the defeat of the Emperor Frederick II at the siege of Parma.[106]

Virgil continued, "See the gloomy women who left their sewing, weaving and spinning to become diviners, casting spells with herbs and images. None of them are worthy of being named."[107]

Virgil then abruptly stopped, "But now let's go. Cain, with his thorns (by which I mean the man on the moon), is directly over the two hemispheres and touches the wave below Seville.[108] Remember well that the moon last night was already full and it has done you no harm at any time in the dark wood." This he said to me as we continued to walk along.

Comment

Canto Twenty is unique because it is the first Canto we've encountered without a single Biblical reference or allusion. From the first line, we get the sense that something different is going on within this Canto because the language is so self-consciously referential. Nowhere else does Dante specifically refer to the Canto itself. It's almost as if the poem itself is the focus here.

What gets explored in this Canto is the fraud of language, something that Teodolinda Barolini is well-known for pointing out.[109] Language can either tell the truth or it can defraud.[110] Remarkably, Dante has Virgil retell several well-known stories from the *Aeneid* in different ways than the original, thus indicting him with literary fraud.

It's the version Virgil tells in the *Inferno* that we're supposed to rely on, not the one preserved for us in Virgil's Latin text of the *Aeneid*. Dante is drawing a distinction between his text (a Comedy, which is true) and Virgil's (a Tragedy, which is fraudulent).[111] This is a pretty stunning claim to make against what heretofore had been considered the greatest epic poem ever written.

The other unique thing about this Canto is that Dante hardly speaks a word. Virgil is the center of attention. Thus we get this ironic interchange of those who spoke too much as soothsayers and astrologers in the life above, who are now muted in the world below. This is contrasted with Virgil who now atypically speaks loquaciously to "correct" his poem.

Although Dante speaks little, he also seems to lack judgment. One of the things Dante needs to learn in the *Inferno* is that God doesn't make mistakes. Sinners are down here for a good reason. Thus the weeping and the natural pity he feels for those stuck in Malebolge show he is inconsistent at learning to see things from God's perspective. Was it not just one Canto prior that Virgil embraced Dante for his strong rebuke of the Papacy? Dante still has progress to make.

Canto Twenty also boasts perhaps the clearest *contrapasso* in the poem. Those who used soothsaying to see too far into the future have their heads turned around; they're forced to walk backwards. They've violated God's natural order and are no longer able to see ahead at all.

Lastly, we receive some specific time indications in the last couple lines of the Canto. We've been in the very early morning on Saturday for the past six or seven Cantos. Suggesting that the moon was directly over the northern and southern hemispheres, and setting in the west, means the sun has started its rise. This implies that the Canto ends at 6:52 AM on Holy Saturday morning (yes, we can figure out exactly what time the sun rose that day).[112] Time moves on in the endless punishments of the Inferno.

21

Barratry (Part I)

MALEBOLGE IV: DITCHES 5-6

Dante encounters one of the darkest areas of the Inferno as they meet those who have bought and sold political offices. These so-called Barraters are punished by being submerged in boiling pitch, emblematic of their sticky fingers when it came to money. The darkness of the scene is symbolic of the secret back-room deals they were known for executing. Virgil exercises poor judgment when he encounters a band of devils, replete with cattle prods, horns and wings. The devils hoodwink Virgil, which Dante sees right through, a sign of progress. This Canto takes place at about 10:00 AM on Saturday morning.

Dark Pitch

We moved on from one bridge to the next, talking about other things my Comedy can't recount. If Virgil's High Tragedy had suspect language, my Comedy, written in the vernacular, needed to tell the truth. After all, linguistic fraud was still on display among those we encountered in this ditch.[113] There was no need to employ Virgil's lofty language around those I saw down here.[114]

Virgil and I were standing at the top of one of the bridges, when we stopped to check out the next pouch in Malebolge. We heard all kinds of futile lamentations coming from the ditch. It was strangely dark.[115] The pouch's pervasive corruption made it so.

The darkness reminded me of the Venetian strongholds I had witnessed in winter, which boil at the center with tacky pitch used to patch up unsound wooden sailing vessels. Since the Venetians can't sail in winter, some yard workers busy themselves constructing new vessels, while others re-caulk flanges on existing ships that have seen many voyages. Some hammer away at the prow; others at the stern. Some make oars; others spin hemp to make ropes. Still others patch the jib and mainsail.

As I recall, the Venetian shipyard was an impressive sight that boasted remarkable teamwork and efficiency. The pitch in the shipyard may have smelled similar to this ditch, but in the presence of fraud, both community and productivity were severely curtailed in this section of Malebolge.[116]

Heated not by fire, but by Divine Art, a thick pitch boiled right there in front of me, covering the bank on each side. This explained the unusual darkness of the place. I saw it, but saw nothing in it, save the bubbles that were rising up from the boiling cauldron. All the bubbles were swelling up and bursting, and then settling back down again.[117] I realized that there was something secretively sinister about this place. The darkness was symbolic of back-handed dealings.

The Barraters

While I was standing there, I was focused intensely on my leader. All of a sudden, Virgil shouted, "Look out!" He grabbed me, pulling me to himself and away from the place where I was standing.

I was scared to death. I turned like a man, trying to figure out what he's fleeing from, and, suddenly overtaken with fear, doesn't stop to compose himself. Behind us, I saw an ugly black devil running up the ridge directly towards us.

The horned devil was haughty in his appearance. He gestured in a menacing way toward me with his wings outspread over his nimble feet. The devil had broad shoulders that were hunched over, burdened by the weight of a sinner he was carrying. The devil was clutching the sinner's legs at the sinews above the heel with his sharp claws.

From the bridge, the devil said, "Hey Nasty Claws, here is one of St. Zita's elders. Plunge him down into the pitch while I go back again for the other one from Lucca."

St. Zita was the patron Saint of Lucca.[118] I guess the devil was using the good Zita, who was well-respected in her day, to let us know these sinners were from the town of Lucca, a place known for its industry and efficiency.[119] I had no idea who the sinner was who found himself on the devil's shoulders since he went unnamed. I guess this was appropriate since he was just one of many nameless bureaucrats who were probably down here.[120]

But there were some rumors that the sinner was Marino Bottario, who was suspected of buying and selling political offices as one of the political bosses in Lucca.[121] I could be wrong, but I think he had come down here straight away having just died.[122]

Looking at us, the devil said, "Each man there (except Bonturo) is a Barrater. There, with money, they manage to turn a 'no' into a 'yes.'"

Bonturo Dati was a corrupt political figure in Lucca who managed to get his position through bribes.[123] In case it's not clear, this is what barratry is — the buying and selling of political office. I guess the devil was just being sarcastic when he claimed that everyone was a Barrater in Lucca except Bonturo.[124]

I watched as the devil threw the sinner over the bridge and turned back along the rock ridge. Never did such a powerful dog make such haste to chase after a thief.

The sinner sank down into the pitch, but floated back up again. Every time this happened, the ugly demon positioned underneath the cover of the bridge cried out angrily: "We have no room for an Image bearer. Here, one swims differently than in the Serchio River by Lucca.[125] So, unless you want to experience death by a thousand cuts, don't let yourself be seen above the pitch."

Then, stabbing him with the pricks of a hundred prongs, the devil said, "Here you have to dance under cover, so grab on in secret if you can." This whole scene reminded me of how cooks make their kitchen hands immerse meat in the broiler with prods so that it doesn't float back up.

Once again, the punishment fit the crime. These Barraters had corrupted city government like the Simoniacs had corrupted the Church in the last Canto.[126] Everything they did was with back-room deals, so the darkness down here seemed especially appropriate. Moreover, the sticky pitch they were immersed in was just like the sticky money that changed hands on their watch.[127]

Evil Tail and the Platoon of Devils

My good master said to me, "Look, you need to be careful. Let's make it less obvious you're here. Crouch down low behind that splintered rock over there so you have something to shield you from the devils' sight. No matter what atrocity they commit against me, don't freak out. I've got everything under control. I already tussled with these devils the last time I was down here."

I have to admit, Virgil was sounding a little over-confident. The last time he spoke with such bluster, up at the gates of Dis, it didn't turn out so well for us. I was just happy to be behind the rocks while Virgil went and drew the devils' attention.

Passing over from the splintered rocks to the bridge, Virgil crossed the border to the sixth ditch. He had to put up a strong front. So, with all the furor and bluster of a dog sicced on the back of a beggar who just starts panhandling where he's been stopped, the devils came out from under the little bridge and trained all their nasty hooks on him.

Virgil said, "Please, good sirs, let none of you do me any harm! Before you ply me with your hooks, if you would, let one of your crew come forward and hear what I have to say. Then, you can take counsel among yourselves whether or not I'm to be pricked and tarred."

All the devils cried out in unison, "Let's send Evil Tail!" So one of them started moving toward Virgil while the others stood still. When Evil Tail came to him, the devil said, "What good will it do?"

Virgil replied, "Evil Tail, do you actually think you could have encountered me coming all this way down here safely without any of your ilk resisting me along the way? Could this possibly have happened without the intervention of the divine will and deft fate?"

Virgil continued, "Let us go, for it is willed in heaven that I show another this savage path."

At that, the Evil Tail's pride deflated so much that he let his prod fall at his feet. Evil Tail said to the other devils, "All right, fine, let none of you hurt him." I noticed he had a strange wry smile as he said this.

Virgil turned around to me, as I was hiding behind the rocks and said, "Ok, you who hide all curled up between the splintered rocks of the bridge, I guess now you can return to my side safely."

At that, I moved and Virgil came over to me quickly. The devils were all thrusting themselves forward aggressively. I was terrified they might not honor their agreement. In fact, I couldn't figure out why Virgil was so confident that these nasty devils were telling him the truth about their intentions. I was really worried that Virgil's high-mindedness wouldn't hold up well against the devils' trickery.[128]

As I found myself among such hostile creatures, it was like observing frightened soldiers coming out of Caprona with promises of safe conduct. I had been there when we laid siege to the Pisan stronghold of Caprona.[129] I knew how important it was to maintain military discipline before an enemy, so I couldn't believe Virgil had given away my position.

I scrunched up as close as I could to Virgil and did not take my eyes away from the devils' faces, which were intimidating and ugly. Their hooks were now trained on me and one devil was saying to the other, "Hey, just for fun, should I prick him on the rump?" The other answered, "Yeah, stick him where the sun don't shine!"

But that demon who was negotiating with Virgil got annoyed at the ruckus, turned around suddenly, and yelled, "Get down, knock it off, Scruffy Hair."[130]

Then Evil Tail said to us, "Unfortunately, you can't go any further through this reef since the sixth bridge is out of order. You see, it's shattered at its base. But, if you do desire to go on further, then just continue on with us through this cliff. There's another passage not too far from here."

Evil Tail continued, "Yesterday, five hours hence, it was 1,266 years since the path down here was mangled. It just so happens that I'm sending some from my cohort there now to see if any sinners are airing themselves out. Why don't you go on with them — they'll cause you no trouble."

I couldn't believe Virgil was actually buying this, but he was. Evil Tail was skillfully weaving together lies and truth. The reference to 1,266 years must have been when the Divine Son came down and harrowed hell. But the very fact that the devil knew about it suggested he couldn't be trusted. He was probably down here when it happened! Virgil was staring evil in the face, but couldn't recognize it. Why wasn't he getting this? Was I the only one suspicious of the devils' motives?

Evil Tail continued, "Hup Two, Bat-Devil and Frost Bite.[131] You, Canine Creep and Frizzy Beard, lead the platoon.[132] Take Pussy Whip with Massive Dragon along with you.[133] While you're at it, bring along Tusked Super Swine, Scratching Dog and Goblin, as well as Crazy Red Face, with you.[134]

Evil Tail said, "Attention! The troop is ready. Go about the boiling glue. Here are the rules of engagement: these two have safe passage to the next ridge that goes over the dens."

I couldn't stand it any longer so I took Virgil aside and pleaded with him, saying, "Come on, Master, can't you see that this is bad? Please, let's go on alone without an escort. I just don't want to be around these infernal creatures."

I continued, "If you're as shrewd as you usually are, can't you see that they're gnashing their teeth at us? Don't you see that they mean us harm?"

Virgil calmly replied, "I don't want you to be afraid. Let them gnash their teeth all they want. They're not threatening us — they're salivating over the ones boiling in the pitch below."

I thought to myself, "What can I say, Virgil just doesn't get it."

The devils made their way toward the left on the bank. But each pressed his tongue between his teeth. Then, turning their rears toward their leader, they all nodded in unison, mooned him and then farted violently through their assholes.

So much for a Comedy. This was looking more and more like a vulgar farce to me.

Comment

The vulgar language and almost slapstick comedy in this Canto hits a fevered pitch. Once again, we're confronted metaphorically with the fraud of language. This time, the big question is whether the devils can be taken at their word to be telling the truth. Dante recognizes immediately that they can't. Virgil, the embodiment of reason, simply cannot see the falsehood inherent in their speech. Reason falls apart as it encounters evil in this place.

What is the root of Virgil's error? This is a hotly debated question. Some see the root problem as being the pride of human reason (*"Knowledge puffs up, but love builds up,"* 1 Cor 8.1). If pride is the root of sin, then it's logical to assume this contributes to Virgil's inability to assess the devils' motivations properly. It's also true that Virgil's overreliance on cool reason causes him to miss the source of the threat. Reason has no way of grasping the irrationality of sin. It's a mystery.[135]

One of the most difficult questions this Canto presents is why Dante chooses to punish the sin of buying political office more severely than the sin of simony, which hurt the Church? Wouldn't hurting the Church be more significant in Dante's day than hurting the government?

To Dante, the clear answer is no. Buying Church offices is terrible, but money sloshing around in the government is far worse. Why? Dante had seen first-hand the effects of political corruption on people.

In other words, this is personal for him, since barratry is the charge that got Dante thrown out of Florence. There is little evidence that Dante actually misused government funds. It's the political nature of the charge, which has little basis in truth, that Dante finds so objectionable.

Thus corruption in government is directly related to the corruption of the human heart.[136] It ruins people's lives, including his own. As a result, Dante thinks corruption in government is worse than corruption in the Church since it affects more people.

Another question that this Canto poses is why the humor is so dark. If Dante is contrasting his Comedy against Virgil's High Tragedy (mentioned in the previous Canto), then why is the humor so vulgar? It's vulgar because corruption itself is vulgar and just plain stupid. It helps no one. Those who benefit from corruption are sinning grievously. Those who are affected by the corruption (everyone in the city) have their lives worsened for the gain of a few. None of this is good.

We find this vulgarity reflected in the language of the Canto itself. In fact, this Canto is interesting from a literary perspective because it includes both tragic and comedic elements. It is no laughing matter to Dante that he has been thrown out of Florence on politically-motivated charges. Thus the reality of Dante's life is tragic. Yet Dante depicts this tragic reality with vulgar humor, gestures and language.

In fact, the state of government in this Canto is completely corrupted. We have devils in Malebolge plying their infernal trade, and they're doing it based on cunning and trickery.[137] This is what we'd expect from devils. But Dante associates this corruption indirectly with those who conspired to throw him out of Florence. The devils in this Canto are emblematic of the corrupt politicians who caused his exile.

Dante may have tried to obfuscate this by suggesting that the sinners were from the nearby Italian town of Lucca, but it seems fairly obvious that his political opponents from Florence motivated the events of the Canto. Those who ruined Dante's life are vulgar, base and almost shocking in how vacuous they are. Dante's political commentary has become very sharp and biting indeed.

22

Barratry (Part II)

MALEBOLGE V: DITCHES 5-6

Dante and Virgil continue exploring the sin of barratry, the buying and selling of political offices. After walking along with a platoon of ten devils, they see them pull a sinner out of the pond of boiling pitch and torture him. In between their assaults, the pilgrims learn the sinner was Ciampolo, a corrupt governmental official from Spain. Ciampolo tells of other sinners submerged in the pool of pitch, such as Don Michael Zanche and Brother Gomita. Ciampolo escapes from the clutches of the devils by playing a dangerous game of deception, which results in a deadly brawl between two of the devils.

After what I had just seen, I thought maybe I should try to make sense of what was going on in this part of Malebolge. What came to mind were horsemen I had observed breaking camp during my military days. Upon commencing an offensive, they would parade their ranks. Then, when the going got tough, some would make a run for it to save their rears in a retreat. I was witnessing the ebb and flow between the highest nobility and the basest desertion as the circumstances changed.[138]

I have also seen scouts in your land, O Aretines. I've even been on military probes with platoons in your area.[139] This was noble and good, at least when I was involved. At the same time, I've witnessed distressing tournaments where knights injure each other and where jousters rush at each other with the express intent of doing harm. The contrast between comedy and tragedy is both thin and stark.

I've also seen participants all decked out with trumpets on high campaigns replete with drums and signals from allied strongholds. I've even seen this done with both foreign and domestic instruments, different forces bandying together to fight a common foe. This is, of course, a noble activity.

But I've never seen such truly strange instruments together — woodwinds at that! Nor have I seen horsemen and infantrymen marching together, nor ships departing at a signal from land or star. After all, there are no stars down here. The devils' practice of signaling each other was as far from noble as one could get.[140]

Barraters Punished

So we went on our way, trailing behind ten infernal demons. Talk about ferocious company. As they say, "In the church with saints, in the tavern with gluttons." With that in mind, I still didn't think Virgil's judgment was particularly good regarding these devils.[141]

I was laser-focused on the pool of boiling pitch in front of us. I wanted to figure out what it was like for those consigned to suffer beneath its bubbles and to understand better the souls who were newly coming down to be immersed in it.

In my mind, it was like the dolphins that proffer warnings for sailors that a terrible storm is coming with the arches of their backs. If the sailors are wise, they'll rig their boats for the inclement weather ahead of time and stay alive. Of course, by the time a soul got down here, things weren't going to turn out so well for him. I bring this up because I was pretty sure a storm was coming our way.[142] I needed to be ready. If only Virgil shared my concern.

I noticed the sinners in the pitch sometimes acted like dolphins. They were in so much pain from the boiling pitch that they would try to sneak a peek above the pitch to get some relief. To do this, they'd let their backs float up a little and then hide them again in a flash.

It was almost like frogs I had witnessed at the water's edge. Sometimes the frogs would crouch down in the pool with only their snouts poking out above the water. This would leave their legs and other body parts concealed below. I saw some sinners crouching down similarly when, unfortunately for them, Frizzy Beard was approaching. In utter terror, they drew their backs underneath the boiling pitch right away.

Ciampolo

Next, I saw — and it still makes my heart shudder — a single sinner off by himself, waiting patiently. He was like a single frog that stays put while the others hop away. The problem was that Scratching Dog, who was fairly close, caught sight of his attempt to get some relief and hooked him by his disheveled, knotted hair and yanked him up. The sinner looked like an otter since the black pitch smeared all over his skin was similar to an otter's coat when it was wet.[143]

Now I already knew the names of the whole company of ten devils who were with us. I made it a point to learn them as Evil Tail was forming the platoon. I also learned some names as they called to each other when they were standing around waiting to depart.

The platoon was getting excited because of Scratching Dog's hooking of the sinner. All the devils by the pool were egging him on, shouting, "Hey Crazy Red, put your claws on him![144] Flay the bastard!" They were all whooping and hollering together in unison.

While the devils were distracted with their infernal trade, I quietly asked Virgil, "Master, if it's possible, could you please inquire who that wretch is they're dangling over the pool? He doesn't look too happy, having come into the clutches of his adversaries."

Virgil then went up close and asked where the sinner was from. The nameless sinner, writhing in pain, answered Virgil directly, saying, "I was born in the kingdom of Navarre. My mother placed me with a nobleman to serve. She conceived me with a good-for-nothing man who destroyed himself and all his possessions. Then I was with the family of the good King Thibaut, where I was turned into a barrater, on account of which, I am suffering in this infernal heat."

Although this barrater never directly disclosed his name, I think it was Ciampolo of Navarre.[145] I take it that just as he employed secret deals during his life on behalf of the king, he was happy for his name not to be disclosed openly down here.[146] Ciampolo was a corrupt Spaniard known for his underhanded dealings in Navarre, in the Catalonia region of Northern Spain.[147] In the end, Ciampolo schemed to betray his king.[148]

Then, Super Swine, from whose jaw a tusk protruded from each side like a hog, made him feel what it was like to be ripped open. The sinner screamed in pain. It was like a mouse had wandered in among a bunch of bad-news cats. But Frizzy Beard put an end to it, wanting to get in on the action himself. He stopped them with his arms and said, "Stay over there while I fork him!"

Before he continued his torture treatment, Frizzy Beard turned to Virgil and said, "If you still want to learn anything more from him, why don't you ask him now...before the others completely disfigure him."

So, while Ciampolo was resting between tortures, Virgil asked him, "Now tell me about the other kings. Do you know any other Italian noblemen who are down here under the pitch?"

Ciampolo answered, "Well, just a little while ago, one came down from a nearby place. I'll tell you what, if I were still covered with him, I wouldn't be dreading these claws or hooks!"

Then Pickpocket, boiling with rage said, "We've had just about enough of you." He took his hook, caught him by the arm and pulled, scooping out some of Ciampolo's flesh.

Massive Dragon didn't want to be left out. So he aimed for Ciampolo's legs, seeking to tear something off. But then Frizzy Beard, the platoon leader, turned around right away and gave Massive Dragon a frowning look. This pacified the bunch a least for time.

Into the pause, Virgil, without delay, asked Ciampolo, who was still licking his wounds, "Who was that you were mentioning before? What Italian came down here whose unwise departure caused you to wash up on shore?"

Ciampolo replied, "The soul was that of Brother Gomita who was from Gallura. That whole area was perpetually laden with fraud, not least of which because of his dealings. Brother Gomita was happy to take bribes from the enemies of King Nino Visconti in Sardinia.[149] Brother Gomita was so good at his deception and the king trusted him so much, that everyone praised him as just. Of course he wasn't."

Ciampolo continued, "Brother Gomita took money and rendered summary judgments on behalf of some wealthy prisoners, as he's freely admitted to us. This wasn't the only thing either. He was no small-time barrater; it was like he was trying to be a sovereign king himself. The king ignored repeated complaints about him until someone discovered Brother Gomita's judicial actions were fraudulent.[150] He shouldn't have let the prisoners go without authorization. He was hanged shortly thereafter."[151]

Ciampolo said, "He's not alone. Don Michael Zanche of Logudoro keeps him company. They never get tired of talking about Sardinia with their tongues."

Zanche was from a very wealthy and influential family in Sardinia, and was governor of the district of Logudoro.[152] He was assassinated by his son-in-law Branca Doria for unknown reasons. I guess now we know what his true character was like.[153]

Defrauding the Devils

Ciampolo said, "Oh my, check out that other one over there, the one gnashing his teeth. I'd keep talking but I'm a little freaked out that the demon is fixing to scratch my itch."

Frizzy Beard took control again. He turned to Goblin, who was rolling his eyes. Ready to lash out, he sneered, "Get lost, you stinking, villainous bird!"

After this outburst, the frightened Ciampolo resumed his speech, this time to the whole group of devils, "If you want to see or hear from the Tuscans or the Lombards below, I'll make them come. Only, to pull this off, let Evil Claws stand aside so they won't fear his vengeance. I'll be sitting over there in my place. I'll whistle and you can pounce on them when they surface."

I thought it was pretty clever that Ciampolo had figured out I was from Tuscany and Virgil was from Lombardy and thus surmised we would be interested in meeting more sinners from our hometowns. I guess he figured it out from our accents.[154]

Ciampolo continued, "For every one of me, I'll be sure to have seven come up when I whistle. You see, this is our pattern when someone manages to get out of the boiling pitch. Think of how much sport you devils could have if all the sinners submerged in the pool suddenly surfaced. You could have a field day hooking them with your forks."

I wondered, was Ciampolo really going to deceive his companions to help us? This was a Faustian bargain if I ever saw one. Ciampolo was actually trying to get the devils to hide while he whistled to his friends to make them think a respite awaits.[155] I doubted this would end well for anyone, save Ciampolo. I couldn't believe he was sinning right in front of us by offering to perpetrate fraud on his unsuspecting companions.[156] I had seen a lot of things in the Inferno so far, but nothing that brazen.

At this, Canine Creep raised up his muzzle and smelling something fishy, he shook his head.[157] With an incredulous tone, he said, "Do you hear the trickery this one has thought up? What if he's just trying to get free for a little while before he jumps back in? I'm not sure I like it."

Ciampolo responded, "What do you think? Am I that much of a trickster that I'd fool my friends just to help myself? I mean, come on, that might result in greater sadness for my friends. I'm not that mean."

I thought to myself, of course, he'd do that. Was anyone buying this ruse? This was yet another lie Ciampolo had just told.

Bat Devil couldn't hold it in any longer. He was itching for a fight.[158] Against the others, he turned and said to Ciampolo, "If you dive back in, I for one am not going to run after you. It'll be far worse. I'll beat my wings over the pitch to make you suffer. You'd better do what you said you were going to do."

Bat Devil continued, speaking to the troop gathered around, "Ok, I like this plan. Let's withdraw from the ridge and hide behind the bank over there. Let's see if Ciampolo would dare to get away from us.[159] We'll crush him if he does."

He then turned and spoke directly to Ciampolo, "We'll see if you're equal to us on your own. I sincerely doubt you are."

Now, Dear Reader, I couldn't believe how ludicrous this game was becoming. Bat Devil had really convinced everyone just to back off and trust that Ciampolo, a known fraudster, would do what he said he'd do. Why would anyone trust him? From here, you're going to hear about a whole new game.

At this, the devils all turned their backs away from Ciampolo, including Canine Creep, who at first had most opposed it.

Then the predictable happened. I'll say this much: Ciampolo's timing was perfect. He had his feet firmly planted on the ground. As soon as the devils turned their backs and withdrew, he immediately sprang up and dove off the ridge, thus escaping their clutches. He had outsmarted them all.[160] They never saw it coming.

When the Devils realized they had been tricked, they were ticked off. Bat Devil took off after Ciampolo, crying out "Now I've got you!" But it did no good since his wings couldn't flap fast enough. Ciampolo's frightened flight was far more motivated than a devil just playing a deadly game.

Ciampolo nose-dived into the pool at supersonic speed. When Bat Devil realized he couldn't catch him, he straightened his chest and flew back upward to the ridge. The whole scene was no different from when a duck suddenly dives down into the water to escape an approaching falcon. Then, after the prey is gone, the falcon turns back, cross and weary.

Frost Bite, however, was irate at the hoax. He was flying behind Bat Devil and decided to take out his anger on him. He was angry because Bat Devil's gullibility allowed the escape of a barrater.[161] This was decidedly not appropriate, so Frost Bite turned his claws on his fellow-devil and fought with him above the ditch.

But Bat Devil was like an embattled hawk, rapacious with claws. As a result of their fight, both of them lost control and fell headlong into the boiling pond. The intense heat seized them as soon as they hit the surface, causing them to detach their claws from one another.

There was no getting up, however. They had both gotten their wings so entangled in the gluey slime of the pond, they couldn't get out.

Frizzy Beard, sorrowing with the others, had four of the devils fly to the other bank, each with their hooks in hand. Just then, with four on each side, they descended to their appointed posts and stretched out their hooks toward the pitch-encrusted pair to lift them out. Both Bat Devil and Frost Bite were burned to a crisp.

The other devils shrugged their shoulders and just stared at the pair, roasted beyond recognition. Meanwhile, Virgil and I slipped passed the bewildered devils unnoticed.

Comment

Once again, all order is overturned in this section of the *Inferno*. The devils, who are supposed to be punishing fraud, have fraud practiced on them when they decide to trust one of the sinners, Ciampolo. They play his game, hoping to inflict even more torture on other sinners. All sense of measure and propriety has left as we encounter this scene.

Dante, who himself was charged with barratry, is making an important statement about what happens to a community when fraud goes unchecked. The society falls apart because no one can trust anyone else. No one's word means anything and the only way to get something done is through graft. Not only the business economy, but the political economy gets caught up in this problem.

This Canto continues the theme of the fraudulence of language. When even the devils are getting tricked into doing something they shouldn't, the situation, as Dante depicts it, is dire.

An important transition is occurring in these Cantos dealing with the sin of barratry because Dante is starting to take more responsibility for himself and his own spiritual progress. This is easy to miss since Dante still asks Virgil to go procure information for him. Yet note that it's Dante, not Virgil, who is setting the agenda for the questions.

For much of the *Inferno*, Dante has often been a relatively passive participant with those they encounter. He's had trouble figuring things out and has needed his guide to point the way. Yet, at this point, Virgil isn't particularly helpful. He's not protecting Dante from fraud and is not doing a good job of keeping Dante safe. All Virgil can do is be a messenger. Thus Dante has to start taking responsibility for his own actions and his own spiritual life. This sense of independence and responsibility will become ever-more pronounced as we proceed.

Most importantly, it's Dante who once again sees right through the fraud where others cannot. This is a sign of spiritual progress on Dante's part. He observes everyone as implicated in fraud in this Canto, and concludes that it has ruined society. Those steeped in sin and self-dealing can't accurately observe what is right in front of them. This includes Virgil who still cannot see through the malevolent intentions of the devils.

I have deliberately introduced several anachronisms into this Canto that are not in the text of the poem. For example, a fourteenth-century audience would have known nothing of a "Faustian bargain" since the legend of Faust derives from a sixteenth-century German legend made famous by Goethe. Also, no one at the time would have understood what "supersonic" speed was. I've employed these figures to reinforce the issue of the fraudulence of language in the Canto.

Language does not stay stable in its meaning as time goes on. Consider the word "gay," which had a decidedly different nuance seventy-five years ago than it has today. The implication from this is that literature gets reinterpreted over time as society and language change. It may be questionable to use terms and images not available to the original readers, but I am trying to underscore the inherent difficultly that passing down truths with human language presents for us. It always creates interpretive difficulties.

Lastly, I made the decision both in this Canto and as well as the last to transpose the devils' names into English. Please note that some of these translations are, shall we say, "creative." The reason for doing this is that it adds to the sense of frivolity and play that is at work in this section. The devils, while they're doling out pain, think this is a game. If I had kept the names in Italian, it would have left out something important for the reader.

To be sure, the devils are upset that Ciampolo gets the better of them. Dante specifically uses the language of gaming and play here. Yet torture is no laughing matter. Thus we again observe the interchange between comedy and tragedy.

This also brings up a special issue for us as readers, especially since we are addressed directly in this Canto. Do you find yourself drawn in by the excitement of seeing a sinner tortured by devils? If so, we should be asking ourselves why, since Dante is showing us that our base natures naturally gravitate to things we shouldn't find pleasure in, but do. This is who we are as sinners.

Almost every survey taken of readers of the *Comedy* concludes that the *Inferno* is the most popular of the three sections of the poem. Why? Largely because people get tortured by devils and we can't wait to find out what is going to happen next.

Dante wants us to question ourselves. Why do we have such prurient interests? We should be very careful that we're not defrauding ourselves. We must examine why we're drawn to such things. While we're not supposed to be sympathetic toward the sinners, we are supposed to learn from them.

In no uncertain terms, the torture of a soul is a terrible sight. Why we are drawn to such awful things leads us to the mystery of sin that Dante is trying to get us to explore in our own lives.

23

The Hypocrites

MALEBOLGE VI: DITCH 6

Virgil and Dante narrowly escape from Evil Tail and his band of devils. They meet the hypocrites who are clothed in glittering monastic robes, weighed down by leaden interiors. There is a serious disconnect between their outward appearance and their interior lethargy, which accounts for their extremely slow and pensive movements. The pilgrims encounter Catalano and Loderigno, two monastic leaders who were thrown out of Florence for their hypocritical political dealings. The pilgrims then come across Caiaphas, the High Priest who condemned the Divine Son to death on the cross, who is himself being crucified. He is naked and lying across the path while on his cross, which forces him to bear the weight of those who pass along the trail. At the end, Virgil (finally) comes to the realization that he has been badly misled by the devils in the previous Cantos.

Having ditched our demonic chaperones, we went along silently, independently and without escort. We walked single file. Virgil was in front and I in back, as usual. We looked like first-order Franciscan Friars as we went, walking slowly and pensively.

All the turmoil we had just encountered reminded me of one of Aesop's tales, the one about the frog and the mouse. My reflections on this fable became a source of anxiety for me because of the devils burned to a crisp who we left in the dust above.[162]

In the fable, a mouse came to a stream and asked a frog to ferry him across. But once they were out on the water, the frog tried to drown the mouse by plunging into the deep.[163] A hawk saved the day by rescuing the mouse and eating the frog.[164] In this fable, I saw the problem of fraud at work, and the disorder it brings to a community.[165]

Here, the frog represented the demons who came to their demise because of their malevolence. Both Virgil and I were like the mouse, simple creatures just trying to make our way across the ditch. Like the frog, the devils had offered to help us since we couldn't get across the fifth ditch without it. We barely survived by the grace of the Maker who was acting in the role of the hawk. He was dishing out his retributive justice on the devils, similar to what the hawk did to the frog.

My anxiety stemmed from the mouse's innocence. In the story, the mouse did nothing wrong. But were we really so innocent? Hadn't a bunch of creatures been harmed just to allow us to pass through? It troubled me that fraud, which so often seeks to hoodwink the innocent, only brings destruction on itself.[166] This was true in my life, and it was certainly true in the ditch we had just exited.

In fact, the word "now" in English and its cognate "nu" in Old English weren't closer in meaning than the fracas and the fable. The stories began and ended in just the same way.

Just as one thought erupts from another, so the thought of the fight in the last Canto led to another one. Truth be told, it made me even more frightened than I was before. I thought about it this way: on account of our inquiries, those sinners probably had it even rougher now. I didn't want to cause pain to satisfy my idle curiosity, but I couldn't shake the thought that we hadn't done much good for anyone except ourselves. If this pattern of things worsens as our descent continues, the devils would likely come at us with even more viciousness than a dog chasing after a rabbit.

The Great Escape

I could almost feel my hair standing on end. Out of fear, I kept looking over my shoulder to see if anything was behind us. Finally, I said to

Virgil, "Master, if you don't hide us lickety-split, I'm afraid Evil Tail is going to find a way to get us. I just know he's right behind us somewhere with his band. I can almost hear them sneaking up on us."

Virgil said, "If you were made of leaded glass, I wouldn't catch your outer image faster than I can feel your inner angst. Look, we're on the same page; I'm worried, too. Your thoughts came alongside mine in both thought and result."

Virgil continued, "I've already thought about what to do. If the bank on the right can get us down to the next ditch, we'll escape the hunt we're both picturing."

Virgil had been reading my mind the whole time we had been down here. I was grateful for it now. It was almost like we were mirroring each other in our thoughts. Our minds were tied together in a uniquely intimate way.

In fact, Virgil hadn't finished talking before I saw the band of devils furiously making their way toward us, their wings outstretched. They weren't far off, and their intent was clearly malicious. They wanted to snatch us and take us back to their pool of pitch.

Virgil immediately grabbed me. He was like a loving mother who, awakened by a loud noise and seeing flames springing up near her, grabs her child and flees without hesitation. That kind of mother shows more concern for the child than for herself and doesn't even pause to put on a dress when escaping the flames, thus running out of the house naked.[167]

Once down from the upper edge of the rocky bank, Virgil set himself face up at the edge of the overhanging rock that borders the other side of the next ditch. Water never coursed so quickly through a channel to turn a waterwheel with its paddles than when my master dove down that edge. Virgil carried me on his breast, like his son, not like a mere acquaintance. We were that close.

Just as Virgil's feet touched the adjoining rock-bed at the bottom, the devils reached the bank above us. We had escaped just in a nick of time. For once, there was no cause for fear since the High Providence, who appointed them keepers of the fifth ditch, took away their ability to depart from there. We were safe, at least for the moment. All I can say is that Virgil was pretty courageous in getting us down here.[168]

The Cluniac Hypocrites

As we looked around the sixth ditch, we encountered a painted people who were going about weeping with slow steps. Their quiet, almost contemplative pace, was a nice break from the rapid and furious tempo we had just witnessed.[169]

These sinners sported tunics with low hoods over their eyes, made in the fashion of Cluniac monks. On the outside, their robes were so gilded that they dazzled, but on the inside they were weighed down with lead. They were so heavy that the ones Frederick used were but straw by comparison.

The French Benedictine Abbey at Cluny was one of the most famous of my day. Known for its reform efforts started under Abbot Peter the Venerable, Cluny played a key role in maintaining European civilization during the eleventh century.[170] The Cluniac reforms led to increased power for the Pope, a greater commitment to clerical celibacy, an increase in literacy throughout the society and an elevation of the priesthood.[171]

Despite these outcomes, the Cluniac monks were implicated as hypocrites. The great monk Bernard of Clairvaux had once criticized the "soft and delicate" robes of the Cluniac monks, preferring the more austere lifestyle of the Cistercian order.[172] Thus these sinners had glittering robes on the outside, but on the inside they were weighed down by their hypocrisy.

Frederick II used to execute those who had offended him by covering them with lead and having them melted in a furnace.[173] This was a terrible way to die. I couldn't help remembering what the Divine Son said about these souls: *"Woe to you...hypocrites! For you are like whitewashed tombs which outwardly appear beautiful, but within are full of dead men's bones and all uncleanness"* (Matt 23.27). Oh, what a wearisome mantle to be worn forever!

Catalano and Loderigno

We turned again to our left, going along with the procession of sinners. I personally preferred their gloomy wailing to what we had observed before with Evil Tail. But, because of their burden, the sinners were moving so slowly it seemed like we had new companions every time we took another step.

I said to Virgil, "Could you please keep your eyes open as we go along and find someone I might recognize by deed or reputation?"

One of them overheard my Tuscan accent and cried out behind us, "Hold it right there, you who run so fast through this murky air. Perhaps you could get from me what you're looking for."

Then, my leader turned around and said to me, "Hold up, just a sec. Let's proceed at his turtle pace."

I stopped and saw two sinners with expressions suggesting they desired to converse with me. The problem was their burden and their narrow gait slowed them down. Once again, there was hypocrisy at work here. Their faces were sincere on the outside, but they were weighed down by sin on the inside.[174]

As they came near, they had dubious looks and approached me without saying a word. They then turned to each other and said in unison: "That one's throat is moving so he must be alive. If he were dead, by what right does he go about down here without a heavy cloak?"

One of them then turned to me and said, "Oh Tuscan, you've come to this gathering of miserable hypocrites. If you don't mind, tell us who you are."[175]

I said to him, "I was born and grew up in the great city of Florence, by the fair Arno River. You've discerned right. I'm in the body I've always had."

I went on, "But who are you whose sorrow is so distilled that I see it running down your cheeks? And what pain is in you that makes them sparkle so?"

One of them answered me, "Our golden hoods are so heavy because they're made of lead. Like a balance that measures with weights, our bodies are weighed down.[176] We were Jovial Friars from Bologna.

I'm named Catalano and the one over there is Loderingo. We were both seized by officials from your city."

He continued, "Although the powers-that-be usually chose only one man to keep peace in the city, we did it together so effectively that you can still see the ruins that came from our efforts!"

His snarky irony wasn't lost on me.[177] The ruins were the result of his hypocrisy. Catalano founded the order of the Knights of the Blessed Virgin Mary that was originally formed to protect widows and orphans.[178] These monks liked to party, however. As a result, they became known as the Jovial Friars.[179] They got involved in all kinds of political intrigue, backing a plot by Pope Clement IV to oust the Ghibellines from Florence.[180] The citizens of Florence eventually ran Catalano and his band out of the city entirely.

Loderingo was also a member of the Jovial Friars. Together with Catalano, Loderingo acted as a governor of Florence, trying to keep the peace between the Guelfs and the Ghibellines — but, in reality, favoring the Guelfs.[181] Accused of corruption, Loderingo was banished from Florence as well.[182]

Caiaphas and Annas

I began to speak: "Oh friars, your wicked acts..." But I stopped mid-sentence because, out the corner of my eye, I saw a soul being crucified on the ground on three stakes. When he saw me, he contorted his face and puffed into his beard with sighs. Just like the Divine Son was crucified on a cross, this sinner had stakes through his two hands and one through his conjoined feet.[183]

Brother Catalano noticed him and said to me, "That one you see staked over there advised the Pharisees that it would be expedient for one man to die for all the people." Naked, he is stretched out across the path. As you can see, he is forced to bear the weight of those who pass by as they step on him."

From Catalano's description, I figured out this was Caiaphas, the High Priest, who sent the Divine Son off to Pilate to be executed. It was

Caiaphas who advised the Jewish council that it was expedient for *"one man [to] die for the people"* (John 18.14). Caiaphas' hypocrisy was stunning, but his punishment certainly fit the crime. Even though Caiaphas was naked (unlike the other sinners in their leaden cloaks), he was still weighed down as the travelers stepped on him to make their way down the path.[184]

Catalano continued, "In this way, Caiaphas' father-in-law, Annas, who was also complicit in the death of the Divine Son, suffers down here, too. He headed the council from which so much Jewish wickedness sprang up."

I looked as Virgil stood there marveling at Caiaphas stretched out on the cross. He couldn't take his eyes off the sight. Caiaphas looked so ignoble in his eternal banishment. But I couldn't figure out why it captivated Virgil so much. Hadn't he seen all this before?

Well, no, apparently. Virgil hadn't seen the Divine Son's crucifixion himself since he died in 19 BC. I think the reason Virgil reacted this way is because Caiaphas' statement that "it was expedient for one man to die" reminded Virgil of his own line in the *Aeneid* when he wrote, *"One man will give his head for many."*[185] He must have been disturbed at the similarity between his words and those of Caiaphas. It was all a little too close for comfort.

Virgil then aimed his words at the friars, saying, "Please don't let it displease you. Please tell us if, off to our right, there lies an opening where both of us can escape without the help of the black devils who are coming to haul us out from this depth."

Catalano replied, "You're nearer than you might think. You're approaching a ridge jutting out from the great circle that crosses the whole of the miserable valley. The only problem is that the bridge to get there has completely collapsed. You can climb over the ruins that lie along the sides and are bunched up at the bottom."

Virgil just stood there silently with his head bowed. He shook his head and said, "Evil Tail, who pokes sinners over there in the fifth ditch gave a completely misleading report of this place. I shouldn't have listened to him."

I thought to myself, "Virgil finally gets it. The Devils above, implicated in fraud, were not telling us the truth. The bridge to the sixth ditch was out all along and they were leading us to our doom. I suspected it from the start, but Virgil is just figuring it out."

The friar said, "At Bologna, I heard it said once about the devil's numerous vices that *"He's a liar and the father of lies"* (John 8.44).

You've got that right, I thought. Then, my leader departed with quick steps. He was disturbed in his spirit and had anger on his face.

We took our leave of those burdened sinners. I happily followed Virgil's dear footsteps. Virgil may have been fooled by the devils, but he was still my leader and I was sticking with him.

Comment

Canto Twenty-Three contains a clear example of *contrapasso*. Because Caiaphas sent Jesus off to Pontius Pilate to have him put to death, he now suffers by being endlessly crucified himself and trod upon. Caiaphas had lots of power, but used it for ill; now he is powerless and naked. His sin lies exposed for all to see.

But was Caiaphas a hypocrite? Caiaphas was no doubt threatened by Jesus. He was trying to maintain an uneasy peace between the Romans and the Jews in Jerusalem during Jesus' day. Jesus' apocalyptic claims and the resulting excitement of the crowds were not helping his plan for civic calm.

But we also have hints that Caiaphas was viewed unfavorably — even by fellow Jews in his day — because he was so power hungry and a collaborator with the Roman government. According to the historian Josephus, Caiaphas ruled for a record eighteen years as High Priest. This could not have happened without a close (and perhaps corrupt?) relationship with the Roman authorities. He was hypocritical to claim piety and yet sell out to the Romans. As a result, Caiaphas suffers in the ditch of the hypocrites.

There is an inherent irony in the key Biblical quote — *"It was expedient for one man to die for the people."* Caiaphas no doubt did not originally intend it, but he was proclaiming the Gospel while pronouncing Jesus guilty of blasphemy. One would die for all. Yet, in doing so, Caiaphas sowed the seeds of his own demise. Notice that Caiaphas spoke better than he knew. Now, he is the one being crucified in this Canto.

But why does Virgil express such wonder at the sight of Caiaphas on the cross? Virgil perhaps had no real familiarity with Christ's crucifixion. But this is an odd assertion because Virgil at other times has shown himself quite conversant with Christian theological ideas. Is it really likely that Virgil knows details about Christian theology, but has never heard of the resurrection or the crucifixion?[186]

As noted, Virgil is probably amazed at how his own text in the *Aeneid* anticipated the crucifixion.[187] This much seems likely. But one wonders if Virgil isn't thinking that perhaps *he's* the one who is going to have to sacrifice himself for Dante. After all, his powers of reason aren't working so well. They barely escaped the last ditch. How were they possibly going to navigate the Inferno?

One of the hardest things to figure out in this Canto is why Dante is so freaked out in the beginning. After all, has he not had enough experience in the Inferno to realize that he's under God's grace? The question we have to grapple with is whether Dante can really suffer harm or not.

Dante clearly thinks he can, which is why he is so scared. Dante and Virgil barely escape the clutches of Evil Tail and the rest of the demons. While the danger is real, Dante still has to learn something about God's grace. Heaven cares about him and will see him through this journey, even if it seems unlikely at times. Dante can recognize the danger of fraud, but apparently he still needs help having faith.

Interestingly, this Canto represents the only time Virgil gets angry because someone gets the best of him.[188] He's been upset before, but not tricked. This is probably why Catalano reminded us that the devil *"is a liar and the father of lies."*[189] Once again, Virgil is almost helpless in the face of pure evil. Reason is no match for a society turned on its head by fraud. Yet, by the end of the Canto, we come back to a sense of balance as Dante follows happily in Virgil's "dear" footsteps. Apparently reason knows plenty about hypocrisy.

Both Dante and Virgil do not seem up to the task at this point. Perhaps they're learning something about humility. Either God will see them through this journey or he won't. But heaven has promised to bring Dante along. He needs to learn to trust this. Yet Dante cannot do it on his own. This would seem to be the very opposite of hypocrisy, which desires to assert itself beyond where it should.

As a result, we end the Canto with a rare sight of Virgil's anger and a touching sight of Dante's exercising faith in Virgil, despite all they've been through. Reason and faith have been reunited as they continue their travels.

24

The Thieves (Part I)

MALEBOLGE VII: DITCHES 6-7

Dante begins the Canto shaken because of Virgil's recent misjudgments. Yet Virgil returns to himself and reconciles with Dante, thus restoring confidence. They encounter a series of naked thieves who are bound by serpents who have thrust themselves through the sinners' guts. The serpents, which represent deception, bind the thieves' hands that were used for stealing, and also penetrate their bodies, symbolic of the corruption of the body politic. One sinner spontaneously combusts and then comes back to life again, a kind of corrupt resurrection. He is forced to repeat this action over and over again for eternity, emblematic of the fluctuating nature of human endeavor. At the end of the Canto, Dante meets Vanni Fucci, a confessed thief from Pistoia who issues a prophecy about the demise of the White Guelfs specifically to injure Dante.

In the early part of the year, in January and February, the sun concentrates its rays under the waters of Aquarius as the night sky pivots south at the winter solstice.[190] During this season, the hoarfrost of the ground imitates the image of its snowy-white sister, but as it warms in the day, it doesn't last long.[191]

This is like a small peasant, who awakens and looks around to see a landscape blanched completely white. Upset because his things are hidden under the hoarfrost, he strikes his thigh and returns to the house, complaining everywhere he goes like a wretch not knowing what to do. Then, after a bit, he goes back outside and his hope revives again. He sees in a flash the world has changed its appearance once the frost melts. Then, taking his shepherds' staff, he drives his sheep to the pasture.

This is how my master disturbed me when I saw how troubled his brow was and how quickly the remedy reached the wound. For when we came to the broken-down bridge, my leader turned to me with a kindly, sweet look, which I had first seen near the foot of the mountain at the start of our journey.

I was speaking figuratively here about how Virgil had walked away from Catalano at the end of the last Canto.[192] I was still worried about Virgil's lack of understanding.[193] The hoarfrost on the ground was like Virgil's frown that melted away once we got away from the devils.[194] Yet nature, personified by the frost on the ground, was also a text from which we were supposed to learn something.[195] The problem was that Virgil kept taking the text too literally and was making mistakes. He was like the reader of a figurative text who had become confused by focusing only on the literal sense of it.[196]

In this simile, I was the humble wretch who didn't know what to do.[197] Once the deceptive cover of the frost had melted, I saw things for what they were, and was able to get my sheep to pasture and find safety. My hope resulted from perseverance in the midst of uncertainty.[198]

By contrast, that humble peasant was many things Virgil was not.[199] The peasant was simple and had faith. Virgil represented the glories of intellectual learning, but all he had to go on was reason.[200] This was a major cause of why our journey almost ended with the devils above. Virgil relied on reason too much. He had little faith. We had barely made it this far. I still had some hope I would make it through the Inferno, but not necessarily because of Virgil.

Then Virgil did something that restored my confidence. He took some time to think, carefully studied the ruins around us, like one who thinks as he acts, and who plans before he goes ahead. Virgil spread open his arms and hugged me, heaving me up to the top of the next ridge.[201] Thus Virgil made a display of the virtues of prudence, temperance and fortitude.

Virgil had his eye on a different crag of rocks. He told me to hold on carefully to the rocks, adding that I should first test them to see if they could hold my weight. I'll tell you what: this was no path for hypocrites with leaden cloaks. Even though, as a shade, Virgil didn't weigh a thing, and even though I was being pushed along, it was really difficult for us to go from one rock face to another.

In fact, if we had been on the other side that divides the sixth ditch from the seventh where the slope was substantially shorter, I don't know about Virgil, but I certainly would have been vanquished by it. But, since Malebolge slopes down toward the opening of the lowest shaft, the shape of the ditch required that one side be higher than the other. In other words, I think I only made it because the path was sloping downward most of the way.[202]

We finally came to the point where the last stone was rent asunder. My lungs were completely spent. I now needed to climb up a bit to get over the rock formation. Once I climbed up to the rock, I simply couldn't go any farther. I was done, finished, kaput. I sat down right away when I reached the ledge.

Virgil didn't like this move at all. He said, "You're going to have to cast off your sloth since sitting on feathered seats or under a warm blanket isn't going to bring you fame. After all, without fame, one who spends his life on earth leaves just a vestige of himself like smoke in the air or froth in the water."

Virgil continued, "So get up! Overcome anguish with the fortitude of soul that conquers every battle if it doesn't collapse under the weight of the body. Eventually, you're going to have to climb up a much longer stairway if you get to Mt. Purgatory.[203] It's not enough to leave the hypocrites behind. If you understand me, then get moving."

Virgil, of course, was right. I did need to get up and get moving. But I was completely exhausted. And yet on we went. After all, I certainly didn't want to stay down here. However, Virgil's reason to get going was curious. Like all Florentines, I wanted fame. But was I supposed to be seeking it?[204] Virgil seemed to have forgotten why I was on this journey in the first place.

Transition to the Seventh Ditch

So I got up. To be honest, I was just faking it. I was acting like I didn't need to rest and that I was feeling fine. In reality, everything hurt and I was still pretty tired. I then said to Virgil, "Let's go. I'm strong and hardy." I assume, since he could read my mind, Virgil knew I was lying as I asserted this.

We took a path along the rock ridge that was jagged, narrow and treacherous. It was even steeper than before. Thankfully, the rest had done me some good so I was no longer so out of breath.

I was talking to Virgil as we were going along, when a voice came out from the next ditch. It was a strange voice, almost inept at forming words. I had no idea what it was trying to say. While I was on the arch of the crossing, I think I saw the speaker moving.[205]

I was looking down, but my eyes couldn't see much because of the thick darkness below us. I said to Virgil, "Master, go on to the next bank and descend alongside the wall since, from here, I can't make out anything but muffled sounds. I can't see a thing."

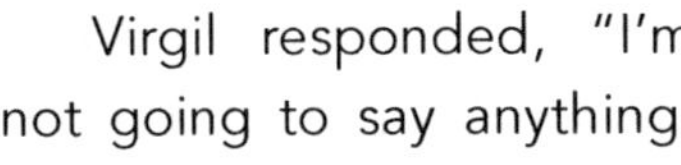

Virgil responded, "I'm not going to say anything, except to act. An honest request should be followed with quiet action, nothing more."

The Serpents

We descended down the bridge at the head where it's joined to the eighth bank. For the first time, I was able to see the seventh ditch. The sight stunned me.

I saw a terrible multitude of different kinds of serpents. The memory still chills my blood.[206] Let the Libyan sands not brag anymore. If Libya produced Chelydruses, Iaculuses, Pariases,

Cenchrises and Amphisbaenas, never did it have so many pestilential animals as I was seeing before me. Not throughout the whole of Ethiopia, nor even along the land above the Red Sea, were there this many poisonous snakes.

These snakes all came from classical literature. The Libyan sands were a reference to Ovid's story of Perseus' flight over the desert with the head of Medusa.[207] Perseus was just like me since he had been exiled and sentenced to death in his day.[208] All the rest were species of serpents that came from Lucan. These monsters were grotesque — not only in appearance, but also in name.[209]

Amidst this cruel and dismal profusion of serpents, naked and frightened sinners were running everywhere without hope of finding a hiding place or a heliotrope stone. This stone reportedly would make its bearer invisible.[210]

The sinners' hands were bound behind their backs with snakes, which then shoved their tails and heads through their guts, knotting themselves in front.[211] Thus the sinners' hands, which had been used for stealing and pickpocketing, were now of little use to them.[212]

One of the sinners was near us on the bank when a serpent darted up and pierced him right where the neck and the shoulders came together. You couldn't write an "O" or even an "I" in the time it took the sinner to combust and burn.

The sinner turned completely to ashes right before our eyes. It was like spontaneous combustion. His remains were lying there destroyed on the ground when suddenly his pulverized dust gathered itself up and he immediately became himself again. It was a distorted resurrection that seemed to be happening over and over again…for eternity.[213] I never thought the resurrection could be corrupted, but little down here surprised me anymore.

This sight was similar to Ovid's Phoenix that dies and then is reborn as its five-hundredth year approaches.[214] Through its life, the Phoenix grazes on neither grass nor grain, but only leaves droplets of frankincense and fragrant perfume behind; nard and myrrh occupy its last nest.[215]

The risen one was like someone who didn't know how he fell down, whether by demonic power that pulled him to the ground, or by another physical malady that made him pass out. But, when he got up and looked around, he was completely befuddled by the great distress he suffered. As he looked around, he sighed. This was similar to the sinner after he got up. Oh the power of God when he is firm, raining down vengeance with such blows!

Vanni Fucci

Virgil then asked him who he was. The sinner answered, "Not that long ago, I fell down here from Tuscany into this cruel gorge. I preferred the animal life to the human. I was just like an ass. I am Vanni Fucci. 'The Beast' was my nickname, and Pistoia was my worthy lair."

I said to Virgil, "Make sure you tell Vanni not to slip away. We can't trust him. Then ask him what specific fault has thrust him down here, since I knew him before as a bloody, violent man, not a thief."

Fucci was listening and didn't play-act, but directed his mind and face towards me. Painted with sad shame, he said, "You see this misery in me? It pains me more than if you had caught me before I was taken away from the other life."

Fucci continued, "I can't refuse your questions. I'm so far down here because I stole the valuable decorations from the sacristy and the blame was falsely affixed to another."

I knew Fucci had been a leader of the Black Guelfs in Pistoia. He reportedly was one of the thieves who broke into the church of San Zeno in Pistoia and tried to rob the chapel of San Jacopo of its solid-silver tables.[216] Fucci let several others rot in jail for a year before someone confessed that he was in on the infernal deed.[217] He was a snake if there ever was one.

After a pause, Fucci continued, "But so you don't enjoy this sight, I'm going to tell you something you're not going to like.[218] If you ever get out of this Inferno, open your ears to my prophecy and listen to what I have to say. The first thing is Pistoia is going to kick out all her Black Guelfs. This will affect Florence and will change its personnel and ways."

Fucci went on, "Then Mars will draw up a bolt from the Val di Magra, enveloped in chaotic clouds and with ferocious and bitter storms. The fighting will start at Camp Piceno. Quickly, the bolt will break through the clouds so that every White Guelf will be struck by it."

Fucci concluded, "I have told this to you so that it might sadden you. I hope it breaks your heart."[219]

Comment

This Canto finds the image of snakes joined with the theme of deception. The snake is a symbol of theft and, by extension, of deceit. We shouldn't miss the allusion to the biblical story of the Fall when the serpent was described as the "craftiest" of all the creatures God had made (Gen 3.1). As a symbol of deceit, the serpent in the Fall inflicted great damage on God's creation. Subsequent thieves did the same to whole societies.

In this Canto, Vanni Fucci didn't simply steal, but he robbed valuable items from the Church, engaged in deception to cover up his crime, and then let innocents rot in jail while he remained free. Thus Fucci is condemned for his deception as much as for his hubris in stealing from the Church. Such robbery transforms whole societies in a negative way.

When all authority breaks down (in both government and church), chaos is let loose in a society. Property rights are not respected, and the innocent are convicted of crimes they didn't commit. Thus the breakdown of order in a society is a very serious crime because, to the medieval mind, property was an extension of a person.[220] To steal property was like inflicting damage on the owner's physical body.[221] When this happens to the Church, the robber is inflicting damage on the body of Christ. Further, when a society's leaders allow this to happen for personal gain, this is a very grievous sin worthy of serious punishment.

This is why the imagery of the snakes that push their heads through the bodies of sinners is a powerful one. This is symbolic of what happens to the body politic when fraud infects all the major institutions of the society. Everything falls apart. Even the hope of resurrection is tainted in such a society.

What should we make of Fucci's prophecy at the end of the Canto? He offers it with the self-righteous glee of a sinner, and seems to be motivated to inflict harm on Dante as he issues it. He really wants Dante to suffer with his words.

Fucci predicts that the White Guelfs (Dante's party) will drive out the Black Guelfs in Pistoia. The Blacks will get revenge on the Whites by taking back control. This pattern will repeat itself in Florence. The Black Guelfs will throw out the Whites. This, of course, really happened in 1300 and led to Dante's exile. Thus Fucci is rubbing in the Blacks' victory over the Whites, an event that has caused Dante so much pain.

But this is not just about the corruption of individuals — it's about the corruption of the whole city. We learned in Canto Thirteen[222] that Mars, the God of war, was rejected as being the patron of the city of Florence in favor of John the Baptist.[223] Mars will get his revenge when the leaders of the White Guelfs, including Dante, are thrown out of Florence.

The vapor drawn from the Val di Magra is a reference to Moroello Malaspina, a Guelf military leader, whom Vanni predicts will be the agent of the White Guelf demise when he takes their armed fort. [224] This will happen at Camp Piceno, a likely reference to the plains of Pistoia.[225]

Thus the Canto ends the opposite way to how it began. What began as a pastoral scene of reconciliation, ends in war and societal breakdown. This is what robbery, fraud and deception do to a society.[226] It has not only ruined Dante's life; it has ruined the body politic as well.

25

The Thieves (Part II)

MALEBOLGE VIII: DITCH 7

Vanni Fucci concludes his antics by making an obscene gesture directed at God. When he does, a set of snakes devour him. We then meet Cacus, a kind of Centaur, who was famous for theft in one of Lucan's tales. Next, several shades experience transformations, one group that combines natures (Cianfa and Agnello) and another that mutates their natures (Francesco and Buoso). In the end, the breakdown of order in the society, brought about by theft, leads to loss of all permanence. Not even one's nature can be preserved.

When Vanni was finished, he lifted up both his hands with clenched fists, his thumb shoved between his index and middle fingers.[227] In an outburst of angry defiance, he shook his raised fists and yelled, "Up yours, Yahweh! Look here, I've shaped my figs just for you!"

I couldn't believe what I had just seen and heard. Vanni's obscene gesture was like giving the Master the finger. It was so offensive that several neighboring cities had outlawed this gesture entirely.[228] In fact, most knew that his outburst about his shaped figs was a subtle reference to a woman's vagina.[229] You couldn't get much more blasphemous than this. If Fucci was done being violent, it certainly didn't seem like it.[230]

From then on, the serpents banded together like friends. One wrapped himself around Vanni's neck as if to say, "I won't let him speak anymore," while another bound his arms, wrapping him so tight that Fucci couldn't even move his limbs.

Oh, Pistoia, Pistoia, why don't you just go incinerate yourself? Get it over with. How can you survive anymore since you've so obviously surpassed your ancestors in wickedness? In thinking this, I was deliberately patterning my rebuke after the Divine Son when he cried out, *"Oh Jerusalem, Jerusalem, killing the prophets and stoning those who are sent to you"* (Matt 23.37).

I have to say, through all the murky circles of the Inferno we had travelled, I hadn't seen any shade act so haughtily toward the Creator, not even the blasphemer Capaneus.[231] What I had just seen was far worse — Vanni wasn't just an individual blasphemer like Capaneus. Oh no, he represented what it was like when an entire society starts blaspheming.[232] The results are catastrophic.

Cacus

Fucci fled without uttering another word. Right after he left us, I saw a Centaur, half-man and half-horse, who was full of rage.[233] He came looking for Vanni, asking in a snarling tone, "Where is he? Where's the green one?" The Centaur was acting like the Maker when he was looking for Adam and Eve after the Fall in the Garden, asking, *"Where are you"* (Gen 3.9)?

I don't even think Maremma, the swampy area in Tuscany infested with serpents, had so many snakes as the Centaur bore on his back all the way from the rump of the horse to where the human part begins.[234] On his shoulders, at the back part of his neck, was a dragon with its wings spread. It could incinerate anything it encountered.

Virgil said, "This is Cacus. He's the one who time and again left a trail of blood in the cave at the Aventine Hill. He doesn't go with his brethren on the road because he fraudulently stole the great herd that was grazing nearby. His crooked works ceased under the club of

Hercules who thumped him a hundred times, even if he felt perhaps only ten of them."

A fire-breathing dragon, Cacus was the offspring of Vulcan, who lived in a cave and wreaked havoc on the inhabitants of the area surrounding the Aventine Hill in Rome.[235] It was well-known in mythology that Cacus had stolen some of Hercules' cattle.[236] As soon as Hercules found out about the theft, he killed Cacus with his club, beating him over and over again, even after he was dead.[237] This is why he only felt about ten of the blows. I couldn't help but notice once again the combination of violence and theft.

While Virgil was still speaking, Cacus ran by — along with three shades — on the bank beneath us.[238] Since we couldn't see them, neither Virgil nor I really noticed them until they shouted, "Who are *you*?" At this, our discourse ceased and we paid attention to them alone.

Cianfa and Agnello (Mutation of Natures)

I had no idea who the three shades were, but it so happened, like it often does by chance, that one proceeded to name the other, saying "Where did Cianfa go?"

I was pretty sure this Cianfa was a son from the powerful Donati family in Florence.[239] Corso Donati, Cianfa's father, was the leader of the Black Guelfs in Florence.[240]

I really wanted Virgil to pay attention to this so I put my index finger over my lips, barely touching my nose, as a gesture that we should be quiet and watch.

Dear Reader, if you're finding it hard to believe what I've recounted to you so far, let me encourage you — don't marvel at this. I really saw what I've written down, even if I could hardly believe my eyes.

As I kept gawking at them while looking down on the ditch below,[241] a reptile with six short legs launched itself toward another shade and clung to him everywhere he went.[242] With its middle feet, the reptile gripped the shade's tummy. Then, with its front feet, it seized his arms, puncturing both his cheeks with its fangs. Then, the reptile distended its rear feet and shoved its tail through both thighs, straightening itself out over the shade's backside.

Although no one's identity was clear, I think it was Cianfa, who had morphed into the serpent, who then attacked the shade.[243] This is why the other two shades were looking for him before, but couldn't find him.[244] They didn't expect him to come at them in the form of a reptile!

This is how confused things were. Not even a shade's form was safe! It was almost like someone was stealing what was supposed to be changeless.

No ivy ever clung so tightly to a tree as that horrible serpent entwined itself around the other's members. They were wrapped together so compactly that it was like they were made from hot wax that mixed its colors and produced something new.[245] The result was that neither appeared as it was at first.

This combination was also like a scrap of parchment combusting. A brownish color comes before the flame. It's no longer black, but it also makes the white of the parchment die out.

Meanwhile, the other two shades were checking things out. Each was shouting, "Oh no, Agnello, look how you're changing! Already, you're neither two nor one."

I'm pretty sure this Agnello was from the Ghibelline Brunelleschi family in Florence.[246] He was reportedly a thief who hid his identity during his crimes.[247] I guess this is why the reptile was so quick to change his identity; it was part of his punishment.[248]

If I've got this all straight, apparently it was Cianfa, transformed into a snake, who had attacked Agnello, the thief. When they mixed themselves together, you couldn't even tell what they were anymore, man or beast. It was like they were mixed up in some sort of sexual embrace.

Their two heads became one when their two forms melded together into one face, wherein both were lost. Their four appendages became two arms, the thighs melded into legs, the tummy with the chest. The body parts became appendages never witnessed before. Each original appearance was quashed. Each perverse image appeared to be both alike and unlike at the same time. With slow steps the grotesque, mutated creature slunk away.

This was all beyond comprehension to me. How could someone, even a shade, combine its form with another? How could a reptile, which used to be human, turn back into a mixture of beast and man?[249] Nothing was stable. Everything was flux. This truly was hell.

Francesco and Buoso (Union of Natures)

As a green lizard under the harsh conditions of summer moves between one hedge and another, crossing the road in a flash, so a fiery serpent appeared, whizzing toward the bellies of the other two thieves. The serpent was livid, black as a granule of pepper.

One of the serpents latched onto the shade's belly button and then fell down, outstretched toward him. The one was staring in a kind of daze, but didn't say anything. Since his feet stopped, he was yawning like sleep or a fever was overtaking him. Maybe the yawning was the result of an infernal snakebite.[250]

The serpent and he were eyeing one another, one through his wound, the other through his mouth. Thick smoke was pouring out of both as their natures clashed.

The smoke here was like a corrupt spirit, which once again was confusing the natures of beast and shade.[251] Yet another metamorphosis was going on before our eyes, but this time, it was even worse.

Lucan had once described the physical metamorphosis of poor old Sabellus and Nasidius who were Roman soldiers in Cato's army.[252] Sabellus was stung by a venomous snake, which caused his body to deteriorate in the Libyan Desert.[253] Something similar happened to Nasidius, except his body swelled up before he died. However,[254] Lucan's tales couldn't compare to what I saw next.

In fact, Ovid's tales of Cadmus, who was turned into a serpent;[255] and of Arethusa, who was turned into a fountain,[256] couldn't even come close to what I saw.

Never before did anyone see two natures, one shade and one beast, completely mixed together so that both their forms actually exchanged their substances. I know, it sounds impossible, but I saw this!

Let me describe what I observed. The reptile split its tail into a fork, which it then used to join the wounded shade's feet together. The shade's legs and his thighs were then tied together so tightly that there was no sign of a juncture. The split tail then took on the shape of the lost shade. Further, its reptile hide softened even as the skin of the shade became hard and scaly.

This wasn't all. I saw the arms of the shade being drawn in at his armpits, while the two feet of the beast, that had been short, become as long as the shade's. Then, the shade's legs shortened into that of a reptile. The hind feet of the reptile twisted together and became the penis of a man, while the penis of the man turned into the two back paws of the reptile. The two turned into each other! What an ugly sight!

As this was happening, the smoke was obfuscating the two creatures. I couldn't tell which was which. I guess this was emblematic of the obfuscation they used to hide their thieving activities in the world above.[257]

Each also took on different sets of color. One generated human hair, while the other saw it peel off. One of them got up, while the other fell down. One's face became a reptile's, while the other's became a man's.

The one who stood upright grew some ears that looked like they spontaneously popped out of his upper cheeks. They came out from the excess flesh that was around his temples. The flesh that wasn't used for the ears then became a nose for his face, while lips jutted out to an appropriate thickness.

The one lying on the ground pushed out his nose and drew in his ears to his head. He looked like a snail pulling in its horns. Moreover, his tongue, which was previously whole, and ready to speak, suddenly split while the other's forked tongue joined and became smooth. At this, with the metamorphosis complete, the smoke ceased. They had transmuted into completely different creatures, having exchanged their natures.[258]

The shade who had become a beast took off through the valley hissing as he went. The other directed his spit towards him. It was a pathetic sight. The reptile who had turned into a shade was trying to spit out poison even though he didn't have any, so ingrained were his habits.[259] Where words should have come out, only unintelligible sounds came forth.

Then he turned his new shoulders and said to Puccio, "I want Buoso to run on all fours along the bottom of the ditch like I've had to do for ages."

I'm not even really sure who this Buoso was. I knew some Buosos in my day in Florence, but I couldn't always tell who was who down here.

So I saw the full panoply of beasts down here in this seventh ditch do nothing but change and then change again. I'm sorry that I've spent so much time describing this spectacle. I fear it has caused me to transgress as I write.

Although my eyes were pretty confused and my mind bewildered, I wasn't going to let some of these sinners get away that easily without being called out. I could plainly make out Puccio Sciancato who, alone among the three companions I encountered at the beginning of the Canto, had not been changed. The other was Francesco de' Cavalcanti from the town of Gaville, who just makes you want to weep.[260]

Comment

This Canto manages to be both complex and straightforward at the same time. Canto Twenty-Five continues the theme of theft from Canto

Twenty-Four, but examines it corporately. We observe the damage done to the society when property isn't respected.

Dante carries this breakdown to its chaotic conclusion when he shows that even the very nature of a person — which is supposed to be changeless — can be completely transformed into the classic symbol of sin, a serpent.[261] Those who engage in theft have lost their humanity to the point where they have brought ruin to the good order of community.

At the same time, however, Canto Twenty-Five can be very confusing. It's hard to keep straight all the changing characters and their forms.

But this is the point. This Canto is supposed to be confusing because theft confuses everything.[262] I have tried to keep some of the ambiguity Dante intended, while providing enough clarity to make it readable for those not very familiar with the poem. Beware, however: I've made this much clearer than the original.

Dante wants us to conclude from this episode that this world of the *Inferno* is impossible and utterly unlivable.[263] Things are not supposed to work this way. But, in the presence of sin, everything gets upended.

There are two basic transformations that occur. In the first, Cianfa and Agnello morph into a completely new creature, thus mutating their natures.[264] When Francesco and Buoso, the other two thieving shades, notice the transformation, they exclaim to Agnello that he is no longer "two nor one." They're saying that his being has been completely corrupted.[265] In essence, Agnello has ceased to bear the Divine Image and has been reduced to nothing.[266]

On the other hand, Buoso and Francesco combine natures to form something new.[267] But, this doesn't happen just once. It seems to be an on-going process.[268] Everything becomes confused when property isn't respected in the society.

Thus, to Dante, theft is not about the material goods stolen as much as it is about the damage done spiritually both to an individual and a society that does not protect property. We shouldn't forget that to the medieval mind, property was an extension of the person. Thus a culture of theft affects the entire society.

One only has to look at certain developing countries to observe the profound damage done to a society infected with fraud or theft. When no one can trust each other, it destroys industry, creativity and efficiency in a city or a country. A select few often get very wealthy in such a system. But the society as a whole suffers. Thus Dante's analysis anticipates the corrupt societies even of our day.

26

Fraudulent Counsel (Part I)

MALEBOLGE IX: DITCH 8

"Rejoice, O Florence, since you're so great. You beat your wings through sea and land so that your name resonates throughout the entire Inferno!"

I was saying this ironically, of course.[269] The reason Florence resounds throughout the Inferno is because she's doomed.[270] It seems like I've met half her citizens down here. Given all the fraud in Florence's midst and her clear penchant for injustice, the city's greatness is just a mirage. In fact, Florence's huge wings were a kind of foreshadowing of the devil himself.[271]

I continued, "Just among the thieves in the last ditch, I found five of your citizens, all from decent families.[272] And, you, despite your venerable reputation, won't recover your former greatness. Yet, as morning nears, if dreams come to you, you'll experience what Prato and others crave for you a short time from now."

Prato was a town close to Florence.[274] But I was really referring to all the towns in and around Tuscany.[275] None were particularly virtuous since they were ruled by Florentine authority which was corrupt.

As most in my day were aware, dreams that occurred right before dawn carried the greatest prophetic power. I was sure Florence was going to face tough times ahead.[6273]

I continued, "And if that disaster had already come to you, it wouldn't be too soon. Would that it had come, since disaster certainly must come! And it will weigh on me more as I grow old."

This disaster I was foreseeing was a terrible fire that would come to Prato in 1304, ignited by Pope Benedict XI.[276] The fire was to burn over two-thousand houses and to destroy countless families. If both the church and the government are corrupt, it can bring about great misery.[277] The older I was getting, the more suffering I kept encountering, while waiting for divine justice to come. [278] I'm still waiting even now.

Describing the Eighth Ditch

Virgil and I then departed. We were on the stairs that previously left me breathless and pale while we were descending. Virgil pulled me close to him and heaved me up onto the bridge.[279] We went on our way alone between the rock reefs and the outcroppings. It was narrow enough that our feet weren't able to make headway without the help of our hands.

I was grieved before, but now, I grieve even more as my thoughts processed what I saw next. In fact, I'm going to curb my creative powers more than usual, certainly more than the last couple of Cantos, lest I let them run without virtue to guide them. There's little room for great literary flourishes amidst the ruin of the seemingly noble men I found down here.[280]

In fact, even if the constellation Gemini, or one superior, had granted me its own great wit,[281] I wouldn't deprive myself of the same. I was really trying to not to get lured into the same boundless rhetoric I would encounter from the sinners in this ditch.[282]

There were an awful lot of souls down here. I felt like a peasant, resting in peaceful repose on top of a mountain, around the time of the summer solstice when the sun was out in full force.[283] It looked like early evening when the fly gives way to the mosquito.

Then this peasant sees a bunch of fireflies down in the valley, perhaps as he harvests grapes or tills the ground. The sinners were as numerous in my sight as the fireflies were to the peasant.[284] It was so bright from the light of the flames, I could even make out the bottom of the ditch.

I was picturing this peasant as a kind of model of salvation, as one resting on top of a steep hill, the arduous portion of his spiritual journey complete.[285] Of course, I was hoping to be that peasant, but his repose was very different than the sinners I encountered in this ditch. When I saw the peasant overlooking his vineyard, I realized this was a symbol of the Christian Church at rest.[286]

This light I was observing must have been what it was like for those who watched Elijah when he "***went up by a whirlwind into heaven***" (2 Ki 2.11). Elisha, his successor, was thereafter mocked by some young boys who were then killed when "***two she-bears came out of the woods and tore forty-two of the boys to pieces***" (2 Ki 2.24). The boys doubted Elisha's prophetic authority, just like Florence was now doubting mine.[287]

As Elisha watched Elijah's chariot departing for heaven, he couldn't follow it with his eyes as the horses lifted up toward heaven because he could see nothing except the flames. The chariot was hidden within them. The horses were ascending upward like a small cloud in a similar way to how each flame moved through the narrow neck of the ditch down here.

To be sure, I was no Elijah (I was journeying through the Inferno, after all), but I felt like his successor Elisha must have, as one who was bearing witness to what he saw.[288] The flames in the ditch managed to move while concealing each one's larceny. In a remarkable sight, each flame enveloped the sinners within it.

A Perverted Pentecost

I was standing on top of the bridge looking down below. If I hadn't grabbed onto a rock, I could have fallen down to the ditch below without being pushed. There were flames cloaked the sinners.

Virgil noticed me standing there longing to understand what was below. He said, "The spirits are within the flames; each is wrapped in that which burns him."

This was a remarkable sight. It was like the inner passions of each sinner were externalized and were now scorching them forever.[289] The flames reminded me of the Biblical scene from Pentecost when "*divided tongues of fire appeared to them and rested on each one of them*" (Acts 2.2, ESV). The difference, of course, was that the Spirit who was in the tongues of fire at Pentecost was nowhere to be found in this place.

These tongues of fire represented both the gift of prophecy as well as the rhetorical ability that communicated it.[290] As St. Peter put it when describing King David's anticipation of resurrection, "*Being therefore a prophet and knowing that God had sworn with an oath to him that he would set one of his descendants upon his throne, [David] foresaw and spoke of the resurrection*" (Acts 2.30-31).

I responded to Virgil, "I'm more assured to hear you say this about the flames. But I'm also not surprised; this was already what I thought. I want to ask you, who is in that flame that is so divided on top it seems to be rising up from the funeral pyre where Eteocles was laid with his brother?"

Eteocles was the son of Oedipus (king of Thebes) and Jocasta.[291] Having forced Oedipus to abdicate the throne, Eteocles and his twin-brother Polynices took power, agreeing to trade off rule at one-year intervals.[292] But, when Eteocles' term ended, he refused to leave the throne, resulting in a conflict with his brother. This led to their killing each other.[293]

Most in my day thought of Thebes as the archetypal tragic city.[294] Even the normally-joyous idea of birth was corrupted when these brothers turned against their father and killed each other. This was as far away from virtue as I could imagine.

Ulysses and Diomed

Virgil said, "Inside that flame, Ulysses and Diomed are tormented together and thus they go on toward the vengeance of the Master and his wrath. Within a single flame they bemoan the trickery of the Trojan horse that fashioned the door where the noble seed of the Romans came forth. This was their first crime."

In the famous story of the Trojan horse, the Greeks made the Trojans believe they were sick of war after ten years of inconclusive fighting and were about to sail home.[295] They elected Sinon to sell the ruse, claiming the Greeks left the giant horse as a peace offering to the people of Troy.[296]

Ulysses, ever the clever one, convinced the Greek soldiers to hide themselves in the horse. Apparently Diomed, king of Argo, was in on the deal.[297] When the horse, over the strenuous objections of the Trojan Calchas, was wheeled into the city of Troy, this enabled the Greeks to gain access and burn the place to the ground.[298] Out of this disaster, Aeneas and his crew left Troy and made their circuitous voyage to go establish Rome.

Virgil continued, "Within the flames, Ulysses and Diomed together weep for their fraudulent craft since they both bear the guilt of the Palladium. This was their second crime."

The Palladium was a statue of Athena that Ulysses and Diomed stole from Troy as they were fleeing. In Virgil's version of the story, Aeneas made off with this Palladium to secure Athena's favor when he founded the city of Rome. This was clearly an impious act on Aeneas' part.[299]

Virgil said," In death, Deidamia still mourns for Achilles. This was their third crime."

Deidamia was the daughter of the King of Scyros.[300] The sea nymph Thetis, aware of the prophecy that her son Achilles would die in Troy, left him among the daughters of the king, disguised as a woman to keep him out of the war.[301] This ruse failed.

Achilles ended up impregnating Deidamia. When Achilles was lured away to war by the persuasive Ulysses, Deidamia died of grief.[302] Thus, in all three crimes, fraudulent counsel was the source of great misery to many.

I asked Virgil, "Can they speak within those flames? I'm going to ask you again; please, I beg you, don't make me stay here and wait for the split flame to come over here. You can see how I bend toward it with desire."

Virgil said, "Your prayer is worthy of much praise and I will yet accept it. But you simply must stay your tongue. I think I know what you want. Since we're dealing with untrustworthy Greeks, they might just shirk your words when they hear your speech."

I couldn't be sure, but I think Virgil was saying that one could only address these Greeks in the lofty style of classical rhetoric.[303] As I had already observed, the fraudulent nobility can sound very convincing.[304]

Since I had curtailed my speech to protect myself from the sin I was observing, I figured I would just let Virgil take the lead. Being Italian and thus a descendent of Troy, the Greeks would probably hate me anyway, as soon as they heard my accent.[305]

When the flame had come close, and Virgil thought the time was right, I heard him speaking this way: "O you who are two within one flame; if I have merited your consideration while I lived and if I have merited your consideration as I wrote my lofty verses while in the world, don't move away. But please, one of you, tell me where you went, lost, to die."

The larger horn of that old flame began to shake and murmur. It was like a flame, wearied by the wind, which waves its tip here and there as if it were a tongue speaking."

On the surface, the larger horn was a reference to Ulysses, whose greater stature within the flame was noticeable. But it was also a reference to Daniel's prophecy from the Bible when "*the he-goat magnified himself exceedingly; but when he was strong, the great horn was broken and instead of it there came up four conspicuous horns toward the four winds of heaven*" (Dan 8.7-8). As the prophet Daniel later pointed out (Dan 8.21), the he-goat represents the kingdom of the Greeks and the big horn was a reference to its great leader, Alexander the Great. Just as Alexander won for himself great fame through his military craft, so Ulysses became famous in war, as well.[306]

The big-horned flame opened up his voice and said, "My story begins with the enchantress Circe, the daughter of Helios, god of the sun, and Perse, a nymph.[307] For over a year, Circe kept me near Gaeta before Aeneas named it so."

I thought this was a bit ironic that Ulysses was using the name for the island that Aeneas had coined. It was almost like Ulysses was trying to stand in the shoes of Aeneas as he told this tale.[308]

Ulysses went on, "Nothing could overcome the ardor that was within me, not sweetness for my son, nor duty to my aged father, nor my love promised to Penelope, which would have pleased her. No, nothing could keep me from experiencing the world and learning about the vices and worth of men."

This was interesting. For Ulysses, it was all about his lust for experience and knowledge. On his voyage, he wasn't seeking greater knowledge of himself or even enhanced virtue. He just wanted to know what was unknown. He seemed to be mistaking knowledge for the possession of virtue.[309]

Ulysses continued, "But setting out onto the high seas, I only had one ship and a small company of mates made up of those who hadn't deserted. From one shore to the other, I saw as far as Spain and Morocco, the island of Sardinia and the others washing into that sea."

"My mates and I were old and slow when we came upon the Strait of Gibraltar where Hercules positioned his markers that prevented men from going out any father. On the right hand, I left Seville in Spain. On the left, I had already departed the city of Ceuta in Morocco."

Once again, this was remarkable. What Ulysses was confessing was that he had transgressed all boundaries set for him. No one was supposed to go beyond Hercules' markers, since they indicated the end of the world. And, yet, here was Ulysses admitting he did that very thing on his voyage, thus arrogantly transgressing the limits of knowledge set by the gods.

Ulysses said, "O brothers, who for one-hundred-thousand perils have come to the west, to this fleeting vigil of our senses left to us, you don't want to deny yourselves the experience of the sun beyond the unpeopled world, do you? Consider your origins: you weren't made to live like beasts. You were made to pursue virtue and knowledge!"

What soaring rhetoric, I thought. No wonder Ulysses' shipmates signed up to go with him.[310] He could sound convincing, but great virtue is not the same thing as great rhetorical ability.[311] Ulysses didn't seem to realize this. His mates followed a bad counsellor to their doom.

Ulysses said, "I caused my mates to be so keen to follow me on the journey with this short speech, that afterwards I could barely hold them back. Turning our stern to the east, we made wings out of our oars for our mad flight, always gaining on the port side."

Ulysses, I thought, was certainly right. This was a mad flight. But, then again, so was my journey. The big difference was that mine was enabled by grace while Ulysses' was enabled by his boundless passions.[312] Ulysses' unbridled passion was literally consuming him. Perhaps this was the reason he was consigned to burn eternally within a flame.

Ulysses continued, "When we crossed the equator, the night passed the other pole.[313] Its stars and our own were so low that they didn't rise above the ocean floor. Five months passed when the light under the moon waxed and waned until we came upon a high brown mountain. In the distance it seemed loftier than any other I had seen."

"We immediately cheered, but our joy quickly turned to tears when, out of the new land, a whirlwind arose that accosted the prow of the ship. Three times it made her turn with all the waters. At the fourth, the stern rose to high heaven and the prow plunged beneath until the sea closed up over us, sinking the ship."

This was just like the Psalmist had described: "*Some went down to the sea in ships, doing business on the great waters; they saw the deeds of the Lord and his wondrous works in the deep for he commanded, and raised the stormy wind, which lifted up the waves of the sea. They mounted up to heaven, they went down to the depths; their courage melted away in their evil plight; they reeled and staggered like drunken men, and were at their wits' end*" (Ps 107.23-27).

Ulysses' lack of restraint had sealed his doom.[314]

Comment

Dante's vivid depiction of Ulysses' journey and ultimate doom is one of the most famous scenes in the *Comedy*. Further, the poetry in this section is perhaps the greatest of the entire work. When Dante tells us at the beginning of the Canto that he is going to hold back on his talent (literally, his genius), this is an example of his stunning artistic achievement. Coming off the high poetic style of the last couple of Cantos, where he surpassed the poetic abilities of those who had come before him, Dante now restrains his poetry with great economy of vocabulary and simplicity of style. Yet the result is even more powerful. Few poets have been able to pull off what Dante has done here.

It might be helpful to realize that Dante essentially makes up his own version of the famous story of Ulysses' journey. In case it's not clear, Ulysses is the Latinized name of Odysseus, the star of Homer's *Odyssey*. Dante had no access to Homer since it had not yet been translated from Greek into Latin in Dante's day. So Dante is drawing on sources as diverse as Virgil, Horace, Statius and Ovid for his depiction of what happens. He picks and chooses what he wants from these sources, and draws his own conclusions.

In Dante's day, Ulysses was seen as the ultimate hero. He was smart, resourceful and loyal. He returned to his wife Penelope in Ithaca who faithfully waited for him even when she thought he was dead, spurning other suiters in the process. Even Ulysses' dog Argos was loyal and faithful. Thus Ulysses represented the ideal virtuous hero. He exhibited most of the classic philosophical virtues such as temperance, courage, wisdom and justice.

But Dante doesn't see it like this. He upends the classical view of Ulysses by depicting him as someone who arrogantly transgressed natural boundaries, thus leading those around him to their deaths. Ulysses' bad counsel results in disaster for his crew and ultimately for himself since he is consigned to one of the lowest reaches in the Inferno. Whereas Elijah, Elisha, David and Daniel humbled themselves before God, Ulysses transgressed natural constraints (the markers of Hercules) in a mad rush for knowledge.

Dante appears to be drawing on Augustine's critique of curiosity in this Canto, a critique that had lasting significance throughout the Middle Ages.[315] Writing in the *Confessions,* Augustine thought curiosity was a problem that the untrammeled lust for knowledge created.[316] The problem was not knowledge itself (since all truth first comes from God), but the potential for excessiveness that can attach to the pursuit of knowledge.[317] Hence the mad pursuit of knowledge outside of the love of God can lead one toward sin, not toward human flourishing.

Ulysses' pursuit of knowledge ends in the tragedy of self-deception.[318] He takes the good gifts that God had given to him and twists them for his own glory, thus transgressing the bounds of reason and propriety set by God himself.

We see the tragedy of this in the end. Once Ulysses has gone past Hercules' markers, he comes upon a tall, brown mountain. Dante recognizes this mountain because it's the one that began the Inferno, the hill Dante tried to climb on his own before being forcefully repelled by three sinful beasts. As we will learn later, this is the mountain of Purgatory, the hill Dante will have to climb in the second stage of his spiritual journey.

In fact, Ulysses comes up in all three sections of the *Comedy.* Dante will allude to Ulysses right at the beginning of *Purgatorio* when he reaches the shore that Ulysses couldn't reach. Then, when Dante makes it to heaven, Ulysses comes up yet again. Dante ends up seeing God face to face because his own "mad journey" is enabled by grace. In contrast, Ulysses spends eternity within the flame of his desire since he did not respect the boundaries that God had set for him.[319]

Thus this Canto presents an important dichotomy between salvation and damnation. Ulysses was one of the greatest of God's creatures, endowed with wit, talent, courage and cleverness. Ulysses employs these gifts to trick others for his own pleasure. He comes up with the idea of the Trojan horse to trick the Trojans. He convinces his crew to follow him into unknown waters, leading to their deaths. Ulysses, one of the cleverest literary characters ever created, did not care about those under his charge. At least in Dante's view, he is worthy of condemnation, not approbation.

Yet Dante himself was a great poet on a mad journey, who in the preceding Cantos had surpassed everyone else in poetic talent and skill. He had just finished showing off his remarkable abilities. But, unlike Ulysses, Dante reins it in so that he might learn something. Dante has made it this far with God's enablement and his own decision to trust God's sanctifying grace rather than his own genius.

The difference between salvation and damnation is inches, not miles. The difference is whether we, as readers, will have courage to humble ourselves, recognize our limitations and be grateful for constraints. This embrace of limitation is the sign of spiritual maturity. This maturity Ulysses sorely lacks.

Dante keeps learning and growing. He humbles himself here, accepting limits for his own good. This enables his journey to continue.

27

Fraudulent Counselors (Part II)

MALEBOLGE X: DITCH 8

Dante encounters another fraudulent counselor, Guido da Montefeltro, a military leader who repented and became a Franciscan monk. Guido accuses Pope Boniface VIII of causing him to go against his monastic vows by threatening excommunication and by forcing him to give military counsel to the Pontiff in the midst of a conflict with the Colonna family. After his death, St. Francis came down to the Inferno to rescue Guido, but was repelled by a fallen Angel, thus showing that Guido's repentance was suspect. Justice without virtue threatens the very foundations of society and causes great confusion among its citizens and saints.

When the flame that enclosed Ulysses' tongue went silent, it ceased flickering and started moving away with dear Virgil's consent.[320] But, just then, another flame came, appearing just behind where Ulysses' flame had been. The prattle spewing out from the new flame caught our attention and caused our eyes to fixate on its tip.

The sight of the flame reminded me of the bronze Sicilian bull that the artist Perillus sculpted for Phalaris, the tyrannical ruler of Syracuse.[321] This contraption was designed to torture Phalaris' enemies by roasting them alive within the sculpted beast.[322] While inside, the tortured would emit cries that sounded like bellowing bulls.[323]

This situation was similar because the one within the flame was bellowing like a victim in pain. There was so much clamor, it sounded like a brazen bull was being agonizingly stabbed. This is the closest thing I could think to describe what it sounded like to hear the soul contained within the flame crying out to us.

What started out as incomprehensible shrieks without means of escape were eventually changed into conventional language, albeit words I couldn't make out particularly well. Once the shrieks made their way up to the tip of the flame, the flame would flicker like a tongue producing speech.

Here, we were observing tongues of fire, just like we had with Ulysses previously. Once again, the perversion of the miracle at Pentecost was at work. Whereas the tongues of fire at Pentecost brought spiritual life, the lying tongues in this ditch brought death.

Guido da Montefeltro

While watching the flickering of the flame, we heard it say, "You over there. I'm talking to you, who just now was speaking with Ulysses in the Lombard dialect, saying, 'Now go on; I ask for nothing more.'"

By this, I realized the flame was addressing Virgil directly. Virgil was the only one who could really understand the dialect of Lombardy, where he was from.

The voice continued, "Maybe I've arrived too late, but please rest with me a while here. You can note it doesn't irk me. And, as you can see, I'm burning in this flame."

The voice within the flame went on, "If just now you've fallen into this blind dark world from that sweet Italian land from which I carry all my guilt, tell me if Romagna makes peace or war. I was from the hills between Urbino and the Apennine mountains where the Tiber finds it source."

I inferred once again that shades in the *Inferno* had no knowledge of current events, which is why they were so eager to learn of what was happening above. From the details the voice had given, I realized this was none other than Guido da Montefeltro, one of the great leaders of the Ghibellines.[324]

Count Guido was a famous military man, whose strategic prowess enabled him to control the Italian region of Romagna in the latter part of the thirteenth century.[325] As a good Ghibelline, Guido had been an antagonist of the Papacy. But he had made peace with the Church at the end of his life, becoming a Franciscan friar and taking up the monastic life.

However, Pope Boniface VIII got Guido to go against his Franciscan vows of non-violence by calling on him for military advice in order to repel the powerful Colonna family from their stronghold in Palestrina. The Colonnas had questioned the circumstances around Boniface's rise to the Papacy.[326] I thought there had always been something sinister in the way Celestine V, his predecessor, had abdicated the Papacy. The conflict that ensued ultimately led to Guido's death at the battle of Campaldino in 1298.[327] The peace of Romagna had not yet been negotiated when Guido was killed in battle.[328]

Because Guido was a little hard to understand, speaking as he was from within the flame, I had been straining toward him to hear. But Virgil pulled me aside and said, "You speak to this one; he's Italian and can understand you."

Now this was new. After all, Virgil had done almost all the talking to Ulysses in the last Canto because they were speaking in a Lombard dialect. Their lofty rhetoric was too much for me. But, now, Guido was speaking in unadorned Italian. Guido was a whole lot more verbose than Ulysses ever was.[329]

Reporting Current Events

I was glad for the chance to talk to this suffering soul about what was going on in the world. In fact, I already had my reply ready. Without delay, I began saying, "O soul hidden within the flame, your Romagna is not (and never was) without war, at least within the hearts of your princes. That said, there's no open warfare that I have to report right now. The region is at peace."

I continued, "Ravenna is like it was for many years. Guido Vecchio, the head of the Polenta family, broods over the region still, so that he covers up the small town of Cervia on the Adriatic with his wings."[330]

I went on, "The land that endured the long siege at Forli, the Ghibelline fortress, which ended in a massacre of French Nobles, who were put to rest in a bloody heap, finds itself under the control of the Ordelaffi family and its distinctive green lion crest."[331]

I continued, "The old ruler of Rimini, Malatesta, along with his son, Malatestino, governed cruelly (as was their custom) from their family castle at Verrucchio. They completely overran Montagna de Parcitati, former head of the Ghibellines in Rimini. They treated him terribly and had him killed."[332]

"Moreover," I said, "the cities of Lamone and Santerno today are ruled by Mainardo Pagano. He's known as 'the little lion with the white nest' and is notorious for changing sides. Sometimes, he fights for the Ghibellines in Romagna to the north of the mountains, other times he fights for the Guelfs to the south of the mountains.[333] There's no real faithfulness or stability with him."

I continued, "The city of Cesena, which lies between Forli and Rimini, has changed its government so many times that it's known for living between tyranny and freedom, even if it is at peace right now."[334]

I concluded, "So I've answered your questions. Now it's time for you to answer ours.[335] I ask you kindly, please tell us definitively who you are. Don't be harder than the other has been toward you. If you tell me, I'll make sure your name continues on in the world."

Guido's Apology

After the fire had finished roaring a bit, it started moving its tip again, now here, now there. Guido then exhaled these words:

"If I thought I was talking to someone who would return to the world, this flame would no longer tussle. I'd keep quiet. But, from this depth, no one that I know of has ever returned alive. If I've heard you right, I'm at no risk of further disgrace by responding to you. So I'll tell you my tale."

Now this was awkward. Apparently, Guido didn't realize I was just passing through. He thought he could talk to me and nothing ill would be reported of him. I didn't bother to correct him.

Guido continued, "I was a man of arms and then a Franciscan, girt with the cord. Believing myself forgiven after my conversion to monastic life, I thought there was little risk in trying to make amends with the Pope. But that great Padre, Boniface VIII, did me in. (I'm speaking ironically, of course. He wasn't so great.)[336] Boniface returned me to my former guilt. It's all his fault! I want you to know exactly the how and the why of what happened."[337]

I thought Guido's rather formal way of expressing himself was interesting since he was relying on a scholastic formulary. He was going to try to make his methodical case to me. But I thought to myself, here we go again. No one thinks he's guilty down here!

Guido went on, "While I was in my body, with the flesh and bones my mother gave me, my actions were not that of a lion, but that of a fox. The ruses and hidden ways: I knew them all. I practiced their arts so *"that their voice [went] out to the all the earth"* (Rom 10.18).

This was amusing. Guido was actually admitting he had engaged in fraudulent activity. How this was supposed to exculpate him was beyond me. He probably wouldn't be speaking like this if he knew I wasn't planning on staying.

Guido continued, "When I saw that I had reached that age of my life when one ought to let the sails down and to gather in the ropes, a marked change occurred. What used to please me, started to grieve me. With penitence and confession, I surrendered. *'Oh wretched man that I am! Who will deliver me from this body of death'* (Rom 7.24)? It might have worked for good."

Guido continued, "But then the head of the new Pharisees, Boniface, was waging war near the Colonna family's stronghold outside Rome.[338] Mind you, Boniface's war wasn't with the Saracens, the Muslims who had just retaken Acre, the last Christian stronghold in the Holy Land.[339] Likewise, Boniface's war wasn't with the Jews, who were supporting the Sultan with trade.[340] No, his enemies were fellow Christians!"

Guido went on, "Boniface cared neither for the Highest Office that he held nor for Holy Orders themselves. He certainly didn't care about my Franciscan vows. He inwardly scoffed at the Franciscan cord I wore and the Order's demand for frequent penance and fasting, which made us more emaciated."

Guido continued, "But like the Emperor Constantine who reportedly asked Pope Silvester I to cure his leprosy while the Pope was hiding out in the cave at Soracte, fearing for his life, so Boniface asked for my help in curing his feverish pride. As he asked me for counsel, I initially kept quiet since the Pope seemed inebriated he was raving so much."[341]

Guido continued, "When the Pope saw my reticence, he objected: *'Don't let your heart be troubled'* (John 14.27), I'll absolve you here and now if you'll just advise me how I can destroy the town of Palestrina.[342] Understand, I have the power to bind and loose heaven (Matt 16.19), as you well know. My predecessor, Celestine V, didn't much prize this power of binding and loosing. But I wield it willingly."

I couldn't believe what I was hearing. My nemesis, Pope Boniface, gets worse every time I hear about him. The Pope had no power to exonerate someone for a sin not yet committed.[343] Worse yet, Boniface was threatening Guido with excommunication if he didn't comply. He was employing his power to manipulate Guido into giving him military advice. Boniface was misusing his office and tempting another to sin. Guido, in his self-deception, apparently fell into it.[344]

Guido continued, "Boniface's weighty arguments prompted me to speak. Silence didn't seem appropriate in the presence of the Pope. So I said, 'Padre, since you cleanse me from that sin which, you know, I have to incur, I'll speak. Promise Palestrina the world, but keep little of what you promise. Sue for peace, but when they've laid down their arms, destroy them. This will cause you to triumph over the Colonnas from your lofty seat."[345]

This was even worse, I thought. Guido just encouraged the Pope to lie to the people to get what he wanted. This was terrible advice! And there's no doubt about it — Guido knew he was sinning. He was just hoping the Pope's absolution would get him out of any consequences without having to offer contrition for it.

Guido continued, "St. Francis came here just after I died and tried to rescue me from this infernal place. But one of the black Cherubim, said to him, 'Don't even think about taking him away. That would injure me. This one has to come live with my wretched slaves since he gave fraudulent counsel. I've been waiting to seize him. One can't be absolved without repenting, nor can he repent of something and then will it to take place. Because of the contradiction, it's simply not allowed.'"

This was shocking, I thought. Even the great St. Francis was hoodwinked in this whole affair. St. Francis actually thought Guido was innocent. How could a Saint in heaven get something this wrong?

Guido said, "*'O wretched man that I am'* (Rom 7.24)! How I shook when the black angel grabbed me and said to me, 'You didn't think I'd be a logician, did you? Ha! This is where your reason has sent you.'"

Guido continued, "The angel brought me to Minos, the Inferno's judge, who coiled his tail eight times around his hardened back. And then, gnawing himself with great rage, he said, 'This one must go into the thieving fire. This is why I'm down here among the damned. Clothed within this flame, I go on grieving for this injustice which has come upon me.'"

When Guido came to the end of his talk, the grieving flame departed, twisting and tossing his sharp horn. This made his punishment obvious. The contortions of the tip of his flame were emblematic of Guido's troubled thoughts.[346] He would be unsettled forever, trying to make sense of how he ended up down here. Amazingly, Guido was still trying to convince himself he had done nothing wrong.

Virgil and I then passed over the ridge until we came to the other arch that covers the ditch where the penalty is paid by those who acquired the wages of sin by instigating conflict.[347]

Comment

One of the key questions the reader ought to answer is whether or not we can trust Guido in this Canto. We've already discovered that sinners often lie in the *Inferno* (remember the lying devils just a few Cantos prior). As we travel lower and lower, it becomes increasingly important to take the claims of sinners with some skepticism.

Guido is trying to convince Dante (and us) that he's done nothing wrong. It was the Pope who made him sin. He was a man under authority, so why should he be held responsible for something an authority figure commanded him to do? After all, Boniface, by referencing the power of binding and loosing heaven, is implicitly threatening excommunication. Guido's lengthy speech is designed to shift blame onto Pope Boniface VIII.

But we have every right to ask whether Guido was really duped or not.[348] The short answer is that Guido wasn't duped at all. He knew exactly what he was doing, but doesn't like the consequences ensuing from his bad behavior. Although trying to depict himself as a friend of St. Francis, his own words give him away.[349]

Guido even describes himself as a fox, which in the Middle Ages was associated with fraud. He's sly and slick, hardly the stuff of a humble Franciscan. Just about everything he tells us is either a lie or a half-truth. He only agrees to speak with Dante under the mistaken assumption that since Dante is in hell, this conversation will never again be told in the world. In short, Guido can't be trusted.

This had led some to question whether "fraudulent counsel" is really the sin in focus in this Canto. True, it's the sin the Black Angel cites for why Guido needed to stay in the Inferno. But we're never told explicitly this is the case either for Guido or for Ulysses, who are both suffering in the same ditch.[350] Despite this uncertainty, it still seems to be the best reading.

What is fraudulent counsel? One could commit this sin by giving bad counsel that takes advantage of other people.[351] This appears to be what Guido does. But one can also give fraudulent counsel by advising another to use fraud. In this case, Guido didn't commit fraud against the Pope, he advised the Pope to commit fraud.[352] No matter what, it seems obvious that Guido is guilty.

Yet, if Guido is guilty, this makes Pope Boniface even more so. Dante, of course, is no fan of Boniface VIII. Dante still blames him for his exile. But the sheer scope of damage from the Pope's actions is breathtaking. When Guido asks Dante how Romagna is doing, Dante replies that, at present, there is no war, but that they live under constant tyranny because of the bellicosity of the princes' hearts. This is a legacy of the Pope's actions. Peace is tenuous and true freedom non-existent.

In Boniface's struggle against the Colonna family, the Pope had promised them peace if they surrendered. But, following Guido's counsel that the Pope should promise peace and then crush them, Boniface went back on his word, breaking a peace treaty in the process. Boniface's armies completely destroyed the family compound at Palestrina after offering the family amnesty.

But this isn't all. Boniface also violated a covenant with God. The Sacraments are the key ways that God and man have a relationship with each other under the New Covenant. Thus, when Boniface misuses his authority to grant absolution, he is violating the very foundations of the New Covenant.[353]

When religious leaders undermine the foundations of the divine-human relationship, this results in terrible discord in society. Dante is linking the fraud of bad counsel to the breakdown of peace. This is why Boniface's sin is so grievous and affects so many people. Fraudulent counsel is tearing apart the very fabric of the society.

This even leads one of the greatest Saints, St. Francis, to commit a misdeed (literally, 'a legal tort,' in Italian).[354] That a Saint in heaven could be duped caused all sorts of consternation to the poem's first readers. But we probably should not read this too literally. Although Jesus warned "*The sons of this world are more shrewd in dealing with their own generation than the sons of light*" (Luke 16.8), Dante is probably trying to show just how confusing things become when religious leaders engage in fraud. It wrecks the good order of the society. Even Saints can get confused.

As Justin Steinberg has pointed out, the tension Dante builds into the poem is deliberate. He wants us to see what justice divorced from virtue looks like.[355] It causes the society to crumble.

But, as many readers have noticed, Guido is not sorry at all for what he's done. He refuses to believe his actions have injured many. His repentance is not genuine.[356] As a result, he winds up toward the very bottom of Malebolge. He's guilty of perpetrating fraud.

What Dante keeps trying to teach us is that sin has implications beyond the individual. We are a long way from Francesca and Paolo whose sexual sin primarily affected them. When sin infects the entire society, things fall apart quickly, order is mislaid, and the very foundation of man's relationship with God is imperiled. The impact of sin becomes ever graver the lower we travel into the Inferno.

28

Sowers of Division and Discord

MALEBOLGE XI: DITCH 9

Dante encounters the sowers of discord. The punishments are disgusting, as each sinner has an appropriate body part severed. These sinners are forced to walk in an endless loop. At a certain point, a devil slices them open. The sinners then heal and are sliced open again and again, forever. We encounter Mohammed and Ali, whom Dante thinks are schismatics. We meet Pier da Medicina, who caused family divisions. Curio, Caesar's former tribune, gave advice to cross the Rubicon, thus destroying the unity of the Roman republic. We also encounter Bertran de Born, a troubadour poet, who wrote glowingly about war and helped sow division between Henry II and his son in England.

I'm going to have a hard time describing in words what came next. Even if I unbound my poetry from rhyming and could adequately recount what those wounded in front of me were like, who would believe me? I could tell this tale over and over and still not convince anyone. I have little doubt that the tongue that tried to describe it would fall short, since our minds and our speech have little ability to comprehend this terrible scene.

In fact, if all the maimed and dead, who have ever run over the storm-tossed lands of northern and southern Italy were gathered together, they couldn't compare to what I saw.[357] For example, if Aeneas and his men, while mourning over the blood spilled in the Trojan War, were gathered together, they couldn't compare to what I saw. If Aeneas' Roman descendants, who fought in the second Punic war, when they lost badly to Hannibal, who scooped up all their golden rings from the dead corpses as booty, were gathered together, they couldn't compare to what I saw.[358] Remember, Livy, who doesn't err, wrote about this.

There's more. Even if Roberto Guiscard, Count of Apulia, were here, the Norman Duke who fought innumerable battles across these lands to consolidate his power, his collected exploits wouldn't compare to what I saw.[359] Moreover, if Charles of Anjou were here, who marched against Manfred, King of Sicily, at the behest of the Pope, but lost the battle at Benevento when the Apulian Barons deserted, this couldn't compare to what I saw, either.[360]

Oh, but there's more. If the Ghibellines at the battle of Tagliacozzo were here, whose armies Charles of Anjou destroyed in a later battle, they couldn't compare to what I saw.[361] Charles' victory really came from the cleverness of his general, Erard de Valery — better known as Alardo, whose cunning strategy managed to win the day despite being outnumbered.[362] Erard won not primarily by force of arms, even though there was plenty of that, but by brainy tactics.[363] And even considering the accumulated carnage that is the result of all war, with the requisite sight of perforated and severed limbs, this is nothing compared to the filthiness of the ninth ditch. It was that bad.

Mohammed

No broken cask, missing its center board or half-moon-shaped end piece was so split open as the shade I saw next. From his chin down to his butt-crack, his entrails were hanging out, suspended between his legs. His heart, liver and lungs as well as the ugly sack (his stomach) that manufactures shit out of everything one has guzzled down were hanging out, too.[364] He was completely disjointed.

While I was fastening my sight on him, the shade was staring at me. With his hands, he ripped open his chest, saying, "Now see how I split myself open! See how crippled Mohammed is!"

I had heard of this Mohammed. From what I knew, he was a Christian schismatic whose war-like activities led to a split in the Christian Church.[365] I thought he rebelled against the cardinals so he himself could be named Pope. I thought that Mohammed held to a so-called Nestorian Christology, which radically separated the divine and human natures of the Divine Son. This made Mohammed both a heretic and a schismatic.[366] He was also a charismatic imposter.[367]

Mohammed continued, "Before me, Ali goes along, weeping, his face split open from his chin to the top of his forehead."

Ali was Mohammed's son-in-law and cousin. The first Imam of Shiism, Ali was the first of four successors to Mohammed. The dispute over Ali's right to head the Caliphate led to the Sunni-Shiite split. Thus Ali was an author of discord among the sects that came from Mohammed.[368]

Mohammed continued, "All the others whom you see here in this ditch were disseminators of scandal and schism in life and this is why their bodies are so split apart. There's a devil lurking behind these shades who treats us all cruelly. Once we've completed our miserable trek around the ditch, the devil slices us to pieces with the edge of his sword. Our wounds then close up and heal. But we have to return again and again to appear before him and be cut open forever."

Mohammed continued, "But who are you who loiters on this reef? Perhaps you're tarrying to delay going off to your own punishment for the charges pronounced over you."

At this point, Virgil cut in, addressing Mohammed: "Death has not reached this one yet nor has the blow that leads to torment. He's down here to get a fuller experience."

Virgil continued, "I, however, am dead and have to lead him through the Inferno from one Circle to another. This is as plain and true as I can tell it."

After Virgil finished speaking, more than one-hundred shades made a full stop in the ditch to check me out. They were all marveling that someone alive was down here. In the distraction, each forgot his pain just for a moment.

Mohammed said to me, "You, who will perhaps soon see the sun, give Brother Dolcino a message, won't you? Tell him, if he doesn't want to follow me down here, he'd better stock up on food. If he doesn't, the grip of snow will hand the victory to the Novarese who otherwise wouldn't find it so easy to acquire."

Mohammed was talking about the breakaway sect of the Apostolic Brothers, founded by Dolcino. After being charged with heresy for suggesting the group hold all goods in common and admit women, Dolcino escaped to the hills of Novara.[369] He was in danger of being starved, discovered with his beautiful mistress Margaret and burned alive. Like Mohammed, Dolcino was both a heretic and a schismatic.[370] I take it that Mohammed shared Dolcino's views on women in religious life.[371]

With one foot lifted to depart, Mohammed spoke these words to me. After finishing, he lowered the foot to the ground and departed.

Pier da Medicina

After Mohammed left, another appeared who had his throat perforated and his nose cut open all the way up to his eyebrows. Having only one ear, he halted with the others to gaze in amazement at me. Before the others could, he opened up his trachea, his ruby red flesh exposed for all to see.

He said, "O you whose guilt does not convict, I saw you up above in Italy. If I'm not mistaken about your likeness, make sure you remember the name Pier da Medicina when you return to the sweet plain that descends from Vercelli to Angiolello."

This was a grotesque sight. Since Pier was missing part of his face, he had to speak through a hole in his throat, presumably that had been cut open by the one of the devils.[372] Pier was taking his hands and holding the bloody flaps open to speak.

I didn't know much of anything about Pier. All I knew was that Medicina was a relatively large town near Bologna.[373] I had heard rumors Pier had sowed division between the Malatesta and Polenta families, but was never quite sure if that was true.[374]

Pier went on, "Make it known to Guido and Angiolello that unless our foresight here is in vain, they'll be thrown out of their ship and drowned at Cattolica because of the treachery of a terrible tyrant."

Pier went on, "Between the islands of Cyprus and Majorca, Neptune never witnessed so great a crime, not by pirates nor by the Greeks of Argolis. Malatestino, who sees with only one eye and holds Rimini, the land that one down here would wish he had never seen, will make the two leaders come to a conference. As a result, these doomed souls will have no need for vows or prayer against the treacherous winds of Focara."[375]

Both Guido Del Cassero and Angiolello da Calignano were noblemen of Fano.[376] I had heard that Malatestino of Rimini invited these nobles to a conference at La Cattolica.[377] I guess Pier wanted me to warn Guido and Angiolello that Malatestino was going to have them drowned before they arrived.[378] Betrayal is a heinous sin.[379]

I responded to Pier, "If you want me to bring news of you to the world above, point the one out to me who wished he had never seen that land. Who is he whose sight is so bitter?"

In response, Pier set his hand on the jaw of one of his companions and pulled open his mouth. Crying out he said, "This is the one I was talking about. He can't speak a word. Once he was cast into exile, this one was overwhelmed. He advised Caesar to cross the Rubicon and attack Rome, thus encouraging the civil war.[380] His quip to Caesar: 'Don't delay — waiting always harms those who are prepared,' was one of the most famous sayings recorded in Lucan's writings."[381]

I realized this bitter figure was Curio, Caesar's former tribune.[382] After Curio helped Caesar cross the Rubicon, Caesar made Curio a leading official in Sicily.[383] After Curio booted Cato from Sicily, he went to Africa where he was killed. I take it that for speaking so daringly to Caesar and others, his punishment was to have his tongue cut out.[384]

There was another shade who had his hand severed that caught my attention. He raised his detached stumps through the murky air so that blood besmirched his face.

Pier said, "You'll remember Mosca, as well. Mosca said, 'What's done is done — kill him'.[385] For the Tuscan people this was the start of great evil."

I remembered hearing about Mosca all the way back at the beginning of my journey.[386] His reputation above was as a do-gooder.[387] The problem was that he advised the murder of Buondelmonte after he ended his engagement to the Amadei girl, thus inciting the Guelf-Ghibelline split.[388] This affected just about everyone in Florence for a long time.

Fed up with all this wickedness, I said, "May death come to your line as well." It wasn't lost on me that his family was thrown out of his city, too. After accumulating sorrow upon sorrow, Mosca took off like one sad and a little bit crazy.

Bertran de Born

But I stayed to watch the flock. What I saw, however I would be afraid to recount at all without more proof than my own senses. If my conscience, that good companion that encourages a man under the chain mail of pure feeling, hadn't assured me, I would have stayed quiet.

I'm sure I saw (and it still amazes me) a torso without a head going along with the others in that mournful herd. That's right — a headless torso was walking along like it was a normal occurrence. The torso held its severed head at its side. It was dangling from his hand like a lantern. Despite his severed head, the figure was not deprived of speech.[389]

The head looked at us and "Oh, my." Out of his own head, he had made himself into a lantern. The head and the torso were of one person, but severed into two parts. How this could be, I can hardly explain. Probably only the Creator who governs it knows for sure.

When the grotesque figure was right at the foot of the bridge, he raised his arm high, together with his severed head to bring his words closer to us.

His words were as follows: "You who gaze on the dead, is there anything you've seen that's as awful as this? Note the terrible retributive judgment you see on the one over there breathing."

This sinner was making reference to Jeremiah's words in Lamentations: "*Is it nothing to you, all you who pass by? Look and see if there is any sorrow like my sorrow which was brought upon me, which the Lord inflicted on the day of his fierce anger*" (Lam 1.12).

He continued, "Because you carry news of me, know that I am Bertran de Born, who gave the young king bad encouragements."

Bertran was a poet who wrote great verses in praise of war.[390] To Bertran, the constant flux in society in which men make and dissolve factions is normal and is one way to deal with the growing idleness of the burgeoning merchant class.[391]

Bertran went on, "I caused father and son to rebel against each other. Ahithophel did no worse by Absalom and King David with his wicked provocations."

Bertran was referencing the story from the Bible when Absalom, David's son, rebelled against his father in an attempt to usurp power. Asking for counsel from David's most trusted advisor on how to overthrow his father, Ahithophel said, "*Go in to your father's concubines, whom he has left to keep the house; and all Israel will hear that you have made yourself odious to your father, and the hands of all who are with you will be strengthened*" (2 Sam 16.21). This counsel came with unfortunate results because, in short order, both Absalom and Ahithophel lost their lives.

One of the earliest Troubadour poets, Bertran became famous for his literary lament for the death of Prince Henry, son of Henry II in England.[392] Apparently, Bertran had convinced Prince Henry to rebel against his father.[393]

Bertran continued, "Since I divided persons so joined, I carry around my brain severed from my body, for now. From its starting point in this stump, you can observe the *contrapasso* in me."

Comment

As we've seen throughout the *Inferno*, the concept of *contrapasso* is central to Dante's work. In almost every Canto, we have observed how God makes sinners' punishments fit their crimes. Thus punishment in the *Inferno* is simply an outgrowth of sinners' misplaced desires. It reflects their sin.

In life, Bertran wrote so eloquently about war that the twentieth-century English poet Ezra Pound became a great admirer of his verses. Pound's so-called "Hell Cantos" reimagined a hell full of politicians, professionals and writers who corrupt society with their words. These verses depict the terrible descent of twentieth-century societies into chaos through fascism, anti-Semitism and other madness.[394]

As Pound puts it, "I saw in the place...politicians...their wrists bound to the ankles, standing bare bum, faces smeared on their rumps, wide eye on flat buttock, bush hanging for beard, addressing crowds through their arse-holes, addressing the multitudes in the ooze."[395] This imagery and his later attacks on those who "forge false news" (the BBC) are inspired by this Canto.[396]

Thus Dante is exploring the power that words have to fragment a society.[397] Each shade we encounter has caused significant division among his contemporaries, divisions that have affected many people. From Dante's point of view, when leaders speak in ways that deliberately cause division, this causes a significant problem because of the lack of stability it brings to a society. One can only imagine what Dante would say about our society today with its twenty-four hour news cycle.

In this Canto, we encounter sinners who are forced to make an infinite loop around a circuit.[398] A devil slices and dices them, causing great pain and anguish. They quickly heal as they move along their infinite circle, but then are sliced open again when they get back to the devil. This is an indication of what discord brings. The body politic can never heal if its leaders foment division.[399]

One character easy to misunderstand is Mohammed. Dante, like many late medieval Christians, had little conception that Mohammed had founded a separate religion. He thought of Mohammed as a Christian schismatic.

In the era before the Reformation, the aggressive military expansion of Mohammed's followers into the formerly Christian lands of North Africa, Asia Minor and the Middle East was the most significant "Church" split they could think of. Dante probably doesn't realize that Mohammed had founded a "new" religion that was not Christian. Thus we shouldn't read Dante's polemic against Mohammed and Ali as an anti-Islamic statement. We should read it that Mohammed's actions were seen by Dante as a schism within the Church.

The sinners in this Canto wear their punishments outwardly on their bodies. As they severed the unity of communities, so their members are severed from their bodies. Words employed with the intention of sowing division harm everyone.

Dante is unable to interpret what he sees adequately. He tells us from the start that poetry cannot adequately express what he saw. If words can cause great harm, it is a dangerous practice to use more words to describe them. When Dante sees the damned in this Canto, he feels even more overwhelmed than in other places. Language cannot describe the scene properly.

In medieval legal terms, the crime of schism was grave. Since the crime was outside standard boundaries, the punishment could be spectacular.[400] That is what we get in this Canto. It is grotesque and unparalleled. Only God had the right to punish like this.[401]

Why is division so heinous? Schism is terrible not only because it affects a lot of people and creates confusion, but also because it runs directly counter to the will of God. As Jesus prayed to the Father, "*I do not pray for these only, but also for those who believe in me through their word, that they may all be one; even as you, Father, are in me and I in you, that they also may be in us so that the world may believe that you have sent me*" (John 17.20-21).

Division is contrary to the harmony of the godhead, is contrary to the work of the Gospel and also harms the society as a whole. Thus, to split the Church — or the society — is one of the worst things a person can do.

29

The Falsifiers, Part I

MALEBOLGE XII: DITCHES 9-10

The Pilgrims reach the tenth ditch and the penultimate Canto of Malebolge. Before they reach the ditch, they encounter Geri del Bello, the first blood relative that Dante has encountered. Having been murdered, Geri del Bello indirectly expresses his displeasure that his death has not been avenged. This causes Dante to struggle with what his reaction ought to be, given the Biblical prohibitions against private retribution. Once in the tenth ditch, Dante and Virgil encounter the falsifiers who used alchemy for various selfish purposes. Both Griffolino and Capocchio are depicted among those in a stinking pit of disease, symbolic of what falsity does to a society. This Canto takes place in the afternoon on Saturday.

What I saw next, the multitudes of people with their very strange wounds, so befuddled my eyes that I just wanted to stay there and weep. I was experiencing what Jeremiah, the so-called "weeping prophet," must have encountered when he cried out, "*O that my head were waters, and my eyes a fountain of tears, that I might weep day and night for the slain of the daughter of my people...For they are all adulterers, a company of treacherous men. They bend their tongue like a bow; falsehood and not truth has grown strong in the land*" (Jer 9.1-3).

When Virgil saw my look, he said to me, "Why are you stopping here to stare? What good does it do to fix your gaze on these miserable, mutilated shades? You haven't done this in the other ditches we've come through. Even if you wanted to number them all, you couldn't count that high. This valley alone is twenty-two miles around."

Virgil continued, "Look, already the moon is under our feet. The time we've been allotted has almost run out and there are other things to see. So we need to get moving."

Virgil was referencing a long-held tradition that visits to the netherworld had to be completed in twenty-four hours.[402] It was already early Saturday afternoon so I guess time was running out for our visit to the Inferno, but I decided to respond to him anyway. I snapped, "Look, Virgil, if you had bothered to figure out why I was staring, maybe you'd have let me linger a little longer down here."

Geri del Bello

Virgil had already starting walking, so I scurried to take up my usual place behind him. Having already made my reply, I decided to add something else while we were going along since I didn't want Virgil to think I was staring out of idle curiosity.[403] So I said: "Within that pit, where I was fastening my eyes, I think I saw a spirit weeping over the wound that costs so much down here. I could have sworn I just saw one of my blood relatives.[404] I haven't seen any relatives down here until now."

Virgil said, "From here on, don't even waste a thought on him. Pay attention to the other things and just let him be. Here's why: while you were focused on other shades in the last ditch, I saw him at the foot of the bridge. He was pointing right at you, threatening menacingly with his finger. I even heard him speak. Apparently his name is Geri del Bello. You were so preoccupied with Bertran de Born that you didn't notice him before he departed."

Geri was one of my relatives from Florence. He was my father's cousin.[405] About thirty years ago, he was murdered by someone from the

Sacchetti family. He must be angry because my family never got around to avenging his death.

I said, "O my leader, Geri's violent death has not yet been avenged by anyone related to him.[406] I think this has made him indignant. I guess that's why he left without talking to me. This makes me pity him all the more."

I knew by now that I wasn't supposed to be pitying Geri, but I couldn't help it. There was something just not right about his death, which went unanswered. Vendettas were legal in my day as long as they weren't carried out excessively.[407]

At the same time, however, I recognized that my judgment was going against God's will. As St. Paul wrote (quoting Moses in Deuteronomy), "***Beloved, never avenge yourselves, but leave it to the wrath of God; for it is written, 'Vengeance is mine, I will repay, says the Lord'***" (Rom 12.19). [408] So I understood Geri's grievance against me, but I also wasn't going to do anything about it. All that was left to do was to pity him.[409]

The Tenth Ditch

Virgil and I went on talking as we walked. We reached the first point where we could make out the next ditch. If there had been more light, I probably could have seen down to its bottom. When we were above the final cloister of Malebolge, so that its lay brothers appeared to our sight, odd laments gripped me like iron arrows tipped with pity at which I covered my ears with my hands. All this pity was probably doing me harm.

Imagine the grief if the sick in the hospitals at Valdichiana during the summer malarial outbreaks were all together in one wretched ditch with the sick from the swampy regions of Maremma and Sardegna that bred so much malarial misery. That's what it was like here. There was this awful stench coming out of the ditch, which smelled like festering limbs.

Virgil and I descended to the last crag of the long reef, continuously moving to our left. At this point, my vision became clearer and I could see down into the next pit where unerring justice from the Most High punishes the falsifiers registered down here.

I don't think the agony would have been any greater if I had witnessed with my own eyes all the infirm in Aegina when the air was so full of sickness that the animals, down to the smallest worm, all fell. (As the ancients and poets have firmly held, they were restored from the seeds of ants.)

I was referring here to Ovid's myth about Aegina, an island not far away from Athens, ransacked by plague, which came about because of Juno's jealousy.[410] When Jupiter bore Aeacus with the sea nymph Aegina and named the island after his lover, this riled up Jupiter's rival, Juno.[411] Every creature but Aeacus died in the plague.[412] The island was rescued when Aeacus begged Jupiter for help and in a dream saw ants transformed into people.[413] Thus the island, completely depopulated from plague, was saved from destruction when Jupiter transformed ants into men.[414]

What I saw in front of me was grotesque. Some of the sinners were lying on their stomachs, some on their backs. Another was crawling around on all fours along the miserable path.

Stride after stride we went along without talking. We were watching and listening to the ailing spirits who weren't able to raise themselves up.

Griffolino and Capocchio

I saw two shades sitting, resting against each other. They were like two pans leaning against one another to transfer heat. Each was pocked from head to toe with scabs.

They were also like stable boys hurriedly brushing a horse while their master looked on. Additionally, they were like horse trainers grooming a horse late at night, who rush through the process since they just want to go to bed.[415]

These shades were furiously trying to scratch themselves with their nails, but this was providing no relief. Their nails were ripping off scabs from their hardened skin like a knife whittles flakes from a wooden beam.

Their skin was so hardened it was like the rough scales of carp fish.[416] It reminded me of what it must have been like to dig through a suit of chain mail.[417]

Virgil started speaking to one of them, "Oh you who are dismembering yourself with your fingers, employing them as pincers, tell us if any Italians are among those who are within this ditch. Perhaps then your nails will be eternally able to complete this work."

The shade replied mournfully, "Both of us, who you see mutilated, are Italians. But who are you that you ask about us?"

Virgil said, "I am one descending below with this living one. We're going from shore to shore. I intend to show him the whole Inferno."

At this, their mutual support was broken. Trembling, each turned toward me with the other listening in as the sound reverberated.

Virgil moved up closer and told me, "Say whatever you want to them."

Following his instructions, I began to speak: "If you don't want your memory to be diminished in the minds of men in the world above, but want your memory to live on for years, tell me who you are and from which cities you come. Don't let your indecent and burdensome punishments prevent you from disclosing yourself to me."

The first shade, Griffolino, responded, "I was from Arezzo. Albert of Siena had me burned alive for heresy. But what I died for doesn't lead me here."

He continued, "I was just kidding when I told Albert that I knew how to rise up through the air and fly. He was too slow to get the humor. He thought I was serious and wanted me to show him how. He got pretty mad when I couldn't teach him how to fly.[418] He had the Bishop burn me at the stake for heresy, something I didn't commit."[419]

Griffolino continued, "I pled my case before Minos at the gates of the Inferno, but he had other ideas. Minos doesn't err. He told me that I'm down here because of the alchemy that I performed in the world."

This puzzled me. I didn't think alchemy was that bad in and of itself. Of course, not everyone agreed with me. The problem appeared to be the fraudulent way Griffolino was practicing alchemy.[420] He was a kind of charlatan, using alchemy to perpetrate fraud.[421]

I turned to Virgil and quipped, "Now was there ever anyone as vain as those from Siena? Certainly even the French can't compare!"

Then the other leper, Capocchio, who overheard me, responded to my quip: "Well, except Stricca, of course, who knew how to rein in his spending."

I knew Stricca was a famous profligate spender in Siena.[422] Capocchio was being ironic.

Capocchio continued, "Consider as well Niccolo, Stricca's brother, who first discovered the luxurious use of the clove as a condiment from the garden. He specialized in gourmet luxury. In the same club is Caccia d'Ascian, who completely dissipated his vineyard and his great fields and to whom Abbagliato, the dazed one, proffered his judgment."

I thought, "Ah, the Sienese. So unwise, so foolish."[423] I think all these souls blew their treasures in riotous living.[424]

Capocchio went on, "But to let you know who backs you up against the Sienese, fix your eyes on me so that my face might answer you well. You'll see that I'm the one who distorted metals with alchemy. And you should recall, if I eye you well, how I could imitate nature in making false gold out of other metals."[425]

Comment

As we enter the tenth ditch, this is the last of the divisions of Malebolge. We'll be in this ditch for both this Canto and the next, meaning that it will have taken us thirteen Cantos to explore the sin of fraud. Clearly, fraud was a major concern for Dante as he wrote.

The beginning part of the Canto gives us some information about what time it is, the first indication we have had in a while. We learn that it's about 1:00 in the afternoon because of the position of the moon. This means time is running out for this visit to the Inferno. Virgil urges Dante to move along. The reason for the rush is that they are going to need to emerge from the Inferno (which means getting back to the surface from the middle of the earth) by Sunday morning.

Before entering the tenth ditch, we encounter Geri del Bello who brings up the issue of vengeance. Dante is clearly torn here. He knows, from Christian teaching, that vengeance is God's alone. Yet he lives in a culture where vengeance was a kind of noble right. If someone killed a relative, it was lawful to seek proportional vengeance against the family who carried it out. Geri's wagging finger reminds Dante that his relative's death had never been avenged.

This was true in 1300 when this story supposedly takes place. But, as Dante was writing, he would have known that Geri's murder was avenged by one of his nephews, who killed someone from the Sacchetti family while he was at home.[426] It took until 1342 for the Alighieri and the Sacchetti families to make peace.[427]

But what should we make of this? The Bible prohibits vengeance. So what does Dante do while he's in the Inferno? Dante seems to be striking a kind of *via media* position. On the one hand, he's sympathetic to Geri's complaint that he was murdered, supposedly without cause. Yet Dante also realizes that God's judgment is infallible. Geri belongs in the Inferno.

So Dante balances these competing claims on Geri by expressing pity and then moving on. Dante thus handles himself fairly well. The difference now is that he is no longer questioning God's justice. Dante simply has sympathy for a relative who died under suspicious circumstances.

The rest of the Canto deals with the falsifiers. Because they are so far down at the bottom of Malebolge, the falsifiers are punished as the worst manifestation of fraud. We've seen all kinds of souls tell lies so far. Why does Dante single out this kind of falsity for such condemnation?

To make sense of this, we're going to have to dig a bit deeper under the surface level of the text. As noted in the Canto, alchemy wasn't prohibited in Dante's day. In fact, the research that went into alchemy laid the groundwork for the modern field of chemistry.

Too many in our day have an incomplete idea of what alchemy was. Many assume these sinners were trying to get rich by turning base metals into gold. There were some who did such things, and were get-rich-quick schemers.

But medieval alchemy was much more than an investigation into the physical sciences. It had an even more important spiritual component to it. The alchemist was a mystical seeker who was trying to uncover a kind of universal medicine to heal the soul.[428] In essence, alchemists were trying, through scientific research, to get back to Eden — thus reversing the tragic implications of the Fall.

Part of the problem with the alchemists whom we encounter at the end of this Canto is that they have entirely lost this spiritual sense of their work. They're supposed to be helping people find their way back to God. Instead, these alchemists ply their trade fraudulently.

For the sinners in this Canto, it appears their sin wasn't primarily engaging in alchemy, but about the misrepresentations that grew out of the work. This makes it likely that their falsity extends to their very persons. In other words, by pursuing their work with false motives, these sinners are sinning against their own natures.

This is why these sinners are pictured as diseased and lying in a putrid, stinking heap. We shouldn't just imagine a series of sick individuals in this heap. We should instead understand this as Dante's picture of what the whole society looks like when it is corrupted by falsity.[429] Falsity hinders relationships, harms the economy and makes political stability impossible. In short, corruption ruins everything. Dante himself has paid the price for it with his exile.

Thus neither Griffolino nor Capocchio is condemned for alchemy *per se*. Each one is base but not terribly interesting. The simple language each employs reflects this. In fact, both Griffolino and Capocchio appear to have been accepted at court, at least until they ran afoul of the authorities.

The big problem is that Griffolino and Capocchio tampered with nature itself by plying their trade. They did this by falsifying their results. These sinners are trying to tamper with what God has made, for their own use. In so doing, they're bringing ruin on the society as a whole, not just themselves.

30

The Falsifiers, Part II

MALEBOLGE XIII: DITCH 10

Dante begins by admitting the craziness of what he saw next with examples of insanity from classical mythology. Dante learns that Gianni Schicchi, whom we encountered at the end of the last Canto, impersonated someone else for the purposes of fraud. We then meet Master Adam, a notorious counterfeiter, who is rendered immobile and thirsty from dropsy. Master Adam represents the corruption that comes to the body politic when its blood supply (money) is exploited for unjust gain. Master Adam gets into a fight, both verbal and physical, with Sinon the Greek, who tricked the Trojans by lying at the end of the Trojan War. Dante, who enjoys their wrangling, receives a stern rebuke from Virgil.

The Impersonators

At one point long ago, Juno, Jupiter's wife, became angry over Semele and the blood of Thebes. Juno was constantly getting mad at her husband Jupiter because of his unfaithfulness.[430] In this case, Jupiter got Semele, daughter of Cadmus, the King of Thebes, pregnant.[431] The son she bore to Jupiter was named Bacchus. When Semele asked Jupiter to turn up before her in the same splendor he appeared to Juno, he reluctantly complied.[432] However, since Jupiter appeared before Semele as the god of thunder, Juno took out her wrath by having Semele consumed by lightning, thus implementing her revenge.[433]

What does this have to do with insanity? Well, Athamas, king of Orchomenus in Boetia, married Nephele at Juno's behest, but was secretly in love with Ino, a daughter of Cadmus and sister of Semele.[434] Still enraged by Jupiter's betrayal with Semele, Juno caused Athamas to go insane.[435] One day, when Athamas saw Ino going along with her two sons, each in one arm, he cried out, "Let's stretch out the nets so I can trap the lioness and her cubs at the gate."

Athamas, confusing Ino and sons for lions, extended his pitiless claws, grabbed one of her sons, Learchus, whirled him around and smashed him on a rock. This was similar to the judgment that would come to Babylon: "***Happy shall he be who takes your little ones and dashes them against the rock***" (Ps 137.9).[436] When Ino saw what Athamas had done, she drowned herself, together with her other son Melicertes.[437]

The story of Athamas occurred in ancient Thebes, but I'll recount another tale of insanity from Troy.[438] When Fortune had brought down the loftiness of the Trojans after the trickery of the Greeks with the Trojan horse, King Priam was killed and his rule wrecked.[439] The wretched and miserable Hecuba, the former Queen of Troy, along with Polyxena, her daughter, were enslaved by the Greeks and forced to go with them.

The spirit of Achilles, still angry over his surprise defeat and subsequent death, demanded the life of Polyxena in return.[440] When Hecuba saw not only her daughter Polyxena dead, but also her son Polydorus washed up on the shore of the sea, she went out of her mind. She began frantically barking like a dog, so much did her distress twist her psyche.

As bad as these stories turned out, neither compared to what I saw next. Neither a Theban like Athamas nor a Trojan like Hecuba could make anyone as crazy as the next two shades I encountered.

Gianni Schicchi and Myrrha

These two shades ran around on all fours chomping in the manner of pigs when let out of the sty and into the pasture. They were both like rabid animals.[441] The one lunged at Capocchio and sunk his tusks into his neck. The other then dragged him off, making his belly scrape the hard ground as he went.

The one dragging off Capocchio must have been Gianni Schicchi, who Griffolino identified in the last Canto. Schicchi, a member of the Cavalcanti family, was from Florence and was famous for his ability to mimic others.[442] Schicchi was well-known for using his skills of mimicry to perpetrate fraud.[443]

In fact, when Buoso Donati, father of Simone Donati, died, Simone was so afraid his father had left an unfavorable will, that Simone hid his father's body.[444] When Simone had explained his dilemma to Schicchi, Gianni had Simone call a notary. Curling up sick in bed and pretending to be the father, Buoso, Schicchi then dictated a fraudulent will that left a hefty sum to Simone.[445] Thus Gianni conspired to commit fraud by impersonating another.

Trembling, Griffolino, stayed behind. He confirmed the gremlin that had taken away Capocchio was indeed Gianni Schicchi. Griffolino told me that the other shade rabidly went about mangling others since he was never satisfied.

I turned to Griffolino and asked, "Could you please tell me who the other shade is? Perhaps if you're talking to me the other one won't sink his teeth into you before he takes off from here."

Griffolino said to me, "That other one is the ancient soul of the wicked Myrrha, daughter of Cinyras, King of Cyprus. Myrrha became infatuated with her father outside the bounds of sanctioned love. She wanted to have an incestuous sexual relationship with her dad."

Griffolino continued, "Myrrha went in to have relations with Cinyras by falsely cloaking herself in a different shape. This wasn't that dissimilar to what Gianni did for himself with the fraudulent will, bequeathing the most beautiful she-mule in all of Tuscany, the queen of the herd, to himself. Griffolino confirmed that Gianni had falsely disguised himself as Buoso Donati, dictated the will and put it in the right legal form."[446]

Master Adam, the Counterfeiter

At this, both Griffolino and Myrrha passed from my sight. Since my gaze had been fixated on them, I hadn't noticed that there were others who were badly born. For example, I saw one, made to look like a lute, because of his swollen belly and craned neck.[447] That is, he would have looked like a lute if his legs had been cut off.[448]

Because of his distended belly that almost swallowed up his legs, I think he had dropsy. Medieval doctors would have diagnosed this one has having "drum dropsy," whose main symptom is intense thirst that comes about because of a liver malfunction.[449] With dropsy, the belly swells, and the face loses its shape.[450]

This grotesque shade had lips that were pulling apart like one afflicted with a wasting disease. He was obviously thirsty, was drawing one lip down toward his chin while twisting the other one up in an attempt to get something to drink.

This shade said, "I don't know why it is that you're the only one down here without punishment in this miserable place, but look over here and pay attention. I want you to observe the suffering of Master Adam."

Similar to Bertran de Born in Canto Twenty-Eight, Master Adam described his situation in terms like Jeremiah had used in the book of Lamentations: *"Is it nothing to you, all who pass by? Look and see if there is any sorrow like my sorrow which was brought upon me, which the Lord inflicted on the day of his fierce anger" (Lam 1.12).*

Master Adam continued, "When I was living, I had whatever I wanted. And now, wearied as I am, I crave a single drop of water. The recollection of little streams that descend from the green hills of Casentino down to the Arno River, making their channels cold and soft, are always before me (and not for nothing). This memory tortures me, drying me out even more than the infirmity that deprives me of my proper shape."

Master Adam went on, "The unyielding justice that intrudes on me uses each place where I sinned to intensify my punishment, making my sighs come out ever quicker. For example, there's Romena where I falsified the alloy stamped with the face of John the Baptist. Because of that, I was burned at the stake."

I was pretty sure this Master Adam was Adam of Brescia, who was an employee of the court in Romena.[451] He was caught adding dross to the coinage in Florence that was stamped with the face of John the Baptist to ensure the coins' quality and authenticity.[452] Adam of Brescia was burned alive, the typical punishment for counterfeiting.[453] His fraud was done on such a large scale that the entire monetary system in Tuscany was affected.[454]

When Master Adam came down to the Inferno, this must have been quite an adjustment for him. He must have missed his luxurious lifestyle dedicated to the pursuit of gold, since he's now reduced to longing for a single drop of water.[455]

I couldn't help but be reminded of the parable of the rich man and Lazarus where a similar role reversal took place. As St. Luke put it,

> *There was a certain rich man who was clothed in purple and fine linen and fared sumptuously every day. And at his gate lay a poor man named Lazarus, full of sores who desired to be fed with what fell from the rich man's table; moreover the dogs came and licked his sores. So it was that the beggar died and was carried by the angels to Abraham's bosom. The rich man also died and*

> *was buried. And in Hades, being in torment, he lifted up his eyes and saw Abraham far off and Lazarus in his bosom. And he called out, 'Father Abraham, have mercy upon me and send Lazarus to dip the end of his finger in water and cool my tongue; for I am in anguish in this flame' (Luke 16.20-24).*

Master Adam was this rich man.

Master Adam continued, "Let me tell you, as thirsty as I am, I'd gladly give up a drink from the springs at Fonte Branda to see the miserable souls of Guido, Alessandro and their brother down here.[456] They were my employers and are more to blame than I am!"

Master Adam went on, "I think Guido has already come down here, if such shades can be trusted to tell the truth. But what good does that do me since my limbs are all tied up?"

It was at this point that I realized Master Adam, suffering as he was from dropsy, was rendered immobile by his ailment.[457] His immobility must have been part of his punishment for his frenetic lifestyle in the world above.

Master Adam said, "If only I were a little bit lighter. Even if it takes one-hundred years to go one inch, I would have already been started on my way, searching for Guido among these obscene shades. Even if this ditch is eleven miles around and not less than a mile across, I'd find him somewhere."

I just shook my head at Master Adam's bizarre wish for revenge. At that pace, it would take him almost 700,000 years to find Guido.[458] I'm not kidding. The math checks out.

Master Adam said, "It's the brothers' fault I'm down here among such an infernal family. They're the ones who induced me to mint the ill-weighted florins. They told me to add three carats of dross to the mix."

Right, I thought, it's always someone else's fault. The irony of all this wasn't lost on me. The coins that Master Adam were minting had the seal of John the Baptist on them. The baptism of John was supposed to lead to repentance and ultimately to salvation.

Because of Master Adam's fierce envy, pride and need for revenge, he corrupted what was supposed to save. Not only did he undermine the entire monetary system of Tuscany, but he actually falsified the Divine Image in his soul.[459] Thus those three carats of dross he added to the coins to debase the currency were a kind of perversion of the Image of the triune God found in his reasoning faculty.

I asked him, "Who are these two fellows who are lying so close to you on your right side? Their steaming hands look like they're being washed outside in hot water during the cold of winter."

Master Adam replied, "I found them when I got down here and they haven't turned over since. Frankly, I don't think they'll ever move again, even if I gave them all eternity. The female one is Potiphar's wife who falsely accused Joseph."

I remembered the story of Potiphar's wife from the Bible. Joseph, who had been promoted to be caretaker of Potiphar's household, ran afoul of Potiphar's wife when he refused to give in to her repeated sexual entreaties. She falsely accused Joseph of rape, saying, "*See, he came in to me to lie with me, and I cried out with a loud voice*" (Gen 39.14-15). Based on her false testimony, Joseph was thrown into prison.

Sinon, the Liar

Master Adam continued, "The other one beside me is Sinon. He's the one who tricked the citizens of Troy into letting the Trojan horse into their city, thus sealing their demise. Both Sinon and Potiphar's wife are suffering from high fevers, which is why they are throwing off a terrible stench."

Then I witnessed a remarkable sight. Sinon, who was apparently annoyed at Master Adam's description of him, took his fist and punched Master Adam in his gut. His stiff stomach sounded like a hollowed-out drum when the punch landed. In return, Master Adam punched Sinon in the face with his arm, which was no less hardened.

Master Adam said to Sinon, "I may not be able to move my limbs, but my arm is free to knock you around."

Sinon answered, "When you were being burned at the stake, you didn't have much dexterity then, did you? But you sure had some fancy footwork when you were counterfeiting coins!"

Master Adam retorted, "You're right on that point. But what do you know about telling the truth? You swore an oath before the Trojans that the horse you wheeled up to the gates was a peace offering. You're a liar. So why should anyone bother listening to you?"

Sinon answered, "I may have spoken falsely, but you falsified the coinage. I'm down here for just one misdeed. You did more damage to Tuscany by corrupting its monetary system than any demon ever did."

Master Adam said, "Look, you perjurer, remember the Trojan horse. That's evidence enough you destroyed a whole city. May it torment you forever to realize the whole world knows about it and will always see you as a villain."

Sinon said, "Villain? May the thirst that cracks your tongue and the running water that swells your belly always make your stomach bloat so you can't even see your legs. May it torment you forever."

Master Adam replied, "So your mouth hangs open wide because of your sickness. I may be thirsty because of dropsy, but your fever and aching head will never go away. You're as desperately thirsty as I am, so much so you wouldn't even need an invitation to stare at yourself in the water like Narcissus. Your own narcissism is your undoing."

I was ready to keep listening to this entertaining verbal joust, but Virgil said to me, "If you keep looking on this ugliness, you and I are going to have a problem."

When I heard Virgil speaking to me so forcefully, I realized I had erred. Ashamed, I turned toward him. I still remember it vividly. I felt like someone dreaming about his own harm. It was like a bad dream, when one wants so badly for it just to be a dream.

Thus I found myself longing for what it is, as if it were not. I really didn't know what to say. I earnestly desired to ask forgiveness, and was apologizing for myself all along without knowing it. I guess the only thing separating me from Sinon or Master Adam is that I recognized my guilt.[460]

Virgil said to me, "This is good. Less shame would wash away a greater fault than yours has been. Put away your sadness. I'm right here. If it should happen that Fortune puts us somewhere where shades are fighting, remember, listening to such things is base."

Comment

Canto Thirty is remarkable for the typology that lies beneath the surface of the text. As always, the surface level of the text is absorbing, but there is much more richness here than a purely literal reading would reveal. It is especially important to see the underlying typology that weaves John the Baptist, counterfeiting and spiritual regeneration together.

We should note that Master Adam is typologically connected to the archetypal Adam of the creation narratives in the Bible.[461] For example, when Master Adam tells us upfront that he had everything he needed, we should immediately see this as a reference to the Garden of Eden.

Then, Master Adam falls, just as the original Adam did. Even though Master Adam is at the bottom of Malebolge, he doesn't understand that his self-love and greed destroyed his spiritual life and caused him to fall from grace.[462]

Similarly, the original Adam fell from Eden after being created through the primal waters. In turn, Master Adam corrupted the waters of baptism by debasing the coinage sealed by John the Baptist. John, of course, is the forerunner of the spiritual regeneration that comes in water baptism, since he baptized Jesus who sanctified the waters of the Jordan. When the Spirit is called down upon the water in the Church's baptismal rite, this similarly sanctifies the water.

Because of Master Adam's dropsy, he's constantly thirsty and forced to remember for all eternity the flowing, pleasant streamlets of his hometown. He's been led to water, but cannot drink because his lust for vengeance gets in the way of the spiritual healing that would come through the water. As a result, spiritual health is completely lacking in Master Adam, the typological equal of the first Adam.

As for the coin itself, we should read this through Jesus' parable of the lost coin. In this parable, Jesus gives a description of redemption as being like a woman who finds a coin she had lost and "*calls together her friends and neighbors, saying, 'rejoice with me, for I have found the coin which I lost.*'" (Luk 15.9). Jesus interprets this parable, saying, "*Just so, I tell you, there is joy before the angels of God over one sinner who repents*" (Luke 15.10).

What is completely lacking among the sinners in this Canto? Repentance. The glaring exception to this is Dante's repentance after Virgil's rebuke at the end of the Canto.

We should also remember the story Jesus tells when one of the Pharisees asks Jesus whether Jews should pay taxes to Caesar or not. Jesus responded as follows: "*'Whose likeness and inscription is this?' They said, 'Caesar's.' Then he said to them, 'Render therefore to Caesar the things that are Caesar's and to God the things that are God's'*" (Matt 22.19-21).

The coin becomes a symbol of the soul that Jesus will redeem by his sacrifice on the cross.[463] Master Adam, by counterfeiting coins, has chosen fraud over redemption, greed over generosity and sickness over healing. His fraud not only affects his soul, but his actions also affect the entire society. To the Medieval mind, which saw money as the lifeblood of the body politic, this image is particularly arresting.[464]

Thus our old Adamic natures can be renewed and redeemed through the saving waters of baptism. When incorporated into the Church, the redeemed look forward to salvation and resurrection. The problem with Master Adam is that he has forfeited these goods because he has chosen hatred over love.

We observe the results of this decision at the end of the Canto when Master Adam and Sinon devolve into a shouting match. There is a subtle word play going in Sinon's name. His name is a combination of the Italian words for yes and no ("*si*" and "*non*").[465] The Dante is playing on the idea that Sinon, a famous liar and trickster, has lost his identity because of fraud.

Sinon and Master Adam hit each other, trade insults and wallow in their misery. They are the very picture of a society that, through fraud, has killed the life-giving spirit. It's so bad that Master Adam would rather get his revenge than reach out for a single drop of living water.

Even worse, we will learn when we get to the *Paradiso* that the first Adam has repented and is in heaven. Master Adam, typologically connected to the Fall, cannot be redeemed because his love has grown cold. He chooses to perpetrate fraud on the whole society rather than turn from his sin and be saved. This is the sad reality of a soul gripped by fraud.

At the end of the Canto, Virgil rebukes Dante for his *schadenfreude*. Dante apparently enjoys looking on the strife between Sinon and Master Adam (didn't we as well?). Interestingly, Virgil doesn't only rebuke Dante for taking pleasure in watching another sin. He also rebukes Dante even for the shame he feels, which is out of proportion to the sin itself.

Dante's point is important because he's trying to show us that with a greater awareness of sin, there is greater risk of allowing improprieties to thrill us.[466] We risk looking on others in a condescending way who are struggling with sins we consider ourselves to have dealt with. This is a very real danger for those who have made progress in the spiritual life. Becoming more aware of sin is helpful. But it is entirely possible to open ourselves up to even greater sin by our improved awareness.[467] This is Dante's error and can be ours as well.

Cocytus:
The Sins of Complex Fraud

31

Corrupting Language

COCYTUS I: THE THREE GIANTS

Leaving Malebolge, Dante and Virgil encounter a series of giants that Dante initially mistakes for towers. Dante first encounters Nimrod, whose pride was responsible for the confusion of language at the tower of Babel. Nimrod speaks incomprehensible gibberish. He next meets Ephialtes, a giant from mythology, who took on Jupiter and the other gods with his great strength. Ephialtes is bound and is without speech. In his rage over his inability to communicate, Ephialtes causes a great earthquake. Finally, we meet Antaeus, who is unbound and can speak. Antaeus gently transports the pilgrims to the frozen lake of Cocytus, the lowest section of the Inferno.

I was embarrassed by Virgil's rebuke at the end of the last Canto, so much so, it caused me to blush. So I was holding out for the medicine of some comforting words.[1]

Virgil's reproach, followed by his kindness, reminded me of what I've heard about Achilles' spear.[2] In mythology, Achilles' spear, which originally belonged to his father Peleus, could heal the wound it had opened up.[3] This is similar to what Virgil did for me. First there was pain and then a good gift, the gift of continuing moral development.

We turned our backs on the last miserable ditch of Malebolge and climbed up the bank that encircles it, crossing over without uttering so much as a word. Here, it was not quite night, but not quite day, either. I couldn't see much, as my vision only reached a little way ahead.

But I did hear sounds from a high horn. The horn was so loud that it would make any peal of thunder sound faint. Following the sound, it drew my eyes entirely to one place.

This reminded me of what happened when Charlemagne lost his rear guard under the command of his nephew, Roland.[4] The Saracens attacked from behind, thus surprising Roland and the rear guard.[5] Using his last breath, Roland blew his horn to warn Charlemagne of the enemy's impending attack.[6] Although eight miles away, Charlemagne heard the horn because it was so loud.[7]

I hadn't turned my head in that direction too long, when I thought I saw a whole series of tall towers. I asked Virgil, "Please tell me, what city is this?"

Virgil said to me, "You're confused. You're trying to see in this dim light, but are too far away to make out the shapes properly. You'll understand better once we get there. Your sight deceives you from afar. So push on a bit more and it will become clearer."

Virgil took me by the hand and said, "Before we go too far, I should tell you (and I'm hoping this makes things a little clearer for you) that those aren't towers. Those shapes in the distance are giants. Each of them is standing in a pit that comes up to their navels."

The landscape looked like it does when fog is burning off. As one comes closer to one's destination through the fog, little by little, it reveals what the vapor packs into the air. It was like that down here, as I made my way through the murky and dark atmosphere.

As I got nearer and nearer to the bank, error fled away and fear grew within me. The bank that encircles the pit looked like the round walls at Monteriggioni outside Siena. In this strongly fortified castle, there were fourteen towers at regular intervals that guarded the entrance.[8]

As I got closer, I realized the horrible giants were towering over the bank. About half of their trunks were visible, the other half were hidden within the deep pit. They reminded me of the giants from the famous battle at Mt. Olympus when Jupiter used his thunder bolts to put down their attempted insurrection.[9]

Nimrod

I was already recognizing the face of one of the giants. His chest and shoulders made up his midsection, while both his arms were hanging by his side. Of course, nature, when she gave up making such creatures, showed wisdom in dispossessing Mars, the god of war, of such warriors.[10]

I can hardly imagine what it was like when giants "*were on the earth in those days*" (Gen 6.4). But it must have been quite a sight, especially since the giant in front of me was standing about sixty feet above the surface and that's only the part I could see.[11] He must have been twice that height from head to toe.

On the other hand, nature also showed her wisdom when she allowed huge creatures like elephants and whales to live. Whoever examines this closely will see these animals were allowed to live because their reasoning faculties were more discerning than the giants'.

When the reasoning faculty is joined with ill-will and great might, mankind can't find any refuge against these creatures. The Maker couldn't allow the giants to rule over man, the apex of His creation. So, as one writer put it, "*God did not choose [the giants], nor give them the way to knowledge. So they perished because they had no wisdom; they perished through their folly*" (Baruch 3.27-28).[12]

As I got up closer, I saw the giant's face. It seemed to be as long and large as St. Peter's pine cone in Rome. The bronze figure of the pine cone stood a good thirteen-feet high.[13]

From the bank, which served as a kind of loincloth, the giant's midsection was revealing quite a bit above the surface. It reminded me of what it would look like if three Frieslanders, the tallest men I had ever seen, had stood on top of each other. I think they would have barely reached the giant's chin. I counted about thirty large spans from his waist, meaning that the part I could see made him almost sixty-feet tall.[14] I guess I had been accurate in my initial assessment of his height.

The giant began to speak a load of gibberish out of his infernal mouth: "*Raphael, mai amecche zabi almi.*" I couldn't understand a word he was saying. Maybe he was reciting a Psalm, but I couldn't make it out.[15] Whatever it was, he didn't seem happy.

My leader looked at the giant and said, "O foolish soul. Stick to your horn and vent yourself with that. When anger or another passion wells up, search your neck and you'll find the cord that keeps it taut. O confused soul, see how the horn decorates your large chest."

Virgil then looked at me and said, "This one is Nimrod and he accuses himself. He's the one who corrupted language when, in his pride, he built the tower of Babel that reached toward the heavens. The Maker took care of Nimrod's building project when he "*confused the language of all the earth*" (Gen 11.9).

I was beginning to realize the sheer gravity of Nimrod's sin. Like everything else at creation, the original language given to Adam and Eve (some thought it was Hebrew, but I wasn't so sure) was incorruptible.[16] After all, that first common language continued on even after the Maker created all the languages. But afterwards, everything became confused. Few communicate easily across borders today because of the confusion of different languages. Human language can no longer do what it was intended to do — facilitate easy correspondence.[17]

This confusion is the result of Nimrod's pride as he tried to reach toward the heavens. This terrible scene represented the epitome of misplaced reason and foolishness.[18] Nimrod's building project split the society like no other, making fellowship between people of different tongues very difficult.

Virgil continued, "Let's let him be and not waste our breath. He can't understand us anyway.[19] Every language is like all the others to him. Language is all babble to Nimrod."

Ephialtes

Leaving Nimrod, we keep going along. Turning to our left, about a bowshot away, we encountered another giant, fiercer and taller than the first.

I had to wonder who had the job of tying him up. I can't say, but I did notice his left arm was secured in front of him while his right arm was bound behind. A chain wrapped around his body five times and kept him secured from the neck down.

Virgil said, "This prideful one wanted to exercise his might against the most-high Jupiter. He received his recompense for that silly maneuver."

Virgil continued, "His name is Ephialtes and he performed great feats during the time when giants put fear into the gods. His arms, which he used for these deeds, no longer move."

Ephialtes was a famous giant who had unparalleled strength. The son of Neptune and Iphimedia, Ephialtes tried to oust Jupiter in a coup by slamming Mt. Ossa onto Mt. Pelion.[20] Of course, since he's down here, his efforts failed. Apollo killed Ephialtes and his brother Otus during the coup attempt.[21]

I said to Virgil, "If it's possible, I'd like to see the immense Briareus with my own eyes while we're here." Briareus was one of the mythical giants who participated in the coup attempt against Mt. Olympus.[22] Jupiter killed Briareus with a thunderbolt.

The reason I made this request is I thought Virgil's inclusion of Briareus in the *Aeneid* was absurd. Homer had described Briareus as having one-hundred arms and fifty heads.[23] This was just too much to be believed.

I was playing with Virgil here by bringing up what I thought was one of the worst parts of the *Aeneid*, the ridiculous inclusion of Briareus.[24] Even Virgil, with all his poetic skill, couldn't make it believable. I bet the giant would look much more convincing in my version of the story.

Catching my drift, Virgil responded, "I'm going to take you to see Antaeus instead. He is both speaking and unbound. He'll set us down at the bottommost point of the pit, the gulch of all guilt."

Virgil continued, "Briareus is a bit farther over there. He is tied up and shaped like Antaeus, expect he's more ferocious by his looks."

But, before we could move, we experienced the most intense earthquake I had ever felt. Never before did an earthquake shake a tower so violently as when Ephialtes shook himself just then. I take it that

Ephialtes was angry because we had little interest in him. His inability to speak must have really frustrated him.

At the earthquake, I dreaded death more than ever before. What if the mighty Ephialtes got loose? The experience would have been worse had I not seen the ropes that bound him. If that giant got free, we would be done for.

Antaeus

Proceeding further, we came to Antaeus who stood a good sixty-three feet above the edge of the pit.[25] Antaeus was renowned for his remarkable strength, which grew greater every time he touched the ground.[26]

He came to his end when Hercules figured out the source of his strength, lifted him up, and crushed him.[27] Antaeus was unbound because, unlike the others we had seen, he didn't participate in the insurrection against the gods at Mt. Olympus, which led to the giants' defeat.[28]

Virgil looked up at Antaeus and said, "O you who formerly took as prey one thousand lions, had you been in the other war alongside your brethren, the sons of earth, they would have won. (Well, at least this is what some still believe.) Set us down below and don't be annoyed at our request. Put us down where the cold makes Cocytus freeze over."

Virgil continued, "Don't make us to go to Tityus or Typhon for transport. We don't want to since you're stronger.[29] Here's what's in it for you: the one beside me can give us what we really want. So don't get all bent out of shape or twist your snout. My friend here can still give you the fame you crave in the world above. He's alive and still hopes for a long life to write down what he's seeing here. He'll do it unless grace recalls him before his time."

Virgil's speech seemed to convince Antaeus, who extended his hand and took my leader's. Virgil thus felt the strong grip Hercules once handled when he crushed Antaeus.

Feeling himself grasped, Virgil said to me, "Come here, let me take hold of you." Then he made a single bundle of himself and me."

This reminded me of how the Garisenda tower appears from its overhang when a cloud goes by in the opposite direction from which it seems to lean. Garisenda was a famous leaning tower in Bologna.[30] When Antaeus bent over to pick us up, he looked a lot like that tower.

As I watched Antaeus bend over, I really didn't want to be anywhere near him. He seemed so ferocious and mighty. If I could have gone another way, I would have.

But, to my surprise, he gently let us down at the bottom of Cocytus, the place that devours Lucifer together with Judas. Antaeus didn't stay bent over, however. Like a ship's mast, he arose.

Comment

Canto Thirty-One is transitional.[31] In it, Virgil and Dante descend to the Ninth Circle, which is called Cocytus. This Circle is at the center of the earth and is ice cold. Thus, when we think about the "pit of hell," Dante wants us to envision the center of hell as freezing cold, not burning hot. The reason for this is that Cocytus is completely devoid of love.

After thirty Cantos, we should by now be used to the idea that sin incurs ever-greater punishment as we proceed lower. But does it surprise you that one of the worst sins possible is the corruption of language?

The obvious way to explain this is that the corruption of language affects everyone in the society since language is so fundamental to the human experience. Because of the confusion of language at the tower of Babel, societies are divided instead of united. Nimrod's pride made this a reality.

As a poet, Dante, of course, would be very sensitive to corruptions in language. This is probably one of the reasons Dante composes his poem in the so-called *terza rima*, which he invents. As I pointed out in the Introduction, this rhyme scheme made his poem very hard to corrupt or miscopy, which kept its integrity intact from those who might try to alter it (a frequent problem before the invention of the printing press).

In fact, scholars have noted several numerical patterns that Dante placed within the poem, perhaps to ensure its integrity. To name just one, each line of the poem has eleven syllables.[32] Since each tercet has three lines, this makes for thirty-three syllables, which perfectly matches the number of Cantos in each of the *Paradiso and Purgatorio.*[33] (The *Inferno* also contains thirty-three Cantos, if one considers Canto One an introduction to the *Comedy* as a whole.) Thus the poem is meant to be a perfectly ordered whole, reflecting the perfection of God's created universe.

But what we observe in Canto Thirty-One is not perfect. In fact, Dante has constructed a kind of "linguistic fall."[34] Where language used to be united before the tower of Babel, it splinters after Nimrod's prideful actions. So Dante has been trying to recreate a slice of God's perfect creation in poetry. Is this even possible in a fallen world?

The answer is no. This is why Dante is taking the corruption of language so seriously. It threatens his whole project. In the *Comedy*, Dante has been trying to bridge the gap between words and things, much like a Sacrament brings together a thing and something else signified.[35] Each Canto has had a *contrapasso* that directly connects sin to its consequences.

What's uncomfortable for Dante is the realization that his project might be similar to what Nimrod tried to do. Nimrod doesn't just fall because of pride. He falls because he attempts to reach beyond human limits. But isn't Dante doing the same in this poem? Isn't Dante's goal to find Beatrice in heaven? If Dante is trying to reach toward heaven with human tools, Nimrod did it first. Nimrod presents a grave warning to those who reach for the stars with human effort alone.

As such, what Dante is attempting in this *Comedy* might just be prideful and, ultimately, unattainable.[36] In the end, he can't join things with what they signify because of the limitations of language. Only Jesus, in the Incarnation, can marry Word and flesh. A human author cannot.

This may be why, even at this point, Dante keeps failing on his journey. Only grace, moving through love, can bring him home. Unaided human effort cannot finally be efficacious. And, within the *Inferno*, we see the results of the absence of grace on display all over the place.

One detail easy to miss is Dante's take on the Biblical story of the tower of Babel.[37] Dante largely follows Augustine's interpretation from *The City of God* that the giant Nimrod was the founder not only of Babel, but of the city Babylon, as well.[38] Babylon, the archetypal pagan city, is the source of all the confusion in the world, according to Augustine. This contrasts to the humility of the heavenly city built by Christ in his Incarnation. Augustine puts it this way:

> *We conclude that [Nimrod] raised a tower with the help of his people against God, and by the 'tower' is meant 'impious pride'. However, though a wicked conception is never brought to perfection, it deserves to be punished. But notice the kind of punishment. It was because the tongue is the means for expressing a domineering command that pride was punished in such a way that the man who refused to understand and obey the commands of God should not be understood by men when he tried to command them. Thus was the plot foiled. Since no one could understand him, they abandoned him and he could associate only with those who understood him. Thus were nations divided by language barriers and scattered over the earth.*[39]

Augustine's interpretation makes the *contrapasso* in this Canto clear. Nimrod, whose prideful actions resulted in the confusion of language, finds himself in hell unable to speak intelligibly. He has become the tall tower he himself tried to build, impressive on the outside, but utterly devoid of communicative ability. Because he cannot communicate, Nimrod cannot love. Nimrod is forced to live in his own hell because of the confusion he unleashed on the world.

This is true of the other giants we meet as well. Ephialtes is silent, enraged and bound. He is a reflection of irrational violence that has been rendered impotent.[40] Antaeus, while unbound, never speaks. Yet he is still swayed by promises of fame. Antaeus, infected by the desire for fame, represents a society preoccupied, but ultimately weakened by pride.[41]Once again, sin has disordered what once was in perfect harmony.

Thus it becomes incumbent on us, as readers, to make our own spiritual journeys. Dante cannot do it for us. At this point, Dante's literary project must fail to reach perfection because of the limitations and confusions of human language in the absence of grace.

As pilgrims, we must go into the unknown to be made whole, through grace.[42] Dante's poetry is ultimately an inadequate guide not because it's poor (remember, it's probably the greatest epic poem ever written), but because language is always a limiting factor in a literary depiction of a spiritual journey.

Dorothy Sayers puts it well: *"[The giants] are the images of the blind forces which remain in the soul, and in society when the 'general bond of love' is dissolved and the 'good of the intellect' [is] wholly withdrawn and when nothing remains but blocks of primitive mass-emotion."*[43] In other words, we must examine our own souls and uncover the deep structures of sin that plague us. No one can do it for us.

32

The Pain of Cain

COCYTUS II: BETRAYAL OF CLAN AND COUNTRY

Dante encounters the first two subdivisions of Cocytus, where treachery against clan and country are punished. After Virgil releases Dante to conduct his interrogation, we encounter sinners encased in ice up to their necks. They weep, but their tears freeze in the cold, thus heightening their torture. In Caina, the first section, Camicione de' Pazzi accuses everyone in sight. In the second section, Antenora, we encounter Bocca degli Albati, who betrayed his country. In turn, he betrays everyone around him. The Canto concludes with an as-yet unnamed shade cannibalizing the brain of his neighbor. In this place, love has grown completely cold and the society has disintegrated.

It's getting harder and harder to describe in words what I saw down here. Even if I had verses of poetry rough and jarring enough, I don't think human language is up to the task of illustrating this dismal pit. How can I describe the complete disintegration of society?[44] The entire weight of the world seemed to be bearing down on this very place.

I could try to squeeze more fruit from my recollection, but since I don't have any words to do it justice, I bring myself to speak only with great trepidation. This is no task to be seized lightly. In some ways, not even the infant tongue that cries out "*mamma*" or "*babbo*" is adequate to what I'm trying to do.

Given the enormity of the task in front of me, I call out to the Muses to help me. Let my words be no different than the reality I witnessed.

Oh, sweet ladies who aided Amphion, son of Zeus, who built the walls that closed off Thebes, come to my aid![45]

I keep mentioning Thebes at this lowest point of the Inferno for good reason. Thebes was the archetypical city of suicidal civil war.[46] Founded by Cadmus and Oedipus, Thebes was a city famous for its tragic history of horrific violence.[47] It was reportedly built when the verses of Amphion's poetry caused rocks to come together miraculously and form the walls of the city.[48] I was asking the Muses to help me wall in this terrible place with my verses.[49]

I cried out to all the inhabitants of Cocytus, "Oh you who surpass all badly-born plebes, you're in a place almost impossible to describe. It would have been better if you had been sheep or goats."

I was really directing my comments to Judas, the ultimate betrayer, who I suspected was down here somewhere. I was reminded of what the Divine Son said about him: "*Woe to that man by whom the Son of man is betrayed! It would have been better for that man if he had not been born*" (Matt 26.24).

We were down in the deep dark pit, quite a bit beneath the feet of the giants. I was still looking up at the high wall above. Antaeus and the other giants were standing on some sort of ledge above us. They may have stood over one-hundred feet tall, but we were still quite a ways beneath them.[50]

I heard a voice I didn't recognize say to me, "Watch where you're going. Be careful not to trounce our heads with your feet. We're miserable and exhausted enough. We don't need any more pain from you."

At this, I turned around and looked ahead. Under my feet, I saw a lake that was completely frozen over. It was so icy that it appeared to be made more of glass than water. The best analogy I can draw was to the Danube River in Austria when it freezes in the winter. But it was also like the River Don in the Ukraine that completely freezes over as well.

Even if the full weight of Mt. Tambera or Mt. Pania in the Alps had collapsed on it, I doubt it would have made a crack in the ice, even at its edge.[51] Like most lakes, the center of it was completely frozen, the edges a little bit less.

Caina

The creatures I witnessed next looked like frogs squatting with their snouts above the water, or like a peasant women longing for the summer gleaning season. I have to assume these souls were desperate for some thaw in the ice, a hope that would never come to fruition.

The souls were encased up to their necks in the ice. Through the ice, I could see the rest of their shapes frozen below. Only their heads showed above the ice. I could hear their teeth chattering, which sounded like the clacking that comes from a stork's beak.

Each sinner kept his face turned down. No one wanted to be seen. Each bore witness to the cold with clacking mouths, and to saddened hearts with eyes that were filled with tears.

As I looked around just a bit, I glanced at my feet and saw two shades so close it seemed like the hair on their heads was all mixed together. They were facing each other and had their heads pushed up against the other.[52] I turned to the pressed-together souls and said, "Who are you?"

They craned their necks back and raised their faces toward me. I could see their eyes were still moist inside. They were dripping tears down onto their lips. The cold trapped the tears within their eyes and froze them solid. All these infernal souls could do was to knock their heads together like angered goats.[53] The image looked like a single clamp binding two boards together so they couldn't move.

I noticed one shade had lost both his ears because of the cold. He kept his face turned down, and said, "Why are you standing there staring at us? It's like you're holding up a mirror to yourself. If you want to know who these two are, I'll tell you."

He continued, "The valley where the Bisenzio River descends belonged to these two brothers and their father Alberto. They all came from one family. Even if you search through all of Caina, you won't find a shade more worthy to be put on ice."

From this reference to "Alberto," I realized the two brothers with their heads pressed together were Alessandro and Napoleone degli Alberti. Apparently the two brothers got into a fight over their inheritance and killed each other.[54]

I also couldn't help but notice the close reference to Cain and Abel from the Bible in the name of this first subdivision, Caina. Angry over the Maker's reaction to his brother's sacrifice, "***Cain rose up against his brother Abel and killed him***" (Gen 4.8). I guess this was similar to what happened to Alessandro and Napoleone.

The voice continued, "In fact, not even Mordred, bastard son of King Arthur, is worthy of comparison.[55] The story I heard is when Arthur killed Mordred, light went through his stab wound which broke up his shadow." [56]

He continued, "I'll go even further. Vanni dei Cancellieri from Pistoia, better known as Focaccia, who is rumored to have killed his cousin Detto, can't compare. Focaccia annoys me because his head is constantly in my way and is locked against mine so I can't see."[57]

He said, "Sasol Mascheroni, who murdered his cousin over an inheritance, can't compare either.[58] Sasol's crime was bad enough that he was rolled through the streets of Florence in a barrel full of nails and then beheaded. [59] If you're Tuscan, you know full well who he was."

He concluded, "And so you won't direct any more sermons my way, please know that I was Camicione de' Pazzi and I wait for Carlino to exonerate me."

I had heard of this Camicione. He killed his relative Ubertino to get sole ownership of the property he shared with him.[60] Even worse, he was using his ability to see the future to predict his relative Carlino's death (apparently with glee).[61] Carlino, a White Guelf, would take a bribe to surrender the castle of Piantravigne to the Black Guelfs, a terrible case of betrayal.[62]

Antenora

Next, I saw a thousand faces turned purple from the cold. Unlike in Caina, their faces were looking straight ahead.[63] I shuddered when I saw it and always will whenever I come across a frozen ford. While we were going toward the center of the lake (toward which all gravity is amassed), I was trembling from an unending chill.

Whether it was by destiny or fortune, I don't know, but as I walking among the heads protruding from the ice, my foot stumbled forcefully into the face of one of them. Bawling, one of them asked, "Why are you plaguing me? If you didn't come to get your revenge against Montaperti, why are you abusing me?"

This soul must have been at the Battle of Montaperti in 1260 when the Ghibellines destroyed the Guelfs. This was the battle where Farinata (whom we met above in Canto Ten among the heretics), along with his Sienese allies expelled my party, the Guelfs, from Florence.[64]

I said to Virgil, "Master, please wait for me here. I want to remove any doubt about this one. After I'm done questioning him, you can hurry me along all you want." I said this because it was evident that Virgil was still worried about the waning time we had left.

Virgil stood still while I spoke to the shade encased in ice who was still swearing rudely. I asked, "Who are you that insults another?"

He answered brusquely, "Who are *you* that you go through Antenor, trouncing another's cheeks? If I were still alive, it would be too much to bear."

I answered with equal brusqueness: "I *am* alive. If it's fame you crave in the world above, I have the ability to place your name among the others I've noted during my time down here."

He said to me, "I crave just the opposite. Get out of here and leave me alone. You apparently have no idea how to flatter someone in this swamp."

I couldn't stand this one. So I grabbed him by the back part of his neck and said, "Either you agree to tell me your name or I'll scalp you right here. I'll make sure not one hair will remain on your head."

I hope he didn't miss the irony of what I was saying. The Divine Son had promised his followers that "*not a hair of your head will perish*" (Luk 21.18). This one was about as far away from that promise as you could get. I wanted to finish him off.

He sneered as he replied to me, "Even if you make me bald, I won't tell you who I am nor will I reveal myself. Even if you jump on my head a thousand times, I won't do it. So get lost!"

I had already wrapped his hair in my hand and had ripped out more than one lock. He kept barking away while keeping his eyes deliberately pointed down.

Just then another voice cried out, "What's happening to you, Bocca? Isn't it enough that you pop off with your mouth? Do you have to bark, too? What the devil has gotten into you?"

The adjoining voice revealed this soul as Bocca degli Abati. I shook my head in amazement when I figured out who it was, because "*Bocca*" means mouth in Italian. He was truly a big mouth. But his biggest problem was betrayal.

Bocca was a fellow Guelf who betrayed his party at the Battle of Montaperti. He was a big reason why the Guelfs lost to the Ghibellines that day and had to suffer exile and humiliation. Just at the moment when the Guelfs were being pressured by Manfred and his Ghibelline troops, Bocca cut off the hand of the Guelf standard bearer, which started a panic in the army. [65] This led to the Guelf defeat. Bocca was despicable, if you ask me.

He said, "Be gone, and say whatever you want to say. If you actually escape from here, don't keep silent about the one whose tongue is so ready to speak. The tattle-tale bewails the silver of the French down here. You might say I saw him at Duera where sinners stand cooling off."

Bocca was betraying Buoso da Duera. It was rumored that Buoso had accepted a bribe from the French, which allowed the troops of Charles of Anjou to gain access to Lombardy on their way to taking over Naples in 1265.[66] He was a Ghibelline who was supposed to be protecting a strategic pass for his leader, Manfred, whom he apparently betrayed.[67]

Bocca continued, "I believe you'll see Gianni de' Soldanieri further over there along with Ganelon and Tebaldello who opened up Faenza while it was asleep."

Gianni de' Soldanieri was also a Ghibelline who joined a popular uprising against his leaders in Florence just after the death of Manfred in 1266.[68] He did this despite the honest attempts of the Guelf government of Guido Novello and the Ghibelline nobles to make peace.[69] He betrayed almost everyone, it seems.

Ganelon was famous for being the traitor who caused the demise of Roland, the head of Charlemagne's rear guard.[70] Moreover, Tebaldello, a Ghibelline, treacherously opened the gates of the town of Faenza to the Guelf armies under Geremei of Bologna to get revenge against the Lambertazzi family.[71] His grudge match with this family was apparently over a couple of pigs.[72] For this, scores of soldiers died when they were attacked in their sleep.

The Cannibals

Virgil and I left Bocca behind, but, as we were leaving, we ran into two souls frozen together in one single hole so that their individual heads served as the hat of the other. In one of the most gruesome sights I've ever seen, the one above was sinking his teeth into the one below. He was cannibalizing him and doing it with such apparent zeal that he looked like someone eating bread after being starved. Where the brain joins the spinal column, he was just chomping away.

This was really no different than when Tydeus gnawed at the temples of Menalippus. He munched his skull and everything else with the maximum level of disdain.

Tydeus was a character in Statius' *Thebaid.* While dying from a blow inflicted by Menalippus' spear, Tydeus requested Menalippus' head, whom he had just killed.[73] When the head was presented to him, Tydeus gnawed on it with apparent joy.[74]

I said, "Hey you, who shows such contempt by this bestial sign for the one you're eating, tell me why you're doing this. If you do, I guarantee I'll repay you for it in the world above if I manage to stay alive and see it again.[75] Just give me a reason for your lament. Tell me who you are and what his sin is!"

Comment

We are really starting to hit bottom. There is little order left in this society. Everyone is betraying everyone else. There are no loyalties left. There is no respect for others. There is no love. This society has completely fallen apart, which is what happens when we get as far away as possible from God and his love.

Dante's mention of the "bestial sign" is curious. This is an apparent reference to St. Paul's statement, "***But if you bite and devour one another, take heed that you are not consumed by one another***" (Gal 5.15). Paul likely did not mean this literally, but Dante exploits this text to its full effect if read with wooden literalism. In this world, there is only literalism. These sinners are being devoured by one another and yet are never consumed.

In this terrible place, violence and vengeance are the norm. Everyone has appointed himself as his own god. [76] The existence of another just gets in the way.[77] There is no value to human life in such a society.

This is an important point because Dante is arguing that human dignity derives from our status as bearers of the Image of God. To discard God entirely from a society, as these souls have done, is to discard any basis for valuing another person. All that is left is violence and vengeance.

Dante is again drawing on St. Augustine for his understanding. In Augustine's *City of God,* he writes the following:

> *Here we have the very heart of the earthly city. Its God (or gods) is he (or they) who will help the city to victory after victory and to a reign of earthly peace; and this city worships, not because it has any love for service, but because its passion is for domination. This, in fact, is the difference between good men and bad men, that the former make use of the world in order to enjoy God, whereas the latter would like to make use of God in order to enjoy the world.*[78]

Thus we are left with two choices in the body politic. The society can collectively serve God, which, to Augustine, brings harmony and peace. Or we can focus on ourselves, which brings domination and division. To go a step further and abandon God, as the souls in this Canto have done, is to abandon any permanent basis of value. All that's left to do is to fight and get one's revenge. In a post-modern world that reduces everything of value to power relations, this is what results. It's hell. Cannibalism, the bestial sign, is the absurd extreme of a society completely devoid of love.

To Augustine, it was Cain who was the author of the earthly city. When Dante names the first subdivision of this Canto "Caina," he is making explicit the allusion to Augustine's earthly city. Augustine puts it this way:

> *Now the city of man was first founded by a fratricide who was moved by envy to kill his brother, a man who, in his pilgrimage on earth, was a citizen of the City of God....the root of the trouble [between Cain and Abel] was that diabolical envy which moves evil men to hate those who are good for no other reason than that they are good...Thus we have two wars, that of the*

> *wicked at war with the wicked and that of the wicked at war with the good.*[79]

As John Freccero points out, "Caina" is Augustine's City of Man taken to its absurd extreme. In a society, we can ultimately have communion among the citizens or we can have cannibalism.[80] This is obviously an extreme view. But Dante is picturing what a society would look like without any transcendent reference point to determine value. Without love, there are no relationships and there is no society.

This is especially troubling because the breakdown is almost complete in Canto Thirty-Two. The traitors in this Canto are beyond law breaking. It's far worse. They've destroyed the whole system on which order depends.[81] There is no more law, only might and revenge. If these sinners were released from their icy prisons, they would unleash fury on anything in their sight. If evil is the absence of good, they are the personification of it. As a result, they can never be released.

But what are we to make of Dante's complicity in all this? After all, Dante appoints himself judge, jury and executioner over Bocca.[82] He leaves the constraints Virgil has put on him behind and not only interrogates Bocca, but tortures him. Dante grabs him by the scalp and starts pulling out his hair.

By the way, this is probably a reference to Isaiah's suffering servant who "*gave my back to the smiters and my cheeks to those who pulled out the beard*" (Isa 50.6). As the Church has usually read the passages involving Isaiah's servant as looking forward to Christ, this sufferer in the *Inferno* does so without purpose or redemption.

It is fitting that Dante gets nowhere with this power play. Bocca gives up no useful information. But this act unleashes a flurry of vengeance from those around him. All Dante has done has been to sink to the level of the sinners.[83] Down here, he is little different than they are.

But what does this say about Dante's spiritual progress? It says we all run the risk of stooping to such depravity. Even someone like Dante, who has shown signs of spiritual development, can't help himself. While

Dante may be unwittingly carrying out the vengeance of God, he adjudicates himself poorly when he is shorn of restraint.

Think of how far we have come. What began in a simple, ill-fated sexual embrace between Francesca and Paolo concludes with hatred and betrayal.[84] Just so we don't miss it, Francesca predicts in Canto Five that her husband and murderer Gianciotto would be housed right here in Caina. We are coming full circle from the ill-fated embrace of love to the complete lack of it. The result of sin, at every level, is misery and division.

Moreover, just as Francesca made an important allusion to Augustine's *Confessions* when she stopped reading (presumably to consummate her illicit affair with Paolo), so in this Canto we again encounter an important allusion to Augustine, this time from the *City of God*. The reality of Augustine's earthly city is on full display.

Now we see why Dante says this sight is so hard to describe. It's impossible to understand how people (or shades) can sink to this level. The only relief from the intense cold is the hot hatred within their hearts.[85] This is the picture of a society where love has grown cold and meaningful relationships have been utterly stamped out. This really is hell.

33

The Death of Children

COCYTUS III: CANNIBALS, TRAITORS AND THE DEMON POSSESSED

Dante and Virgil speak with Ugolino who is feasting on the brain of Archbishop Ruggieri. Ugolino tells the tragic story of how Ruggieri starved to death not only Ugolino, but his children as well. This leads to a strong polemic against not only the city of Pisa but also Genoa. Dante then enters the area of Cocytus called Ptolomea, likely named after Ptolemy who betrayed his father-in-law and two sons at a banquet. The sinners in Ptolomea are punished for betraying guests. Once there, Dante meets Brother Alberigo, a Jovial Friar, and Branca Doria who had guests killed. Branca has the strange distinction of still being alive, suggesting that he is possessed by a demon.

Ugolino and Ruggieri

The sinner stopped and lifted up his mouth from his cruel meal. With impeccable, but bestial manners, he wiped his mouth on the hairs of the head he had been gnawing.

Then, the sinner began: "You want me to renew the hopeless grief that already presses on my heart before speaking of it? As Virgil can attest, the remembrance of it is grievous, the sorrow too deep to tell."[86]

Francesca had used this same line from Virgil's *Aeneid* back in Canto Five to justify herself. I was betting this sinner was about to do the same.

He continued, "But if my words are to become seeds which bear infamous fruit against the traitor whose head I'm gnawing, you'll see me speaking and weeping together. I accept your charge to tell my story as long as you agree to keep alive the terrible things this sinner did among the living."[87]

He went on, "I don't know who you are or how you've managed to come down here. But, as soon as I heard you speak before, you certainly sounded like a Florentine to me. You must know that I was Count Ugolino and this sinner whose brain is my eternal meal is Archbishop Ruggieri. I mistakenly put my trust in the Archbishop who had me arrested, locked up and killed. That's a story that doesn't need any more explanation."

I knew Ugolino was a powerful Ghibelline political figure in Pisa.[88] But he was also a traitor, switching his political loyalties, out of expediency, to the Guelf side.[89] When his treachery became known, he was exiled from Pisa.[90] He tried to take over Genoa, but failed. Yet, in a strange turn of events, Ugolino managed to come to power in Pisa with the backing of the authorities in Florence and Lucca who were allied against the existing Pisan leadership.[91]

Despite his best efforts, Ugolino caused a split in the authority structure in Pisa while he was in power.[92] Ugolino then allied himself with the Ghibelline Archbishop Ruggieri in an attempt to take firmer control of the city.[93] Ruggieri then betrayed Ugolino by accusing him of surrendering certain castles to the Florentines.[94] Ruggieri then seized control of the city and imprisoned Ugolino in a tower for nine months where he starved to death after Ruggieri locked the doors and threw away the key.[95]

I couldn't help but notice that Ugolino was, like everyone else, pleading his case to me. He was trying to gain sympathy by placing his own guilt in the past while emphasizing the on-going role Ruggieri played in his demise. This was a clever strategy, but, by now, I was on my guard against such devices. I was used to sinners giving self-serving versions of their stories. [96]

Ugolino said, "Let me tell you why Ruggieri and I are neighbors now. You must realize just how cruel my death was. You simply can't understand this fully unless you've experienced it yourself. I want you to hear and understand how Ruggieri ruined me."

"There was a tower of torture called "hunger" because this was Ruggieri's weapon of choice. You should check it out, others are still yet to be shut up in it. Many moons ago, as if peering through a small slit in the tower, I was having a bad dream. It was like I was in a version of the passion narrative when *'the veil of the temple was torn in two'* (Luk 23.45). The veil that was torn in my dream was the veil of my future. Ruggieri appeared to me as both Lord and Master, hunting the wolf and wolf-cubs on the mountain through which the Pisans can't see Lucca."

I couldn't miss the remarkable resemblance to what I had experienced on the mountain at the start of my journey. Remember, right at the start of my story, I tried to go up the mountain, but ran into a ravenously hungry she-wolf who made sure I came right back down. Somehow, Ugolino was making reference to my own experience to gain sympathy.

I couldn't miss the allusion to the Bible either. Maybe Ugolino himself was speaking better than he knew, since it reminded me of what a traitor he was. Jude said, "*For admission has been secretly gained by some who long ago were designated for this condemnation, ungodly persons who pervert the grace of our God into licentiousness and deny our only Master and Lord*" (Jude 1.4). I don't know if Ugolino intended the reference, but it damned him nevertheless.

Ugolino continued, "With trained hounds, keen and skilled, Gualandi with Sismondi and Lanfranchi were placed in front of Ruggieri in my dream. In a short time, the father and son seemed to tire and I saw their thighs ripped open with the front teeth."

This was ironic since he was telling the truth now. Ugolino was being very accurate in his description of his dream, which corresponded exactly to what happened when Ruggieri turned on him. All three of these names were from famous Ghibelline families in Pisa who joined with Archbishop Ruggieri in his uprising against Ugolino.[97] I recognized that the wolf in the dream was Ugolino while the wolf-cubs were Ugolino's children who were locked up with him.[98]

"When I was awoken from my dream before dawn, I heard in the midst of my sleep my sons with me in prison, crying out and asking for bread."

Ugolino then turned and said, "You are really cruel if you aren't already commiserating with me. Think about what my heart was foretelling. I was going to watch my children starve. If you don't weep at that, what would make you weep?"

Ugolino continued, "My children were already awake and the hour drew nigh when food used to be brought to us. Because of the dream, each child was troubled. Down below, I heard them nailing shut the exit to the tower. It was clear Ruggieri was locking us in and throwing away the key. He would provide us no more food."

"Then, I looked my sons in the face without saying a word. Although I was petrified within, I didn't weep. They were weeping, however. Through his tears, my dear little Anselm said, 'You look funny, father, what's happening to us?'"

"Therefore, I didn't cry nor did I answer that whole day, nor when night drew near. I said nothing until the next sun came into the world. As a small ray found its way into the miserable prison, I noticed through the reflection in their four faces my own appearance. It was gaunt, pale and wasting away."

"In my grief, I bit into both my hands. My children misinterpreted this, thinking I was doing it out of a desire for food. The children arose and said, 'Father we would have less grief if you ate our flesh instead. You clothed us with this miserable flesh, so strip it off now!'"

"So as to not make them sadder, I quieted myself and stayed silent that day and the next. Everything became silent. O hard earth why didn't you just swallow us whole?"

"When, on the fourth day, my son Gaddo came to me and threw himself at my feet, saying, 'My father, why won't you help me?'"

Here, I couldn't miss the allusion to the Divine Son's words on the cross to his own Father, "*My God, My God, why have you forsaken me*" (Ps 22.1)?

Ugolino said, "Right there Gaddo died. As you see me, I saw the other three fall, one by one. On the fifth day, one died, and, on the sixth, another.[99] Already blind from starvation, I found myself fumbling over each of their dead corpses.[100] For days I called to them although they were already dead. At this point, fasting was more potent than grief."

Having recounted his tale of woe, Ugolino, with crazed eyes, took Ruggieri's miserable skull into his mouth. His teeth were strong on the bone, like that of a dog.

Oh, Pisa, reproach of the people. You are that fair city were "*si*" is sung since your neighbors are slow in punishing you. May Capraia and Gorgona, the two small islands in the Mediterranean at the mouth of the Arno that belonged to Pisa, move in and drown every person in it.

I wasn't speaking against Pisa here for killing Ugolino. That seemed perfectly just to me. But killing children by starvation? That was another matter. It was almost incomprehensible to me how a state could justify killing innocent children because a father ran afoul of the powers-that-be. Even if Count Ugolino was connected with the surrender of Pisa's castles to Florence and Lucca, Ruggieri and his thugs shouldn't have taken the lives of his sons by forcing them to endure such a cross.[101]

Their young years made Uguiccione, Ugolino's fifth son, and Brigata, his second grandson, innocent as well.[102] This goes for little Anselm and Gaddo whom I've already mentioned. They all died because of the treachery of Pisa, the new Thebes. Thebes was the archetypical city of wickedness in antiquity.[103] Pisa was following right along in this wake.

Ptolomea

We went on further to where the ice encases others in a rough way. In contrast to Antenora, in the region of Cocytus we had just left, here the faces of the souls were turned up, not down. In Ptolomea, the same wailing we encountered before doesn't actually allow weeping, since perpetual tears freeze into mounds of ice.[104] The grief that finds a barrier at the eyes turns inward, causing anguish to grow. It looked painful because ice expands as it freezes.[105]

When their tears turn to ice, crystals fill up the sinners' eyes all the way up to their eyebrows. As I saw this, I couldn't help remembering the Divine Son's statement, "*While seeing, they do not see, and while hearing they do not hear, nor do they understand*" (Matt 13.13).

It was so cold that all feeling had gone from my face, kind of like the lack of feeling in a callus on the skin. Despite the numbing cold, I could feel a bit of wind blowing across the iced-over sea of Cocytus. I asked Virgil, "Who got this wind going? I thought all vapor was switched off down here."

Virgil responded, "You'll understand in just a bit. You'll see its source for yourself when you discover the cause of the wind."

I thought Virgil's answer was a bit cryptic. I couldn't help but think this wind was the ultimate perversion of the Spirit that was supposed to "*give life*" (John 6.63). Unlike the life-giving Spirit, which "*blows where it wishes*" for those "*born of the Spirit*" (John 3.8), this wind destroys life and inhibits movement. It causes spiritual blindness.

One of the miserable souls in the cold crust cried out to us, "O cruel souls, for some reason you've been given leave to come down to this lowest point. Please clear these blocks of ice from my face for just a bit. I'd like to let out the grief that fills my heart, at least until my tears congeal again."

I responded to him, "If you want me to help you, tell me who you are. If I don't provide relief for you, may I go down to the bottom of this ice formation myself."

Of course, this wasn't a completely honest oath. I had every intention of going down to the bottom of this place to see what was there. For some reason, it didn't seem wrong to me to betray a betrayer.[106]

He answered, "I am Brother Alberigo. I'm the one who offered the fruit of the evil garden. So here, for figs, I'm paid back in dates."

I had seen a number of shocking things down here, but this was just bizarre. I knew full well that Brother Alberigo, a prominent Guelf who had joined the so-called Jovial Friars, was still alive.[107] How could he be down here if his body was still on earth?

There was a rumor going around that Brother Alberigo had his cousin killed during a banquet that he hosted. He was said to have been actively involved in the conspiracy to murder his cousin since he apparently signaled the assassins to ply their trade with the phrase "bring the fruit."[108] I guess this section of the Inferno was reserved for those who had betrayed their guests.[109]

I asked Brother Alberigo, "How is it that you're down here if you're still alive"?

He answered, "I don't really know how my body still exists in the world above. But apparently it's possible. A whole bunch of souls fell down here before Atropos finished her work and sent them out."[110]

Alberigo continued, "Because you're willing to clear away these glazed tears from my face, I'll tell you that as soon as a soul betrays a guest like I did, his body is taken over by a demon who governs it. This can happen well before a soul is ready to die. The soul falls straight into this cistern. Perhaps the body of the shade who winters with me here still appears up there on the earth."

Branca Doria

Now this was just strange. Those who are demon-possessed are already damned and in the Inferno? I hadn't heard that one before. I'm not sure I even believed what he was telling me.

Alberigo went on, "You must know that if you've just come down here, the shade of Branca Doria is right over there. Apparently he's been down here for several years."

I shot back, "I think you're deceiving me. Branca Doria isn't dead yet. He eats and drinks, sleeps and puts on clothes. In fact, when I met Evil Tail above, where the tacky pitch boils, Michael Zanche was nowhere to be found. How can Branca be down here?"

I knew about this Branca. Aided by his nephew, Branca was rumored to have murdered his father-in-law, Michael Zanche, at a banquet.[111] It would have been appropriate that he be punished alongside others who had betrayed their guests, but I knew for a fact that he was still alive.

Alberigo said, "I've now told you plenty. Please now stretch out your hand and clear off my eyes."

I did no such thing. I got what I wanted from him. He made me sick and I wanted nothing more to do with him. The betrayer got betrayed. There was at least some justice in that.

O men of Genoa, separated from every good virtue and full of every corruption, why have you not been dispersed from the world? With the worst spirit of Romagna, I found one of yours, whose soul, because of his works, already bathes himself in Cocytus. While still in the body, he finds himself among the living.

Comment

Dante's depiction of demon-possession is far from Christian teaching. He invents this up and frankly his description, while fascinating, does not work very well. For example, if demon-possessed souls are already in hell, how would Dante explain the souls Jesus freed from demons on earth? Did their souls somehow escape the Inferno after being released? There is little evidence from either Scripture or Tradition to suggest that demon-possessed souls are already in hell.

What is more interesting is Dante's depiction of Ugolino, one of the most lurid characters in the entire poem. We saw in the last Canto how Dante tied Ugolino to Francesca and Paolo from Canto Five through a common allusion to Book Two of Virgil's *Aeneid*. We also observed how Caina presented an allusion to Augustine's earthly city from *The City of God*.

Augustine's theology underlies many aspects of the *Comedy*. For example, Dante has embraced Augustine's view of sin as misplaced love. Augustine's teaching on the corruption of the human heart underlies much of what Dante has been envisioning.

Augustine himself stays in the background of the poem until the very end of the *Paradiso* when we find him at one of the highest points of heaven. This is the first real appearance Augustine makes.

But what is important to notice is the prominent role that Augustine's ideas play at key turning points. We have already seen this with the allusion to the eighth book of the *Confessions* at the key point in Canto Five. Whereas Augustine stopped his reading from a passage in the Bible, made a commitment to celibacy and had an outsized influence on the Church, Francesca and Paolo kept reading their medieval romance, which led to their affair, and their untimely deaths.

Augustine's *Confessions* comes up again in this Canto through a very subtle allusion. One of the climaxes in the *Confessions* is the mystical experience Augustine has with his mother Monica in Book Nine. After experiencing a spiritual vision of God, Augustine writes the following:

> *Therefore we said, if for someone the commotion of the flesh were silent, if the phenomena of the earth, water and air were silent, if the heavens themselves were silent and if the soul itself were silent that it might go beyond itself by not thinking about itself, and if all dreams and imaginary revelations were silent, and if whatever was transient were silent...Oh that this could continue! Then other visions, so far inferior, could be taken away. This vision alone would ravish, engulf and hide the beholder in interior blessedness. Hence eternal life is like that single moment of understanding, which we sighed after. Is this not what is written: 'Enter into the joy of your lord' (Matt 25.21)?*[112]

I think Dante has this climactic passage of the *Confessions* in mind as he describes the silence of Cocytus. Whereas Augustine's vision brings peace, joy and harmony, Ugolino's experience is only suffering, deprivation and division.

This vision of Ugolino at the bottom of the *Inferno* serves as the corruption of the climactic experience Augustine has in the *Confessions*. Given the tie between the *Confessions* and Canto Five of the *Inferno*, it seems appropriate that this allusion comes right as the *Inferno* is about to conclude.

The allusion to the *Confessions* stresses the perfection and unchangeable character of God and the utter futility of ignoring him. Could there be a starker contrast than between Ugolino's cannibalism and Augustine's conversion? Augustine and Ugolino go on to diametrically opposed fates.

But there is another key point to be made with respect to Ugolino and his children. The topic of the corruption of language has come up several times in the second half the *Inferno*. For example, we saw how Nimrod corrupted language at the Tower of Babel in Canto Thirty-One. We also observed the corruption of language in Bertran de Born in Canto Twenty-Eight, who used it to sow division in England. Finally, we encountered the fraudulent use of language among the Soothsayers in Canto Twenty and the Barraters of Canto Twenty-One. The idea that language can be misused has been an especially important theme for Dante.

The story of Ugolino is not so much about the fraud of language, but about a pervasive interpretive misunderstanding. I am following John Freccero's controversial, but brilliant analysis of this Canto. Freccero points out there are allusions to the passion all over the place. For example, Ugolino makes a direct reference to Psalm 22.1 ('*My God, my God, why have you forsaken me*?'), which are some of Jesus' last words on the cross. Dante, in his polemic against Pisa, states that Ruggieri made the children "endure such a cross." The children become innocent sufferers, much like Christ was.[113]

The interpretive misunderstanding starts with the children who misinterpret their father's action of gnawing on his own hand. In response, Ugolino's youngest, Anselm, seems to offer up his own life so that his father might live, a beautiful depiction of the atonement. We shouldn't miss the clear reference Dante makes to St. Anselm, the greatest medieval writer on the need for substitutionary atonement and the Incarnation, in his masterwork *Cur Deus Homo (Why the God-Man).*

But the problem is that Ugolino can't find the spiritual significance in his son Anselm's words.[114] He's a literalist and can only see impending death. His literalism turns him away from the repentance that might have brought spiritual life. The children, speaking spiritually, offer redemptive hope.[115] Ugolino misreads Anselm's statement. This is why Ugolino says "hunger was stronger than grief."

What is the spiritual significance Ugolino was supposed to grasp? If he misinterprets Anselm's offer, thinking he's offering his flesh to cannibalize, what would the proper spiritual interpretation be? It seems clear that what would turn this image around would be the Eucharist. The Eucharist, to a naïve literalist, seems like cannibalization, but is essential for bringing spiritual life.[116]

Thus the key interpretive crux in the Canto is seeing that little Anselm's offer of himself was not only spiritually redemptive, but Sacramental as well.[117] Anselm's statement juxtaposes hunger in the spiritual and material realms. Physical hunger can only be sated for a brief time until it comes again. Spiritual hunger, which similarly needs to be satisfied, can only be sated through spiritual food, namely the Christian Sacraments.

Ugolino, who cannot see the Eucharistic mystery unfolding before him, spends eternity feasting on the brain of a corrupt churchman, Ruggieri. Hence, to denigrate the Sacraments out of naïve literalism is pretty much the worst thing we can do. Dante places this error at the bottom of hell.

While he knew little of the subsequent debates about the Eucharist, Dante anticipates the controversies that would come, particularly after the Reformation. Spiritual starvation is the result of failing to interpret the central Christian mystery properly.[118] Christ offered up himself in a literal body, and Christians participate in his sacrifice through the Eucharist.

The death of children for the purposes of political power is reprehensible and worthy of the worst condemnation. But to miss redemption because of crass literalism is even more tragic. As St. Paul puts it, *"The letter kills, but the spirit gives life"* (2 Cor 3.6).

34

The Emperor of Hell

COCYTUS IV: SATAN AND THE BETRAYAL OF FRIENDS

Dante and Virgil encounter Satan, a massive figure fifty to one-hundred stories tall. As a fallen angel, Satan has six wings and three heads, a perversion of the Trinity. Satan's wings generate massive amounts of frigid air, the reason why Cocytus is frozen over. With his three heads, Satan is continuously cannibalizing three men who betrayed close friends: Judas, Brutus and Cassius. Judas is the worst of the worst. Dante and Virgil then climb down Satan's body, stretched out in the form of a cross, and escape through a narrow opening in the rock. Having passed to the Southern Hemisphere, they now see Satan turned upside down, symbolic of their passage away from the evil that has turned things right-side up. Dante experiences a kind of resurrection in imitation of Christ. Dante and Virgil then emerge on Easter morning and once again see the stars of the sky.

Virgil said, "*Vexilla regis prodeunt inferni,*" which means "abroad the regal banners of the Inferno fly towards us." This is how the entrance hymn for the vespers liturgy on the evening of Holy Saturday goes.[119]

Of course, that's not exactly how the hymn goes.[120] The entrance hymn I knew said nothing about the Inferno when I heard it originally.[121] This was a sign of an important transition about to take place.[122]

Virgil said, "Look on ahead and see if you can make him out." Sure enough, off in the distance, I could see the regal banner of the Emperor of the Inferno.[123] It was quite a sight.

This scene reminded me of a thick fog that rolls in when our hemisphere darkens into night. A long way off, I saw something that looked like a windmill turning round and round. But there was something very odd about it. The windmill was in the shape of a cross.

There was a strong wind blowing through the place, apparently generated by the windmill. This wind seemed like a perversion of the love that is supposed to be shed abroad by the procession of the Spirit (Rom 5.5).[124] Because of the wind, I withdrew behind Virgil since there was no other place to hide.

Satan, Emperor of the Inferno

It's with significant trepidation that I place this next part in verse. I had already retreated behind Virgil to a place where the shades were completely covered and translucent like straw inside of glass. Some shades were lying down. Others were upright. Some had their heads up. Others had their feet up. Still others, like bows, had their faces bent down to their toes. Everything seemed scattered.

We had gone forward far enough that it pleased Virgil to help me see the creature who had once seemed so fair. I recognized immediately that this grotesque figure was none other than Lucifer himself. As his name implies, he was the "light-bearer," and was reputed to be the most beautiful of the angels.[125] This is why Isaiah wrote, ***"How you are fallen from heaven, O Day Star, son of Dawn! How you are cut down to the ground, you who laid the nations low"*** (Isa 14.12)!

Virgil stood aside and made me stop. Pointing toward Satan, he said, "Behold Dis! Behold the place where you have to arm yourself with courage." Virgil was sounding like Pilate here when he exclaimed, ***"Behold the man"*** (John 19.5)! Virgil's reference to Dis suggested that it wasn't just a city, but that Dis was embodied in Satan himself.

Dear Reader, if you're wondering how I became so frozen and faint, don't bother asking, since I'm not going to write about that. All language would miscarry anyway if I tried to explain it. I didn't die, but I didn't stay alive either. From here on out, if you have the wit, think whatever you want about what I became, deprived of one state or the other.

All I'll say was that by not dying, but not living, I was about to experience new birth, the dawn of Easter morning.[126]

Satan, the Emperor of this miserable realm, was standing right-side up, encased in ice up to the middle of his breast.[127] Satan seemed to be occupying the very center of the earth where Fall and Redemption come together.[128] But he was as far away from the Maker as one could get.[129]

Satan seemed to have sunk lower into the ice than Nimrod and the other giants above.[130] In fact, I was standing closer to a giant than Nimrod and his ilk were to Satan's arms. I say this because Satan was simply enormous. I'd say he rose up fifty to one-hundred stories above the ice.[131]

Lucifer might once have been fair, but now he's nothing but ugly. All grief now proceeds from him. He raised his brow against his Maker and is paying the price for his rebellion. As Isaiah put it, "*You said in your heart, 'I will ascend to heaven; above the stars of God I will set my throne on high; I will sit on the mount of assembly in the far north; I will ascend above the heights of the clouds, I will make myself like the Most High'. But you are brought down to Sheol, to the depths of the Pit*" (Isa 14.13-15).

I marveled at what I saw next. Satan had three faces on his head. The first one in front was crimson in color. The other two joined themselves to him above the mid-point and were set at right angles in profile.[132] They united themselves at the place of the crest. The one on the right side was white and yellow, while the one on the left looked black like those who come from Ethiopia.

Satan had three faces. This was an obvious perversion of the Trinity! Their unity at the crest was a symbol of pride.[133] Their being joined together was a further perversion of the unity of the Maker.

Satan desperately wanted to be like God and now his punishment was to embody a deformed image of his desire.[134] Satan was a pure image of evil, the complete absence of goodness.[135]

As for the colors of the faces, they were all related to the Son's passion in some way. The red was emblematic of his sacrificial blood, the yellow to his flesh and the black to his wounds.[136] But the colors also signified the moral decay that Satan had caused.[137] These were the colors of death, not life.

Under each face protruded two large wings, making six wings in all. The wings were huge and looked like those of a large bird. They also looked like a sail on a massive boat, but never had I seen something this large at sea. They had no feathers, but looked like the wings of a bat.

The six wings demonstrated that Lucifer was a fallen angel since the seraphim, the highest rank of angels, boasted of such an expansive set of wings. Isaiah described it this way: "*Above him stood the seraphim; each had six wings: with two he covered his face, and with two he covered his feet, and with two he flew*" (Isa 6.2).

When Satan fluttered his wings, three winds came forth from them. At this point, I realized it wasn't a windmill that was generating the wind down here, but rather Satan's wings. In fact, the reason Cocytus was frozen over was because of the frigid air that proceeded from him. Given the coldness of the place, Satan caused it to be completely devoid of love. He breathed forth hate, division and discord, not love.[138]

From his six eyes, Satan was weeping. His tears dripped down over his three chins. The steady flow of water was like a perverted mixture of tears and bloody drool. This gross mixture was emblematic of Satan's impotent anger.[139]

Judas, Brutus and Cassius

In each of his three mouths, Satan was munching on a sinner. This was evidently a perversion of both a mouth's speaking and eating functions.[140] Satan sunk his teeth continuously into the sinner. His teeth looked like a rake that separates the hemp from the flax. But Satan made sure all three sinners suffered continuously. Frankly, the chopping of the one in front was nothing compared to the awful flaying of his backside. He clawed at one of the sinners so hard the skin of his back was torn off.

Virgil said, "The one who's enduring the worst pain is Judas Iscariot." Judas' head was completely inside Satan's center mouth, while his legs dangled outside. Judas, of course, was the betrayer of the Divine Son, who was his close friend.

Virgil continued, "Now the other two have their heads face down. The first one hanging from Satan's black muzzle is Brutus. See how he twists about and doesn't offer up a word? The other is Cassius. His raw muscles are hanging out because his skin is almost completely torn off from Satan's incessant clawing."

Both Brutus and Cassius conspired to betray their leader and friend Julius Caesar.[141] Caesar had even pardoned Cassius for his alliance with Pompey.[142] But Cassius was clearly the ringleader of this conspiracy, which is why he's in more pain.[143]

Resurrection and Redemption

Virgil continued, "We need to get going. Night is again rising and it's time for us to depart. At this point, we've seen everything."

At Virgil's request, I clung tightly to his neck. At the appropriate time and place, after Satan had opened his wings wide enough, Virgil grabbed onto his furry sides. From one tuft to the next he dropped down between the thick hair and the crusted ice.

When we reached the point where Satan's thigh pivots, at the center point of his haunch, my leader — with great labor and exertion — turned his head to where Satan had his shanks.[144] From there, he grabbed onto Satan's furry pelt as one who climbs. I thought for a minute we were returning to the Inferno.

But Virgil corrected me, saying, "Hold on tight. We've got to get away from so much evil."

Gasping like a man exhausted, we exited the Inferno through a hole in the rock. With wary steps, Virgil reached out for me.

Virgil then set me on a ledge to rest. I lifted up my eyes, thinking I could see Lucifer as I had left him. But, to my surprise, I now saw him upside down. His legs were now upward and his torso was pointing down. If this is confusing, let the uninformed consider this. Think about what point I had just passed.

After we had rested a bit, Virgil said, "Get up onto your feet. The road ahead is long and treacherous. Already the sun is returning to the middle tierce. Morning is upon us."[145]

There, where we were, it wasn't like the promenade of a palace. It was more like a natural dungeon that had bad soil and was bereft of life.

I said to Virgil as I stood up, "Master, before I uproot myself from this abyss, explain some things to me so error might fly far away from me. Where is the ice? And why is Lucifer now upside down? Finally, how in just a few hours, has the sun made the journey from evening to morning?"

Virgil said to me, "You're imagining you're still there in the center of the earth where I grabbed the furry pelt of the guilty worm who pierces the world. You *were* there as long as I was descending. But when I turned, you passed the point at which all weights are drawn from every side."

I guess what Virgil meant is that we had passed into the Southern Hemisphere. Since, according to Aristotle, gravity is centered at the middle of the earth, this was why Lucifer looked like he was upside down.[146]

Virgil continued, "Now you're beneath the hemisphere opposite to the one canopied by dry land. It was right underneath this point that the Divine Son was slain, the one who was born and lived without sin. From this side, that is, the southern hemisphere, Satan fell down from heaven. The land, which previously was here, fled away from him, making a veil of the sea."

I think what Virgil was trying to say was that Jerusalem was the central point of the earth on land, just like Cocytus was the center point of the core of the earth. They were on top of each other. It was just like Ezekiel said: "*This is Jerusalem; I have set her in the center of the nations with countries round about her*" (Eze 5.5). Thus the city of Jerusalem stands directly over where Satan hangs in Cocytus.[147] The cross of the Divine Son stands in triumph over the perversion of the cross in Cocytus.

Virgil said, "You have your feet on a small sphere that forms the other face of Judecca from which we've just exited. Here it's morning when there it was evening. Things have been turned right-side up. The miserable beast whose shaggy pelt made a ladder for us is still encased in ice just as he was before."

Virgil continued, "When Satan was thrown out of heaven (at the moment of creation), our hemisphere fled from him. He crashed into the earth, forming the Inferno. In fleeing from him, the mountain we'll find anon escaped from him and went back above. This is Mt. Purgatory; it's a long way from Beelzebub, the prince of the demons. The mountain is located in the farthest place imaginable from Satan's tomb."

As Virgil said this, I began to realize that Satan had acted as a kind of cross for me. We had climbed up his shaggy body to reach the exit from the Inferno. Thus, unbeknownst to him, the devil's cross had served as a symbol of redemption. Everything in the Inferno had been upside down.[148] But, by coming out the way we did, we were turned right-side up.[149]

Virgil and I followed the sound of a streamlet. Through the hollow of a rock cleft, its course wrapped around and slanted down a bit. Following the stream, my leader and I stayed on that hidden road.

Then we returned to the world of brightness. Without caring to rest, we climbed upward — Virgil in the lead and I behind — until I saw the beautiful things, which heaven brings, through a round opening.

We exited and once again I saw the stars.

Comment

Thus ends the final Canto of the *Inferno*. Some readers have expressed disappointment with this ending. Satan never speaks, which is a great irony, since it contributes to the perversion of how he uses his mouth. Instead of speaking, he devours three sinners in an act of cannibalism. This irony of silence seems to be purposeful. There are no words appropriate to describe pure evil, the complete absence of all good.

While some may wish for an erudite Satan (like Milton's) to explain why he traded in his beauty, intelligence and grandeur in heaven to rebel against God, this is not what Dante gives us. I think he does this because there is nothing remotely erudite about what Satan did. Like everything in the *Inferno*, Satan has misused his God-given endowments. In Dante's view, Satan contributes nothing to the pilgrim's spiritual progress and thus is unworthy of real discussion.

Moreover, unlike popular conceptions of hell as red-hot, we see the exact opposite description that Dante brings to this scene. As we've seen, all of Cocytus is ice cold because of its lack of love. This lack of love leads to a particularly delicious irony.

When Dante figures out that the air that is freezing Cocytus is coming from Satan's wings, he describes this as a "procession." The Italian word Dante uses ("*procedere*") sounds like the English. But, earlier in the Canto, when Dante sees the windmill in the distance that he thinks is generating the wind, he uses a different verb, calling it a "spiration." The Italian word in this case is "*spira*".

Charles Singleton noticed that "spiration" and "procession" are two distinct ways of describing the Holy Spirit.[150] The language of procession should sound familiar. The western version of the Nicene Creed says that the Spirit "*proceeds* from the Father and the Son." Thus procession is that which distinguishes the Holy Spirit from the Father or the Son.[151] The Spirit *proceeds* from the Father and the Son as a means of distinguishing the Spirit as a Person.

According to Thomas Aquinas, however, there are two processions of the Spirit, not one. St. Thomas writes the following:

> *The procession of love in God ought not to be called generation...What proceeds in God by way of love, does not proceed as begotten, or as son, but proceeds rather as spirit; which name expresses a certain vital movement and impulse, accordingly as anyone is described as moved or impelled by love to perform an action.*[152]

Thus the procession of the Holy Spirit that is not generative is called spiration. Said simply, spiration is the "breathing forth" of the love the Father has for the Son, which is expressed to the whole creation through the giving of the Spirit.[153] This spiration, the breathing forth of love, is thus distinct from procession.

The irony is that there's no love in Canto Thirty-Four. The "*spira*" of the windmill blows forth hatred, malice and coldness. What proceeds from Satan is misery and bereavement, not love. Everything has been turned on its head. This place is completely devoid of love.

This leads to one of Dante's most bold inventions, the story of how Satan was thrown out of heaven. Most of this story would have been well-known to Dante's original readers. To a medieval reader, Lucifer was the greatest of all of God's creatures. But, in pride, he wanted to be like God.[154] Satan couldn't be equal to God, but still wanted to be.[155] So the only way to become equal to God was to try to do it by his own might. This was an irrational choice on Lucifer's part, an impious act of pride. Thus Satan initiated a rebellion against God. God threw Satan and one-third of the angels out of heaven in response.

When did this happen? Once again, it's Thomas Aquinas who suggests that Lucifer rebelled at the first possible second after creation, the point at which the exercise of free will becomes possible. Thus the rebellion didn't happen right away after Satan was created, since angels, as spiritual beings, were not created before the physical world came into being. It happens directly afterwards.

According to Augustine, when the Bible says that God created light (Gen 1.3), this is a reference to angels. Augustine writes, "*And since men ask when the angels were made, they are perhaps signified by this light.*"[156] Then, when God separated the light from darkness (Gen 1.4), this is the separation of good angels from bad. The bad angels fall to earth as demons and the good angels stay in heaven.

Here is where Dante starts to innovate. He has Lucifer crashing down into the center of the earth. The displaced landmass creates Mt. Purgatory, which Dante will explore in the next part of the *Comedy.* Satan is stuck at the center of the earth and the giant cavern he creates becomes the Inferno.

Once again, Dante simply invents this. There's no evidence for it in the Christian Tradition or in the Bible. Satan is stuck at the center of the earth. His punishment is to spend eternity breathing out the cold air of malice via his massive wings, which, in turn, keeps him immobile. Pure evil cannot move; it can only devour others. This is as far away from the grace of God as one can go.

Notice, as well, that by being a perversion of the Trinity, Dante also depicts Satan as a perversion of the Eucharist. Instead of feeding on the flesh of Christ, which brings grace, he feeds on the heads of three betrayers, which brings nothing but sterility.

But, ultimately, Satan is a perversion of the healing that comes through the cross. Despite this, by crawling up the immobilized body of Satan, extended in the form of a cross, Dante is saved. Dante tells us that he's not dead, but he's not alive, either. He has to be reborn into new life.

This is why it's so significant that Dante emerges from the Inferno on Easter morning. Dante consciously depicts this scene in imitation of Christ, who descended to hell, but on the third day rose again from the dead. He passes to the southern hemisphere and now everything that was upside down is turned right-side up.

Dante has experienced redemption through the cross. He has transitioned from an examination of sin to an embrace of penance for that sin.[157] But, ultimately, Dante will ascend into heaven, completing his journey and his imitation of Christ. Wholeness, joy and peace await. The dawn of a new day has come.

Endnotes

Notes to Preface/Introduction

1 Dante Alighieri and Dorothy L. Sayers, *The Divine Comedy, Part 1: Hell*, Reprint edition (Harmondsworth etc.: Penguin Classics, 1950), 9.

2 Etienne Gilson, "Forward," in *Saint Augustine: The City of God, Books I-VII*, ed. Hermigild Dressler, Fathers of the Church (Washington DC: Catholic University of America, 1962), xii.

3 Dante Alighieri, *The Banquet* (Lexington, KY: Hard Press, 2006), 1.3.

4 Giuseppe Mazzotta, "Life of Dante," in *The Cambridge Companion to Dante*, ed. Rachel Jacoff, 2nd ed. (Cambridge: Cambridge University Press, 2007), 8.

5 Dante Alighieri, Robert Martinez, and Robert M Durling, *The Divine Comedy of Dante Alighieri: Volume 1: Inferno* (New York: Oxford University Press, 1997), 12.

6 Quoted in Dante Alighieri and Dorothy L. Sayers, *The Divine Comedy, Part 1: Hell*, Reprint edition (Harmondsworth etc.: Penguin Classics, 1950), 50–51.

7 William Anderson, *Dante the Maker* (Brooklyn, NY: S4N Books, 2010), 157.

8 Ibid., 158.

9 This is my translation.

10 Ibid., 210.

11 Richard Lansing, ed., *The Dante Encyclopedia* (London; New York: Routledge, 2000), 480.

12 R. W. B. Lewis, *Dante: A Life*, Reprint edition (New York: Penguin Books, 2009), 125.

[13] Lansing, *The Dante Encyclopedia*, 480.
[14] Lewis, *Dante*, 161.
[15] Lansing, *The Dante Encyclopedia*, 396.
[16] Richard A. Goldthwaite, *The Economy of Renaissance Florence* (Baltimore: JHU Press, 2009), 21.
[17] Ibid., 22.
[18] Ibid., 23.
[19] Prue Shaw, *Reading Dante: From Here to Eternity* (New York: Liveright, 2014), 11.
[20] Goldthwaite, *The Economy of Renaissance Florence*, 5.
[21] Shaw, *Reading Dante*, 11.
[22] Lansing, *The Dante Encyclopedia*, 390.
[23] Ibid., 437–438.
[24] Ibid., 457.
[25] Alighieri, Martinez, and Durling, *The Divine Comedy of Dante Alighieri*, 7.
[26] Anderson, *Dante the Maker*, 154.
[27] Lansing, *The Dante Encyclopedia*, 403.
[28] Alighieri and Sayers, *The Divine Comedy, Part 1*, 34.
[29] Mazzotta, "Life of Dante," 6.
[30] Anderson, *Dante the Maker*, 150.
[31] Ibid.
[32] Ibid., 65.
[33] Peter S. Hawkins, *Dante: A Brief History*, 1 edition (Malden, Mass: Blackwell Publishing, 2006), 10.
[34] Alighieri, Martinez, and Durling, *The Divine Comedy of Dante Alighieri*, 8.
[35] Mazzotta, "Life of Dante," 8.
[36] Alighieri, Martinez, and Durling, *The Divine Comedy of Dante Alighieri*, 9.
[37] Mark Musa, "Introduction," in *Vita Nuova* (Oxford ; New York: Oxford Paperbacks, 2008), vii.
[38] Ibid.
[39] Lansing, *The Dante Encyclopedia*, 874.
[40] Musa, "Introduction," xiii.
[41] Ibid., xiv.

42 Alighieri and Sayers, *The Divine Comedy, Part 1*, 27.

43 Dante Alighieri, *Vita Nuova*, trans. Mark Musa (Oxford ; New York: Oxford Paperbacks, 2008), xlii, P. 84.

44 Anderson, *Dante the Maker*, 3.

45 Alighieri, *The Banquet*, 1.3, P. 11.

46 Shaw, *Reading Dante*, 206.

47 Ibid., 263.

48 "Amazon.com Link," 117', accessed July 7, 2015, http://www.amazon.com/Dante-Maker-William-Anderson/dp/0979870739/ref=sr_1_1?ie=UTF8&qid=1436228462&sr=8-1&keywords=dante+the+maker.

49 Shaw, *Reading Dante*, 191.

50 Lansing, *The Dante Encyclopedia*, 220.

Notes to Canto 1

1 Joseph Gallagher, *A Modern Reader's Guide to Dante's The Divine Comedy* (Liguori, MO: Liguori Publications, 1999), xxi.

2 R. W. B. Lewis, *Dante: A Life*, Reprint edition (New York: Penguin Books, 2009), 74–75.

3 Prue Shaw, *Reading Dante: From Here to Eternity* (New York: Liveright, 2014), 14–15.

4 Peter S. Hawkins, *Dante: A Brief History*, (Malden, Mass: Blackwell Publishing, 2006), 37–39.

5 Francis Ambrosio, "The Divine Comedy: Dante's Journey to Freedom" (presented at the Georgetown X: HUMX421-01x, Georgetown, November 26, 2014), https://courses.edx.org/courses/GeorgetownX/HUMX421-01x/3T2014/info.

6 Hawkins, *Dante*, 32.

7 Dante Alighieri and Charles S. Singleton, *The Divine Comedy, I. Inferno. Part 2* (Princeton: Princeton University Press, 1990), 8.

8 John Freccero, *Dante: The Poetics of Conversion*, ed. Rachel Jacoff, Reprint edition (Cambridge, Mass.: Harvard University Press, 1988), 29.

9 Dante Alighieri and Dorothy L. Sayers, *The Divine Comedy, Part 1: Hell*, Reprint edition (Harmondsworth etc.: Penguin Classics, 1950), 71.

[10] Alighieri and Singleton, *The Divine Comedy, I. Inferno. Part 2*, 11.

[11] Dante Alighieri and Robert M. Durling, *The Divine Comedy of Dante Alighieri: Volume 1: Inferno* (New York: Oxford University Press, 1997), 65.

[12] Alighieri and Sayers, *The Divine Comedy, Part 1*, 77.

[13] Charles S. Singleton, *Dante's Commedia: Elements of Structure* (Baltimore: The Johns Hopkins University Press, 1977), 14.

[14] Jane Chance, *Tolkien and the Invention of Myth: A Reader* (Louisville, KY: University Press of Kentucky, 2004), 210.

[15] I'm aware of the intense scholarly debate concerning the authenticity of this letter, but am assuming its veracity.

[16] Singleton, *Dante's Commedia*, 14.

Notes to Canto 2

[17] Dante Alighieri and Charles S. Singleton, *The Divine Comedy, I. Inferno. Part 2* (Princeton: Princeton University Press, 1990), 27.

[18] Dante Alighieri and Robert Hollander, *The Inferno*, trans. Jean Hollander (New York; London: Anchor Books, 2002), 38.

[19] Prue Shaw, *Reading Dante: From Here to Eternity* (New York: Liveright, 2014), 41–42.

[20] Richard Lansing, ed., *The Dante Encyclopedia*. (London; New York: Routledge, 2000), 576.

[21] The idea of seeing this scene in light of the Annunciation came from Francis Ambrosio, "The Divine Comedy: Dante's Journey to Freedom" (presented at the Georgetown X: HUMX421-01x, Georgetown, November 26, 2014), https://courses.edx.org/courses/GeorgetownX/HUMX421-01x/3T2014/info.

[22] Gregory Nagy, *The Ancient Greek Hero in 24 Hours* (Cambridge, Massachusetts: Belknap Press, 2013), 50.

[23] John Freccero, *Dante: The Poetics of Conversion*, ed. Rachel Jacoff (Cambridge, Mass.: Harvard University Press, 1988), 139.

Notes to Canto 3

[24] Allen Mandelbaum, Anthony Oldcorn, and Charles Ross, eds., *Lectura Dantis: Inferno: A Canto-by-Canto Commentary* (Berkeley: University of California Press, 1999), 36.

25 Ibid., 37.

26 John Freccero, *Dante: The Poetics of Conversion*, ed. Rachel Jacoff (Cambridge, Mass.: Harvard University Press, 1988), 100–101.

27 Dante Alighieri and Robert Hollander, *The Inferno*, trans. Jean Hollander (New York; London: Anchor Books, 2002), 57.

28 Freccero, *Dante*, 114.

29 Ibid., 117.

30 Mandelbaum, Oldcorn, and Ross, *Lectura Dantis*, 41.

31 Ibid.

32 Dante and Charles S. Singleton, *The Divine Comedy, I. Inferno. Part 2* (Princeton: Princeton University Press, 1990), 50.

33 Richard Lansing, ed., *The Dante Encyclopedia*. (London; New York: Routledge, 2000), 151–152.

34 Mandelbaum, Oldcorn, and Ross, *Lectura Dantis*, 44.

35 Ibid., 41.

36 Dante Alighieri and Robert M. Durling, *The Divine Comedy of Dante Alighieri: Volume 1: Inferno* (New York: Oxford University Press, 1997), 65.

37 Dante and Singleton, *The Divine Comedy, I. Inferno. Part 2*, 53–54.

38 Freccero, *Dante*, 56.

39 Paget Toynbee, *Concise Dictionary of Proper Names and Notable Matters in the Works of Dante* (New York: Phaeton Press, 1968), 119–120.

40 Francis Ambrosio, "The Divine Comedy: Dante's Journey to Freedom" (presented at the Georgetown X: HUMX421-01x, Georgetown, November 26, 2014), https://courses.edx.org/courses/GeorgetownX/HUMX421-01x/3T2014/info.

41 Leo F. Stelten, *Dictionary of Ecclesiastical Latin* (Peabody, MA: Hendrickson Publishers, 1995), 188.

42 Lansing, *The Dante Encyclopedia*, 221.

43 John Ciardi and Dante Alighieri, *The Divine Comedy* (New York: New American Library, 2003), 30.

44 Ibid.

45 Helen M. Luke, *Dark Wood to White Rose: A Study of Meanings in Dante's Divine Comedy*, 1st Paperback Edition (Pecos, NM: Dove Publications, 1975), 17.

[46] Freccero, *Dante*, 105.

[47] Alighieri and Hollander, *The Inferno*, 59.

Notes to Canto 4

[48] Dante Alighieri, Robert Martinez, and Robert M. Durling, *The Divine Comedy of Dante Alighieri: Volume 1: Inferno* (New York: Oxford University Press, 1997), 80.

[49] Dante Alighieri and Robert Hollander, *The Inferno*, trans. Jean Hollander (New York; London: Anchor Books, 2002), 78.

[50] Richard Lansing, ed., *The Dante Encyclopedia* (London; New York: Routledge, 2000), 567.

[51] Ibid., 568.

[52] Ibid.

[53] Manlio Pastore Stocchi, "A Melancholy Elysium," in *Lectura Dantis: Inferno: A Canto-by-Canto Commentary*, ed. Allen Mandelbaum, Anthony Oldcorn, and Charles Ross (Berkeley: University of California Press, 1999), 51.

[54] Dante Alighieri and Charles S. Singleton, *The Divine Comedy, I. Inferno. Part 2* (Princeton: Princeton University Press, 1990), 585.

[55] Stocchi, "A Melancholy Elysium," 55.

[56] Ibid., 53.

[57] Alighieri and Singleton, *The Divine Comedy, I. Inferno. Part 2*, 60.

[58] Alighieri, Martinez, and Durling, *The Divine Comedy of Dante Alighieri*, 82.

[59] Ibid.

[60] Dorothy L. Sayers, *Introductory Papers on Dante : The Poet Alive in His Writings*, ed. Barbara Reynolds (New York: Harper Brothers, 1954), 7.

[61] Alighieri and Hollander, *The Inferno*, 82.

[62] Lansing, *The Dante Encyclopedia*, 494.

[63] Dante Alighieri and Mark Musa, *The Divine Comedy: Volume 1: Inferno*, Revised edition (New York: Penguin Classics, 2002), 103.

[64] Ibid.

[65] Lansing, *The Dante Encyclopedia*, 572.

[66] Alighieri and Hollander, *The Inferno*, 83.

[67] Ibid., 84.

[68] Alighieri, Martinez, and Durling, *The Divine Comedy of Dante Alighieri*, 82–83.
[69] Dante Alighieri and John Ciardi, *The Divine Comedy* (New York: New American Library, 2003), 44.
[70] Lansing, *The Dante Encyclopedia*, 336.
[71] Dante Alighieri and Dorothy L. Sayers, *The Divine Comedy, Part 1: Hell* (Harmondsworth etc.: Penguin Classics, 1950), 96.
[72] Alighieri and Hollander, *The Inferno*, 86.
[73] Paget Toynbee, *Concise Dictionary of Proper Names and Notable Matters in the Works of Dante* (New York: Phaeton Press, 1968), 104.
[74] Alighieri and Musa, *The Divine Comedy*, 105.
[75] Lansing, *The Dante Encyclopedia*, 557.
[76] Ibid.
[77] Ibid., 129.
[78] Ibid., 252.
[79] Alighieri, Martinez, and Durling, *The Divine Comedy of Dante Alighieri*, 84.
[80] Toynbee, *Concise Dictionary of Proper Names and Notable Matters in the Works of Dante*, 187.
[81] Alighieri and Musa, *The Divine Comedy*, 106.
[82] Lansing, *The Dante Encyclopedia*, 481.
[83] Ibid., 771–772.
[84] Alighieri and Musa, *The Divine Comedy*, 108.
[85] I'm grateful to Steve Wilensky for pointing this out to me.
[86] Alighieri and Sayers, *The Divine Comedy, Part 1*, 95.
[87] Sayers, *Introductory Papers on Dante*, 133.
[88] Ibid., 134.

Notes to Canto 5

[1] Alighieri and Singleton, *The Divine Comedy, I. Inferno. Part 2*, 74.
[2] Lansing, *The Dante Encyclopedia*, 615.
[3] Alighieri and Sayers, *The Divine Comedy, Part 1*, 101.
[4] Alighieri and Ciardi, *The Divine Comedy*, 51.
[5] Alighieri and Hollander, *The Inferno*, 101.

[6] Alighieri, Martinez, and Durling, *The Divine Comedy of Dante Alighieri*, 95.

[7] Alighieri and Hollander, *The Inferno*, 103.

[8] Alighieri and Sayers, *The Divine Comedy, Part 1*, 102.

[9] Alighieri and Musa, *The Divine Comedy*, 115.

[10] Alighieri and Singleton, *The Divine Comedy, I. Inferno. Part 2*, 77.

[11] Lansing, *The Dante Encyclopedia*, 771.

[12] Alighieri and Singleton, *The Divine Comedy, I. Inferno. Part 2*, 77–78.

[13] Lansing, *The Dante Encyclopedia*, 178.

[14] Alighieri and Musa, *The Divine Comedy*, 116.

[15] Toynbee, *Concise Dictionary of Proper Names and Notable Matters in the Works of Dante*, 408.

[16] Alighieri and Musa, *The Divine Comedy*, 117.

[17] Lansing, *The Dante Encyclopedia*, 832.

[18] Paolo Valesio, "The Fierce Dove," in *Lectura Dantis: Inferno: A Canto-by-Canto Commentary*, ed. Allen Mandelbaum, Anthony Oldcorn, and Charles Ross (Berkeley: University of California Press, 1999), 67.

[19] Alighieri and Singleton, *The Divine Comedy, I. Inferno. Part 2*, 87.

[20] Lansing, *The Dante Encyclopedia*, 409.

[21] Prue Shaw, *Reading Dante: From Here to Eternity* (New York: Liveright, 2014), 102.

[22] Lansing, *The Dante Encyclopedia*, 412.

[23] Ibid., 135.

[24] Toynbee, *Concise Dictionary of Proper Names and Notable Matters in the Works of Dante*, 101.

[25] Alighieri and Singleton, *The Divine Comedy, I. Inferno. Part 2*, 92–93.

[26] Alighieri, Martinez, and Durling, *The Divine Comedy of Dante Alighieri*, 98.

[27] Alighieri and Musa, *The Divine Comedy*, 118.

[28] Alighieri and Singleton, *The Divine Comedy, I. Inferno. Part 2*, 94.

[29] Alighieri and Sayers, *The Divine Comedy, Part 1*, 103.

[30] Sayers, *Introductory Papers on Dante*, 134.

[31] Ibid., 135.

[32] http://digitaldante.columbia.edu/dante/divine-comedy/inferno/inferno-5/, Accessed 12-20-14.

[33] Saint Augustine, *Confessions*, trans. Henry Chadwick (Oxford: Oxford University Press, 2009), 8.12.29, P. 153.

Notes to Canto 6

[34] Alighieri and Hollander, *The Inferno*, 122.

[35] Robert Dombrowski, "The Grain of Hell: A Note on Retribution in Inferno VI," *Dante Studies* 88 (1970): 104.

[36] Alighieri, Martinez, and Durling, *The Divine Comedy of Dante Alighieri*, 108.

[37] Lansing, *The Dante Encyclopedia*, 154.

[38] Maria Picchio Simonelli, "Canto VI: Florence, Ciacco and the Gluttons," in *Lectura Dantis: Inferno: A Canto-by-Canto Commentary*, ed. Allen Mandelbaum, Anthony Oldcorn, and Charles Ross (Berkeley: University of California Press, 1999), 89.

[39] Alighieri, Martinez, and Durling, *The Divine Comedy of Dante Alighieri*, 109.

[40] Simonelli, "Canto VI: Florence, Ciacco and the Gluttons," 90.

[41] Alighieri, Martinez, and Durling, *The Divine Comedy of Dante Alighieri*, 110.

[42] Lansing, *The Dante Encyclopedia*, 13.

[43] Ibid., 629.

[44] Ibid., 130.

[45] Alighieri and Musa, *The Divine Comedy*, 127.

[46] Simonelli, "Canto VI: Florence, Ciacco and the Gluttons," 99.

[47] Toynbee, *Concise Dictionary of Proper Names and Notable Matters in the Works of Dante*, 430.

[48] Sayers, *Introductory Papers on Dante*, 135.

[49] Ibid., 134.

Notes to Canto 7

[50] Dante Alighieri and Robert M. Durling, *The Divine Comedy of Dante Alighieri: Volume 1: Inferno* (New York: Oxford University Press, 1997), 120.

51 Paget Toynbee, *Concise Dictionary of Proper Names and Notable Matters in the Works of Dante* (New York: Phaeton Press, 1968), 430.

52 Dante Alighieri and Dorothy L. Sayers, *The Divine Comedy, Part 1: Hell*, Reprint edition (Harmondsworth etc.: Penguin Classics, 1950), 114.

53 Alighieri and Durling, *The Divine Comedy of Dante Alighieri*, 121.

54 Philip Berk, "The Weal of Fortune," in *Lectura Dantis: Inferno: A Canto-by-Canto Commentary*, ed. Allen Mandelbaum, Anthony Oldcorn, and Charles Ross (Berkeley: University of California Press, 1999), 103.

55 Dante Alighieri and Robert Hollander, *The Inferno*, trans. Jean Hollander (New York; London: Anchor Books, 2002), 141.

56 Ibid., 142.

57 Berk, "The Weal of Fortune," 104.

58 Alighieri and Durling, *The Divine Comedy of Dante Alighieri*, 122.

59 Berk, "The Weal of Fortune," 105.

60 Dante Alighieri and Charles S. Singleton, *The Divine Comedy, I. Inferno. Part 2* (Princeton: Princeton University Press, 1990), 115.

61 Berk, "The Weal of Fortune," 106.

62 Alighieri and Sayers, *The Divine Comedy, Part 1*, 115.

63 Ibid.

64 Ibid.

65 http://www.etymonline.com/index.php?term=Styx, Accessed 1-4-2015.

66 Berk, "The Weal of Fortune," 108.

67 Richard Lansing, ed., *The Dante Encyclopedia* (London; New York: Routledge, 2000), 405.

Notes to Canto 8

68 Dante Alighieri and Robert Hollander, *The Inferno*, trans. Jean Hollander (New York; London: Anchor Books, 2002), 158.

69 Ibid.

70 Dante Alighieri and Robert M. Durling, *The Divine Comedy of Dante Alighieri: Volume 1: Inferno* (New York: Oxford University Press, 1997), 134.

71 Caron Ann Cioffi, "Fifth Circle: Wrathful and Sullen," in *Lectura Dantis: Inferno: A Canto-by-Canto Commentary*, ed. Allen Mandelbaum, Anthony

Oldcorn, and Charles Ross (Berkeley: University of California Press, 1999), 112.

[72] Richard Lansing, ed., *The Dante Encyclopedia* (London; New York: Routledge, 2000), 697.

[73] Dante Alighieri and Mark Musa, *The Divine Comedy: Volume 1: Inferno*, Revised edition (New York: Penguin Classics, 2002), 143.

[74] Cioffi, "Fifth Circle: Wrathful and Sullen," 112.

[75] Ibid.

[76] Alighieri and Hollander, *The Inferno*, 139.

[77] Augustine, *Confessions*, 13.9.10.

[78] Dante Alighieri and Dorothy L. Sayers, *The Divine Comedy, Part 1: Hell* (Harmondsworth etc.: Penguin Classics, 1950), 121.

[79] Lansing, *The Dante Encyclopedia*, 59.

[80] Cioffi, "Fifth Circle: Wrathful and Sullen," 116.

[81] Ibid., 115.

[82] Alighieri and Musa, *The Divine Comedy*, 145.

[83] Lansing, *The Dante Encyclopedia*, 306.

[84] Dante Alighieri and Charles S. Singleton, *The Divine Comedy, I. Inferno. Part 2* (Princeton: Princeton University Press, 1990), 129.

[85] Alighieri and Hollander, *The Inferno*, 161.

[86] William Franke, *Dante's Interpretive Journey* (Chicago: University Of Chicago Press, 1996), 82.

[87] Dante Alighieri and John Ciardi, *The Divine Comedy* (New York: New American Library, 2003), 73.

[88] Thomas Aquinas, *The Summa Theologica of St. Thomas Aquinas* (New York: Christian Classics, 1981), I–II.46.8.

[89] *Dante's Deadly Sins: Moral Philosophy In Hell* (John Wiley & Sons, 2011).

[90] Aquinas, *The Summa Theologica of St. Thomas Aquinas*, II–II.158.1.

[91] Ibid., II–II.158–2.

[92] Franke, *Dante's Interpretive Journey*, 82–83.

Notes to Canto 9

[93] Dante Alighieri and Charles S. Singleton, *The Divine Comedy, I. Inferno. Part 2* (Princeton: Princeton University Press, 1990), 133.

94 Dante Alighieri and Robert Hollander, *The Inferno*, trans. Jean Hollander (New York; London: Anchor Books, 2002), 176.

95 Francis Ambrosio, "The Divine Comedy: Dante's Journey to Freedom" (presented at the Georgetown X: HUMX421-01x, Georgetown, November 26, 2014), https://courses.edx.org/courses/GeorgetownX/HUMX421-01x/3T2014/info.

96 Dante Alighieri and Robert M. Durling, *The Divine Comedy of Dante Alighieri: Volume 1: Inferno* (New York: Oxford University Press, 1997), 149.

97 Amilcare Iannucci, "The Harrowing of Dante from Upper Hell," in *Lectura Dantis: Inferno: A Canto-by-Canto Commentary*, ed. Allen Mandelbaum, Anthony Oldcorn, and Charles Ross (Berkeley: University of California Press, 1999), 123.

98 Alighieri and Hollander, *The Inferno*, 178.

99 Richard Lansing, ed., *The Dante Encyclopedia* (London; New York: Routledge, 2000), 429.

100 Dante Alighieri and Dorothy L. Sayers, *The Divine Comedy, Part 1: Hell*, Reprint edition (Harmondsworth etc.: Penguin Classics, 1950), 127.

101 Paget Toynbee, *Concise Dictionary of Proper Names and Notable Matters in the Works of Dante* (New York: Phaeton Press, 1968), 439.

102 Dante Alighieri and Mark Musa, *The Divine Comedy: Volume 1: Inferno*, Revised edition (New York: Penguin Classics, 2002), 153.

103 Alighieri and Singleton, *The Divine Comedy, I. Inferno. Part 2*, 138.

104 Freccero, *Dante*, 125.

105 Alighieri, Martinez, and Durling, *The Divine Comedy of Dante Alighieri*, 149.

106 John Freccero, *Dante: The Poetics of Conversion*, ed. Rachel Jacoff, Reprint edition (Cambridge, Mass.: Harvard University Press, 1988), 125.

107 Lansing, *The Dante Encyclopedia*, 603.

108 Toynbee, *Concise Dictionary of Proper Names and Notable Matters in the Works of Dante*, 275.

109 William Franke, *Dante's Interpretive Journey* (Chicago: University Of Chicago Press, 1996), 84.

110 Ibid., 85.

111 Alighieri and Durling, *The Divine Comedy of Dante Alighieri*, 151.

112 Iannucci, "The Harrowing of Dante from Upper Hell," 124.

113 Alighieri and Hollander, *The Inferno*, 180.

114 Iannucci, "The Harrowing of Dante from Upper Hell," 124.

115 Alighieri and Musa, *The Divine Comedy*, 156.

116 Alighieri and Durling, *The Divine Comedy of Dante Alighieri*, 152.

117 Alighieri and Hollander, *The Inferno*, 142.

118 Thomas Aquinas, *The Summa Theologica of St. Thomas Aquinas* (New York: Christian Classics, 1981), II–II.5.3.

119 Freccero, *Dante*, 87.

120 Alighieri and Musa, *The Divine Comedy*, 157.

121 Franke, *Dante's Interpretive Journey*, 56.

122 Saint Augustine, *Confessions*, trans. Henry Chadwick (Oxford: Oxford University Press, 2009), 13.9.10.

Notes to Canto 10

123 Dante Alighieri and Robert M. Durling, *The Divine Comedy of Dante Alighieri: Volume 1: Inferno* (New York: Oxford University Press, 1997), 162.

124 Dante Alighieri and Charles S. Singleton, *The Divine Comedy, I. Inferno. Part 2* (Princeton: Princeton University Press, 1990), 144.

125 Ibid.

126 Dante Alighieri and John Ciardi, *The Divine Comedy* (New York: New American Library, 2003), 162.

127 Dante Alighieri and Allen Mandelbaum, *Inferno* (New York: Bantam Classics, 1982), 360.

128 Richard Lansing, ed., *The Dante Encyclopedia*, 1st ed. (London; New York: Routledge, 2000), 347.

129 Dante Alighieri and Robert Hollander, *The Inferno*, trans. Jean Hollander (New York; London: Anchor Books, 2002), 194.

130 Alighieri and Singleton, *The Divine Comedy, I. Inferno. Part 2*, 146.

131 Alighieri and Hollander, *The Inferno*, 194–195.

132 Robert M. Durling, "Farinata and Calvalcante," in *Lectura Dantis: Inferno: A Canto-by-Canto Commentary*, ed. Allen Mandelbaum, Anthony

Oldcorn, and Charles Ross (Berkeley: University of California Press, 1999), 138.

133 Lansing, *The Dante Encyclopedia*, 371.

134 Alighieri and Singleton, *The Divine Comedy, I. Inferno. Part 2*, 148.

135 Alighieri and Mandelbaum, *Inferno*, 360.

136 Alighieri and Durling, *The Divine Comedy of Dante Alighieri*, 163.

137 Durling, "Farinata and Calvalcante," 139.

138 Alighieri and Hollander, *The Inferno*, 196.

139 Durling, "Farinata and Calvalcante," 139.

140 Dante Alighieri and Mark Musa, *The Divine Comedy: Volume 1: Inferno*, Revised edition (New York: Penguin Classics, 2002), 163.

141 Alighieri and Hollander, *The Inferno*, 196.

142 Dante Alighieri and Dorothy L. Sayers, *The Divine Comedy, Part 1: Hell*, Reprint edition (Harmondsworth etc.: Penguin Classics, 1950), 133.

143 Alighieri and Durling, *The Divine Comedy of Dante Alighieri*, 166.

144 Alighieri and Musa, *The Divine Comedy*, 165.

145 Alighieri and Durling, *The Divine Comedy of Dante Alighieri*, 144.

146 Ibid., 167.

147 Alighieri and Singleton, *The Divine Comedy, I. Inferno. Part 2*, 156.

148 Ibid.

149 Alighieri and Hollander, *The Inferno*, 201'.

150 Durling, "Farinata and Calvalcante," 148.

151 John Freccero, *Dante: The Poetics of Conversion*, ed. Rachel Jacoff, Reprint edition (Cambridge, Mass.: Harvard University Press, 1988), 72.

152 Ibid., 85–86.

Notes to Canto 11

153 Dante Alighieri and Robert Hollander, *The Inferno*, trans. Jean Hollander (New York; London: Anchor Books, 2002), 212.

154 Richard Lansing, ed., *The Dante Encyclopedia*, 1st ed. (London; New York: Routledge, 2000), 36.

155 Dante Alighieri and Robert M. Durling, *The Divine Comedy of Dante Alighieri: Volume 1: Inferno* (New York: Oxford University Press, 1997), 178.

[156] Dante Alighieri and Mark Musa, *The Divine Comedy: Volume 1: Inferno*, Revised edition (New York: Penguin Classics, 2002), 173.

[157] Alfred Triolo, "Malice and Mad Bestiality," in *Lectura Dantis: Inferno: A Canto-by-Canto Commentary*, ed. Allen Mandelbaum, Anthony Oldcorn, and Charles Ross (Berkeley: University of California Press, 1999), 151.

[158] Alighieri and Hollander, *The Inferno*, 213.

[159] Dante Alighieri and Dorothy L. Sayers, *The Divine Comedy, Part 1: Hell*, Reprint edition (Harmondsworth etc.: Penguin Classics, 1950), 140.

[160] Dante Alighieri and Charles S. Singleton, *The Divine Comedy, I. Inferno. Part 2* (Princeton: Princeton University Press, 1990), 171.

[161] Triolo, "Malice and Mad Bestiality," 155.

[162] Ibid., 158.

[163] Ibid., 159.

[164] Ibid., 160.

[165] Dante Alighieri and Allen Mandelbaum, *Inferno* (New York: Bantam Classics, 1982), 362.

[166] Alighieri and Durling, *The Divine Comedy of Dante Alighieri*, 183.

[167] Alighieri and Singleton, *The Divine Comedy, I. Inferno. Part 2*, 182.

[168] Alighieri and Musa, *The Divine Comedy*, 175.

[169] Alighieri and Hollander, *The Inferno*, 212.

[169] Irenaeus, *Against Heresies*, vol. 1 (New York: Paulist Press, 1992), 90.

Notes to Canto 12

[1] Dante Alighieri and Charles S. Singleton, *The Divine Comedy, I. Inferno. Part 2* (Princeton: Princeton University Press, 1990), 184.

[2] Paget Toynbee, *Concise Dictionary of Proper Names and Notable Matters in the Works of Dante* (New York: Phaeton Press, 1968), 529.

[3] Dante Alighieri and Mark Musa, *The Divine Comedy: Volume 1: Inferno*, Revised edition (New York: Penguin Classics, 2002), 181.

[4] Alighieri and Singleton, *The Divine Comedy, I. Inferno. Part 2*, 185.

[5] Dante Alighieri and Robert M. Durling, *The Divine Comedy of Dante Alighieri: Volume 1: Inferno* (New York: Oxford University Press, 1997), 192.

[6] Richard Lansing, ed., *The Dante Encyclopedia*, 1st ed. (London; New York: Routledge, 2000), 615–616.

[7] Alighieri and Durling, *The Divine Comedy of Dante Alighieri*, 192.

[8] Vittorio Russo, "The Violent against Their Neighbors," in *Lectura Dantis: Inferno: A Canto-by-Canto Commentary*, ed. Allen Mandelbaum, Anthony Oldcorn, and Charles Ross (Berkeley: University of California Press, 1999), 169.

[9] Alighieri and Singleton, *The Divine Comedy, I. Inferno. Part 2*, 187.

[10] Russo, "The Violent against Their Neighbors," 171.

[11] Alighieri and Singleton, *The Divine Comedy, I. Inferno. Part 2*, 191.

[12] Dante Alighieri and John Ciardi, *The Divine Comedy* (New York: New American Library, 2003), 102.

[13] Lansing, *The Dante Encyclopedia*, 153.

[14] Ibid.

[15] Ibid., 646.

[16] Dante Alighieri and Allen Mandelbaum, *Inferno* (New York: Bantam Classics, 1982), 363.

[17] Lansing, *The Dante Encyclopedia*, 696.

[18] Dante Alighieri and Robert Hollander, *The Inferno*, trans. Jean Hollander (New York; London: Anchor Books, 2002), 232.

[19] Ibid., 193.

[20] Ibid., 232.

[21] Alighieri and Durling, *The Divine Comedy of Dante Alighieri*, 195.

[22] Alighieri and Singleton, *The Divine Comedy, I. Inferno. Part 2*, 194.

[23] Ibid., 196.

[24] Ibid., 198.

[25] Lansing, *The Dante Encyclopedia*, 365–366.

[26] Alighieri and Singleton, *The Divine Comedy, I. Inferno. Part 2*, 199.

[27] Alighieri and Musa, *The Divine Comedy*, 184.

[28] Alighieri and Hollander, *The Inferno*, 233.

[29] Alighieri and Mandelbaum, *Inferno*, 364\.

[30] Russo, "The Violent against Their Neighbors," 175.

[31] Alighieri and Hollander, *The Inferno*, 234.

[32] Ibid.

[33] Alighieri and Singleton, *The Divine Comedy, I. Inferno. Part 2*, 201.

34 Alighieri and Hollander, *The Inferno*, 234.
35 Alighieri and Musa, *The Divine Comedy*, 185.
36 Ibid.
37 Dante Alighieri and Dorothy L. Sayers, *The Divine Comedy, Part 1: Hell*, Reprint edition (Harmondsworth etc.: Penguin Classics, 1950), 146.

Notes to Canto 13

38 Dante Alighieri and Charles S. Singleton, *The Divine Comedy, I. Inferno. Part 2* (Princeton: Princeton University Press, 1990), 205.
39 Dante Alighieri and Mark Musa, *The Divine Comedy: Volume 1: Inferno*, Revised edition (New York: Penguin Classics, 2002), 191.
40 Dante Alighieri, Robert Martinez, and Robert M Durling, *The Divine Comedy of Dante Alighieri: Volume 1: Inferno* (New York: Oxford University Press, 1997), 208.
41 Richard Lansing, ed., *The Dante Encyclopedia*, 1st ed. (London; New York: Routledge, 2000), 469.
42 Dante Alighieri and Robert Hollander, *The Inferno*, trans. Jean Hollander (New York; London: Anchor Books, 2002), 250.
43 Alighieri, Martinez, and Durling, *The Divine Comedy of Dante Alighieri*, 209.
44 Alighieri and Hollander, *The Inferno*, 251.
45 Alighieri, Martinez, and Durling, *The Divine Comedy of Dante Alighieri*, 209.
46 Ibid., 211.
47 Justin Steinberg, *Dante and the Limits of the Law* (Chicago: University Of Chicago Press, 2013), 76.
48 Alighieri, Martinez, and Durling, *The Divine Comedy of Dante Alighieri*, 211.
49 Alighieri and Hollander, *The Inferno*, 251.
50 Alighieri and Singleton, *The Divine Comedy, I. Inferno. Part 2*, 209.
51 Ibid., 210.
52 Lansing, *The Dante Encyclopedia*, 699.
53 Alighieri and Hollander, *The Inferno*, 253.

[54] Dante Alighieri and Dorothy L. Sayers, *The Divine Comedy, Part 1: Hell*, Reprint edition (Harmondsworth etc.: Penguin Classics, 1950), 154.

[55] Alighieri and Singleton, *The Divine Comedy, I. Inferno. Part 2*, 217.

[56] Alighieri, Martinez, and Durling, *The Divine Comedy of Dante Alighieri*, 214.

[57] Steinberg, *Dante and the Limits of the Law*, 75.

[58] Lansing, *The Dante Encyclopedia*, 554.

[59] Paget Toynbee, *Concise Dictionary of Proper Names and Notable Matters in the Works of Dante* (New York: Phaeton Press, 1968), 310–311.

[60] Alighieri and Musa, *The Divine Comedy*, 194.

[61] Alighieri and Singleton, *The Divine Comedy, I. Inferno. Part 2*, 223.

[62] Giorgio Petrocchi, "Canto XIII: The Violent Against Themselves," in *Lectura Dantis: Inferno: A Canto-by-Canto Commentary*, ed. Allen Mandelbaum (Berkeley: University of California Press, 1999), 179.

[63] U. S. Catholic Church, *Catechism of the Catholic Church: Second Edition*, 2nd ed. (New York: Doubleday Religion, 2003), para. 2281.

[64] Prue Shaw, *Reading Dante: From Here to Eternity* (New York: Liveright, 2014), 96.

[65] Steinberg, *Dante and the Limits of the Law*, 75.

[66] Alighieri and Sayers, *The Divine Comedy, Part 1*, 153.

[67] Giuseppe Mazzotta, *Reading Dante* (New Haven: Yale University Press, 2014), 67.

[68] Lansing, *The Dante Encyclopedia*, 469.

[69] Alighieri and Singleton, *The Divine Comedy, I. Inferno. Part 2*, 223–224.

Notes to Canto 14

[70] John A. Scott, "Capaneus and the Old Man of Crete," in *Lectura Dantis: Inferno: A Canto-by-Canto Commentary*, ed. Allen Mandelbaum (Berkeley: University of California Press, 1999), 185.

[71] Alighieri and Singleton, *The Divine Comedy, I. Inferno. Part 2*, 227.

[72] Alighieri, Martinez, and Durling, *The Divine Comedy of Dante Alighieri*, 226.

[73] Scott, "Capaneus and the Old Man of Crete," 186.

74 Lansing, *The Dante Encyclopedia*, 146.

75 Alighieri and Hollander, *The Inferno*, 269.

76 Alighieri and Singleton, *The Divine Comedy, I. Inferno. Part 2*, 228.

77 Alighieri and Hollander, *The Inferno*, 269.

78 Scott, "Capaneus and the Old Man of Crete," 186.

79 Ibid.

80 Alighieri and Musa, *The Divine Comedy*, 201.

81 Alighieri and Singleton, *The Divine Comedy, I. Inferno. Part 2*, 234.

82 Lansing, *The Dante Encyclopedia*, 141.

83 Ibid.

84 Scott, "Capaneus and the Old Man of Crete," 188.

85 Ibid.

86 Alighieri, Martinez, and Durling, *The Divine Comedy of Dante Alighieri*, 229.

87 Scott, "Capaneus and the Old Man of Crete," 189.

88 Alighieri and Musa, *The Divine Comedy*, 203.

89 Ibid.

90 Alighieri and Sayers, *The Divine Comedy, Part 1*, 161.

91 Alighieri and Musa, *The Divine Comedy*, 203.

92 Louis Francis Hartman and Alexander A. Di Lella, *The Book of Daniel*, The Anchor Bible (New York: Doubleday, 1978), 146.

93 Ibid., 31–32.

94 Scott, "Capaneus and the Old Man of Crete," 195. This point is hotly debated by Dante scholars. Some say all the rivers run down individually.

95 Alighieri and Sayers, *The Divine Comedy, Part 1*, 161.

96 Alighieri and Hollander, *The Inferno*, 272.

97 Alighieri and Singleton, *The Divine Comedy, I. Inferno. Part 2*, 121.

98 Scott, "Capaneus and the Old Man of Crete," 188.

99 Dorothy L. Sayers, *Introductory Papers on Dante : The Poet Alive in His Writings*, ed. Barbara Reynolds (New York: Harper Brothers, 1954), 141–142.

100 Steinberg, *Dante and the Limits of the Law*, 36.

101 William Anderson, *Dante the Maker* (Brooklyn, NY: S4N Books, 2010), 292.

Notes to Canto 15

102 Alighieri and Hollander, *The Inferno*, 286.

103 Alighieri and Singleton, *The Divine Comedy, I. Inferno. Part 2*, 251.

104 Alighieri and Musa, *The Divine Comedy*, 209.

105 Toynbee, *Concise Dictionary of Proper Names and Notable Matters in the Works of Dante*, 138.

106 Dante Alighieri and John Ciardi, *The Divine Comedy* (New York: New American Library, 2003), 124.

107 Alighieri, Martinez, and Durling, *The Divine Comedy of Dante Alighieri*, 238.

108 Ibid., 239.

109 Alighieri and Hollander, *The Inferno*, 286–287.

110 Lansing, *The Dante Encyclopedia*, 127.

111 Mazzotta, *Reading Dante*, 72.

112 Alighieri and Hollander, *The Inferno*, 287.

113 Joseph Gallagher, *A Modern Reader's Guide to Dante's The Divine Comedy* (Liguori, MO: Liguori Publications, 1999), 34.

114 Dante Della Terza, "The Canto of Brunetto Latini," in *Lectura Dantis: Inferno: A Canto-by-Canto Commentary*, ed. Allen Mandelbaum (Berkeley: University of California Press, 1999), 200.

115 Alighieri and Hollander, *The Inferno*, 288.

116 Alighieri and Musa, *The Divine Comedy*, 211.

117 Alighieri and Hollander, *The Inferno*, 288.

118 Alighieri, Martinez, and Durling, *The Divine Comedy of Dante Alighieri*, 242.

119 Alighieri and Singleton, *The Divine Comedy, I. Inferno. Part 2*, 268.

120 Charles Williams, *The Figure of Beatrice* (Berkeley: Apocryphile Press, 2005), 130–131.

121 Shaw, *Reading Dante*, 76.

122 Lansing, *The Dante Encyclopedia*, 712.

123 Alighieri and Singleton, *The Divine Comedy, I. Inferno. Part 2*, 271.

124 Lansing, *The Dante Encyclopedia*, 36.

125 Alighieri and Musa, *The Divine Comedy*, 212.

126 Alighieri, Martinez, and Durling, *The Divine Comedy of Dante Alighieri*, 245.

127 Alighieri and Musa, *The Divine Comedy*, 213.

128 Daniel I. Block, *The Book of Ezekiel, Chapters 1–24*, New International Commentary of the Old Testament (Grand Rapids, MI: Eerdmans, 1997), 509.

129 E. A. Speiser, *Genesis: Introduction, Translation, and Notes*, vol. 1 (New Haven: Yale University Press, 2008), 142.

130 Steinberg, *Dante and the Limits of the Law*, 35.

131 Alighieri, Martinez, and Durling, *The Divine Comedy of Dante Alighieri*, 180.

132 Ibid., 245.

133 Steinberg, *Dante and the Limits of the Law*, 38.

Notes to Canto 16

134 Dante Alighieri, Robert Martinez, and Robert M Durling, *The Divine Comedy of Dante Alighieri: Volume 1: Inferno* (New York: Oxford University Press, 1997), 254.

135 Dante Alighieri and Charles S. Singleton, *The Divine Comedy, I. Inferno. Part 2* (Princeton: Princeton University Press, 1990), 276.

136 Dante Alighieri and Allen Mandelbaum, *Inferno* (New York: Bantam Classics, 1982), 368.

137 Dante Alighieri and Robert Hollander, *The Inferno*, trans. Jean Hollander (New York; London: Anchor Books, 2002), 304.

138 Richard Lansing, ed., *The Dante Encyclopedia* (London; New York: Routledge, 2000), 461.

139 Alighieri, Martinez, and Durling, *The Divine Comedy of Dante Alighieri*, 255.

140 Paget Toynbee, *Concise Dictionary of Proper Names and Notable Matters in the Works of Dante* (New York: Phaeton Press, 1968), 19.

141 Alighieri and Hollander, *The Inferno*.

142 Susan Noakes, "Canto XVI: From Other Sodomoites to Fraud," in *Lectura Dantis: Inferno: A Canto-by-Canto Commentary*, ed. Allen Mandelbaum (Berkeley: University of California Press, 1999), 217.

143 Alighieri and Hollander, *The Inferno*, 305.

144 Noakes, "Canto XVI: From Other Sodomoites to Fraud," 217.

145 Lansing, *The Dante Encyclopedia*, 125.

146 Alighieri and Singleton, *The Divine Comedy, I. Inferno. Part 2*, 282.

147 Alighieri, Martinez, and Durling, *The Divine Comedy of Dante Alighieri*, 256.

148 Dante Alighieri and Dorothy L. Sayers, *The Divine Comedy, Part 1: Hell*, Reprint edition (Harmondsworth etc.: Penguin Classics, 1950), 172–173.

149 Dante Alighieri and John Ciardi, *The Divine Comedy* (New York: New American Library, 2003), 132.

150 James C. Nohrnberg, "The Descent of Geryon: The Moral System of Inferno XVI-XXXI," *Dante Studies, with the Annual Report of the Dante Society*, no. 114 (January 1, 1996): 130.

151 Charles S. Singleton, *Dante's Commedia: Elements of Structure* (Baltimore: The Johns Hopkins University Press, 1977), 5.

152 Dante Alighieri and Mark Musa, *The Divine Comedy: Volume 1: Inferno*, Revised edition (New York: Penguin Classics, 2002), 221.

153 Alighieri, Martinez, and Durling, *The Divine Comedy of Dante Alighieri*, 257.

154 Alighieri and Hollander, *The Inferno*, 308.

155 Justin Steinberg, *Dante and the Limits of the Law* (Chicago: University Of Chicago Press, 2013), 37.

156 Noakes, "Canto XVI: From Other Sodomoites to Fraud," 214.

157 Ibid., 219.

158 Ibid., 220.

159 Steinberg, *Dante and the Limits of the Law*, 36.

160 Ibid., 29.

161 Ibid., 20.

162 Ibid., 36.

163 Ibid., 29.

164 Ibid., 153.

165 Teodolinda Barolini, *The Undivine Comedy* (Princeton University Press, 1992), 61.

166 Ibid.

[167] Ibid., 67.

[168] Steinberg, *Dante and the Limits of the Law*, 128.

[169] Barolini, *The Undivine Comedy*, 63.

[170] http://rhinoweb.org/the-five-knots-of-the-franciscan-cord, accessed 5-22-15.

[171] Noakes, "Canto XVI: From Other Sodomoites to Fraud," 223.

Notes to Canto 17

[172] Alighieri and Singleton, *The Divine Comedy, I. Inferno. Part 2*, 295.

[173] Paolo Cherchi, "Geryon's Downward Flight; The Usurers," in *Lectura Dantis: Inferno: A Canto-by-Canto Commentary*, ed. Allen Mandelbaum (Berkeley: University of California Press, 1999), 229.

[174] Ibid.

[175] Lansing, *The Dante Encyclopedia*, 58.

[176] Ibid.

[177] Ibid., 436.

[178] Alighieri and Hollander, *The Inferno*, 322.

[179] Cherchi, "Geryon's Downward Flight; The Usurers," 230.

[180] Nohrnberg, "The Descent of Geryon," 135.

[181] Cherchi, "Geryon's Downward Flight; The Usurers," 231.

[182] William Franke, *Dante's Interpretive Journey* (Chicago: University Of Chicago Press, 1996), 108.

[183] Alighieri and Hollander, *The Inferno*, 323.

[184] Cherchi, "Geryon's Downward Flight; The Usurers," 232.

[185] Ibid., 233.

[186] Alighieri and Musa, *The Divine Comedy*, 239.

[187] Alighieri, Martinez, and Durling, *The Divine Comedy of Dante Alighieri*, 271.

[188] Ibid.

[189] Alighieri and Hollander, *The Inferno*, 324.

[190] Alighieri and Singleton, *The Divine Comedy, I. Inferno. Part 2*, 302.

[191] Ibid., 304.

[192] Alighieri and Musa, *The Divine Comedy*, 229.

193 Alighieri, Martinez, and Durling, *The Divine Comedy of Dante Alighieri*, 271.

194 Cherchi, "Geryon's Downward Flight; The Usurers," 234.

195 Alighieri, Martinez, and Durling, *The Divine Comedy of Dante Alighieri*, 272.

196 Toynbee, *Concise Dictionary of Proper Names and Notable Matters in the Works of Dante*, 228.

197 Lansing, *The Dante Encyclopedia*, 690.

198 Ibid.

199 Alighieri, Martinez, and Durling, *The Divine Comedy of Dante Alighieri*, 272–273.

200 Alighieri and Mandelbaum, *Inferno*, 370.

201 Cherchi, "Geryon's Downward Flight; The Usurers," 235.

202 Ibid.

203 Alighieri, Martinez, and Durling, *The Divine Comedy of Dante Alighieri*, 273.

204 Alighieri and Hollander, *The Inferno*, 326.

205 Barolini, *The Undivine Comedy*, 71.

206 Cherchi, "Geryon's Downward Flight; The Usurers," 231.

207 Ibid.

208 Ibid.

209 Alighieri and Sayers, *The Divine Comedy, Part 1*, 178.

210 Cherchi, "Geryon's Downward Flight; The Usurers," 234.

211 Barolini, *The Undivine Comedy*, 72.

212 Helen M. Luke, *Dark Wood to White Rose: A Study of Meanings in Dante's Divine Comedy*, 1st Paperback Edition edition (Pecos, NM: Dove Publications, 1975), 29.

213 Ibid., 30.

Notes to Canto 18

1 Alighieri, Martinez, and Durling, *The Divine Comedy of Dante Alighieri*, 282.

2 Alighieri and Hollander, *The Inferno*, 338.

3 Alighieri, Martinez, and Durling, *The Divine Comedy of Dante Alighieri*, 283.

[4] Ibid.

[5] John Nohrnberg, "Introduction to Malebolge," in *Lectura Dantis: Inferno: A Canto-by-Canto Commentary*, ed. Allen Mandelbaum (Berkeley: University of California Press, 1999), 239.

[6] Alighieri and Singleton, *The Divine Comedy, I. Inferno. Part 2*, 314.

[7] Alighieri and Hollander, *The Inferno*, 339.

[8] Lansing, *The Dante Encyclopedia*, 542–543.

[9] Nohrnberg, "Introduction to Malebolge," 241.

[10] Alighieri and Musa, *The Divine Comedy*, 233.

[11] Toynbee, *Concise Dictionary of Proper Names and Notable Matters in the Works of Dante*, 100.

[12] Lansing, *The Dante Encyclopedia*, 133.

[13] Alighieri and Singleton, *The Divine Comedy, I. Inferno. Part 2*, 317.

[14] Alighieri and Sayers, *The Divine Comedy, Part 1*, 186.

[15] Alighieri and Mandelbaum, *Inferno*, 371.

[16] Alighieri and Singleton, *The Divine Comedy, I. Inferno. Part 2*, 320.

[17] Alighieri and Sayers, *The Divine Comedy, Part 1*, 185.

[18] Ibid.

[19] Ibid., 187.

[20] Lansing, *The Dante Encyclopedia*, 535.

[21] Ibid.

[22] Alighieri and Hollander, *The Inferno*, 340.

[23] Lansing, *The Dante Encyclopedia*, 811.

[24] Alighieri, Martinez, and Durling, *The Divine Comedy of Dante Alighieri*, 287.

[25] Lansing, *The Dante Encyclopedia*, 585.

[26] Ibid.

[27] Alighieri and Sayers, *The Divine Comedy, Part 1*, 133.

Notes to Canto 19

[28] William Franke, *Dante's Interpretive Journey* (Chicago: University Of Chicago Press, 1996), 95.

[29] Prue Shaw, *Reading Dante: From Here to Eternity*, 1 edition (New York: Liveright, 2014), 43.

30 Giuseppe Mazzotta, *Reading Dante* (New Haven: Yale University Press, 2014), 80.

31 Charles S. Singleton, *Dante's Commedia: Elements of Structure* (Baltimore: The Johns Hopkins University Press, 1977), 26.

32 Dante Alighieri and Charles S. Singleton, *The Divine Comedy, I. Inferno. Part 2* (Princeton: Princeton University Press, 1990), 330.

33 Charles Davis, "Canto XIX: Simoniacs," in *Lectura Dantis: Inferno: A Canto-by-Canto Commentary*, ed. Allen Mandelbaum (Berkeley: University of California Press, 1999), 267.

34 Dante Alighieri, Robert Martinez, and Robert M Durling, *The Divine Comedy of Dante Alighieri: Volume 1: Inferno* (New York: Oxford University Press, 1997), 296.

35 Davis, "Canto XIX: Simoniacs," 267.

36 Ibid.

37 Alighieri and Singleton, *The Divine Comedy, I. Inferno. Part 2*, 331.

38 Mazzotta, *Reading Dante*, 81.

39 Alighieri, Martinez, and Durling, *The Divine Comedy of Dante Alighieri*, 297.

40 Dante Alighieri and Robert Hollander, *The Inferno*, trans. Jean Hollander (New York; London: Anchor Books, 2002), 355.

41 Dante Alighieri and Mark Musa, *The Divine Comedy: Volume 1: Inferno*, Revised edition (New York: Penguin Classics, 2002), 246.

42 Alighieri and Singleton, *The Divine Comedy, I. Inferno. Part 2*, 332.

43 Dante Alighieri and Dorothy L. Sayers, *The Divine Comedy, Part 1: Hell*, Reprint edition (Harmondsworth etc.: Penguin Classics, 1950), 192.

44 Alighieri, Martinez, and Durling, *The Divine Comedy of Dante Alighieri*, 299.

45 Alighieri and Musa, *The Divine Comedy*, 247.

46 Richard Lansing, ed., *The Dante Encyclopedia*, 1st ed. (London; New York: Routledge, 2000), 648.

47 Alighieri and Hollander, *The Inferno*, 356.

48 Shaw, *Reading Dante*, 45.

49 Alighieri and Musa, *The Divine Comedy*, 248.

[50] Lansing, *The Dante Encyclopedia*, 177.
[51] Alighieri, Martinez, and Durling, *The Divine Comedy of Dante Alighieri*, 300.
[52] Lansing, *The Dante Encyclopedia*, 177.
[53] Shaw, *Reading Dante*, 43.
[54] Alighieri and Singleton, *The Divine Comedy, I. Inferno. Part 2*, 342.
[55] Mazzotta, *Reading Dante*, 83.
[56] Lansing, *The Dante Encyclopedia*, 157.
[57] Ibid.
[58] Davis, "Canto XIX: Simoniacs," 269.
[59] Shaw, *Reading Dante*, 47.
[60] Lorenzo Valla and Glen Warren Bowersock, *On the Donation of Constantine* (Cambridge, MA: Harvard University Press, 2008), vii.
[61] Alighieri and Singleton, *The Divine Comedy, I. Inferno. Part 2*, 345.
[62] Mazzotta, *Reading Dante*, 82.
[63] Alighieri, Martinez, and Durling, *The Divine Comedy of Dante Alighieri*, 302.
[64] Ibid., 303.
[65] Shaw, *Reading Dante*, 48.
[66] Eusebius, *The History of the Church: From Christ to Constantine*, ed. Andrew Louth, trans. G. A. Williamson (New York: Penguin Classics, 1990), 3.1.
[67] Valla and Bowersock, *On the Donation of Constantine*, ix.
[68] Dante Alighieri, *The "De Monarchia" of Dante*, trans. F. J. Church (New York: Macmillan, 1879), 108–109.
[69] Peter Hawkins, *Dante's Testaments: Essays in Scriptural Imagination* (Stanford, CA: Stanford University Press, 2000), 32.
[70] Davis, "Canto XIX: Simoniacs," 269.
[71] Ibid., 270.

Notes to Canto 20

[72] Dante Alighieri and Charles S. Singleton, *The Divine Comedy, I. Inferno. Part 2* (Princeton: Princeton University Press, 1990), 347.

[73] Ibid., 348.

[74] Ibid., 349.

[75] Dante Alighieri and Robert Hollander, *The Inferno*, trans. Jean Hollander (New York; London: Anchor Books, 2002), 372.

[76] Teodolinda Barolini, "Canto XX: True and False See-Ers," in *Lectura Dantis: Inferno: A Canto-by-Canto Commentary*, ed. Allen Mandelbaum (Berkeley: University of California Press, 1999), 278–279.

[77] Ibid., 278.

[78] Ibid., 279.

[79] Paget Toynbee, *Concise Dictionary of Proper Names and Notable Matters in the Works of Dante* (New York: Phaeton Press, 1968), 32.

[80] Richard Lansing, ed., *The Dante Encyclopedia*, 1st ed. (London; New York: Routledge, 2000), 36.

[81] Ibid., 820.

[82] Dante Alighieri and Mark Musa, *The Divine Comedy: Volume 1: Inferno*, Revised edition (New York: Penguin Classics, 2002), 256.

[83] Toynbee, *Concise Dictionary of Proper Names and Notable Matters in the Works of Dante*, 519.

[84] Alighieri and Hollander, *The Inferno*, 373.

[85] Lansing, *The Dante Encyclopedia*, 66.

[86] Dante Alighieri, Robert Martinez, and Robert M Durling, *The Divine Comedy of Dante Alighieri: Volume 1: Inferno* (New York: Oxford University Press, 1997), 314.

[87] Alighieri and Hollander, *The Inferno*, 373.

[88] Alighieri, Martinez, and Durling, *The Divine Comedy of Dante Alighieri*, 314–315.

[89] Dante Alighieri and Dorothy L. Sayers, *The Divine Comedy, Part 1: Hell*, Reprint edition (Harmondsworth etc.: Penguin Classics, 1950), 200.

[90] Alighieri, Martinez, and Durling, *The Divine Comedy of Dante Alighieri*, 315.

[91] Alighieri and Musa, *The Divine Comedy*, 253.

[92] Ibid., 257.

[93] Barolini, "Canto XX: True and False See-Ers," 275.

[94] Alighieri and Hollander, *The Inferno*, 376.
[95] Barolini, "Canto XX: True and False See-Ers," 283.
[96] Lansing, *The Dante Encyclopedia*, 142.
[97] Alighieri and Hollander, *The Inferno*, 376.
[98] Barolini, "Canto XX: True and False See-Ers," 284.
[99] Barolini, *The Undivine Comedy*, 80.
[100] Lansing, *The Dante Encyclopedia*, 359–360.
[101] Ibid., 360.
[102] Alighieri and Singleton, *The Divine Comedy, I. Inferno. Part 2*, 359.
[103] Toynbee, *Concise Dictionary of Proper Names and Notable Matters in the Works of Dante*, 372.
[104] Alighieri, Martinez, and Durling, *The Divine Comedy of Dante Alighieri*, 317.
[105] Toynbee, *Concise Dictionary of Proper Names and Notable Matters in the Works of Dante*, 85.
[106] Lansing, *The Dante Encyclopedia*, 66.
[107] Alighieri and Singleton, *The Divine Comedy, I. Inferno. Part 2*, 361.
[108] Alighieri and Musa, *The Divine Comedy*, 258–259.
[109] Barolini, *The Undivine Comedy*.
[110] Barolini, "Canto XX: True and False See-Ers," 277.
[111] Ibid.
[112] Alighieri and Sayers, *The Divine Comedy, Part 1*, 200.

Notes to Canto 21

[113] Teodolinda Barolini, *The Undivine Comedy* (Princeton University Press, 1992), 80.
[114] Giuseppe Mazzotta, *Reading Dante* (New Haven: Yale University Press, 2014), 83.
[115] Steve Ellis, "Canto XXI: Controversial Comedy," in *Lectura Dantis: Inferno: A Canto-by-Canto Commentary*, ed. Allen Mandelbaum (Berkeley: University of California Press, 1999), 292.
[116] Dante Alighieri, Robert Martinez, and Robert M Durling, *The Divine Comedy of Dante Alighieri: Volume 1: Inferno* (New York: Oxford University Press, 1997), 326.

117 Dante Alighieri and Mark Musa, *The Divine Comedy: Volume 1: Inferno*, Revised edition (New York: Penguin Classics, 2002), 265.

118 Paget Toynbee, *Concise Dictionary of Proper Names and Notable Matters in the Works of Dante* (New York: Phaeton Press, 1968), 556.

119 Alighieri, Martinez, and Durling, *The Divine Comedy of Dante Alighieri*, 327.

120 Ellis, "Canto XXI: Controversial Comedy," 293.

121 Alighieri, Martinez, and Durling, *The Divine Comedy of Dante Alighieri*, 327.

122 Dante Alighieri and Robert Hollander, *The Inferno*, trans. Jean Hollander (New York; London: Anchor Books, 2002), 393.

123 Richard Lansing, ed., *The Dante Encyclopedia*, 1st ed. (London; New York: Routledge, 2000), 124.

124 Dante Alighieri and Charles S. Singleton, *The Divine Comedy, I. Inferno. Part 2* (Princeton: Princeton University Press, 1990), 369.

125 Ibid., 371.

126 Dante Alighieri and Dorothy L. Sayers, *The Divine Comedy, Part 1: Hell*, Reprint edition (Harmondsworth etc.: Penguin Classics, 1950), 205.

127 Lansing, *The Dante Encyclopedia*, 84.

128 Dorothy L. Sayers, *Introductory Papers on Dante : The Poet Alive in His Writings*, ed. Barbara Reynolds (New York: Harper Brothers, 1954), 172.

129 Alighieri, Martinez, and Durling, *The Divine Comedy of Dante Alighieri*, 329.

130 Ellis, "Canto XXI: Controversial Comedy," 294.

131 Ibid.

132 Ibid., 295.

133 Ibid., 294.

134 Alighieri and Hollander, *The Inferno*, 397.

135 Sayers, *Introductory Papers on Dante*, 172.

136 Ibid.

137 Ellis, "Canto XXI: Controversial Comedy," 291.

Notes to Canto 22

[138] Teodolinda Barolini, *The Undivine Comedy* (Princeton University Press, 1992), 81.

[139] Dante Alighieri, Robert Martinez, and Robert M Durling, *The Divine Comedy of Dante Alighieri: Volume 1: Inferno* (New York: Oxford University Press, 1997), 342.

[140] Ibid.

[141] Dorothy L. Sayers, *Introductory Papers on Dante : The Poet Alive in His Writings*, ed. Barbara Reynolds (New York: Harper Brothers, 1954), 171.

[142] Alighieri, Martinez, and Durling, *The Divine Comedy of Dante Alighieri*, 343.

[143] Dante Alighieri and Charles S. Singleton, *The Divine Comedy, I. Inferno. Part 2* (Princeton: Princeton University Press, 1990), 381.

[144] Dante Alighieri and John Ciardi, *The Divine Comedy* (New York: New American Library, 2003), 174.

[145] Richard Lansing, ed., *The Dante Encyclopedia*, 1st ed. (London; New York: Routledge, 2000), 169.

[146] Giuliana Carugati, "Canto XXII Poets as Scoundrels," in *Lectura Dantis: Inferno: A Canto-by-Canto Commentary*, ed. Allen Mandelbaum (Berkeley: University of California Press, 1999), 302.

[147] Lansing, *The Dante Encyclopedia*, 925.

[148] Joseph Gallagher, *A Modern Reader's Guide to Dante's The Divine Comedy* (Liguori, MO: Liguori Publications, 1999), 45.

[149] Dante Alighieri and Mark Musa, *The Divine Comedy: Volume 1: Inferno*, Revised edition (New York: Penguin Classics, 2002), 274.

[150] Lansing, *The Dante Encyclopedia*, 451.

[151] Paget Toynbee, *Concise Dictionary of Proper Names and Notable Matters in the Works of Dante* (New York: Phaeton Press, 1968), 275.

[152] Dante Alighieri and Robert Hollander, *The Inferno*, trans. Jean Hollander (New York; London: Anchor Books, 2002), 413.

[153] Alighieri, Martinez, and Durling, *The Divine Comedy of Dante Alighieri*, 345.

[154] Ibid.

155 Alighieri and Singleton, *The Divine Comedy, I. Inferno. Part 2*, 387.

156 Alighieri and Musa, *The Divine Comedy*, 275.

157 Alighieri, Martinez, and Durling, *The Divine Comedy of Dante Alighieri*, 345.

158 Alighieri and Musa, *The Divine Comedy*, 275.

159 Alighieri and Hollander, *The Inferno*, 414.

160 Ibid.

161 Ibid.

Notes to Canto 23

162 Neil M. Larkin, "Another Look at Dante's Frog and Mouse," *MLN* 77, no. 1 (January 1, 1962): 97.

163 Dante Alighieri and Allen Mandelbaum, *Inferno* (New York: Bantam Classics, 1982), 376–377.

164 Dante Alighieri and Mark Musa, *The Divine Comedy: Volume 1: Inferno*, Revised edition (New York: Penguin Classics, 2002), 282.

165 Dante Alighieri, Robert Martinez, and Robert M Durling, *The Divine Comedy of Dante Alighieri: Volume 1: Inferno* (New York: Oxford University Press, 1997), 354.

166 Larkin, "Another Look at Dante's Frog and Mouse," 99.

167 Tibor Wlassics, "Canto XXIII: The Painted People," in *Lectura Dantis: Inferno: A Canto-by-Canto Commentary*, ed. Allen Mandelbaum (Berkeley: University of California Press, 1999), 311.

168 Justin Steinberg, *Dante and the Limits of the Law* (Chicago: University Of Chicago Press, 2013), 163–164.

169 Dante Alighieri and Robert Hollander, *The Inferno*, trans. Jean Hollander (New York; London: Anchor Books, 2002), 430.

170 Johannes Fried, *The Middle Ages* (Cambridge: Harvard University Press, 2015), 114–115.

171 William Anderson, *Dante the Maker* (Brooklyn, NY: S4N Books, 2010), 27.

172 Dante Alighieri and Charles S. Singleton, *The Divine Comedy, I. Inferno. Part 2* (Princeton: Princeton University Press, 1990), 396.

173 Alighieri and Hollander, *The Inferno*, 431.

174 Alighieri, Martinez, and Durling, *The Divine Comedy of Dante Alighieri*, 357.

175 Dante Alighieri and Dorothy L. Sayers, *The Divine Comedy, Part 1: Hell*, Reprint edition (Harmondsworth etc.: Penguin Classics, 1950), 218.

176 Alighieri, Martinez, and Durling, *The Divine Comedy of Dante Alighieri*, 358–359.

177 Alighieri and Singleton, *The Divine Comedy, I. Inferno. Part 2*, 402.

178 Richard Lansing, ed., *The Dante Encyclopedia*, 1st ed. (London; New York: Routledge, 2000), 144.

179 Alighieri and Musa, *The Divine Comedy*, 283.

180 Alighieri and Hollander, *The Inferno*, 432.

181 Lansing, *The Dante Encyclopedia*, 571.

182 Alighieri and Singleton, *The Divine Comedy, I. Inferno. Part 2*, 401.

183 Alighieri, Martinez, and Durling, *The Divine Comedy of Dante Alighieri*, 359.

184 Alighieri and Hollander, *The Inferno*, 432.

185 Margherita Frankel, "Dante's Anti-Virgilian 'Villanello' (Inf. XXIV, 1-21)," *Dante Studies, with the Annual Report of the Dante Society*, no. 102 (January 1, 1984): 87.

186 Ibid.

187 Ibid., 88.

188 Ibid., 85.

189 Dorothy L. Sayers, *Introductory Papers on Dante : The Poet Alive in His Writings*, ed. Barbara Reynolds (New York: Harper Brothers, 1954), 172.

Notes to Canto 24

190 Dante Alighieri, Robert Martinez, and Robert M Durling, *The Divine Comedy of Dante Alighieri: Volume 1: Inferno* (New York: Oxford University Press, 1997), 372.

191 Dante Alighieri and Charles S. Singleton, *The Divine Comedy, I. Inferno. Part 2* (Princeton: Princeton University Press, 1990), 409.

192 Richard H. Lansing, *From Image to Idea: A Study of the Simile in Dante's Commedia* (Ravenna: Longo, 1977), 80.

193 Margherita Frankel, "Dante's Anti-Virgilian 'Villanello' (Inf. XXIV, 1-21)," *Dante Studies, with the Annual Report of the Dante Society*, no. 102 (January 1, 1984): 89.

194 Dante Alighieri and Robert Hollander, *The Inferno*, trans. Jean Hollander (New York; London: Anchor Books, 2002), 448.

195 Frankel, "Dante's Anti-Virgilian 'Villanello' (Inf. XXIV, 1-21)," 89.

196 Ibid., 90.

197 Alighieri and Hollander, *The Inferno*, 448.

198 Frankel, "Dante's Anti-Virgilian 'Villanello' (Inf. XXIV, 1-21)," 90.

199 Ibid.

200 Joan Ferrante, "Canto XXIV: Thieves and Metamorphoses," in *Lectura Dantis: Inferno: A Canto-by-Canto Commentary*, ed. Allen Mandelbaum (Berkeley: University of California Press, 1999), 320.

201 Alighieri, Martinez, and Durling, *The Divine Comedy of Dante Alighieri*, 373.

202 Ferrante, "Canto XXIV: Thieves and Metamorphoses," 321.

203 Alighieri, Martinez, and Durling, *The Divine Comedy of Dante Alighieri*, 373.

204 Alighieri and Hollander, *The Inferno*, 449.

205 Alighieri and Singleton, *The Divine Comedy, I. Inferno. Part 2*, 414.

206 Ferrante, "Canto XXIV: Thieves and Metamorphoses," 322.

207 Ibid.

208 Ibid., 323.

209 Dante Alighieri and Mark Musa, *The Divine Comedy: Volume 1: Inferno*, Revised edition (New York: Penguin Classics, 2002), 295.

210 Alighieri, Martinez, and Durling, *The Divine Comedy of Dante Alighieri*, 375.

211 Joseph Gallagher, *A Modern Reader's Guide to Dante's The Divine Comedy* (Liguori, MO: Liguori Publications, 1999), 49.

212 Dante Alighieri and Dorothy L. Sayers, *The Divine Comedy, Part 1: Hell*, Reprint edition (Harmondsworth etc.: Penguin Classics, 1950), 225.

213 Ferrante, "Canto XXIV: Thieves and Metamorphoses," 325.

214 Alighieri, Martinez, and Durling, *The Divine Comedy of Dante Alighieri*.

215 Dorothy L. Sayers, *Introductory Papers on Dante : The Poet Alive in His Writings*, ed. Barbara Reynolds (New York: Harper Brothers, 1954), 30.

216 Alighieri and Singleton, *The Divine Comedy, I. Inferno. Part 2*, 420.

217 Paget Toynbee, *Concise Dictionary of Proper Names and Notable Matters in the Works of Dante* (New York: Phaeton Press, 1968), 247.

218 Sayers, *Introductory Papers on Dante*, 70.

219 Ibid.

220 Alighieri and Sayers, *The Divine Comedy, Part 1*, 224.

221 Ibid., 140.

222 Richard Lansing, ed., *The Dante Encyclopedia*, 1st ed. (London; New York: Routledge, 2000), 539.

223 Ferrante, "Canto XXIV: Thieves and Metamorphoses," 326.

224 Alighieri and Hollander, *The Inferno*, 453.

225 Dante Alighieri and Allen Mandelbaum, *Inferno* (New York: Bantam Classics, 1982), 378.

226 Ferrante, "Canto XXIV: Thieves and Metamorphoses," 327.

Notes to Canto 25

227 Dante Alighieri and Charles S. Singleton, *The Divine Comedy, I. Inferno. Part 2* (Princeton: Princeton University Press, 1990), 428.

228 Anthony Oldcorn, "Canto XXV: The Perverse Image," in *Lectura Dantis: Inferno: A Canto-by-Canto Commentary*, ed. Allen Mandelbaum (Berkeley: University of California Press, 1999), 333.

229 Dante Alighieri and Robert Hollander, *The Inferno*, trans. Jean Hollander (New York; London: Anchor Books, 2002), 468.

230 Oldcorn, "Canto XXV: The Perverse Image," 329.

231 Dante Alighieri, Robert Martinez, and Robert M Durling, *The Divine Comedy of Dante Alighieri: Volume 1: Inferno* (New York: Oxford University Press, 1997), 390.

232 Oldcorn, "Canto XXV: The Perverse Image," 330.

233 Richard Lansing, ed., *The Dante Encyclopedia*, 1st ed. (London; New York: Routledge, 2000), 152–153.

234 Dante Alighieri and Mark Musa, *The Divine Comedy: Volume 1: Inferno*, Revised edition (New York: Penguin Classics, 2002), 302.

235 Paget Toynbee, *Concise Dictionary of Proper Names and Notable Matters in the Works of Dante* (New York: Phaeton Press, 1968), 100.

236 Ibid.

237 Dante Alighieri and Burton Raffel, *The Divine Comedy* (Northwestern University Press, 2010), 567.

238 Alighieri and Singleton, *The Divine Comedy, I. Inferno. Part 2*, 435.

239 Toynbee, *Concise Dictionary of Proper Names and Notable Matters in the Works of Dante*, 140.

240 Lansing, *The Dante Encyclopedia*, 232.

241 Alighieri and Singleton, *The Divine Comedy, I. Inferno. Part 2*, 436.

242 Alighieri, Martinez, and Durling, *The Divine Comedy of Dante Alighieri*, 391.

243 Alighieri and Hollander, *The Inferno*, 470.

244 Alighieri, Martinez, and Durling, *The Divine Comedy of Dante Alighieri*, 392.

245 Alighieri and Singleton, *The Divine Comedy, I. Inferno. Part 2*, 437.

246 Alighieri, Martinez, and Durling, *The Divine Comedy of Dante Alighieri*, 392.

247 Alighieri and Singleton, *The Divine Comedy, I. Inferno. Part 2*, 437.

248 Ibid.

249 Oldcorn, "Canto XXV: The Perverse Image," 342.

250 Alighieri, Martinez, and Durling, *The Divine Comedy of Dante Alighieri*, 394.

251 Ibid.

252 Alighieri and Musa, *The Divine Comedy*, 303.

253 Toynbee, *Concise Dictionary of Proper Names and Notable Matters in the Works of Dante*, 468.

254 Ibid., 384.

255 Ibid., 101.

256 Ibid., 43.

257 Alighieri, Martinez, and Durling, *The Divine Comedy of Dante Alighieri*, 395.

258 Alighieri and Hollander, *The Inferno*, 437.

259 Alighieri, Martinez, and Durling, *The Divine Comedy of Dante Alighieri*, 396.

260 Alighieri and Hollander, *The Inferno*, 472.

261 Richard Terdiman, "Problematical Virtuosity: Dante's Depiction of the Thieves (Inf. XXIV-XXV)," *Dante Studies, with the Annual Report of the Dante Society*, no. 91 (January 1, 1973): 35.

262 Oldcorn, "Canto XXV: The Perverse Image," 340.

263 Terdiman, "Problematical Virtuosity," 35.

264 Alighieri and Hollander, *The Inferno*, 473.

265 James T. Chiampi, "The Fate of Writing: The Punishment of Thieves in the Inferno," *Dante Studies, with the Annual Report of the Dante Society*, no. 102 (January 1, 1984): 54.

266 Ibid., 55.

267 Alighieri and Hollander, *The Inferno*, 473.

268 Terdiman, "Problematical Virtuosity," 33.

Notes to Canto 26

269 Dante Alighieri, Robert Martinez, and Robert M Durling, *The Divine Comedy of Dante Alighieri: Volume 1: Inferno* (New York: Oxford University Press, 1997), 406.

270 Giuseppe Mazzotta, "Ulysses: Persuasion Versus Prophecy," in *Lectura Dantis: Inferno: A Canto-by-Canto Commentary*, trans. Allen Mandelbaum (Berkeley: University of California Press, 1999), 349.

271 Dante Alighieri and Mark Musa, *The Divine Comedy: Volume 1: Inferno*, Revised edition (New York: Penguin Classics, 2002), 310.

272 Dante Alighieri and Charles S. Singleton, *The Divine Comedy, I. Inferno. Part 2* (Princeton: Princeton University Press, 1990), 448.

273 Alighieri, Martinez, and Durling, *The Divine Comedy of Dante Alighieri*, 406.

274 5Alighieri and Musa, *The Divine Comedy*, 310.

275 796Alighieri and Singleton, *The Divine Comedy, I. Inferno. Part 2*, 448.

276 Dante Alighieri and Dorothy L. Sayers, *The Divine Comedy, Part 1: Hell*, Reprint edition (Harmondsworth etc.: Penguin Classics, 1950), 237.

[277] Ibid.

[278] Dante Alighieri and Allen Mandelbaum, *Inferno* (New York: Bantam Classics, 1982), 380.

[279] William Anderson, *Dante the Maker* (Brooklyn, NY: S4N Books, 2010), 393.

[280] Ibid., 394.

[281] Alighieri, Martinez, and Durling, *The Divine Comedy of Dante Alighieri*, 407.

[282] Dante Alighieri and Robert Hollander, *The Inferno*, trans. Jean Hollander (New York; London: Anchor Books, 2002), 487.

[283] Alighieri and Singleton, *The Divine Comedy, I. Inferno. Part 2*, 453.

[284] Edward M. Hood, "The Condition of Ulysses: Expansions and Contractions in Canto XXVI of the 'Inferno,'" *Annual Reports of the Dante Society, with Accompanying Papers*, no. 81 (January 1, 1963): 5.

[285] Margherita Frankel, "The Context of Dante's Ulysses: The Similes in Inferno XXVI, 25-42," *Dante Studies, with the Annual Report of the Dante Society*, no. 104 (January 1, 1986): 105.

[286] Ibid.

[287] Peter J. Leithart, *1 & 2 Kings* (Grand Rapids, Mich: Brazos Press, 2006), 176.

[288] Giuseppe Mazzotta, *Reading Dante* (New Haven: Yale University Press, 2014), 87.

[289] Alighieri and Hollander, *The Inferno*, 488.

[290] Mazzotta, "Ulysses: Persuasion Versus Prophecy," 354.

[291] Richard Lansing, ed., *The Dante Encyclopedia*, 1st ed. (London; New York: Routledge, 2000), 356.

[292] Paget Toynbee, *Concise Dictionary of Proper Names and Notable Matters in the Works of Dante* (New York: Phaeton Press, 1968), 211.

[293] Ibid., 212.

[294] Mazzotta, *Reading Dante*, 88.

[295] Prue Shaw, *Reading Dante: From Here to Eternity* (New York: Liveright, 2014), 122.

[296] Alighieri, Martinez, and Durling, *The Divine Comedy of Dante Alighieri*, 409.

[297] Lansing, *The Dante Encyclopedia*, 303.

[298] Alighieri, Martinez, and Durling, *The Divine Comedy of Dante Alighieri*, 409.

[299] Alighieri and Hollander, *The Inferno*, 490.

[300] Toynbee, *Concise Dictionary of Proper Names and Notable Matters in the Works of Dante*, 186.

[301] Alighieri, Martinez, and Durling, *The Divine Comedy of Dante Alighieri*, 408.

[302] Lansing, *The Dante Encyclopedia*, 295.

[303] John Freccero, *Dante: The Poetics of Conversion*, ed. Rachel Jacoff, Reprint edition (Cambridge, Mass.: Harvard University Press, 1988), 142.

[304] Ibid., 143.

[305] Alighieri and Sayers, *The Divine Comedy, Part 1*, 238.

[306] Louis Francis Hartman and Alexander A. Di Lella, *The Book of Daniel*, The Anchor Bible (New York: Doubleday, 1978), 234.

[307] Charles S. Singleton, *Journey to Beatrice* (Baltimore: The Johns Hopkins University Press, 1977), 463.

[308] Mazzotta, "Ulysses: Persuasion Versus Prophecy," 351.

[309] Ibid.

[310] Shaw, *Reading Dante*, 124.

[311] Mazzotta, *Reading Dante*, 89.

[312] Peter Hawkins, *Dante's Testaments: Essays in Scriptural Imagination* (Stanford, CA: Stanford University Press, 2000), 274.

[313] Alighieri and Mandelbaum, *Inferno*.

[314] Alighieri, Martinez, and Durling, *The Divine Comedy of Dante Alighieri*, 415.

[315] Hawkins, *Dante's Testaments*, 273.

[316] N. Joseph Torchia, "Curiosity," ed. Allan D. Fitzgerald, *Augustine Through the Ages: An Encyclopedia* (Grand Rapids: Wm. B. Eerdmans Publishing Company, July 31, 1999), 260.

[317] Ibid., 259.

[318] Mazzotta, "Ulysses: Persuasion Versus Prophecy," 355.

[319] Ibid.

Notes to Canto 27

320 Dante Alighieri and Robert Hollander, *The Inferno*, trans. Jean Hollander (New York; London: Anchor Books, 2002), 506.

321 Dante Alighieri, Robert Martinez, and Robert M Durling, *The Divine Comedy of Dante Alighieri: Volume 1: Inferno* (New York: Oxford University Press, 1997), 424.

322 Dante Alighieri and Mark Musa, *The Divine Comedy: Volume 1: Inferno*, Revised edition (New York: Penguin Classics, 2002), 319.

323 Dante Alighieri and Charles S. Singleton, *The Divine Comedy, I. Inferno. Part 2* (Princeton: Princeton University Press, 1990), 472.

324 Alighieri and Hollander, *The Inferno*, 506.

325 Richard Lansing, ed., *The Dante Encyclopedia*, 1st ed. (London; New York: Routledge, 2000), 462.

326 Ibid.

327 Paget Toynbee, *Concise Dictionary of Proper Names and Notable Matters in the Works of Dante* (New York: Phaeton Press, 1968), 289.

328 Alighieri and Hollander, *The Inferno*, 507.

329 Joseph Markulin, "Dante's Guido Da Montefeltro: A Reconsideration," *Dante Studies, with the Annual Report of the Dante Society*, no. 100 (January 1, 1982): 27.

330 Alighieri and Musa, *The Divine Comedy*, 320.

331 Alighieri, Martinez, and Durling, *The Divine Comedy of Dante Alighieri*, 426.

332 Alighieri and Singleton, *The Divine Comedy, I. Inferno. Part 2*, 480–481.

333 Alighieri, Martinez, and Durling, *The Divine Comedy of Dante Alighieri*, 426.

334 Dante Alighieri and Dorothy L. Sayers, *The Divine Comedy, Part 1: Hell*, Reprint edition (Harmondsworth etc.: Penguin Classics, 1950), 244.

335 Ibid., 245.

336 Alighieri and Singleton, *The Divine Comedy, I. Inferno. Part 2*, 485.

337 Alighieri, Martinez, and Durling, *The Divine Comedy of Dante Alighieri*, 427.

338 Dante Alighieri and Allen Mandelbaum, *Inferno* (New York: Bantam Classics, 1982), 382.

[339] Alighieri, Martinez, and Durling, *The Divine Comedy of Dante Alighieri*, 428.
[340] Ibid.
[341] Alighieri and Singleton, *The Divine Comedy, I. Inferno. Part 2*, 489.
[342] Ibid.
[343] Jennifer Petrie, "Canto XXVII: False Counselors: Guido Da Montefeltro," in *Lectura Dantis: Inferno: A Canto-by-Canto Commentary*, ed. Allen Mandelbaum (Berkeley: University of California Press, 1999), 363.
[344] Alighieri and Musa, *The Divine Comedy*, 323.
[345] Alighieri, Martinez, and Durling, *The Divine Comedy of Dante Alighieri*, 430.
[346] Ibid., 431.
[347] Alighieri and Musa, *The Divine Comedy*, 319.
[348] Markulin, "Dante's Guido Da Montefeltro," 31.
[349] Ibid.
[350] Ibid., 35.
[351] Anna Hatcher, "Dante's Ulysses and Guido Da Montefeltro," *Dante Studies, with the Annual Report of the Dante Society*, no. 88 (January 1, 1970): 112.
[352] Ibid., 113.
[353] Justin Steinberg, *Dante and the Limits of the Law* (Chicago: University Of Chicago Press, 2013), 138.
[354] Ibid., 140.
[355] Ibid., 141.
[356] Alighieri and Musa, *The Divine Comedy*, 323.

Notes to Canto 28

[357] Dante Alighieri, Robert Martinez, and Robert M Durling, *The Divine Comedy of Dante Alighieri: Volume 1: Inferno* (New York: Oxford University Press, 1997), 440.
[358] Dante Alighieri and Robert Hollander, *The Inferno*, trans. Jean Hollander (New York; London: Anchor Books, 2002), 524.
[359] Richard Lansing, ed., *The Dante Encyclopedia*, 1st ed. (London; New York: Routledge, 2000), 466.

[360] Dante Alighieri and Charles S. Singleton, *The Divine Comedy, I. Inferno. Part 2* (Princeton: Princeton University Press, 1990), 499.

[361] Alighieri and Hollander, *The Inferno*, 525.

[362] Paget Toynbee, *Concise Dictionary of Proper Names and Notable Matters in the Works of Dante* (New York: Phaeton Press, 1968), 14–15.

[363] Dante Alighieri and Mark Musa, *The Divine Comedy: Volume 1: Inferno*, Revised edition (New York: Penguin Classics, 2002), 330–331.

[364] Alighieri and Singleton, *The Divine Comedy, I. Inferno. Part 2*, 502.

[365] Karla Mallette, "Muhammad in Hell," *Dante Studies, with the Annual Report of the Dante Society*, no. 125 (January 1, 2007): 217.

[366] Justin Steinberg, *Dante and the Limits of the Law* (Chicago: University Of Chicago Press, 2013), 42.

[367] Mallette, "Muhammad in Hell," 218.

[368] Alighieri and Singleton, *The Divine Comedy, I. Inferno. Part 2*, 504.

[369] Lansing, *The Dante Encyclopedia*, 311.

[370] Alighieri, Martinez, and Durling, *The Divine Comedy of Dante Alighieri*, 443.

[371] Alighieri and Musa, *The Divine Comedy*, 331.

[372] Thomas Peterson, "Canto XXVIII: Scandal and Schism," in *Lectura Dantis: Inferno: A Canto-by-Canto Commentary*, ed. Allen Mandelbaum (Berkeley: University of California Press, 1999), 372.

[373] Alighieri, Martinez, and Durling, *The Divine Comedy of Dante Alighieri*, 444.

[374] Dante Alighieri and Allen Mandelbaum, *Inferno* (New York: Bantam Classics, 1982), 384.

[375] Alighieri and Hollander, *The Inferno*, 528.

[376] Dante Alighieri and Dorothy L. Sayers, *The Divine Comedy, Part 1: Hell*, Reprint edition (Harmondsworth etc.: Penguin Classics, 1950), 251.

[377] Alighieri and Singleton, *The Divine Comedy, I. Inferno. Part 2*, 512.

[378] Alighieri, Martinez, and Durling, *The Divine Comedy of Dante Alighieri*, 445.

[379] Peterson, "Canto XXVIII: Scandal and Schism," 373.

[380] Lansing, *The Dante Encyclopedia*, 242.

[381] Alighieri, Martinez, and Durling, *The Divine Comedy of Dante Alighieri*, 446.

[382] Toynbee, *Concise Dictionary of Proper Names and Notable Matters in the Works of Dante*, 170.

[383] Alighieri and Singleton, *The Divine Comedy, I. Inferno. Part 2*, 515.

[384] Peterson, "Canto XXVIII: Scandal and Schism," 373.

[385] Alighieri, Martinez, and Durling, *The Divine Comedy of Dante Alighieri*, 446.

[386] Alighieri and Hollander, *The Inferno*, 528.

[387] Alighieri and Singleton, *The Divine Comedy, I. Inferno. Part 2*, 516.

[388] Dante Alighieri and John Ciardi, *The Divine Comedy* (New York: New American Library, 2003), 224.

[389] Marianne Shapiro, "The Fictionalization of Bertran de Born (Inf. XXVIII)," *Dante Studies, with the Annual Report of the Dante Society*, no. 92 (January 1, 1974): 107.

[390] Ibid., 109.

[391] Ibid., 111.

[392] Toynbee, *Concise Dictionary of Proper Names and Notable Matters in the Works of Dante*, 76.

[393] Lansing, *The Dante Encyclopedia*, 100.

[394] David Wallace, "Dante in English," in *The Cambridge Companion to Dante*, ed. Rachel Jacoff, 2nd ed. (Cambridge: Cambridge University Press, 2007), 294.

[395] http://www.poets.org/poetsorg/poem/canto-xiv, accessed 8-5-2015.

[396] George Kearns, *Ezra Pound: The Cantos* (Cambridge University Press, 1989), 11.

[397] Shapiro, "The Fictionalization of Bertran de Born (Inf. XXVIII)," 110.

[398] Joseph Gallagher, *A Modern Reader's Guide to Dante's The Divine Comedy* (Liguori, MO: Liguori Publications, 1999), 53.

[399] Steinberg, *Dante and the Limits of the Law*, 42.

[400] Ibid., 47.

[401] Ibid., 47–48.

Notes to Canto 29

402 Dante Alighieri, Robert Martinez, and Robert M Durling, *The Divine Comedy of Dante Alighieri: Volume 1: Inferno* (New York: Oxford University Press, 1997), 458.

403 Dante Alighieri and Robert Hollander, *The Inferno*, trans. Jean Hollander (New York; London: Anchor Books, 2002), 542.

404 Lino Pertile, "Canto XXIX: Such Outlandish Wounds," in *Lectura Dantis: Inferno: A Canto-by-Canto Commentary*, ed. Allen Mandelbaum (Berkeley: University of California Press, 1999), 379.

405 Pertile, "Canto XXIX: Such Outlandish Wounds," 379.

406 Dante Alighieri and Allen Mandelbaum, *Inferno* (New York: Bantam Classics, 1982), 385.

407 Alighieri, Martinez, and Durling, *The Divine Comedy of Dante Alighieri*, 459.

408 Pertile, "Canto XXIX: Such Outlandish Wounds," 380.

409 Ibid.

410 Alighieri, Martinez, and Durling, *The Divine Comedy of Dante Alighieri*, 460.

411 Dante Alighieri and Charles S. Singleton, *The Divine Comedy, I. Inferno. Part 2* (Princeton: Princeton University Press, 1990), 532.

412 Dante Alighieri and John Ciardi, *The Divine Comedy* (New York: New American Library, 2003), 230.

413 Alighieri, Martinez, and Durling, *The Divine Comedy of Dante Alighieri*, 460.

414 Dante Alighieri and Mark Musa, *The Divine Comedy: Volume 1: Inferno*, Revised edition (New York: Penguin Classics, 2002), 340.

415 Alighieri, Martinez, and Durling, *The Divine Comedy of Dante Alighieri*, 461.

416 Alighieri and Singleton, *The Divine Comedy, I. Inferno. Part 2*, 534.

417 Alighieri, Martinez, and Durling, *The Divine Comedy of Dante Alighieri*, 461.

418 Alighieri and Hollander, *The Inferno*, 545.

419 Alighieri and Singleton, *The Divine Comedy, I. Inferno. Part 2*, 538.

420 Lansing, *The Dante Encyclopedia*, 12.

421 Ibid., 13.

422 Paget Toynbee, *Concise Dictionary of Proper Names and Notable Matters in the Works of Dante* (New York: Phaeton Press, 1968), 504.

423 Alighieri and Musa, *The Divine Comedy*, 341.

424 Alighieri and Ciardi, *The Divine Comedy*, 231.

425 Alighieri, Martinez, and Durling, *The Divine Comedy of Dante Alighieri*, 462.

426 Toynbee, *Concise Dictionary of Proper Names and Notable Matters in the Works of Dante*, 71.

427 Ibid.

428 Sally A. Mussetter, "'INFERNO' XXX: DANTE'S COUNTERFEIT ADAM," *Traditio* 34 (January 1, 1978): 431.

429 Dorothy L. Sayers, *Introductory Papers on Dante : The Poet Alive in His Writings*, ed. Barbara Reynolds (New York: Harper Brothers, 1954), 147.

Notes to Canto 30

430 Dante Alighieri and Mark Musa, *The Divine Comedy: Volume 1: Inferno*, Revised edition (New York: Penguin Classics, 2002), 348.

431 Dante Alighieri, Robert Martinez, and Robert M Durling, *The Divine Comedy of Dante Alighieri: Volume 1: Inferno* (New York: Oxford University Press, 1997), 472.

432 Dante Alighieri and Charles S. Singleton, *The Divine Comedy, I. Inferno. Part 2* (Princeton: Princeton University Press, 1990), 544.

433 Dante Alighieri and Robert Hollander, *The Inferno*, trans. Jean Hollander (New York; London: Anchor Books, 2002), 558.

434 Ibid.

435 Paget Toynbee, *Concise Dictionary of Proper Names and Notable Matters in the Works of Dante* (New York: Phaeton Press, 1968), 56.

436 Frank-Lothar Hossfeld and Erich Zenger, *Psalms 3: A Commentary on Psalms 101-150*, ed. Klaus Baltzer, Hermeneia: A Critical and Historical Commentary on the Bible (Minneapolis: Fortress Press, 2011), 520.

437 Dante Alighieri and Allen Mandelbaum, *Inferno* (New York: Bantam Classics, 1982), 386.

[438] Alighieri and Hollander, *The Inferno*, 558.

[439] Alighieri and Musa, *The Divine Comedy*, 348.

[440] Alighieri, Martinez, and Durling, *The Divine Comedy of Dante Alighieri*, 473.

[441] Richard Lansing, ed., *The Dante Encyclopedia* (London; New York: Routledge, 2000), 765.

[442] Ibid.

[443] Toynbee, *Concise Dictionary of Proper Names and Notable Matters in the Works of Dante*, 263.

[444] Alighieri and Singleton, *The Divine Comedy, I. Inferno. Part 2*, 551.

[445] Ibid., 552.

[446] Ibid., 553.

[447] Alighieri, Martinez, and Durling, *The Divine Comedy of Dante Alighieri*, 474.

[448] Alighieri and Singleton, *The Divine Comedy, I. Inferno. Part 2*, 554.

[449] Alighieri, Martinez, and Durling, *The Divine Comedy of Dante Alighieri*, 475.

[450] Denise Heilbronn, "Master Adam and the Fat-Bellied Lute ('Inf'. XXX)," *Dante Studies, with the Annual Report of the Dante Society*, no. 101 (January 1, 1983): 57.

[451] Lansing, *The Dante Encyclopedia*, 599.

[452] Sally A. Mussetter, "'INFERNO' XXX: DANTE'S COUNTERFEIT ADAM," *Traditio* 34 (January 1, 1978): 428.

[453] Alighieri and Singleton, *The Divine Comedy, I. Inferno. Part 2*, 556.

[454] Dante Alighieri and Dorothy L. Sayers, *The Divine Comedy, Part 1: Hell*, Reprint edition (Harmondsworth etc.: Penguin Classics, 1950), 263.

[455] Allen Mandelbaum and Robert M. Durling, eds., "Canto XXX: Dante among the Falsifiers," in *Lectura Dantis: Inferno: A Canto-by-Canto Commentary* (Berkeley: University of California Press, 1999), 394.

[456] Alighieri and Hollander, *The Inferno*, 560–561.

[457] Mandelbaum and Durling, "Canto XXX: Dante among the Falsifiers," 394.

[458] Alighieri and Hollander, *The Inferno*, 561.

[459] Mussetter, "'INFERNO' XXX," 433.

[460] Alighieri, Martinez, and Durling, *The Divine Comedy of Dante Alighieri*, 481.

[461] Mussetter, "'INFERNO' XXX," 428.

[462] Ibid., 429.

[463] Ibid., 433.

[464] Alighieri, Martinez, and Durling, *The Divine Comedy of Dante Alighieri*, 477.

[465] Giuseppe Mazzotta, *Reading Dante* (New Haven: Yale University Press, 2014), 107.

[466] Helen M. Luke, *Dark Wood to White Rose: A Study of Meanings in Dante's Divine Comedy*, 1st Paperback Edition edition (Pecos, NM: Dove Publications, 1975), 32.

[467] Ibid., 33.

Notes to Canto 31

[1] Dante Alighieri and Charles S. Singleton, *The Divine Comedy, I. Inferno. Part 2* (Princeton: Princeton University Press, 1990), 563.

[2] Dante Alighieri and Mark Musa, *The Divine Comedy: Volume 1: Inferno*, Revised edition (New York: Penguin Classics, 2002), 357.

[3] Dante Alighieri, Robert Martinez, and Robert M Durling, *The Divine Comedy of Dante Alighieri: Volume 1: Inferno* (New York: Oxford University Press, 1997), 490.

[4] Richard Lansing, ed., *The Dante Encyclopedia* (London; New York: Routledge, 2000), 156.

[5] Paget Toynbee, *Concise Dictionary of Proper Names and Notable Matters in the Works of Dante* (New York: Phaeton Press, 1968), 397.

[6] Ibid., 119.

[7] Dante Alighieri and Allen Mandelbaum, *Inferno* (New York: Bantam Classics, 1982), 387.

[8] Alighieri and Singleton, *The Divine Comedy, I. Inferno. Part 2*, 567.

[9] Alighieri, Martinez, and Durling, *The Divine Comedy of Dante Alighieri*, 492.

[10] Alighieri and Musa, *The Divine Comedy*, 360.

[11] Richard Kay, "Vitruvius and Dante's Giants," *Dante Studies, with the Annual Report of the Dante Society*, no. 120 (January 1, 2002): 26.

[12] Alighieri and Singleton, *The Divine Comedy, I. Inferno. Part 2*, 568.

[13] Alighieri, Martinez, and Durling, *The Divine Comedy of Dante Alighieri*, 492.

[14] Kay, "Vitruvius and Dante's Giants," 26.

[15] Giuseppe Mazzotta, *Reading Dante* (New Haven: Yale University Press, 2014), 108.

[16] Stanley Benfell, "Nimrod, the Ascent to Heaven and Dante's 'Ovra Inconsummabile,'" *Dante Studies, with the Annual Report of the Dante Society*, no. 110 (January 1, 1992): 77.

[17] Ibid., 78.

[18] Helen M. Luke, *Dark Wood to White Rose: A Study of Meanings in Dante's Divine Comedy*, 1st Paperback Edition edition (Pecos, NM: Dove Publications, 1975), 32–33.

[19] Dante Alighieri and Robert Hollander, *The Inferno*, trans. Jean Hollander (New York; London: Anchor Books, 2002), 579.

[20] Lansing, *The Dante Encyclopedia*, 344.

[21] Toynbee, *Concise Dictionary of Proper Names and Notable Matters in the Works of Dante*, 228–229.

[22] Ibid., 91.

[23] Dante Alighieri and Dorothy L. Sayers, *The Divine Comedy, Part 1: Hell*, Reprint edition (Harmondsworth etc.: Penguin Classics, 1950), 270.

[24] Alighieri and Hollander, *The Inferno*, 580.

[25] Kay, "Vitruvius and Dante's Giants," 26.

[26] Dante Alighieri and John Ciardi, *The Divine Comedy* (New York: New American Library, 2003), 246.

[27] Toynbee, *Concise Dictionary of Proper Names and Notable Matters in the Works of Dante*, 36.

[28] Lansing, *The Dante Encyclopedia*, 49.

[29] Alighieri and Singleton, *The Divine Comedy, I. Inferno. Part 2*, 578.

[30] Alighieri and Musa, *The Divine Comedy*, 361.

[31] Teodolinda Barolini, *The Undivine Comedy* (Princeton University Press, 1992), 92.

[32] Prue Shaw, *Reading Dante: From Here to Eternity* (New York: Liveright, 2014), 192.

33 Ibid.

34 Barolini, *The Undivine Comedy*, 92.

35 Benfell, "Nimrod, the Ascent to Heaven and Dante's 'Ovra Inconsummabile,'" 80.

36 Ibid., 88.

37 Massimo Pesaresi, "Canto XXXI: The Giants — Majesty and Terror," in *Lectura Dantis: Inferno: A Canto-by-Canto Commentary*, ed. Allen Mandelbaum (Berkeley: University of California Press, 1999), 409.

38 Saint Augustine, *The City of God, Books VIII-XVI*, ed. Hermigild Dressler, trans. Gerald G. Walsh and Grace Monahan, vol. 14, The Fathers of the Church (Washington, D.C.: The Catholic University of America Press, 2008), XVI.4, P. 495.

39 Ibid., 14:XVI.4, pp. 496–497.

40 Luke, *Dark Wood to White Rose*, 33.

41 Ibid., 34.

42 Benfell, "Nimrod, the Ascent to Heaven and Dante's 'Ovra Inconsummabile,'" 91.

43 Alighieri and Sayers, *The Divine Comedy, Part 1*, 269.

Notes to Canto 32

44 John Ahern, "Canto XXXII: Amphion and the Poetics of Retaliation," in *Lectura Dantis: Inferno: A Canto-by-Canto Commentary*, ed. Allen Mandelbaum (Berkeley: University of California Press, 1999), 415.

45 Paget Toynbee, *Concise Dictionary of Proper Names and Notable Matters in the Works of Dante* (New York: Phaeton Press, 1968), 32.

46 Ahern, "Canto XXXII: Amphion and the Poetics of Retaliation," 414.

47 Richard Lansing, ed., *The Dante Encyclopedia* (London; New York: Routledge, 2000), 811.

48 Dante Alighieri, Robert Martinez, and Robert M Durling, *The Divine Comedy of Dante Alighieri: Volume 1: Inferno* (New York: Oxford University Press, 1997), 507.

49 Dante Alighieri and Robert Hollander, *The Inferno*, trans. Jean Hollander (New York; London: Anchor Books, 2002), 596.

50 Dante Alighieri and Charles S. Singleton, *The Divine Comedy, I. Inferno. Part 2* (Princeton: Princeton University Press, 1990), 584.

51 Dante Alighieri and John Ciardi, *The Divine Comedy* (New York: New American Library, 2003), 253.

52 Alighieri and Singleton, *The Divine Comedy, I. Inferno. Part 2*, 587.

53 Alighieri and Hollander, *The Inferno*, 598.

54 Lansing, *The Dante Encyclopedia*, 12.

55 Alighieri, Martinez, and Durling, *The Divine Comedy of Dante Alighieri*, 510.

56 Dante Alighieri and Allen Mandelbaum, *Inferno* (New York: Bantam Classics, 1982), 389.

57 Alighieri, Martinez, and Durling, *The Divine Comedy of Dante Alighieri*, 510.

58 Dante Alighieri and Dorothy L. Sayers, *The Divine Comedy, Part 1: Hell*, Reprint edition (Harmondsworth etc.: Penguin Classics, 1950), 276.

59 Toynbee, *Concise Dictionary of Proper Names and Notable Matters in the Works of Dante*, 363.

60 Lansing, *The Dante Encyclopedia*, 136.

61 Alighieri and Hollander, *The Inferno*, 599.

62 Dante Alighieri and Mark Musa, *The Divine Comedy: Volume 1: Inferno*, Revised edition (New York: Penguin Classics, 2002), 368.

63 Alighieri and Hollander, *The Inferno*, 599.

64 John Najemy, "Dante and Florence," in *The Cambridge Companion to Dante*, ed. Rachel Jacoff, 2nd ed. (New York: Cambridge University Press, 2007), 240.

65 Toynbee, *Concise Dictionary of Proper Names and Notable Matters in the Works of Dante*, 82.

66 Lansing, *The Dante Encyclopedia*, 131.

67 Toynbee, *Concise Dictionary of Proper Names and Notable Matters in the Works of Dante*, 98.

68 Alighieri and Hollander, *The Inferno*, 601.

69 Toynbee, *Concise Dictionary of Proper Names and Notable Matters in the Works of Dante*, 263.

70 Alighieri and Singleton, *The Divine Comedy, I. Inferno. Part 2*, 600.

71 Alighieri and Mandelbaum, *Inferno*, 390.

72 Lansing, *The Dante Encyclopedia*, 807.

73 Alighieri, Martinez, and Durling, *The Divine Comedy of Dante Alighieri*, 513.

74 Alighieri and Hollander, *The Inferno*, 602.

75 Alighieri, Martinez, and Durling, *The Divine Comedy of Dante Alighieri*, 513.

76 John Freccero, *Dante: The Poetics of Conversion*, ed. Rachel Jacoff, Reprint edition (Cambridge, Mass.: Harvard University Press, 1988), 154.

77 Ibid.

78 Saint Augustine, *The City of God, Books VIII-XVI*, ed. Hermigild Dressler, trans. Gerald G. Walsh and Grace Monahan, vol. 14, The Fathers of the Church (Washington, D.C.: The Catholic University of America Press, 2008), 15.7, P. 426.

79 Ibid., 14:15.5, P. 421.

80 Freccero, *Dante*, 153.

81 Justin Steinberg, *Dante and the Limits of the Law* (Chicago: University Of Chicago Press, 2013), 80.

82 Ibid., 79.

83 Ibid., 81.

84 Dorothy L. Sayers, *Introductory Papers on Dante : The Poet Alive in His Writings*, ed. Barbara Reynolds (New York: Harper Brothers, 1954), 148.

85 Charles Williams, *The Figure of Beatrice* (Berkeley: Apocryphile Press, 2005), 140.

Notes to Canto 33

86 Dante Alighieri and Charles S. Singleton, *The Divine Comedy, I. Inferno. Part 2* (Princeton: Princeton University Press, 1990), 605. The allusion is to *Aeneid* 2.3-6.

87 Dante Alighieri, Robert Martinez, and Robert M Durling, *The Divine Comedy of Dante Alighieri: Volume 1: Inferno* (New York: Oxford University Press, 1997), 525.

88 Richard Lansing, ed., *The Dante Encyclopedia* (London; New York: Routledge, 2000), 839.

89 Dante Alighieri and Robert Hollander, *The Inferno*, trans. Jean Hollander (New York; London: Anchor Books, 2002), 616.

90 Alighieri and Singleton, *The Divine Comedy, I. Inferno. Part 2*, 606.

91 Paget Toynbee, *Concise Dictionary of Proper Names and Notable Matters in the Works of Dante* (New York: Phaeton Press, 1968), 536.

92 Lansing, *The Dante Encyclopedia*, 839.

93 Dante Alighieri and Mark Musa, *The Divine Comedy: Volume 1: Inferno*, Revised edition (New York: Penguin Classics, 2002), 375.

94 Alighieri and Hollander, *The Inferno*, 616.

95 Dante Alighieri and Allen Mandelbaum, *Inferno* (New York: Bantam Classics, 1982), 390.

96 Robert Hollander, "Inferno XXXIII, 37-74: Ugolino's Importunity," *Speculum* 59, no. 3 (July 1, 1984): 550, doi:10.2307/2846299.

97 Alighieri and Singleton, *The Divine Comedy, I. Inferno. Part 2*, 614.

98 Dante Alighieri and John Ciardi, *The Divine Comedy* (New York: New American Library, 2003), 262.

99 Alighieri, Martinez, and Durling, *The Divine Comedy of Dante Alighieri*, 529.

100 Dorothy L. Sayers, *Introductory Papers on Dante : The Poet Alive in His Writings*, ed. Barbara Reynolds (New York: Harper Brothers, 1954), 33.

101 Alighieri, Martinez, and Durling, *The Divine Comedy of Dante Alighieri*, 529.

102 Alighieri and Musa, *The Divine Comedy*, 376.

103 Alighieri, Martinez, and Durling, *The Divine Comedy of Dante Alighieri*, 530.

104 Alighieri and Hollander, *The Inferno*, 621.

105 Alighieri, Martinez, and Durling, *The Divine Comedy of Dante Alighieri*, 530.

106 Alighieri and Singleton, *The Divine Comedy, I. Inferno. Part 2*, 621.

107 Lansing, *The Dante Encyclopedia*, 10.

108 Toynbee, *Concise Dictionary of Proper Names and Notable Matters in the Works of Dante*, 16.

109 Ibid.

110 Alighieri and Hollander, *The Inferno*, 622.

111 Toynbee, *Concise Dictionary of Proper Names and Notable Matters in the Works of Dante*, 90.

112 Kevin Dodge, *Confessions of a Bishop: A Guide to Augustine's Confessions* (Dallas: Incarnation Classics Publishing, 2014), 218.

113 John Freccero, *Dante: The Poetics of Conversion*, ed. Rachel Jacoff, Reprint edition (Cambridge, Mass.: Harvard University Press, 1988), 156.

114 Ibid., 158.

115 Ibid., 161.

116 Ibid., 163.

117 Ibid.

118 Ibid., 164.

Notes to Canto 34

119 Dante Alighieri and Charles S. Singleton, *The Divine Comedy, I. Inferno. Part 2* (Princeton: Princeton University Press, 1990), 626.

120 Remo Ceserani, "Lucifer," in *Lectura Dantis: Inferno: A Canto-by-Canto Commentary*, ed. Allen Mandelbaum (Berkeley: University of California Press, 1999), 434.

121 John Freccero, *Dante: The Poetics of Conversion*, ed. Rachel Jacoff, Reprint edition (Cambridge, Mass.: Harvard University Press, 1988), 169.

122 Ibid.

123 Charles S. Singleton, *Dante's Commedia: Elements of Structure* (Baltimore: The Johns Hopkins University Press, 1977), 37.

124 Ibid., 39.

125 Richard Lansing, ed., *The Dante Encyclopedia* (London; New York: Routledge, 2000), 547.

126 Helen M. Luke, *Dark Wood to White Rose: A Study of Meanings in Dante's Divine Comedy*, 1st Paperback Edition edition (Pecos, NM: Dove Publications, 1975), 38.

127 Ceserani, "Lucifer," 436.

128 Ibid., 435.

129 Lansing, *The Dante Encyclopedia*, 574.

130 Alighieri and Singleton, *The Divine Comedy, I. Inferno. Part 2*, 629.

131 Dante Alighieri, Robert Martinez, and Robert M Durling, *The Divine Comedy of Dante Alighieri: Volume 1: Inferno* (New York: Oxford University Press, 1997), 544.

132 Alighieri and Singleton, *The Divine Comedy, I. Inferno. Part 2*, 630.

133 Ibid.

134 Singleton, *Dante's Commedia*, 41.

135 Ibid., 42.

136 Alighieri, Martinez, and Durling, *The Divine Comedy of Dante Alighieri*, 545.

137 Freccero, *Dante*, 172.

138 Singleton, *Dante's Commedia*, 40–41.

139 Ceserani, "Lucifer," 437.

140 Lansing, *The Dante Encyclopedia*, 575.

141 Ibid., 130.

142 Ibid., 144.

143 Paget Toynbee, *Concise Dictionary of Proper Names and Notable Matters in the Works of Dante* (New York: Phaeton Press, 1968).

144 Dante Alighieri and Mark Musa, *The Divine Comedy: Volume 1: Inferno*, Revised edition (New York: Penguin Classics, 2002), 386.

145 Dante Alighieri and Allen Mandelbaum, *Inferno* (New York: Bantam Classics, 1982), 393.

146 Alighieri and Singleton, *The Divine Comedy, I. Inferno. Part 2*, 638–639.

147 Ibid., 639.

148 Freccero, *Dante*, 184–185.

149 Ibid., 182.

150 Singleton, *Dante's Commedia*, 39.

151 Frank Leslie Cross and Elizabeth A. Livingstone, "Procession (Theological)," *The Oxford Dictionary of the Christian Church* (Oxford: Oxford University Press, 2005), 1341.

152 Thomas Aquinas, *The Summa Theologica of St. Thomas Aquinas* (New York: Christian Classics, 1981), 1.27.4.

153 Singleton, *Dante's Commedia*, 40–41.

154 Robert Pasnau, *Oxford Studies in Medieval Philosophy* (OUP Oxford, 2013), 78.

[155] Aquinas, *The Summa Theologica of St. Thomas Aquinas*, 1.63.3.

[156] Augustine, *Saint Augustine: On Genesis: Two Books on Genesis Against the Manichees*, ed. Roland Teske, vol. 84, Fathers of the Church (Washington DC: Catholic University of America Press, 1991), 5.21, P. 158.

[157] Freccero, *Dante*, 185.